D1784953

East Asian Economic Integration

ASIAN COMMERCIAL, FINANCIAL AND ECONOMIC LAW
AND POLICY

Series Editors: Douglas Arner, Xian Chu Zhang and Chin Leng Lim,
University of Hong Kong

Asia is home to the world's most dynamic and increasingly interlinked
economies. At the heart of their future development are issues of commercial, financial and economic law and policy. This series brings together
volumes addressing related issues, across the region, in individual
economies and between Asia and the rest of the world.

East Asian Economic Integration

Law, Trade and Finance

Edited by

Ross P. Buckley

University of New South Wales, Australia

Richard Weixing Hu

University of Hong Kong

Douglas W. Arner

University of Hong Kong

ASIAN COMMERCIAL, FINANCIAL AND ECONOMIC LAW
AND POLICY

Edward Elgar
Cheltenham, UK • Northampton, MA, USA

© The Editors and Contributors Severally 2011

All rights reserved. No part of this publication may be reproduced, stored in a retrieval system or transmitted in any form or by any means, electronic, mechanical or photocopying, recording, or otherwise without the prior permission of the publisher.

Published by
Edward Elgar Publishing Limited
The Lypiatts
15 Lansdown Road
Cheltenham
Glos GL50 2JA
UK

Edward Elgar Publishing, Inc.
William Pratt House
9 Dewey Court
Northampton
Massachusetts 01060
USA

A catalogue record for this book
is available from the British Library

Library of Congress Control Number: 2010939363

MIX
Paper from
responsible sources
FSC® C018575

ISBN 978 1 84980 868 2

Typeset by Servis Filmsetting Ltd, Stockport, Cheshire
Printed and bound by MPG Books Group, UK

Contents

v

PART III   FINANCIAL INTEGRATION

Editors and contributors

EDITORS

Douglas W. Arner, Director, Asian Institute of International Financial Law, and Professor, Faculty of Law, University of Hong Kong; and Visiting Research Fellow, University of New South Wales.

Ross P. Buckley, Professor of Law, University of New South Wales; and Fellow, Asian Institute of International Financial Law, Faculty of Law, University of Hong Kong.

Richard Weixing Hu, Associate Professor, Department of Politics and Public Administration, Faculty of Social Sciences, University of Hong Kong.

CONTRIBUTORS

Henry Gao, Associate Professor, School of Law, Singapore Management University.

Paul Lejot, Visiting Fellow, Asian Institute of International Financial Law, Faculty of Law, University of Hong Kong; and Visiting Research Fellow, ICMA Centre, University of Reading.

C.L. Lim, Associate Dean for Academic Affairs and Professor, Faculty of Law, University of Hong Kong; and Visiting Professor, School of Law, King's College London.

Bryan Mercurio, Professor and Associate Dean (Research), Faculty of Law, Chinese University of Hong Kong.

Miron Mushkat, Adjunct Professor of Economics and Finance, Syracuse University (Hong Kong Programme); Honorary Research Fellow, Hong Kong Institute for the Humanities and Social Sciences, University of Hong Kong; and Responsible Officer and Senior Economic Adviser, Artis Capital Partners.

Roda Mushkat, Professor of International Law and Director, Centre of International and Public Law, Brunel Law School, Brunel University;

Honorary Professor, Faculty of Law, and Visiting Professor, Kadoorie Institute, University of Hong Kong; and Visiting Scholar, Institute of Advanced Legal Studies, University of London.

Junji Nakagawa, Professor of International Economic Law, Institute of Social Science, University of Tokyo.

Cyn-Young Park, Principal Economist, Office of Regional Economic Integration, Asian Development Bank.

Injoo Sohn, Assistant Professor, Department of Politics and Public Administration, Faculty of Social Sciences, University of Hong Kong.

Lisa Toohey, Senior Lecturer, Faculty of Law, University of New South Wales.

Nhu Vu, Legal Counsel, Seravia (Beijing).

Trinh Hai Yen, Lecturer in International Law, Diplomatic Academy of Vietnam.

Introduction

Ross P. Buckley, Richard Weixing Hu and Douglas W. Arner

The economic integration of East Asia is a remarkably uneven phenomenon.

Production of goods is highly integrated. Many products labeled 'Made in China' would be more accurately identified as 'Made in East Asia', as over 40 per cent of the content of manufactured exports from China typically consists of components or other inputs imported from the region. This system of production is replicated in other nations of the region – the nation that finally assembles a product may well contribute less than one-half of the actual value of the final product. Indeed, manufacturing in East Asia today can often more accurately be viewed as a regional, rather than national, endeavour.

This production integration is supported by a high degree of formal trade integration achieved by way of a noodle bowl of regional and bilateral trade agreements. It is also supported by a high degree of direct investment integration, with nations in the region investing in production facilities in other nations. This investment integration in support of production activities is in turn supported by a network of multilateral and bilateral investment treaties. Regional portfolio investment, however, is less well developed.

In stark contrast, financial integration in the region is underdeveloped. Most East Asian nations are more closely integrated financially with nations outside the region, typically in Europe or North America, than they are with other nations in the region. This would make sense if the region were capital poor and the principal sources of capital were external. Yet the region enjoys the largest foreign exchange reserves, and the highest personal savings rates, in the world. So this lack of financial integration is a product of historical factors and underdeveloped financial sectors – particularly underdeveloped equity and capital markets – not supply-side factors.

This volume explores these fascinating inconsistencies in regional integration. It is a volume in three parts. Part I explores the changing regional

institutional order and the dynamics of the rapidly evolving regional cooperation. Part II explores the functional and formal integration in trade
and investment within the region. Part III analyses the anomalous case of
financial integration and explores ways forward this integration may take.

Part I commences with a chapter by Richard Hu that provides an overview of the state of regional institution building and an analysis of the
influences in this regard of China and the United States. This is followed
by Chin Leng Lim's contribution, exploring who is afraid of East Asian
regionalism and why. This chapter puts the increasing integration of this
region in a broader context and explores which countries beyond the
region might oppose these developments and why they might do so.

In the final chapter in Part I, Roda and Miron Mushkat use the case
of transboundary pollution in Hong Kong to analyse the institutional
fragility of the region particularly when it comes to balancing the tension
between economic and ecological imperatives.

Part II – trade integration – begins with chapters by Junji Nakagawa
and Henry Gao which explore the regional free trade agreement (FTA)
strategies of Japan and China respectively. Nakagawa concludes that
competitive dynamics best explain Japan's policy shift, in the past decade,
towards preferential trade arrangements and away from its traditionally staunch support of multilateral initiatives. Gao on the other hand
concludes that the principal drivers of China's use of preferential trade
arrangements have been geo-political factors rather than economic ones.

Bryan Mercurio then takes a sceptical look at the dramatic expansion in
intra-regional trade in the past three decades and concludes that while this
growth occurred at the same time as the growth in regional trade agreements, there is no causal link between the two; that is, trade grew despite,
rather than because of, the proliferation of formal trade agreements.
Mercurio then goes on to explore the changes in regional trade agreements
which would serve to promote intra-regional trade.

The next chapter in this part is by Lisa Toohey. She analyses ASEAN
trade dispute resolution and explores the cultural, political and other
factors which explain why ASEAN's members have consistently avoided
resolving trade disputes by using the region's own dispute resolution protocols and instead, when it is unavoidable, taken their trade disputes to
the Dispute Settlement Understanding of the World Trade Organization
(WTO).

In the final chapter of Part II, Trinh Yen examines the role of investment treaties in regional investment integration and analyses preferable
ways forward towards a more coherent and consistent regional investment
regulatory structure.

Part III deals with financial integration. It commences with an analysis by Douglas Arner and Cyn-Young Park of the implications for Asia of the recent global financial regulatory reforms and of the regional and sub-regional mechanisms and institutions that would serve to advance the region's financial growth and integration. It then proceeds with Injoo Sohn's analysis of the political dynamics of East Asia's financial regionalism. The following chapter by Paul Lejot analyses the multilateralized Chiang Mai Initiative (CMIM), the series of bilateral credit arrangements among regional central banks designed to enhance the financial autonomy and stability of the region in times of crisis. Lejot explores the incompleteness of the initiative at its current stage of evolution.

From this basis, Ross Buckley explores one direction in which the CMIM might lead, if developed extensively, which is to an Asian Monetary Fund. Buckley explores what a regional monetary fund has to offer and concludes that while such a fund has an important role in enhancing regional financial autonomy and stability, it may have even more to offer the region, and the world, by developing an Asian Consensus on development and becoming an authoritative voice to enunciate and promote those policies that have worked in Asia to the benefit of the region's further development and that of other developing nations in other parts of the world.

In the final chapter of Part III Nhu Vu explores one of the potential future paths open for regional financial integration: the establishment of an Asian currency unit and, in particular, the potential role of the Asian Development Bank in its creation.

The work concludes with a chapter by the editors in which we summarize some of the themes of the volume and examine the future prospects of regional institution building.

This volume grew out of two workshops held in the region in the second half of 2009. In October, the University of New South Wales and the Asian Institute of International Financial Law of the University of Hong Kong jointly hosted a workshop in Hong Kong on regional economic integration. The following month the University of New South Wales hosted a workshop on the same subject in Hanoi, Vietnam. Most of the chapters in this volume were presented and discussed at these workshops. Discussions have continued since then among authors working in similar areas with a view to producing a cohesive volume.

This books seeks to do more than describe what is, although we trust it does this competently. More importantly, it seeks to explore alternative pathways down which the region could progress, for the region today truly does stand at a cross-roads. In the past regional institution building and cooperation have been stymied by China's distrust of regional institutions, the long-standing tensions between China and Japan as they have competed for influence, and the strong preference of the United States to continue to exert its influence in the region through its series of bilateral relationships – a preference that has resulted in US opposition to most regional initiatives.

In the past decade this landscape has changed. China has come to understand and appreciate the need for, and potential of, regional institutions and has grown comfortable with being a member of such institutions. China and Japan, while certainly still competing for influence, have seemingly come to some rapprochement, an understanding that influence shared might be influence enhanced. And, finally, for most of the first decade of the new century the United States was obsessed with terrorism and the Middle East. By the time the Obama administration came to power and started to give Asia a focus appropriate to the region's economic importance, the region generally, and China in particular, had grown remarkably in confidence and economic power, and the United States has found a return to its old approaches simply untenable.

So East Asia's economic destiny lies today in its own hands more than it has for the past century. It will be Asians who decide on paths of regional cooperation or competition. And it will be the region that decides whether it is sufficiently committed and serious to lift its financial integration to the levels of its integration in production and trade.

The past two decades in East Asia have witnessed economic growth without peer in human history (except perhaps for the two decades of Japan's growth in the 1950s and 1960s, which is in many ways the starting point for the East Asian growth story). The potential for the next two decades is no less exciting. It has been our pleasure to assemble this volume which explores the directions the region might most usefully take in the future.

PART I

The changing regional order and dynamics for cooperation

1. China, the US and regional institution building in East Asia

Richard Weixing Hu

INTRODUCTION

China and the United States are two key players in shaping future East Asian regional order and institutions. For a long time after World War II, East Asia was perceived as being institutionally underdeveloped with no region-wide political and economic institutional structure, except an American-centered network of bilateral security treaties. Yet, after the Cold War and especially after the Asian Financial Crisis of 1997–98, a rising tide of regionalism and institution-building projects appeared. There is a proliferation of regional groupings and dialogues, ranging from the Association of Southeast Asian Nations (ASEAN), the ASEAN Regional Forum (ARF), ASEAN+3 and the East Asia Summit (EAS) to Asia-Pacific Economic Cooperation (APEC). East Asian nations are organizing themselves into an 'alphabet soup' of multilateral groupings and organizations with overlapping membership and different mandates. This makes people wonder what kind of regional order East Asia is building and what role China and the US will play in regional institution building.

China is a rising power on the global and regional stage. China's ascent and its growing influence in East Asia have important bearings on regional order and regional institutional building. Yet, how China comes to terms with regional institutions is still an issue under debate. In order to rise peacefully, China needs a stable and prosperous regional environment for concentrating on its growth. Meanwhile, Beijing also wants to engage in regional institution building to reassure its neighbors as well as to gain normative and institutional power in shaping the future regional order. On the other hand, the United States is a 'non-territorial' but leading power in East Asian affairs. The US has built and maintained a regional security order based on a system of 'hub-and-spokes' bilateral alliances and an open trading system in the post-war era. This regional structure has provided a remarkably comfortable basis for Washington to pursue its economic and security interests in the region. But since the end of the Cold War, the strategic and institutional landscape in East Asia has undergone fundamental changes in the context of the rise of China and East Asian regionalism. The rise of the Chinese influence is viewed as being at the expense of American power in the region.

There are two contending perspectives on the US–China struggle for power in East Asia. One perspective views the growth of Chinese power as being at the expense of American influence. Although China's power at the present time is no match for that of the US and it does not seem quite obvious that Beijing is explicitly driving Washington out of regional institutions, the Chinese influence is quickly picking up while the American influence in the region has been on the decline. On the other hand, the opposing view argues that things cannot be viewed through a zero-sum lens. The rise of Chinese clout in East Asia does not necessarily mean the loss of American influence. The increase in Chinese influence around its periphery and in different realms is not even, and there are still strong barriers to Beijing advancing its influence in East Asian institutions. As one leading US China scholar argues, American and Chinese influence in East Asia is in an interlocking pattern. Even if it is the case that China's influence has increased, 'the overall direction in which China's regional policy has moved is consistent with fundamental US interests.'[1]

The East Asian region and the world are trying to make sense of the US–China relationship in regional institution building. How does the emerging China–US struggle for influence affect future East Asian institution building? Does emerging regional institution building in East Asia benefit or impede Washington's and Beijing's influence in the region? Does the proliferation of Asian institution-building projects benefit the rising China? Does it help or impede China's efforts to advance its regional influence? How should Washington respond to the growing regionalism in East Asia? How should the US engage China in the development of regional political and economic institution building?

This chapter focuses on two questions of this debate. The first question is about what role China and the US play in regional institution building. Both China and the US have their own strengths and weaknesses in the regional institutional competition. As Peter Katzenstein argues, Asia is a 'porous' region.[2] It is an 'open region,' letting through all sorts of

---

[1] David M. Lampton, 'China's Rise in Asia Need Not Be at America's Expense', in David Shambaugh (ed.), *Power Shift: China and Asia's New Dynamics* (Berkeley, CA: University of California Press, 2006), 322–3.

[2] Peter J. Katzenstein, *A World of Regions: Asia and Europe in the American Imperium* (Ithaca and London: Cornell University Press, 2005), 21.

inputs and influence, internal and external. China is an 'insider,' with geographic advantage, economic attractiveness, local neighborhood, rising soft power, and sharing compatible regional governance interests with regional nations. Beijing is also well plugged into many on-going region-building projects. The US, on the other hand, is a 'non-territorial' power. It still has enormous material and normative power and a strong bilateral security structure in East Asia, enjoying the critical position of 'honest broker' and 'balancer' in regional affairs. Being two leading powers in the region, both the US and China have opportunities and capacities to shape or reshape regional institution building. They also have plenty of room to cooperate in regional institution building and governance. East Asia being a 'porous' region, its regional structure takes different institutional forms and has already witnessed an array of region-building programs flourishing. Thus I would argue that it is in both countries' interests to handle regional institution building in an accommodating way, not in a competitive and mutually exclusive way.

The second question concerns how the rise of China affects the US power position in the region. I would argue that China's ascent so far has fared well with the existing power position held by the US. It is true that China's regional influence is on the rise, and the rising China is challenging America's primary role in the region. Yet, we should recognize that the rise of Chinese influence and the decline of American influence are two separate matters, not negatively related. We should not use zero-sum logic to see the two matters; rather, we should study them separately on their own merits. Yet I believe, although they are not causally related, the two major powers and their relations are closely linked to the play of regional institution building and regional order shaping. What really matters here is not the realist type of power balancing (such as containment, alliance, arms race, or hedging) for future US–China competition but rather, a 'soft' type of power balancing. The underlying logic of competition is not 'balance of power'; rather, it is 'balance of influence'. The soft competition is not about coercive power; instead, it is about remunerative and normative power, ideas, intellectual might, and moral appeals.[3] Among them, regional institutions are an important realm for power competition. Both Beijing and Washington have to try to increase 'institutional power' through initiating, transforming and dominating regional institutions in their favor to counterbalance the other's influence in the region.

---

[3]   See David M. Lampton, *The Three Faces of Chinese Power: Might, Money, and Minds* (Berkeley, CA: University of California Press, 2008).

RISING EAST ASIAN REGIONALISM AND INSTITUTION BUILDING

Compared with Europe, East Asia is much less institutionalized. East Asian nations do not have a comparable integrationist tradition, and the region is too vast and diverse to form a coherent regional organization. East Asian cultural and political traditions have also helped to cultivate a greater reluctance to pool sovereign authority together under a regional institutional framework, as the Europeans did through the European Economic Community by the Treaty of Rome in 1957 and eventually the European Union by the Treaty of Maastricht in 1993. For East Asian nations, economic integration is largely driven by market forces, and the benefits of economic cooperation have nurtured an appetite for regional institution building. Growing economic interdependence and the desire for further economic integration have become the sustained driving force for regional institution building in East Asia.

Yet, East Asian regional institutions are 'soft', shallow, and weak. The process of institution building is largely driven and sustained by the Association of Southeast Asian Nations in the so-called 'ASEAN way'. The ASEAN way emphasizes informality, consultation, consensus building, conflict management and confidence building, and progressing institution building at a pace and to a level comfortable to everyone. The pace of East Asian institution building is slow and the level of institutionalization is low. Everyone involved seems more interested in the 'process' and 'form' than the final result of institution building. In the process, ASEAN has been in the driver seat and other players, including regional major powers, in the passenger seats.

ASEAN has built a series of concentric regional institutions with itself at the center. Now there are at least four layers of regional institution-building projects around ASEAN. At the center, ASEAN itself is moving gradually toward an EU-type of regional community, with three pillars in the security, economic, and social-cultural realms. The next layer is what is called ASEAN+3 (APT), ASEAN's engagement with China, Japan and South Korea in functional cooperation. APT has developed some regional cooperative arrangements, such as the Chiang Mai Initiative (CMI) and the Greater Mekong Subregion (GMS).[4] Under the APT process there is also a collateral Northeast Asian dialogues program among China, Japan

---

[4]   For background information about APT, the CMI and the GMS, see http://www.aseansec.org/16580.htm and http://www.aseansec.org/11600.htm, accessed 10 June 2010.

and South Korea through holding annual trilateral summits.[5] The third layer of the concentric structure is the East Asia Summit (EAS), which extends the APT annual summit to include Australia, New Zealand, and India. The EAS inaugural summit was held in Malaysia in 2005, and has open accession rules that could potentially let in more members like the US and Russia at its future meetings. The fourth layer, from the ASEAN perspective, is the overlapping and enlarged dialogues process within the larger Asia-Pacific region – Asia-Pacific Economic Cooperation (APEC). The APEC process, started in 1989, is the premier forum for facilitating economic growth, cooperation, trade and investment in the Asia-Pacific region. It probably is the most significant trans-Pacific institution so far in the region. In addition to these four layers of the concentric and over- lapping regional institutions, there is a complex network of overlapping regional trade arrangements (RTAs) and bilateral free trade agreements (FTAs). These arrangements in turn can be broken down into clus- ters depending on the partners setting their substantive and procedural agendas (US-led, China-led, Japan-led, and so on).

With these distinct 'institutional complexes' existing in East Asia and the larger Asia-Pacific region, we are seeing a multi-layered and multi-textured community-building process in progress. The existence of overlapping and sometimes competing region-building projects and groupings reflects an emerging redistribution of power and influence in the region after the Cold War. Not only the governance of each institution itself is in question, but also how tasks and functions are allocated across these institutions. More specifically, the region faces some fundamental questions in institution building – who is in the region, what agenda, and what kind of institution?

East Asian countries lack a shared vision for future regional institution building. In East Asia, countries are divided on what regional institutions they need and what a future regional architecture should look like. At the heart of the problem are the different views on what constitutes the basis for regional cooperation and integration. The countries have dif- ferent views on whether East Asia should build an Asian-only grouping based on the ASEAN+3 process, or focus on a pan-Asian community embedded in the East Asia Summit (EAS) design, or pursue a pan-Asian- Pacific community erected in the APEC framework. The vision problem is further complicated by fast-growing bilateral FTAs/economic partnership

---

5 In the latest trilateral summit, held in Jeju, South Korea, on 30 May 2010, the three countries issued the 'Trilateral Cooperation Vision 2020' and agreed to establish a Trilateral Cooperation Secretariat in South Korea in 2011, last accessed 12 June 2010, http://www.mofa.go.jp/region/asia-paci/jck/summit1005/joint_pr.html.

agreements, Sino-Japanese power rivalry, and Washington's posture, as well as other regional arrangements such as the Six Party Talks that have the potential to evolve into a more regular security mechanism.

The membership problem is not about the number of members, but rather the criteria for admitting new members. The EU exercises a 'club membership' model, which imposes stringent requirements on new members, a pre-membership hurdle that has promoted the harmonization of national policies with those of existing members. The expansion of membership occurs gradually and is subject to a lengthy negotiation process. In East Asia, countries can join more quickly with fewer entrance requirements as long as they 'belong to' the region. This is what Amitav Acharya calls the 'socializing effect' of Asian regional institution building – harmonization of policies in East Asia is posited to occur through the socialization that follows membership.[6]

CHINA AND EAST ASIAN INSTITUTION BUILDING

China has shown great interest in regional institution building since the mid-1990s. During the Cold War, Beijing's views on regional institutions were largely negative as it regarded them as Western-backed efforts to encircle or contain China's influence in the region. This attitude has changed substantially since the end of the Cold War. It has become more positive and participatory.

China's spectacular economic growth and rising national power have increased its regional influence remarkably. The size of China's GDP is going to surpass that of Japan to be number two in the world this year. With fast-growing economic clout as well as expanding trade and production networks throughout the region, China has already taken over Japan's role as the leading trading house and manufacturing center in East Asia. Regional economic institutions are now perceived by China as an effective means to strengthen regional economic linkages and integrate the Chinese economy into the regional and global economic system.

Beijing has also become more open-minded and participatory in regional political and security institution building, such as the ARF, the Six Party Talks, and the Shanghai Cooperation Organization (SCO). In recent years, Chinese regional diplomacy has shifted its myopic focus on security to a more comprehensive approach toward '*Mulin, Anlin,* and *Fulin*' (amicable,

---

[6] Amitav Acharya, *Whose Ideas Matter? Agency and Power in Asian Regionalism* (Ithaca and London: Cornell University Press, 2009).

peaceful, and prosperous neighborhood). Its participation in regional security institutions, previously cautious and sometimes selective, has become more active. In the early 1990s, Chinese strategists were keen on talking about how to build a multipolar world with China as one 'pole' among major powers in the world. But since 11 September 2001, this multipolaralism has gradually given way to a foreign policy that emphasizes multilateralism and intensive engagement in regional institution building in East Asia. More Asian-oriented regional institutions are considered a means to balance American influence in the region as well as the means to cope with new sources of threat to Chinese security – the 'three evil forces' (terrorism, separatism, and extremism) at China's periphery. The Shanghai Cooperation Organization, originating as an offshoot from the border security regime between China, Russia, and Central Asian states in 2001, stands out as the first regional organization China has ever initiated and organized. Now regional multilateralism and institution building is considered a convenient way for China to utilize and expand its sphere of influence in East Asia. Such regional institutions may be a good organizational tool that can be used to prevent other powers' 'soft containment' of China.[7]

The motivation behind China's activism in regional institution building is complex.[8] To many scholars, the major motivation underwriting China's regional policy is its economic development strategy in the globalizing world and its national security concerns at borders. For these purposes, China has come to see regional institutions as a useful instrument to pursue its economic, political, and security interests in the region. China proposed to negotiate an FTA agreement with ASEAN in 2001, and, after nine years of negotiation, the China–ASEAN FTA finally came into effect in January 2010. Beijing has also actively engaged in negotiation of bilateral FTAs with other countries. To promote its economic and political interests, regional institutions have the utility of providing appropriate platforms to address security concerns, territorial disputes and regional governance issues with neighbors.[9] While all of these imperatives explain

---

[7] The term 'soft containment' was first introduced in the Chinese media; see 'Soft Containment on China's Development?' (in Chinese), *International Herald Daily*, 23 October 2007.

[8] For a good discussion, see Wu Xinbo, 'Chinese Perspectives on Building an East Asian Community in the Twenty-First Century', in Michael J. Green and Bates Gill (eds), *Asia's New Multilateralism: Cooperation, Competition, and the Search for Community* (New York: Columbia University Press, 2009), 55–77.

[9] A collection of articles on this topic can be found in Guoguang Wu and Helen Lansdowne (eds), *China Turns To Multilateralism: Foreign Policy and Regional Security* (London and New York: Routledge, 2008), 303.

the rationale behind China's regional policy, there is another important motive behind China's policy toward regional institutions, that is, to reassure its neighbors and establish the image of being a responsible power in regional affairs. This is a new aspect of Chinese foreign policy in recent years that underscores the normative foundation of China's diplomacy.

Chinese policymakers are now more concerned about the image of a rising China in world affairs. Beijing seeks more institutionalized arrangements to enhance and expand cooperation with its Asian neighbors. Multilateralism and regional institution building is hailed as a new norm of international politics in today's world politics. The rising China has a desire to ensure that it is accepted by regional nations as a legitimate major power in international and regional order. If viewed in this way, a rising China is expected to improve relations with its neighbors and to actively participate in regional institution building. The events and developments in post-Cold War East Asia have opened up new opportunities for China to integrate into regional institutions. Historically, rising powers have been perceived as challengers to the existing order that may instigate major wars. China, however, has been struggling to chart a different course for its rise to great power status by changing its international posture and image in the rapidly evolving East Asian geopolitical landscape.

China and its East Asian neighbors have found ways of mitigating many of their concerns through the process of building regional economic and security architectures and integrating China into the regional system in accordance with the 'Asian way' of cooperation and consultation. Given China's previous inexperience in institutionalized cooperation, these regional institutions have provided mechanisms for China and its neighbors to work together and mitigate incipient conflict. A growing consciousness of international rules and norms and greater commitment to international society as well as regional structures has helped to build a positive image of Beijing both in regional politics and in the eyes of other East Asian nations. All these developments help Beijing to increase its legitimate power. As China increasingly focuses on regional conflict management, its normative and institutional contribution to regional security also helps to transform the source and nature of regional order.

THE US AND EAST ASIAN REGIONALISM

Washington's views on East Asian regionalism and institution building are mixed and evolving. After World War II, the East Asian regional system emerged in stark contrast with that in Europe, where two competing security blocs (NATO and the Warsaw Pact) came into force.[10] In Europe, Washington took the lead in building its alliance system around NATO and a set of multilateral political institutions across the Atlantic. In East Asia, Washington did not see the strategic value of building an institution-alized regional political and security structure in a fragmented region.[11] Instead, Washington preferred bilateralism over multilateralism. It often viewed proposals for regional institutions as an attempt to undermine the US bilateral alliance system in East Asia.

Yet, after the Cold War, the US attitude toward regional community building underwent a pronounced shift during the Clinton Administration. Washington became more positive in identifying and promoting multi-lateral dialogues for a 'new Pacific community'. To promote his Pacific Community vision and trade liberalization, President Clinton proposed and hosted the first APEC summit in 1993 in Seattle. In the same year, Washington also participated in the ASEAN Post-Ministerial Conference (PMC) with ASEAN's other dialogue partners, which was reconvened in 1994 to form the ASEAN Regional Forum (ARF).

During the George W. Bush Administration, however, Washington's policy began drifting toward passivity. Although Washington was gener-ally supportive of or at least not actively opposed to East Asian regional community-building initiatives (such as ASEAN+3 and the EAS), it took a more passive or 'benign neglect' attitude as much of its foreign policy attention was on the 'War on Terror' after September 11, 2001. During the Bush years, East Asian community-building projects were flourishing, but Washington was strategically 'distracted', looking at something else.

Another reason for the George W. Bush Administration's 'benign neglect' is that it had strong reservations about the effectiveness of such East Asian dialogues and community-building projects in promoting American interests. Washington policy analysts often dismissed these exercises either as irrelevant or creating challenges such as divergent and competing man-dates, based on different notions of membership among regional nations.

---

[10]   For a good discussion on the issue, see Christopher Hemmer and Peter J. Katzenstein, 'Why Is There No NATO in Asia? Collective Identity, Regionalism, and the Origins of Multilateralism', *International Organization* 56 (3) (2002): 575–607.

[11]   Yet Washington did try to organize some sub-regional structures, such as the Southeast Asia Treaty Organization (SEATO) and the Central Treaty Organization, in the 1950s, but they were all unsuccessful and short-lived. See Kent E. Calder and Francis Fukuyama (eds), *East Asian Multilateralism: Prospects for Regional Stability* (Baltimore, MD: Johns Hopkins University Press, 2008), Chapter 1.

The Bush Administration thus chose a policy of selective engagement when deciding whether to participate in regional multilateral dialogues (such as the EAS, APEC and the ARF) or ad hoc mini-multilateral talks such as the Six Party Talks on the North Korean nuclear issue.

America's East Asia policy does not revolve around a clear regional agenda, but rather derives more from its national interest, global strategy, policy priority determined by domestic politics, or specific bilateral concerns of the time. Many East Asian countries, from their viewpoints, see their bilateral relationship with the US as an issue of great salience. But they have seen less and less American interest and leadership in regional multilateralism and institution building. To policymakers in Washington, the American experiences in APEC and the ARF indicate that these multilateral organizations can be useful vehicles for promoting US interests, but they have also learned that these organizations have serious limits. The most voiced American criticism of ASEAN-style regional institution building is that it is more confidence-building 'talking shops' than action-focused workshops. Washington seems to have become more reserved as the proliferation of regional multilateral initiatives increases the danger of 'meeting fatigue' in regional institution building.[12]

While Washington has become less connected to regional agendas, China has traveled in the opposite direction. In the post-9/11 world, the US has increasingly found itself in a dilemma as regards the conflict between its global ambitions and its ability to focus on the East Asian region. Distracted by its 'War on Terror' in Iraq and Afghanistan, Washington found regional agendas in East Asia less connected to its global strategy. As Washington's influence in the region began to wane, Beijing took advantage of it, improving its relations with its neighbors. China has carefully crafted its regional strategy. To avoid major confrontation with neighbors, Chinese policy emphasizes finding common ground with Asian neighbors and not pressing them to change policies in sensitive areas, except on the 'core national interest' issues of Taiwan and Tibet.[13] East Asian nations are not pressed to choose between Beijing and Washington. As a result, most of them have chosen to accommodate, rather than fear and resist, the Chinese economic, diplomatic and political

---

[12]   Ralph Cossa, 'East Asian Community and the United States: U.S. View – One Step Forward, Two Steps Back?' in Council on East Asian Community (CEAC), *An East Asian Community and New Dynamism of Regional Governance*, September 2006.
[13]   See Robert G. Sutter, *China's Rise: Implications for U.S. Leadership in Asia* (policy studies 21), Honolulu: East-West Center, 2006.

emergence in the region. China's success and strength highlights American weakness in East Asia today.[14]

After Barack Obama took office in January 2009, his administration began to take a new look at its policy toward East Asian institution building. Facing the challenge of formulating a coherent strategy responding to the emerging institution building in East Asia, Secretary of State Hillary Clinton made a high-profile visit to East Asia in January 2009, sending a strong message that 'the U.S. is back'. President Obama's visit to the region in October 2009 reinforced the message that the US intends to engage fully with regional institution building in East Asia.

Talking about regional institution building, Secretary of State Hillary Clinton argued in a major policy speech on Asian regional architecture in January 2010 that

> U.S. involvement and leadership in Asia-Pacific institutions, ranging from our support for and contributions to APEC to our response to the Indian Ocean Tsunami, can benefit everyone. We can provide resources and facilitate cooperation in ways that other regional actors cannot replicate or, in some cases, are not trusted to do . . . an active and engaged United States is critical to the success of these.[15]

In the same speech, she also spelled out five principles concerning US engagement in regional institution building:

● the American alliance relationships are the cornerstone of its regional involvement;
● regional institutions should work to build a common regional economic and security agenda;
● the importance of result-oriented cooperation and focusing on delivering results;
● the need to enhance the flexibility and creativity of multilateral cooperation;
● building inclusive regional institutions for all the key stakeholders (the US included) that can best protect and promote collective future.

---

[14] T.J. Pempel, 'How Bush bungled Asia: militarism, economic indifference and unilateralism have weakened the United States across Asia', *Pacific Review* 21 (5) (December 2008).
[15] Secretary of State Hillary Clinton's remarks on 'Regional Architecture in Asia: Principles and Priorities', Honolulu, Hawaii, 12 January 2010, accessed 12 June 2010, http://www.state.gov/secretary/rm/2010/01/135090.htm.

Despite the rhetoric, however, Washington's policy is still vague. One of the key questions facing policymakers in Washington is whether it will go along with the existing institution-building projects *or* propose a new regional institutional framework instead. East Asian institution building has evolved at a faster pace and has developed a more complex regional agenda in the last few years. Washington has no choice but to make itself adapt to the new reality. Although the current financial crisis does not hurt East Asia as hard as that of 1997–98, it has still provided a strong stimulus for East Asia to consolidate its intra-Asian cooperation mechanism. On 22 February 2009, ASEAN+3 financial ministers agreed in principle to establish an independent 'surveillance unit' in conjunction with the multilateralization of the CMI. The multilateralized CMI, with a collective funding of US$120 billion, constitutes a significant move that would lead to an embryonic Asian Monetary Fund (AMF). The key issue for the US is to what extent a future AMF would coordinate with the IMF in lending conditionality and other regional monetary policy.

The old problem of 'meeting fatigue' remains a challenge for Washington. The Obama Administration has signed the Treaty of Amity and Cooperation (TAC), agreed to engage with the EAS more formally, and sent high-level delegates to Asia's annual gatherings (like the ARF). But simply 'showing up' at these functions is not sufficient. Although the US does not need to belong to all East Asian organizations, it has to carefully consider how to engage with them in a more effective way. To promote American interests and values in the region, Washington needs to engage in all institution building activities. But the practical challenge is that the US President cannot afford to attend all regional summits and related activities. As Emmerson argues, President Obama cannot afford to commute between the White House and Asia. 'Showing up in all these summit meetings – APEC, East Asia Summit, US–ASEAN summit, G-20 – is easier to advise than do.'[16] Just consider that the US President has to travel two or three times to Asia in two months of a year (in October and November); it is almost impossible to do so politically, given his daunting agenda at home. Due to scheduling problems, for example, President Obama postponed trips to Indonesia and Australia twice in 2010 at the time of writing.

It is true that East Asia is of vital importance to the United States.

---

[16]   Donald K. Emmerson, 'Asian Regionalism and US Policy: the Case for Creative Adaptation', RSIS Working Paper No. 193, S. Rajaratnam School of International Studies, Nanyang University of Technology, Singapore, March 2010, 7.

Washington wants to 'act as a resident power and not just as a visitor, because what happens in the region has a direct effect on [American] security and economic well-being'.[17] But for a more coherent policy toward future regional institution building, Washington needs to answer three fundamental questions. First, does it want to build a trans-Pacific community like APEC, or support an East Asian community without itself, or participate in something in between like the East Asia Summit? The second question concerns the relationship between future regional institutions and its existing bilateral alliance system in East Asia. Can they coexist or do they conflict with each other? Third, does Washington want to rely on ad hoc multilateralism like the Six Party Talks or on building a more coherent regional institutional security structure like that in Europe? The answers to these questions would be helpful in clarifying the competition and cooperation between China and the US in regional institution building.

CHINA–US RELATIONS AND REGIONAL INSTITUTION BUILDING

As two key players in East Asia, the relationship between China and the US today has become strategically more significant and complicated. The relationship is significant because it goes beyond the bilateral basis. Without China's cooperation, the US alone cannot handle emerging global and regional problems. It is complicated because there are elements of both competition and cooperation in the relationship. Both nations want to build a 'positive, cooperative, and comprehensive' relationship.[18] There are differences and disputes over issues such as Taiwan, human rights, Tibet, trade imbalances, intellectual property rights, and the transparency of China's military modernization. Meanwhile, China and the US also have strong common interests working together to deal with a number of issues concerning the global economy, financial reforms, regional conflicts, climate change, and the nonproliferation regime. The China–US relationship has expereinced ups and downs over the last three decades,

---

[17] Kurt Campbell, 'Regional Overview of East Asia and the Pacific', testimony before the House Committee on Foreign Affairs Subcommittee on Asia, the Pacific, and the Global Environment, Washington, DC, 3 March 2010, accessed 12 June 2010, http://www.state.gov/p/eap/rls/rm/2010/03/137754.htm.

[18] President Obama's speech at U.S.–China Strategic and Economic Dialogue, 27 July 2009, accessed 12 June 2010, http://www.whitehouse.gov/the-press-office/remarks-president-uschina-strategic-and-economic-dialogue.

but it has become more mature to handle differences of opinion while continuing to cooperate on issues of mutual concern. Today's China–US relationship cannot and should not be viewed through a zero-sum lens.

The nature of China–US relations today – cooperation cum competition – reflects the logic of 'balance of influence', rather than that of 'balance of power'. Power balancing is a basic principle of political realism in international relations. It argues that a nation chooses to balance against any one nation from becoming sufficiently too strong in the international system through military or non-military means.[19] Yet entering the twenty-first century, the China–US relationship has gone beyond the logic of using military power and traditional alliance politics to balance each other in regional politics. The cooperation-cum-competition relationship reflects a different type of major power relations based on the logic of balance of influence. The concept of 'balance of influence' is built on Joseph Nye's notion of 'soft power'[20] and its later application by other scholars to the study of how weak states increase their power relative to that of strong ones in the international system through a so-called 'soft balancing' strategy.[21] Power and influence could be the same thing, but they could also mean different things when we use them to distinguish between realism and liberal institutionalism in international relations. The 'balance of power' logic stresses an actor's ability to balance against other actors mainly through 'hard power', coercion, arms race, alliance, and other non-peaceful means, while the 'balance of influence' logic accentuates the exercise of influence and balancing through non-coercive or pursuasive means, such as diplomacy, economic benefit, ideology and other cultural attractiveness, and international institutional power. Since China and the US have a high degree of economic interdependence with each other as well as with other regional nations in East Asia, it is almost impossible to imagine that they would fight an all-over war against each other at the present time. In these circumstances, a more sensible strategy for them is to use what is called an 'institutional balancing' strategy to compete as well as cooperate with each other.[22] That makes the regional institution

---

[19]   Kenneth N. Waltz, *Theory of International Politics* (Reading, MA: Addison-Wesley, 1979).

[20]   Joseph S. Nye Jr, *Bound to Lead: the Changing Nature of American Power* (New York: Basic Books, 1990), and *Soft Power: the Means to Success in World Politics* (New York: Public Affairs, 2004).

[21]   See, for example, Robert Anthony Pape, 'Soft Balancing against the United States', *International Security* 30 (1) (Summer 2005).

[22]   The term 'institutional balancing' was introduced by Kai He to describe a state's balancing behavior in participating in and manipulating multilateral

building an important place to discern and measure their cooperation-cum-competition relations.

For the United States, the rise of China in East Asia poses both opportunities and challenges. In history the arrival of new powers sometimes caused war, and sometimes did not. Therefore, a wise strategy for existing powers is to create strategic space for newcomers in the course of power transition, which ensures they emerge peacefully and in a way that supports, rather than undermines, the existing international system. The challenge posed for Washington by the rise of China in East Asia is multidimensional – political, military, and economic – but one of the most important dimensions is what Thomas Christensen calls the 'strategic peace offensive'.[23] This is how China has increased its regional influence vis-à-vis the US. In contrast to the traditional military balancing, China is using a strategy of 'soft balancing' or peaceful rising to challenge the US in East Asia, while avoiding any direct contest to US military preponderance. China's 'soft rising' of non-military means undermines the American leadership in the region. These soft means range from the formation of temporary coalitions and economic statecraft to attentive diplomacy and regional community building. As Washington is preoccupied with other geostrategic issues, Beijing is reaching out to other East Asian states and people, accommodating their benefits, exercising positive diplomacy, and finding common ground with neighbors in regional community building. China has enhanced its popularity through its economic strength as the regional manufacturing center and, increasingly, the hub for regional trading, supported by its high economic growth and trading prowess.

While economic strength adds to Beijing's influence, its attentive good-neighbor diplomacy and the resulting soft power is something that matters more in the changing 'balance of influence' in East Asia.[24] China's pragmatic approach to Asian neighbors suggests Beijing has learned how to broaden international contacts and advance influence in Asia without overt competition with Washington (which may force other Asian states to choose between Washington and Beijing). China's institutional influence

---

institutions (inclusive or exclusive ones) to engage and compete with other actors; see Kai He, *Institutional Balancing in the Asia Pacific: Economic Interdependence and China's Rise* (London and New York: Routledge, 2009), 10.

[23] Thomas J. Christensen, 'Fostering Stability or Creating a Monster? The Rise of China and U.S. Policy toward East Asia', *International Security* 31 (1) (Summer 2006): 98.

[24] For a good discussion on Chinese soft power, see Bates Gill and Yanzhong Huang, 'Sources and Limits of Chinese "Soft Power"', *Survival* 48 (2) (Summer 2006): 17–36.

is on the rise, but it is not causally related to the decline of Washington's influence in East Asia. The US still has enormous power and influence in the region. China tries to earn more institutional currency to balance US influence. China's constructive role in regional institutional building is a source of its rising soft power as well as a tool to undermine US power in East Asia.

China and the US could be both competitive and cooperative in regional institution building and it all depends on their answers to some major issues concerning future regional institutional structure. These issues include the US security alliances in the region, the vision of regional institution building, and the role of ad hoc multilateralism in East Asian politics. Although China does not like to see American military intervention in East Asia, it does not oppose outright the US military presence in the region. On the contrary, Beijing even welcomes the American forward deployment as 'a stabilizing factor' for Asian security. China is a status quo power, not a revisionist state, for the international system. Do emerging Asian multilateral institutions undermine the primacy of the Washington-anchored security bilateralism? Actually, they could coexist and develop in parallel. East Asian nations have divergent security needs, and they do not want to choose between the US and China. They practice different national security strategies, ranging from ASEAN's enmeshment strategy and South Korea's accommodation strategy (under Kim Dah-jung) to Japan's balancing and hedging strategy against the rise of China. Many others are in the middle, playing bandwagoning, buck-passing, and even 'hiding'. Asia's multilateral institutions not only benefit China but also Washington in its efforts at constraining the rise of China.

Washington's half-hearted embrace of multilateral institution building in East Asia reflects an enduring suspicion that its goal is to undermine American leadership in the region. But, as Susan Shirk argues, if the US were to play a more active role in promoting and building multilateral arrangements in East Asia, it might be surprised by how effective multi-lateralism could be in tackling even sensitive foreign policy and security issues.[25] China and the US share common interests in managing regional conflicts through ad hoc multilateralism like the Six Party Talks, and they should increase mutual trust through working together on regional governance and conflict management. As for the future of East Asian regional institutions, whether there should be an Asian-only grouping based on the ASEAN+3 process, or a pan-Asian community embedded in

---

[25]   Susan Shirk, 'American Hopes: An Agenda for Cooperation that Serves US Interests', *Global Asia* 5 (1) (Spring 2010): 27.

the EAS design, or a pan-Asian-Pacific community erected in the APEC framework, it is still too early for Beijing and Washington to give a clear answer. In some way, the future regional institutional structure will not be something by 'design' but rather something emerging 'naturally' or being assembled along the way.

CONCLUSION: WHITHER EAST ASIAN INSTITUTION BUILDING?

The emerging regional institutional framework in East Asia will not resemble that of Europe, where there have been coherent attempts to construct a regional institutional architecture. The end of the Cold War and the Asian Financial Crisis of 1997–98 created a strong stimulus to regional institution building in East Asia. Yet, constructing regional institutions has not always been a process with a shared grand design and vision; rather, it follows the 'law of independent assortment'. As East Asian nations do not share a set of common norms, values, and threat perceptions, they have different views on how to construct regional institutional architecture.

From ASEAN, ASEAN+3, the EAS and the ARF to APEC, East Asian nations have created quite a few institution-building projects but most of them are still 'institution-lite'. The challenge is how to consolidate them and move forward with more effective regional institution building. According to Hadi Soesastro's classification, the present East Asian institutions belong to two categories: supra-structure institutions and infra-structure institutions.[26] The supra-structure institutions, based on an 'idea of the region', serve the purpose of confidence building, socialization, and creating a conscious sense of regional identity. Using the 'ASEAN way', the region has built a number of this type of institution. The infra-structure institutions, on the other hand, are formed to promote functional cooperation among regional nations who share common interests and similar governance problems. The objective of them is to solve problems, encourage cooperation, and adopt best practices.

Both China and the US can engage in and contribute to the construction of the supra-structure and infra-structure institutions in East Asia. China is more advantageously placed in participating in and promoting

---

[26] Hadi Soesastro, 'ASEAN and Institutions for Regionalism in Asia', presentation at the seminar on Enhancing Asian Institutions: ASAEN's Role in Regional Integration, the Asian Development Bank, Manila, 4 May 2009, accessed 15 June 2010, http://www.adb.org/AnnualMeeting/2009/seminars/hsoesastro-presentation.pdf.

regional infra-structure institutions like ASEAN+3, the CMI, and the GMS project, while the US has the upper hand in regional networks of bilateral security arrangements. In the current discussion on East Asian regional institution building, there are proposals to turn some supra-structure institutions into infra-structure ones. The ARF is seen as having too large and too diverse a membership to be effective as a supra-structure institution for promoting security cooperation in Asia. Washington and Beijing can cooperate, together with ASEAN and other regional players, to transform the organization into a more effective structure.

How to define an appropriate division of labor within the existing regional institutional arrangements is another issue on which Beijing and Washington can cooperate. Consolidating regional institutional arrangements requires a forward-looking answer. For instance, ASEAN+3, the EAS and APEC could readjust their agendas and initiative-conscious activities among themselves. ASEAN+3 could focus more on functional cooperation within East Asia, while the EAS serves as a forum for high-level dialogues on strategic issues among wider-regional members, possibly including the United States and Russia. Different initiatives and projects must find their 'market niche' in the future regional institutional architecture. Looking to the future, APEC may consider giving up its ambition to build an Asian-Pacific community and focusing more on functions of trade facilitation and investment service through research and information gathering like those provided by the OECD. 'Rationalization' of this kind would not be easy and may take time to occur. But the benefit is obvious. It at least could prevent 'meeting fatigue' for regional leaders. As for Beijing and Washington, both should be able to better locate themselves in the regional institutional settings and avoid destructive competition.

2. Who's afraid of Asian trade regionalism, and why?

C.L. Lim

THE MODERN HISTORY OF FREE TRADE AGREEMENTS

The 'GATT draftsmen knew whereof they spoke when they termed the regional exception a "standard clause in all commercial treaties"'.[1] From the 1700s to the 1930s, trade agreements were bilateral,[2] and for practical political reasons the GATT 1947 too needed to include various exceptions to cater for regional trade agreements.[3] Such exceptions covered not only the general permission (under GATT Article XXIV) to form customs unions and FTAs, but also the need to accommodate British and French imperial preferences and other pre-existing arrangements such as those between the Lebanon–Syria Customs Union and Palestine and the Transjordan.[4]

These were limited exceptions, however, coupled with the belief on the part of the GATT's framers that regional trade agreements (that is, FTAs and customs unions) could serve as building-blocks towards greater global trade liberalization at a time when such FTAs and customs unions were relatively few in number. Moreover, belief in the multilateral system, and in particular the underlying idea of trade liberalization through successive

---

[1]   John Jackson, *World Trade and the Law of GATT* (Charlottesville, VA: Michie, 1969), 576.

[2]   Frederick M. Abbott, 'A New Dominant Trade Species Emerges', in William J. Davey and John Jackson (eds), *The Future of International Economic Law* (Oxford: OUP, 2008), 133, 134.

[3]   By 'regional trade agreements', we mean both FTAs and customs unions.

[4]   Jackson, *World Trade and the Law of GATT*, op. cit., 264–5. These were political compromises to accommodate British and French colonies, and apparently in response to Syria's ill-fated call for developing country preferences.

rounds of multilateral negotiations,[5] had remained strong in the first decade of the GATT's existence.

The beginning of modern concern with the 'customs union dilemma' can be traced to 1957 or thereabouts when the GATT Parties were compelled to accept the formation of the European Economic Communities. The Contracting Parties doubted the legality of the EEC and its various Association Agreements with European colonies and ex-colonies but they had little choice in the matter. Failure to accept the EEC as a *fait accompli* could have forced the Contracting Parties to undertake the wholesale renegotiation of the GATT and, compared with the post-war environment in which the GATT was born, the mood now was different. Had the GATT been negotiated ten years later, it might never have achieved all that it did.[6]

Ultimately, the years between 1950 and 1960 witnessed not only the creation of the EEC in 1957 but also the Benelux Economic Union in 1958[7] and the European Free Trade Area (EFTA) in 1960.[8] Following the example of the EEC, developing countries in Latin America and elsewhere began to form their own customs unions and free trade areas in the 1960s,[9] such as the Latin-American Free Trade Area (LAFTA) in 1960 under the Treaty of Montevideo, the Central African Customs and Economic Union (CACEU) in 1966,[10] and the Caribbean Free Trade Association (CARIFTA) in 1965 under the Dickenson Bay Agreement.[11] Subsequently, the 1980s witnessed the emergence of the Southern African Development Community (SADC) in 1980[12] and the Gulf Cooperation Council (GCC) in 1981.[13] Between the late 1980s and early to mid-1990s, similar developments occurred in North America, Europe and Latin

---

[5]   Whereby the benefits of concessions negotiated between the larger trading nations would also be spread more widely across the whole GATT membership through the operation of the Most Favoured Nation rule (MFN).

[6]   Robert Hudec, *The GATT Legal System and World Trade Diplomacy*, 2nd edn (London: Butterworths, 1990), 211–14.

[7]   See the Benelux website, accessed 2 September 2010, www.benelux.be/en/home_intro.asp.

[8]   See the EFTA website, accessed 2 September 2010, www.efta.int.

[9]   Robert Hudec, *Developing Countries in the GATT Legal System* (London: Gower, 1987), 50–51.

[10]   P. Tchanque, 'L'Union Douanière et Économique de L'Afrique Centrale', *Journal of African Law* 16 (1972): 339.

[11]   Now the Caribbean Community (CARICOM), accessed 2 September 2020, www.caricom.org.

[12]   Originally, the Southern African Development Cooperation Conference (SADCC). See website, accessed 2 September 2010, www.sadc.int.

[13]   See website, accessed 2 September 2010, www.gccsg.org/eng.

America. In January 1989, the Canada–US FTA came into effect. The European Union was created on 1 November 1993 by the Treaty of Maastricht, while the North American Free Trade Agreement (NAFTA) entered into force on 1 January 1994. The Southern Common Market (MERCOSUR) had been created in 1991.[14] In Southeast Asia, Thailand also produced a 1991 'discussion paper' proposing an ASEAN Free Trade Area in light of the emergence of these other trading blocs and the anticipated conclusion of the Uruguay Round.[15] Beginning with the establishment of the WTO in 1994, FTAs and customs unions grew by an average of 21 new notifications per year, compared with the figure of three per year during the entire GATT period between 1947 and 1994.

There was a second development, occurring roughly in tandem with the proliferation of FTAs and customs unions. Latin American nations sought preferential access to the US market in light of the example of the EEC's Association Agreements.[16] This demand took place largely under the auspices of UNCTAD and led to the US adopting the Generalized System of Preferences (GSP) Scheme, and eventually to the adoption of the Enabling Clause in 1979.[17] The Enabling Clause did two things. It allowed developed countries to offer preferential access to their markets under today's GSP Schemes, and it allowed developing countries relief from the strictures of Article XXIV in concluding regional trade agreements between themselves. This meant another exception to the Most Favoured Nation rule and that GATT disciplines on FTAs and customs unions became even looser. These developments contributed to the delegalization of the GATT from the 1950s to the 1980s. In the case of FTA and customs union regulation, such delegalization has lasted to the present day. The China–ASEAN FTA and the ASEAN Free Trade Area are contemporary examples of FTAs which have been notified to the WTO under the looser terms of the Enabling Clause (and not under GATT Article XXIV).

---

[14]   See the MERCOSUR website, accessed 2 September 2010, www.mercosur. org.uy.

[15]   Rudolfo Severino, *Southeast Asia in Search of an ASEAN Community* (Singapore: ISEAS, 2006), 223. That proposal had been preceded by earlier calls from the Philippines in 1982 and again in 1990 for 'ASEAN Free Trade' and an 'ASEAN Treaty on Economic Cooperation'; ibid., 15–16, 221.

[16]   Note, 'United States Preferences: The Proposed System', *Journal of World Trade* 8 (1974): 216.

[17]   'Decision on Differential and More Favourable Treatment, Reciprocity and Fuller Participation of Developing Countries', BISD, 26th Supplement (1980), 203–4.

ASIA'S FREE TRADE AGREEMENTS

Asia's FTAs have now become the subject of critical press attention. We shall refer to two articles occurring within weeks of each other in *Time* magazine and *The Economist*. Admittedly, such sudden attention was also due to the conclusion of the ASEAN–India and India–Korea FTAs in August 2009, which happened to coincide with the expected coming into full effect of the China–ASEAN FTA (CAFTA) on 1 January 2010.[18] But aside from such coincidence, what is in fact so remarkable about these developments?

One reason may be that while Asia has been a relative late-comer in the FTA game, its entry has been both sudden and swift.[19] True, ASEAN's Free Trade Area (AFTA) had been conceived as far back as 1991, and it subsequently developed in fits and starts before formulating the aim in 2003 to achieve an ASEAN Economic Community by 2015.[20] But in 2001, China unexpectedly offered to enter into an FTA with ASEAN. The result was that the China–ASEAN (CAFTA) negotiations swiftly overtook discussions on having an ASEAN–Japan Comprehensive Economic Partnership Agreement. China and the six original members of ASEAN made 2010 the target date for the completion of an FTA, but in the meantime there was already an 'Early Harvest' scheme.[21] This was soon followed by a goods agreement and a dispute settlement mechanism, both of which were completed in 2004; a services agreement which was completed in 2006 and which entered into force in 2007; and an investment agreement which was signed in August 2009.[22]

---

[18]   Michael Schumann, 'Bloc Party: Asian Nations are Lowering Trade Barriers to Keep their Economies Chugging. Why the West Should be Worried', *Time*, 21 September 2009 (hereafter, 'Bloc Party'); 'The Noodle Bowl: Why Trade Agreements are All the Rage in Asia', *The Economist*, 5 September 2009 (hereafter, 'Noodle Bowl').

[19]   See Barry Desker, 'In Defense of FTAs: From Purity to Pragmatism in East Asia', *Pacific Review* 17 (2004): 3; Won-Mog Choi, 'Regional Economic Integration in East Asia: Prospect and Jurisprudence', *Journal International Economic Law* 6 (2003): 49; Rahul Sen, '"New Regionalism" in Asia: A Comparative Analysis of Emerging Regional and Bilateral Trading Agreements involving ASEAN, China and India', *Journal of World Trade* (2006): 553.

[20]   Declaration of ASEAN Concord II, Bali, Indonesia, 7 October 2003; Declaration on the ASEAN Economic Community Blueprint, Singapore, 20 November 2007.

[21]   See further, C.L. Lim, 'The China–ASEAN Tariff Acceleration Precedent', in M. Sornarajah and Jiangyu Wang (eds), *China, India and the International Economic Order* (Cambridge: Cambridge University Press, 2009), 427–53.

[22]   'ASEAN–China Dialogue Relations', available on the ASEAN Secretariat website, accessed 26 October 2009, http://www.aseansec.org/5874.htm.

At the same time, the Japan–ASEAN process began to move forward, no doubt in response to the China–ASEAN negotiations. This led to the conclusion of the ASEAN–Japan Comprehensive Economic Partnership Agreement in April 2008.[23] One noticeable difference between the AJCEP and CAFTA negotiations was that Japan decided from an early stage to negotiate also with the individual ASEAN nations (Singapore, Malaysia, the Philippines and Thailand) before finally concluding a larger deal with ASEAN as a whole.

In comparison, Korea had been late in starting negotiations with ASEAN. However, Korea has since concluded a goods agreement which entered into force in July 2007, a services agreement which entered into force on 1 May 2009, and an investment agreement which was signed with ASEAN in June 2009.[24]

Currently, we have AFTA as well as FTAs between ASEAN and China, ASEAN and Japan, ASEAN and Korea, the recent conclusion in 2009 of the ASEAN–India FTA,[25] and a recently concluded ASEAN–Australia–New Zealand FTA.

In addition, there are a large number of overlapping, Asian bilateral agreements. Within ASEAN itself, Singapore has bilateral FTAs in the region with China, Korea, Japan, India and Pakistan. Malaysia has bilateral FTAs with Japan and Pakistan in the region. The Philippines has an Economic Partnership Agreement with Japan. Thailand has bilateral FTAs with Japan and India,[26] and as a party to BIMSTEC (Bay of Bengal Initiative for Multi-Sectoral Technical and Economic Cooperation) recently concluded an agreement on trade in goods with Myanmar, Bangladesh, Sri Lanka, Bhutan and Nepal.[27] Brunei has concluded FTAs with Japan and Pakistan, and is also a party to the Trans-Pacific Strategic Economic Partnership Agreement (comprising Singapore, New Zealand,

---

[23]   ASEAN–Japan Comprehensive Partnership Agreement, text available on the website of the Japanese Ministry of Foreign Affairs, accessed 26 October 2009, http://www.mofa.go.jp/policy/economy/fta/asean.html.

[24]   'ASEAN–Korea FTA Completes', *The Nation* (Bangkok), 2 June 2009. Texts of the goods and services agreements are available at the Singapore Government FTA website, accessed 26 October 2009, http://www.fta.gov.sg/fta_akfta.asp?hl=3.

[25]   'India–ASEAN Sign FTA', *Straits Times* (Singapore), 13 August 2009; Niharika Chandola and Ritupama Bhuyan, 'India, ASEAN Resolve Differences over FTA', *Business Standard* (Delhi/Mumbai), 24 September 2009.

[26]   See Thailand's Department of Trade Negotiations' website, accessed 2 September 2010, www.thaifta.com.

[27]   'India Seals Free Trade Pact with Thailand', *Times of India* (Delhi), 7 June 2009.

Brunei, and Chile). In the case of Vietnam, the Vietnam–Japan Economic Partnership Agreement entered into force in 2009.[28]

Turning to FTAs with countries outside Asia (extra-regional FTAs), Singapore has the largest number of these – with Peru, the US, EFTA, Jordan, Panama, and Australia, as well as with New Zealand (NZ) and Chile under the Trans-Pacific Economic Partnership Agreement. An FTA with the Gulf Cooperation Council (Bahrain, Kuwait, Oman, Qatar, Saudi Arabia and UAE) was signed in December 2008 and awaits entry into force, and Singapore recently signed its third bilateral FTA with a South American nation, the Singapore–Costa Rica Free Trade Agreement (SCRFTA), on 6 April 2010. It is currently negotiating with Canada, Mexico, Ukraine, and Pakistan.[29] In contrast, Malaysia's emphasis has been on larger deals with Islamic and developing nations under the Framework Agreement on the Trade Preferential System among the Member States of the Organization of the Islamic Conference (TPS-OIC),[30] and under the Developing Eight (D8) Preferential Tariff Agreement which Malaysia ratified on 20 July 2006.[31] In addition, the Malaysia–NZ FTA awaits implementation some time in 2010, while the Malaysia–Chile FTA is nearing conclusion following the last round of talks in December 2009.[32] Negotiations with the US, Australia and India are on-going.[33] With respect to Thailand, it has FTAs with Australia, NZ and Peru, and an Early Harvest Agreement with Bahrain.[34] Its FTA negotiations with the US have been suspended since the coup in Thailand in 2006,[35] while negotiations with EFTA are also currently on hold.[36]

Turning to Northeast Asia, China, which also has an FTA with

---

[28]   Joint Press Statement on the Occasion of the entry into force of the Agreement between Japan and the Socialist republic of Vietnam for an Economic Partnership, Ministry of Foreign Affairs of Japan Press Release, 1 October 2009.

[29]   See the Singapore Government's FTA website, accessed 2 September 2010, www.fta.gov.sg.

[30]   See the Malaysian Ministry of Trade and Industry's website, accessed 2 September 2010, www.miti.gov.my.

[31]   See ibid. The D8 comprises Bangladesh, Indonesia, Iran, Malaysia, Egypt, Nigeria, Pakistan and Turkey.

[32]   Ibid.

[33]   Ibid.

[34]   See Thailand's Department of Trade Negotiations' website, accessed 2 September 2010, www.thaifta.com.

[35]   See the USTR's website, accessed 2 September 2010, www.ustr.gov.

[36]   Notice posted on the EFTA website, accessed 2 September 2010, www.efta.int/free-trade/ongoing-negotiations-talks/thailand.aspx.

Pakistan, has concluded extra-regional FTAs with Chile, Peru, and NZ. Negotiations with Costa Rica were concluded on 12 January 2010. China is currently negotiating with the Gulf Cooperation Council, Australia, Iceland, Norway, and the Southern Africa Customs Union (SACU).[37] Its negotiations with Australia, however, have stalled.[38]As for Japan, it has concluded Economic Partnership Agreements (EPAs) with India and Korea in the region, and also with Chile, Switzerland and Mexico outside the region. Korea signed the Korea–US FTA (KORUS) in 2007 after concluding an FTA with EFTA in 2006. Following signature of the Korea–India FTA in August 2009,[39] the Korea–EU FTA was also initialed on 15 October 2009.[40] Korea–Japan talks are on-going,[41] and Korea is also examining an FTA with China.[42] It is currently in various stages of talks with Canada and Mexico,[43] and with the Gulf Cooperation Council, Peru, Australia, New Zealand, and Colombia. Korea aims to launch FTA negotiations with Turkey in April 2010.[44]

There is no FTA at the present time which ties China, Japan and Korea to each other (an 'East Asia' FTA), or indeed one which ties these three nations to each other and to ASEAN (an 'ASEAN plus Three' FTA) as well as India, Australia and New Zealand (an 'ASEAN plus Six' FTA). It was only at the ASEAN plus Three Summit in 2009 that ASEAN's leaders issued instructions to their Ministers to commence discussions on an East Asia FTA.[45] Thus far, China, Japan and Korea have appeared

---

[37]   Comprising South Africa, Botswana, Namibia, Lesotho and Swaziland.

[38]   See the Chinese Government's FTA Network website, accessed 2 September 2010, www.fta.mofcom.gov.cn.

[39]   'Korea, India sign Cautious FTA', *Korea IT Times* (Seoul), 12 August 2009.

[40]   'Free Trade Agreement with South Korea', MEMO/09/452, Brussels, 15 October 2009.

[41]   'S. Korea, Japan Fail to Agree on Resuming Free Trade Negotiations', Xinhua News Agency, 22 December 2009.

[42]   'S. Korea to Examine Feasibility of S. Korea, China FTA', Xinhua News Agency, 15 April 2010.

[43]   Kim Sue-young, 'Korea–Mexico FTA Accord May Take Time', *Korea Times* (Seoul), 10 July 2009. For the background to the Korea–Canada FTA negotiations, see Canada's Foreign Affairs and International Trade website, accessed 2 September 2010, www.international.gc.ca/trade-agreements-accords-commerciaux/agr-acc/korea-coree/index.aspx.

[44]   See the website of Korea's Ministry of Foreign Affairs & Trade, accessed 2 September 2010, www.mofat.go.kr.

[45]   See 'China, S. Korea, Japan to Hold FTA Talks', Xinhua News Agency, 25 January 2010; 'China, Japan, S. Korea Launch Joint Research on Free Trade Area', Xinhua News Agency, 6 May 2010.

comfortable 'trading through ASEAN', at least in terms of regional treaty architecture.

REASON TO FEAR ASIA'S TREATY BEHAVIOUR?

There is, admittedly, uncertainty about how Asia will eventually form up, and this in part has to do with the fact that membership is linked to questions of leadership and dominance. But is uncertainty the reason for contemporary anxiety about Asia's FTAs?

A second possible cause might be the 'surprise' factor. The China–ASEAN, Korea–ASEAN, Japan–ASEAN, ASEAN–Australia–New Zealand, and India–ASEAN FTAs were concluded almost contemporaneously; roughly speaking, between 2007 and 2010. *Time* magazine noted that India signed its deals with ASEAN and Korea in the same week and that the China–ASEAN FTA was soon to come into full effect, while *The Economist* remarked upon the 'feverish pace' of Asia's FTA activity.[46]

Thirdly, an ASEAN plus Three, or plus Six, deal could cut North America off from East Asia.[47] An ASEAN plus Three arrangement would also risk domination by China though it is said that a 21-member APEC (Asia Pacific Economic Cooperation) FTA or an 'Asia-Pacific Community' (as suggested by the Australian Prime Minister)[48] would prevent that. This idea of preventing a divide across the Pacific had become the subject of public debate in the summer of 2005 in the pages of the *Financial Times*.[49]

This leads to a fourth concern. A 21-member APEC-wide FTA, even if designed to prevent an East Asian bloc, or to jump-start the Doha talks,

---

[46]   'Bloc Party', above note 18; 'Noodle Bowl', above note 18.

[47]   Saadia M. Pekkanen, 'Assessing the Prospects for a US–Japan FTA', in *The New International Architecture in Trade and Investment* (Singapore: APEC, 2007), 87. For an earlier proposal preceding Pekkanen's suggestion of a US–Japan FTA, see James Michael Lawrence, 'Japan Trade Relations and Ideal Free Trade Partners: Why the US Should Pursue its Next FTA with Japan, Not Latin America', *Maryland Journal of International Law and Trade* 20 (1996): 61.

[48]   'Rudd Pushes for Asia-Pacific Community', *The Age* (Melbourne), 4 June 2008. See further C.L. Lim, 'Australia's "Rudd Proposal": Business as Usual', *Asian YBIL* 14 (2008): 287.

[49]   Fred Bergsten, 'Plan B for World Trade', *Financial Times* (London), 15 August 2006; Sungjoon Cho, '"Plan B" is Always Inferior to "Plan A"', *Financial Times* (London), 22 August 2006.

could replace the WTO altogether.[50] In other words a reaction to East Asian regionalism could have knock-on adverse effects. A step in that direction has already been taken in the Trans-Pacific Strategic Economic Partnership Agreement (TEP) between Singapore, NZ, Chile and Brunei. Two are ASEAN small economies and all four are APEC members, as is the United States, which is now negotiating its entry into the Trans-Pacific Partnership. Whichever form Asian regionalism takes, a far less ambitious TEP is already taking shape and has the appearance of an embryonic FTAAP (Free Trade Area of the Asia Pacific) or Asia Pacific Community.

Assuming that these are some of the possible reasons for today's anxieties about Asia, we might nonetheless ask whether they are the 'usual' kinds of reasons which cause economists, lawyers and trade diplomats to criticize the establishment of FTAs. In other words, does anxiety about Asia's present-day FTAs have anything to do with FTAs in the first place? Is that anxiety due to lawyers', GATTologists' and economists' anxieties about a specific treaty form or trade device, in which case their study would fall squarely within these specialist domains, or to other 'extraneous' fears?

THE 'USUAL' REASONS FOR CRITICIZING FREE TRADE AGREEMENTS

Some Old Problems Concerning the Interpretation of WTO Disciplines

When the GATT was drafted, the assumption was that FTAs were beneficial steps or 'building blocks' to trade liberalization. It was only some years later that Jacob Viner demonstrated that while FTAs could increase consumption of goods that are more efficiently produced in an FTA partner country than domestically, they could also increase consumption of goods that are less efficiently produced in FTA countries than in third (non-FTA partner) countries.[51]

So the economics of GATT Article XXIV was not fully informed at the outset, and its (American) drafting language has never changed. GATT Article XXIV continues to permit FTAs today so long as two conditions

---

[50] 'Noodle Bowl', above note 18 ('the flurry of bilateral deals may have come at the expense of a world trade agreement').

[51] See Kenneth Dam, 'Regional Economic Arrangements and the GATT', *University of Chicago Law Review* (1963): 615, 619–20, 627, 633–5.

are met – (1) an 'external requirement' that the FTA does not generally increase 'duties and other restrictive regulations of commerce' in relation to imports from non-FTA GATT/WTO members,[52] and (2) an 'internal' requirement that 'substantially all the trade' between the FTA partners themselves will be covered by the FTA.[53]

Whether a specific FTA generally increases barriers to trade has tended to be a hard economic question, but, notwithstanding that, these GATT disciplines came under strain when the EEC was created. As we have seen, GATT members had a hard choice – 'Either accept the EEC, or renegotiate the GATT.' So they accepted the EEC,[54] together with what Robert Hudec called the 'delegalization' of the GATT from the 1950s to the 1980s.[55] This politicization of GATT Article XXIV has never gone away, even with the establishment of the WTO. Today, these Article XXIV disciplines themselves have become controversial.[56]

One example of such politicization has had to do with what the 'internal' requirement entails. For example, Japan's FTAs (styled 'Economic Partnership Agreements') tend to omit agricultural coverage altogether. This has led to the belief that FTA negotiators can simply omit the coverage of entire sectors where there is no hope of doing the same in the Doha Round negotiations. Should this be allowed? Aware of those places where Angels fear to tread, the WTO Appellate Body has itself offered precious little guidance on the matter. In the *Turkey–Textiles* case, it ruled that the 'substantially all the trade' requirement amounts to a flexible standard. Wisely did the Appellate Body pronounce that while 'not the same' thing 'as *all* the trade' between the parties, the 'substantially all the trade' standard nonetheless requires the inclusion of 'something more than merely *some* of the trade' between the parties to a regional trade agreement.[57]

As for the 'external requirement', its purpose is clearly to protect FTA non-parties. Here, the famous *Honda* case serves as a useful illustration.[58]

---

[52]   GATT 1947, Article XXIV.5(b).

[53]   GATT 1947, Article XXIV.8(b).

[54]   Hudec, *The GATT Legal System and World Trade Diplomacy*, above note 6, 211–12.

[55]   Ibid., Preface.

[56]   'Synopsis of Systemic Issues Related to Regional Trade Agreements', WT/REG/W/37; WTO, Negotiating Group on Rules, Compendium of Issues Related to Regional Trade Agreements – Background Note by the Secretariat – Revision, TN/RL/W/8/Rev.1, 1 August 2002.

[57]   *Turkey – Restrictions on Imports of Textile and Clothing Products*, Report of the Appellate Body, WT/DS34/AB/R, 22 October 1999, para. 48.

[58]   Frédéric P. Cantin and Andreas Lowenfeld, 'Rules of Origin, the Canada–

FTAs require preferential rules of origin (ROOs) in order to prevent goods from entering an FTA partner territory with the lowest tariffs and thereafter circulating freely in the FTA area. In theory, they fulfill a legitimate function. The *Honda* case was about the rules of origin under the Canada–US FTA (CUSFTA). These rules were aimed against Japanese auto manufacturers which had relocated part of their manufacturing to the United States in order to jump US auto-tariff walls. It was, as is usual in these cases, a respectable motivation on Honda's part for engaging in such foreign direct investment. It resulted, in turn, in a Honda engine built in the United States with the use of Japanese components being treated as sufficiently 'North American' by Canadian customs as they entered Canada. The engines were then used in the Canadian assembly of finished Honda cars for the purpose of re-export to the United States. However, during re-entry, US customs refused to treat the engine as a 'North American-made' engine. The result was that the Canadian-assembled Honda as a whole failed to meet CUSFTA's ROO requirements for entry into the US. Are such rules of origin not trade barriers *in themselves*? A truthful answer would be 'no', not unless you abuse them but then – critics say – what is an FTA if it is not such abuse itself?

A more complex problem involves what is sometimes called 'cross-sector balancing' – that is, raising applied tariffs in particular sectors such as agriculture, while 'balancing' out such higher tariffs with lowered manufacturing tariffs. The result would be trade diversion,[59] but might it not also go against not raising barriers to third (non-FTA) countries on the whole?

Yet another legal (or 'disciplinary') problem today has to do with the way safeguards, anti-dumping duties and countervailing duties are applied unequally against FTA and non-FTA partners. A trading nation enacts safeguard measures in situations where an unforeseen import surge causes or threatens harm to its domestic industries, while anti-dumping and countervailing duties are sought to be justified on the slightly different basis that they address unfairly priced imports. The existence and use of all these devices are not without controversy, but can FTA parties also apply safeguard measures and, for that matter, anti-dumping duties and countervailing duties *selectively*? Can they apply these measures against non-FTA partners while exempting FTA partners? The question has cropped

---

US FTA, and the Honda Case', *American Journal of International Law* 87 (1993): 375.

[59] See further GATT Art. XXIV:6; Understanding on the Interpretation of Article XXIV of the GATT, paras 4–5; discussed in Choi, above note 19, 58.

up due to the selective application of safeguards,[60] and remains unresolved at the present time.[61]

So there are numerous legal problems. One last illustration will more than suffice to conclude the point. Can Article XXIV's authorization of FTAs serve as a *general* defense to what otherwise would be a GATT/ WTO violation? In the *Turkey–Textiles* case, Turkey had argued (quite ingeniously) that had it not imposed quotas on Indian textiles, the EU would not have included textiles within the scope of its agreement with Turkey for fear of Indian textile exports entering through the Turkish back-door. GATT Article XXIV's requirement that a customs union should include 'substantially all the trade' between the parties would therefore not have been fulfilled, and Turkey would have been prevented from entering into a lawful customs union with the EU. Since Article XXIV stipulates that 'nothing shall prevent' a customs union or FTA so long as Article XXIV's other conditions are met, it seemed to Turkey that Article XXIV itself provides a 'defense' to the charge that Turkey had

---

[60] The panel in the *Argentina–Footwear* case observed that most FTAs contemplate safeguard action, and that Article XXIV need not be read so strictly as to prohibit safeguards between FTA partners. If this is correct, a WTO Member which imposes safeguards selectively (i.e. a Member which exempts its FTA partners) cannot argue that WTO law requires it not to apply safeguards against its FTA partners. See *Argentina – Safeguard Measures on Imports of Footwear*, Panel Report, WT/DS121/R, 25 June 1999, paras 8.96–8.98. On appeal, the Appellate Body ruled that the point did not require a decision. See *Argentina – Safeguard Measures on Imports of Footwear*, Report of the Appellate Body, WT/DS121/AB/R, 14 December 1999, para. 114. However, the panel in the subsequent *US–Line Pipe* case considered that an FTA party can exempt its fellow FTA members from safeguard action. See *United States – Definitive Safeguard Measures on Imports of Circular Welded Carbon Quality Line Pipe from Korea*, Panel Report, WT/DS202/R, 29 October 2001, paras 7.140–7.141. Again, the Appellate Body avoided ruling on the point. See *United States – Definitive Safeguard Measures on Imports of Circular Welded Carbon Quality Line Pipe from Korea*, Appellate Body Report, WT/DS202/AB/R, 15 February 2002, para. 198. See also *US–Definitive Safeguard Measures on Imports of Wheat Gluten from the European Communities*, Appellate Body Report, WT/DS166/AB/R, DSR 2001:III, para. 99.

[61] As for anti-dumping and countervailing duties, one view is based on a textual reading of Article XXIV – namely, that trade remedy measures are prohibited between FTA partners. Another view is that trade remedy measures are especially required only when trade is truly free, and that FTAs which create free trade should therefore allow trade remedies to be used when a country is faced with 'unfair' imports or unexpected, harmful import surges as a result of regional liberalization. See Mitsuo Matsushita, 'Legal Aspects of Free Trade Agreements', in Mitsuo Matsushita and Dukgeun Ahn (eds), *WTO and East Asia: New Perspectives* (London: Cameron May, 2004), 497.

imposed illegal quotas on Indian textiles. The Appellate Body accepted the idea that GATT Article XXIV could serve as a defense to a WTO violation, but ruled that Turkey's response was in any event disproportionate.[62] So how widely does the defense operate?

Such questions have become part of the lawyer's (and Geneva trade diplomat's) uncertainty over the legal interpretation of the complex terms of GATT Article XXIV. Together with trade diversion, the prospect of a spaghetti bowl of ROOs and other trade restrictive rules, and the fact that FTAs may be driven by non-trade-liberalizing concerns, or that they may be especially open to special interest capture, these fears have all led to a sizeable body of skeptical opinion about the worth of FTAs – Asian or otherwise.

The Old Compliance Problem

Another long-standing problem has been that before the establishment of the Committee on Regional Trade Agreements (CRTA) in 1996, FTAs were scrutinized by individual GATT working parties. Because of controversy over the interpretation and application of Article XXIV, this procedure, which lasted from 1947 to 1994, only ever found one FTA (between the Czech and Slovak republics) in compliance with Article XXIV. Few, if any, 'Asian' FTAs featured during this period.

The CRTA's establishment in 1996 was meant to create a single, unified body so that 'systemic' issues could be identified and discussed under one roof. But though this improvement led to the compilation of a list of 'systemic issues' of concern to the world trading system,[63] the CRTA itself became bogged down by these controversies. Again, however, Asia's FTAs were not the problem. During this period, many Asian countries which were committed to the multilateral system in fact sought to impose tighter GATT/WTO discipline on FTAs (for example, by insisting on strict interpretations of Article XXIV in its application to various FTAs under review).[64]

Since these interpretative issues have become intractable, the WTO Members have decided to stay their resolution and have chosen instead to focus on disclosure. When should notification of an FTA take place? Where, in the WTO, should notification take place? And, finally, what

---

[62] Since Turkey could have employed rules of origin instead of quotas. See *Turkey – Restrictions on Imports of Textile and Clothing Products*, Report of the Appellate Body, WT/DS34/AB/R, 22 October 1999, paras. 48–63.

[63] WT/REG/W/37.

[64] Ibid. See also TN/RL/W/8/Rev.1, 1 August 2002.

should be notified? A deal was eventually brokered between the developed and developing WTO Members. FTAs notified under the GATT or under the General Agreement on Trade in Services (GATS) would fall within the purview of the CRTA. Those notified under the Enabling Clause would fall under the authority of the Committee on Trade and Development (CTD). Timelines for notification were tightened up, and provision was made for the preparation of a Secretariat 'factual presentation' on individual FTAs.[65] The General Council's Decision of 14 December 1996 established this new 'transparency mechanism' for the 'consideration' of FTAs,[66] and that is where we are presently.

Newer Problems

There are also 'newer' problems such as the problem of overlapping authority, and overlapping jurisdiction between WTO and FTA dispute settlement bodies. This, again, is a problem which lawyers in particular are familiar with (that is, forum shopping).

We have seen fairly recent cases where FTA clauses which allow the State parties to choose either FTA or WTO dispute settlement – so-called *electa una via* clauses – have not worked so well.[67] In the *Argentina–Poultry* dispute, this was because the Brasilia Protocol, which did not contain such a clause, applied to the dispute. Argentina argued that since Brazil and Argentina had also signed the Olivos Protocol, which contained such a clause, Brazil was at least prevented in good faith from resorting to the WTO after having brought the dispute between them before MERCOSUR dispute settlement. Unfortunately, the panel disagreed,[68]

---

[65]   Jo-Ann Crawford, 'A New Transparency Mechanism for RTAs', *SYBIL* 11 (2007): 133, 134–7.

[66]   WTO, General Council, Transparency Mechanism for Regional Trade Agreements – decision of 14 December 2006, WTO Doc. WT/L/671, 18 December 2006.

[67]   See Henry Gao and C.L. Lim, 'Saving the WTO from the Risk of Irrelevance: The Dispute Settlement Mechanism as a "Common Good" for RTAs', *Journal of International Economic Law* 11 (2008): 899–925, reprinted in Debra Steger (ed.), *Redesigning the World Trade Organization for the 21st Century* (Waterloo: Laurier Press, 2009), 389; C.L. Lim and Henry Gao, 'Competing WTO and RTA Jurisdictional Claims: Defusing the Politics by Resorting to Private International Law Analogies', in Tomer Broude, Amelia Porges and Marc Busch (eds), *The Politics of International Economic Law: The Next Four Years* (Cambridge University Press, 2011) (forthcoming).

[68]   *Argentina – Definitive Anti-Dumping Duties on Poultry from Brazil*, Report of the Panel, WT/DS241/R, 22 April 2003, para. 7.30, 7.37–7.39.

thereby raising the question of when a WTO panel might have the discretion to stay its proceedings in favour of another tribunal.

In the *Mexico–Soft Drinks* dispute, the Appellate Body went on to rule on that question; and it ruled that, generally, panels do not have the discretion to stay proceeding in favour of another (FTA) tribunal.[69]

Again, these problems are not uniquely Asian. The problematic cases we have seen thus far – involving disputes between Brazil, Argentina, the US and Mexico – have not been the result of Asian FTAs or any uniquely 'Asian' regional treaty behaviour. As with WTO disciplines and the compliance problem, forum shopping has thus far involved FTAs outside Asia. At the very least, it cannot be said that Asia has been a primary cause of any of these difficulties.

NOT THE USUAL REASONS?

If the usual reservations about FTAs are not the causes of today's concerns over FTA proliferation in Asia, then what is? As we have seen, the use of Article XXIV as a general defense for GATT/WTO violations, exemption of FTA partner countries from trade remedy action, and forum shopping are highly technical, legal issues. That leaves the lack of global legal disciplines, and the absence of a strong compliance mechanism. These are not problems which are peculiar to Asia. All FTAs and customs unions create the risk of trade diversion – that is, shifting consumer preferences towards less efficient producers in FTA partner countries, and away from more efficient production in non-FTA partner countries. Since no one seriously suggests that the European Communities and NAFTA should be dismantled, we have learnt to live with them however offensive they might be to the economic purist.[70] So why should we not live with Asia's FTAs?

True, complex ROOs in FTAs can be so cumbersome that they could themselves become non-tariff barriers. Yet they too are not unique to Asia's FTAs. This brings us to the discussion of the 'spaghetti' or 'noodle bowl' effect of having multiple, overlapping ROOs and other trade rules due to the sheer number of FTAs which have so rapidly emerged in Asia.

---

[69]   *Mexico – Tax Measures on Soft Drinks and Other Beverages*, Appellate Body Report, WT/DS308/AB/R, 6 March 2006, paras 40–57. Admittedly, the *electa una via* clause in NAFTA had not been invoked by Mexico. That said, Mexico could not invoke that clause because the US had blocked the formation of a NAFTA panel by refusing to engage in the selection of panelists.

[70]   Desker, above note 19.

That at least was the central criticism in the article in *The Economist*.[71] We have seen that Japan has been at the forefront of a 'multi-track' approach in negotiating a Closer Economic Partnership Agreement with ASEAN as a whole, as well as with individual ASEAN nations.[72] Arguably, such a negotiating strategy creates a large number of redundant, potentially trade-discriminatory, diversionary, complex and therefore trade-restrictive bilateral deals. Korea has adopted a similar 'simultaneous multiple FTA negotiating strategy'.[73] Singapore could be another example. In Geneva, questions have been asked about the nature of the relationship between the Japan–Indonesia and Japan–Malaysia Economic Partnership Agreements, the ASEAN–Japan Economic Partnership Agreement, and whether traders would need to choose between separate market access schedules.[74] Likewise, questions have been directed at the Trans-Pacific Strategic Economic Partnership (which links Brunei, Chile, New Zealand and Singapore), particularly with regard to the legal relationship between this and pre-existing bilateral FTAs, the benefits of maintaining two FTAs at the same time, and the impact of such an arrangement on transaction costs.[75]

There is some evidence to suggest that producers who find these rules unwieldy or too costly to understand have simply foregone the supposed preferential benefits since mastering these ROOs and other rules incur business costs which threaten to make the use of these FTAs a 'rich man's game' reserved for the larger producers and industry coalitions.[76] In

[71] 'Noodle Bowl', above note 18. See also, Sen, above note 19.

[72] Hatakeyama Noboru, 'A Short History of Japan's Movement to FTAs (Part 3)', *Journal of Japanese Trade & Industry* 22 (March/April 2003): 42. See also Christopher Findlay, Mohd. Haflah Piei and Mari Pangetsu, 'Trading with Favourites: Free Trade Agreements in the Asia-Pacific', in Riyana Miranti and Denis Hew (eds), *APEC in the 21st Century* (Singapore: ISEAS, 2004), 89, 92.

[73] See Dukgeun Ahn, 'Korea's FTA Policy', in *The New International Architecture in Trade and Investment*, above note 47, 49, 51.

[74] WT/REG241/2, WT/REG216/3 and WT/REG216/M/1.

[75] WT/REG229/2 and WT/REG229/M/1.

[76] Previous figures showing the proportion of trade under the ASEAN Free Trade Area's Common Effective Preferential Trade Scheme to total intra-ASEAN trade have been discouraging – estimated at 5 per cent; see Severino, above note 15, 247. For two other, notable studies of Asian FTA utilization rates, see Masahiro Kawai and Ganeshan Wigraraja, 'Multilateralizing Regional Trade Arrangements in Asia', in Richard Baldwin and Patrick Low (eds), *Multilateralizing Regionalism: Challenges for the Global Trading System* (Cambridge: Cambridge University Press, 2009), 495; Inkyo Cheong and Jungran Cho, 'An Empirical Study on the Utilization Ratio of FTAs by Korean Firms', *Journal of Korea Trade* 13 (2009): 109.

any event, political economy teaches us that big producers and powerful industry interests are likely to be more effective in lobbying for ROOs and other protectionist rules in the first place.[77] Here, again, the problem is not peculiarly 'Asian', as the *Honda* case has amply demonstrated.

It appears that the true cause for concern has to do, instead, with Asia's manner or method of regional treaty formation when viewed in light of its diversity, size and economic and geo-political significance.

WHO FEARS ASIA AND WHY?

The European Benchmark

Compared with the European Union's aim of creating a single market and a harmonized regulatory regime, the WTO is a less ambitious enterprise. Its central focus has been non-discrimination in the form of Most Favoured Nation and National Treatment standards and anti-trade protectionism.[78] But while the WTO is arguably inching closer to the EU paradigm, the Asian FTAs may not be. Only time will tell if ASEAN or a larger East Asian grouping might emulate the EU, or if there will be convergence between Asia, Europe, North America and the other regions, as well as greater convergence between the WTO and FTAs. Presently at least, the idea of an East Asian customs union seems inconceivable. Instead, we have – and are likely to continue to have – a large number of overlapping Asian agreements. That is the first criticism: that there is something about the unwieldiness of Asia's regional trade architecture, and in particular the radical proliferation of overlapping FTAs, which gives genuine cause for concern.[79] Unlike in Europe, we cannot speak of

---

[77] See further Joseph A. Lanasa III, 'Rules of Origin and the Uruguay Round's Effectiveness in Harmonizing and Regulating Them', *American Journal of International Law* 90 (1996): 625; John J. Barcello III, 'Harmonizing Preferential Rules of Origin in the WTO System', Cornell Legal Studies Research Paper No. 06-049 (2006).

[78] See further J.H.H. Weiler, 'Epilogue: Towards a Common Law of International Trade', in J.H.H. Weiler, *The EU, the WTO and the NAFTA: Towards a Common Law of International Trade* (Oxford: OUP, 2000), 201–2.

[79] For criticism (although not specifically directed at Asia as such) of complex ROOS, and a comparison with the merits of the system of Pan-European Rules of Origin (PERO) in this regard, see Michael Gasiorek et al., 'Multilateralizing Regionalism: Lessons from the EU Experience in Relaxing Rules of Origin', in Baldwin and Low, above note 76, 146, 156–9. On Asian fears 15 years ago of NAFTA ROOs causing a similar adverse effect on third countries, see Kathryn

an East Asian, or Asian, collective 'vision'. In the absence of a 'teleological trajectory',[80] Asia's FTAs only reflect a series of pragmatic moves and compromises.[81] Readers of Luigi Barzini's elegant work would have been amused by his observations about the spread of English customs, dress and manners in Europe, the emergence of the French *'dandys'*, Rome's huntsmen who cry 'Tallyho', and the number of continental hotels styled *'Oxford et Cambridge'*, *'d'Angleterre'*, *'St James et Albany'*, *'de Grande Bretagne'*, and so on.[82] But underlying it is a more serious point which goes to Europe's history and shared purposes. Asia is different. Asia-wide cooperation, let alone integration, will take time. Paul Evans, while referring only to East Asia, puts it this way:[83]

> As an institution, APT [ASEAN plus Three], like APEC before it, has the double burden of promoting pragmatic, interest-based cooperation at the same time as building the rationale and instruments for deeper integration structured on some kind of 'community' basis . . . The many obstacles to APT success and progress are frequently recited. The diversity of cultures, political and economic systems, and levels of development is only slightly less than in APEC. Unlike the EU, in APT there is no common aspiration to democracy, and there are enormous variations in administrative, technocratic, and intellectual capacity . . . The inherent asymmetry between the economic clout of ASEAN and the Northeast Asian three is considerable.

In short, what is happening in Asia is more akin to the North American method of regional treaty formation. It resembles the economic treaty interaction between Canada, the US and Mexico from the late 1980s to the mid-1990s, where the Canada–US FTA was formed before NAFTA. What we see presently in that region is part of a difficult US attempt to expand that same thinking towards Central and Latin America.[84] So,

---

McCall, 'What is Asia Afraid Of? The Diversionary Effect of NAFTA's Rules of Origin on Trade between the United States and Asia', *California Western International Law Journal* 25 (1995): 389.

[80]   Paul Evans, 'Between Regionalism and Regionalization: Policy Networks and the Nascent East Asian Institutional Identity', in T.J. Pempel (ed.), *Remapping East Asia: The Construction of a Region* (Ithaca: Cornell University Press, 2005), 211.

[81]   For a study of the deeper, underlying reasons from a cultural perspective, see Gilbert Rozman, 'National Identities in East Asia in the Shadow of Globalization', in Kazuko Mori and Kenichiro Hirano (eds), *A New East Asia: Toward a Regional Community* (Singapore: NUS Press, 2007), 221.

[82]   Luigi Barzini, *The Europeans* (London: Penguin, 1983).

[83]   Evans, 'Between Regionalism and Regionalization', above note 80, 200–201.

[84]   At the time of writing, the US has FTAs with Chile, Peru, Central America

while Asia muddles through in similar manner, the results are likely to be as messy. Whether that messiness is the result of a lack of regional institutions which would (and should) do the work of the European institutions in fostering regional integration begs the question since the existence of such institutions could also depend on having the conditions which make such institutions possible.

Shallow Liberalization

A second criticism holds Asia's FTAs against the standard of other FTAs, generally, and not just against the example of Europe and the European Union. Its central proposition is that Asia's agreements tend to be 'quick, dirty and trade light'.[85] Compared with the United States' FTAs, the EU, and the Australia–New Zealand Closer Economic Relations Trade Agreement (ANZCERTA), Asian FTAs generally show less substantive liberalization.[86] Or as the Australian Government would have it, Asian FTAs commit too few concessions up-front.[87]

Similarly, Razeen Sally of the European Centre for International Political Economy has argued that Asia's FTAs are often politically and strategically motivated, leading to the appearance of being no more than empty political gestures.[88] Some tend to represent narrow mercantilist ends, seeking concessions and export-market access in only a limited number of sectors.[89] Yet Sally's criticism is not entirely unproblematic; not because it draws a comparison with other models of regionalism, but because the idea that FTAs and customs unions *must* evince the liberalization of 'substantially all the trade' between the parties is more

---

and the Dominican Republic (the CAFTA–DR). FTAs with Colombia and Panama are currently pending Congressional approval; see the website of the USTR at: <www.ustr.gov/trade-agreements/free-trade-agreements> . For the CAFTA–DR, see Mauricio Salas, 'Central American–Dominican Republic–United States Free Trade Agreement', in Simon Lester and Bryan Mercurio (eds), *Bilateral and Regional Trade Agreements: Case Studies* (Cambridge: CUP, 2009), 44.

[85] For the criticism that Asian FTAs are generally 'quick, dirty and trade light', see Razeen Sally, 'Maintenance of the World Trade Order: Principles and Mechanics for the WTO System in the 21st Century', Policy Research Project, European Centre for International Political Economy (ECIPE).

[86] See Razeen Sally, *Trade Policy, New Century: The WTO, FTAs and Asia Rising* (London: Institute of Economic Affairs, 2008), 126–39. Singapore is singled out as a notable exception.

[87] TN/RL/W/180, Negotiation Group on Rules, Submission on RTAs by Australia, 13 May 2005, para. 7.

[88] Sally, *Trade Policy*, above note 86, 126–39.

[89] Ibid., 136.

controversial than it might first appear. True it is a GATT Article XXIV requirement (which should make it uncontroversial), but it is not clear why this should be so since limited liberalization would still be a step towards free trade, and would tend to involve less discrimination against non-FTA members.[90] Understandably, the GATT's framers might have considered that allowing selective exceptions, as opposed to agreements that are more comprehensive in product coverage, would be going a step too far. Nonetheless, special preferences for developing countries already do precisely that. GSP schemes permit preferential treatment for qualifying products from qualifying beneficiary countries,[91] and the Enabling Clause was intended (rightly) to confirm the legitimacy of such arrangements where they operate in favour of developing nations.

The China–ASEAN FTA is a good example. Because it has been notified under the Enabling Clause, the China–ASEAN nations are not required to show the liberalization of substantially all the trade between them. But because the East Asian governments involved are also mindful of potential criticism, they are eager to show that fairly comprehensive product coverage will be achieved within ten years (being the grace period – or so-called 'interim period' – currently granted under WTO rules).[92]

---

[90]   See Dam, above note 51, 633; Choi, above note 19, 63 (observing the apparent 'incongruity' of the requirement).

[91]   See (e.g.) the *US Generalized System of Preferences Guidebook*, USTR, March 2008.

[92]   China's target is to achieve duty-free treatment for 90 per cent of goods imports within the duration of the ten-year interim period. In this, CAFTA adopts ASEAN's earlier approach for the ASEAN Free Trade Area (AFTA) by according greater flexibilities to the four newer, least-developed ASEAN members (Cambodia, Laos, Myanmar, and Vietnam). This mirrors AFTA's structure, under which a sensitive list and highly sensitive list consisting of unprocessed agricultural products (rice and sugar in particular) were given until 2010 for tariffs to reach a 0–5 per cent and 0–20 per cent tariff rate, respectively. For all other products, the six original ASEAN members committed to zero duties by 2010, while the four newer members have been given until 2015. The same model has generally been applied to the ASEAN–Korea, ASEAN–Japan, and ASEAN–India FTAs. What is noteworthy in respect of the ASEAN–Korea FTA is the separate treatment of Vietnam from Cambodia, Laos and Myanmar, and an admittedly more restrictive approach to liberalization in comparison with CAFTA due to the use of an Exclusion List of products and in relation to the treatment of certain tariff peaks. The ASEAN–Japan FTA also employed such an Exclusion List. However, Japan has committed itself towards zero duty treatment for 88 per cent of its trade measured by volume immediately upon entry into force of the FTA in 2008. As for the ASEAN–India FTA (AIFTA), four ASEAN members objected to the use of an Exclusion List, thereby finally requiring five contested groups of products (palm oil, coffee, black tea, pepper, crude petroleum) to be included in a Highly

True, the China–ASEAN deal has not escaped criticism.[93] Nonetheless, the view that many of Asia's FTAs are 'trade light', while justified in some cases,[94] could risk becoming a purist's retort. It will have to account for the fact that India, Indonesia, Malaysia, the Philippines, Cambodia, Vietnam, Laos, Myanmar are developing nations, and noting the difference between developed and developing countries is why the WTO allows incomplete liberalization under the Enabling Clause in the first place.[95]

Unlike the first criticism, the second is less technocratic and cultural, and reflects Sylvia Ostry's view more closely; namely, that the causes of trade disputes during the Cold War era lie in the 'systemic frictions' caused by the different policy choices underlying American-style capitalism and the European welfare capitalist and Japanese corporatist models.[96]

Sensitive List for phased reductions instead. While AIFTA admittedly appears to be the least substantive of these agreements in terms of the speed and breadth of tariff cuts on products, 80 per cent of the tariff lines of India, Brunei, Indonesia, Malaysia, Singapore and Thailand have been targeted for tariff elimination by 2015. See further David Chin, 'ASEAN's Journey towards Free Trade', in C.L. Lim and Margaret Liang (eds), *Economic Diplomacy: Essays and Reflections by Singapore's Negotiators* (Singapore: Institute of Policy Studies, 2010).

[93] See Stefano Inama, 'The Association of South East Asian Nations–People's Republic of China Free Trade Area: Negotiating Beyond Eternity with Little Trade Liberalization?', *Journal of World Trade* 39 (2005): 559. In particular, Inama criticizes China–ASEAN for reneging on the promise to have the FTA concluded within ten years. Under Annex 1, paragraph 6 of the Agreement on Trade in Goods of the Framework Agreement on Comprehensive Economic Cooperation between ASEAN and the PRC, Vientiane, 29 November 2004 (the 'Vientienne Agreement'), full tariff elimination for products under the 'Normal Track' is scheduled for 1 January 2012 for China and the original 'ASEAN Six', while products under the 'Sensitive Lists' of China and the ASEAN Six are given until 2018 to reach the 0–5 per cent level. As for products on the 'Highly Sensitive List', these are to be brought down to (only) no more than 50 per cent by 2015 for the ASEAN Six, and by 2018 for Cambodia, Laos, Myanmar and Vietnam – See Annex 2 of the Vientienne Agreement. For a study of China's reasons for entering into an FTA with ASEAN, and the structure of the Framework Agreement and 'Early Harvest Scheme', see Qingjiang Kong, 'China's WTO Accession and the ASEAN–China Free Trade Area: The Perspective of a Chinese Lawyer', *Journal of International Economic Law* (2004): 839; Jiangyu Wang, 'China's Regional Trade Agreements: The Law, Geopolitics, and Impact on the Multilateral Trading System', *SYBIL* 8 (2004): 119.

[94] Japan's and some of Thailand's FTAs are given as key examples; Sally, above note 86, 136, 138–9; see further the critical remarks on the Japan–Singapore Economic Partnership Agreement in Choi, above note 19, 70.

[95] See Choi, above note 19, 75.

[96] Sylvia Ostry, *The Post-Cold War Trading System* (Chicago: University of Chicago Press, 1997).

Other criticisms are related to these first two criticisms, concerning the manner or method of regional treaty formation in Asia.

Institutional Weaknesses

One of these further criticisms which does not appear to be directed at Asian trade policies as such (like the 'shallow liberalization' argument above) has to do with the relative weakness of Asian regional institutions when compared with the EU's 'Cartesian legal formalism'.[97] According to Professor Shaun Breslin, it is common to point to the EU's Commission, Parliament and Court of Justice in drawing a comparison with Asia's (and Latin America's) 'loose or informal' arrangements and their lack of 'progress'.[98]

Fortress Asia

The fear that the United States (and Europe) could be cut off from Asia's turn towards a 'guild-like exclusiveness' is a fourth worry. This is similar to Southeast Asian fears in the early 1990s that Asia could become isolated from Europe and North America with the emergence of NAFTA, the European Union and MERCOSUR – a fear which started the FTA race in Asia. In a sense, that fear also risks confusion. Asian regionalism ('Noodle Bowl'-style) is either too loose, messy, cumbersome, and therefore trade distortive,[99] or it is a concerted, highly institutionalized, and cohesive form of bloc protectionism. At most, there are individual nations which currently do not have an FTA with the US and this has raised some fears about the US being cut off from further Asian, especially East Asian, economic integration. Professor Won-Mog Choi has suggested that although 'it is uncertain in the long term whether the proliferation will eventually lead to a single trading bloc in the region (an "East Asian FTA"), one could cautiously anticipate that two or three plurilateral trading blocs might eventually find . . . shape in East Asia', but that in 'the short and medium term . . . East Asian countries are expected to be circumspect in their approach, given sensitivities to US interests in the region and wider

---

[97] See Shaun Breslin, 'Regions in Comparative Perspective', in Shaun Breslin (ed.), *New Regionalisms in the Global Political Economy* (London: Routledge, 2002), 1, 11.

[98] Ibid., 11–16.

[99] See 'Noodle Bowl', above note 18. See further Jagdish Bhagwati, *Termites in the Trading System* (New York: OUP, 2008), 61–71.

security implications'.[100] Fears will only be amplified if the expansive network of small bilateral deals in Asia is replaced by a region-wide East Asian FTA.[101]

Choi's refrain in relation to US and security concerns does reflect a genuine policy sensitivity in Asia towards the need to maintain an open regionalist model and to have an 'overlap' between Asia Pacific and East Asian regional initiatives.[102] Such fears have also driven the US to participate in Trans-Pacific Partnership (TPP) talks, which involve enlarging the Trans-Pacific Strategic Economic Partnership Agreement (between Singapore, NZ, Chile and Brunei). As of May 2010, Australia and Peru have also joined the TPP talks, while Vietnam has observer status.[103] This would enlarge the TPP to seven members, where its real value, both geo-strategically and in economic terms, lies more in its possible enlargement into an Asia-Pacific-wide FTA than the economic benefits it would currently provide.[104]

Factory Asia

More to the point perhaps than fear of an Asian, or East Asian, 'Bloc' are the kinds of anxieties seen in the 1980s in the relations between Japan and the United States – that is, worries about 'unfair' Asian protectionism, Asian 'competitiveness'[105] – or, more recently, about a great sucking sound of jobs relocating to China.[106] A related concern which also overlaps with fear of 'Fortress Asia' may be of the eventual emergence of an

---

[100]   Choi, above note 19, 55.

[101]   Peter A. Petri, 'Multitrack Integration in East Asian Trade: Noodle Bowl or Matrix?', Asia-Pacific Issues, No. 86, East-West Center; Kawai and Wigraraja, above note 76.; Zhang Yunling, 'The Feasibility of Establishing an East Asian FTA: A Chinese Perspective', Seoul: Institute for Global Economics; Occasional Paper Series 07-05.

[102]   See Evans, 'Between Regionalism and Regionalization', above note 80, 211–15.

[103]   Japan, Malaysia and Canada have also expressed their interest.

[104]   See further Deborah Elms, 'National Interests in the Trans-Pacific Partnership (TPP) Talks', paper prepared for the Asian WTO Research Network (AWRN) Meeting, Seoul, 21 May 2010 (unpublished, forthcoming).

[105]   See 'Bloc Party', above note 18. See further Keisuke Iida, *Legalization and Japan: The Politics of WTO Dispute Settlement* (London: Cameron May, 2006), for the history of the auto-talks, and the Kodak–Fuji and other disputes between Japan and the United States.

[106]   William Greider, 'A New Giant Sucking Sound: China is Taking Away Mexico's Jobs, as Globalization Enters a Fateful New Stage', *The Nation* (New York), 31 December 2001.

intra-Asian market where 'larger, developed markets are better endowed than smaller markets in trade negotiations'.[107] This could have wider ramifications not just in trade negotiations, but also geo-politically, just as the proliferation of FTAs may already be symptomatic of geo-political change.[108] Such 'political economy'-type concerns are probably closer to the usual criticisms leveled against FTAs.[109]

Who then fears Asia? The answer depends upon the causes of such fear. Fear of Asian protectionism, protectionist fears about Asian labour and manufacturing, the economic purist's criticisms, geo-strategic fears about Asian or East Asian insularity, fear of systemic friction, fear of the adoption of a divergent 'Asian model' of trade regionalism, fear of an increase in Asia's clout in trade negotiations, and fear of the adverse effects on the multilateral trading system of increased regionalism make up a wide spectrum of concerns about the accelerating pace and prolixity of East Asian trading nations' bilateral and other regional trade agreements. None, except for the economic purist's view and the regulatory and compliance concerns of lawyers and Geneva trade diplomats which we have discussed, reflect the usual reservations lawyers, economists and traditional trade multilateralists share about FTAs.

Today's concerns about Asia's FTAs have far more to do with 'Asia' than they have to do with 'FTAs' as such. In terms of treaty-making behaviour in (and in response to) Asia, trade policy has become the handmaiden of geo-strategy. Traditional multilateral, institutional and global regulatory concerns are ancillary at best.[110]

---

[107]   See John H. Barton et al., *The Evolution of the Trade Regime* (Princeton, NJ: Princeton University Press, 2006), 10–11; an insight reflected in 'Bloc Party', above note 18.

[108]   Abbott, above note 2, 135.

[109]   For example, that domestic interests might be more easily managed by pointing to trade-offs resulting from global, multilateral negotiations than from bilateral trade deals. Conversely, bilateral negotiations may be more prone to domestic industry capture than global trade talks.

[110]   See (e.g.) the Testimony of the American Federation of Labor-Congress of Industrial Organizations (AFL-CIO), 25 February 2009, cited in Elms, above note 104, 51.

3. Endemic institutional fragility in the face of dynamic economic integration in Asia: the case of transboundary pollution in Hong Kong*

Miron Mushkat and Roda Mushkat

INTRODUCTION

Environmental degradation poses a serious challenge in Asia, albeit not in a uniform fashion because of divergences in socio-economic conditions and variations in policy responses. The problem typically has domestic origins and manifests itself on the home front. However, it often possesses an international dimension due to cross-border spillovers and the difficulties stemming from coordination in circumstances characterized by conflicting preferences and fragmented authority. The absence of effective regional institutions and, selectively, the proliferation of semi-autonomous sub-national power centres aggravate the ecological strains emanating from that source.[1]

* Roda Mushkat wishes to thank the Kadoorie Institute for its research support, but the authors of this chapter are solely responsible for the views expressed herein.

[1] For example see Ian Townsend-Gault, David Vander Zwaag and Robert Adamson, 'Transboundary Ocean and Atmospheric Pollution in Southeast Asia' in Amitav Acharya and Richard Stubbs (eds), *New Challenges for ASEAN: Energy Policy Issues* (Vancouver: University of British Columbia Press, 1995); San-Gon Lee, 'Transboundary Pollution in the Yellow Sea' in H. Edward English and David Runnals (eds), *Environment and Development in the Pacific: Problems and Policy Options* (Melbourne: Addison-Wesley Longman in association with the Australia–Japan Research Centre, the Australian National University, 1997), 117–30; Ben Boer, Ross Ramsey and Donald Rothwell, *International Environmental Law in the Asia Pacific: Problems and Policy Options* (London: Kluwer Law International, 1998), 52; Peter Eaton and Miroslav Radojevic (eds),

The predicament Asia confronts, whether in the domestic arena or in the realm of inter-State relations, is a familiar one in that it has been witnessed abundantly elsewhere at different historical junctures: how to strike a balance between economic and ecological imperatives. What perhaps distinguishes the region from other parts of the world in this respect is consistently (with some exceptions) robust output expansion, commitment to export-led growth (and hence foreign trade and investment), shallow (again, with some exceptions) democratic roots, a vibrant business sector (a pillar of the corporatist order) and a fledgling civil society (long contained by the forces of market-preserving authoritarianism).[2] This has rendered the trade-off between economic prosperity and environmental preservation distinctly acute.[3]

Forest Fires and Regional Haze in Southeast Asia (New York: Nova Science, 2001); Euston Quah, 'Transboundary Pollution in Southeast Asia: The Indonesian Fires', *World Development* 30 (2002): 429–41; Allen L. Springer, 'The Indonesian Forest Fires: Internationalizing a National Environmental Problem' in Paul G. Harris (ed.), *International Environmental Cooperation: Politics and Diplomacy in Pacific Asia* (Boulder: University Press of Colorado, 2002), 291–315; Roda Mushkat, *International Environmental Law and Asian Values* (Vancouver: University of British Columbia Press, 2004), 121–6; Zachary Tyler, 'Transboundary Water Pollution in China: An Analysis of the Failure of the Legal Framework to Protect Downstream Jurisdictions', *Columbia Journal of Asian Law* 19 (2006): 572–613; Colleen A. Fox and Chris Sneddon, 'Transboundary River Basin Agreements in the Mekong and Zambezi Basins: Enhancing Environmental Security or Securitizing the Environment?', *International Environmental Agreements: Politics, Law and Economics* 7 (2007): 237–61; Inkyoung Kim, 'Environmental Cooperation of Northeast Asia: Transboundary Air Pollution', *International Relations of the Asia-Pacific* 7 (2007): 439–62; Koh Kheng-Lian, 'A Breakthrough in Solving Indonesian Haze?' in Sharelle Hart (ed.), *Shared Resources: Issues of Governance* (Gland: World Conservation Union, 2008), 225–46; Paruedee Nguitragool, *Environmental Cooperation in Southeast Asia: ASEAN's Regime For Transboundary Haze Pollution* (London: Routledge, 2010).

   [2]   See generally World Bank, *The East Asian Miracle: Economic Growth and Public Policy* (Washington: World Bank, 1993); Steve Chan, Cal Clark and Danny Lam (eds), *Beyond the Developmental State: East Asia's Political Economies Reconsidered* (New York: St. Martin's Press, 1998); Li Shuhe and Peng Lian, 'Decentralization and Coordination: China's Credible Commitment to Preserve the Market under Authoritarianism', *China Economic Review* 10 (1999): 161–90; Meredith Woo-Cummings (ed.), *The Development State* (Ithaca: Cornell University Press, 1999); Frank-Jurgen Richter (ed.), *The East Asian Development Model: Economic Growth, Institutional Failure and the Aftermath of the Crisis* (Basingstoke: Macmillan, 2000); Jong H. Park, 'The East Asian Model of Development and Developing Countries', *Journal of Developing Societies* 18 (2002): 330–53; Ha-Joon Chang, *The East Asia Development Experience* (Penang: TWN, 2006).

   [3]   See Mushkat, above note 1, 86–104; Jack N. Barkenbus, 'Reconciling Trade

Another key factor complicating Asia's efforts to harmonize economic and environmental goals, and possibly differentiating it from less rigidly configured regions, is the intensity of the attachment to symbols of State sovereignty, even if the practice in that respect at times falls short of the theory. This impedes horizontal cooperation and vertical institution-building, preventing the adoption of a more decisive approach to symptoms of transboundary pollution. Sovereignty continues to be guarded closely in the face of the inevitable and powerful encroachments of globalization.[4]

There is a tendency to attribute the persistence of that pattern to a legacy of inter-State conflicts, lingering territorial disputes and serious national security concerns.[5] This is a valid interpretation, but additional influences are believed to be at work. Specifically, in many cases, the process of national integration in Asia is incomplete, in the socio-psychological sense of the term. Group identities – communal, ethnic, geographical, linguistic, political and religious – remain strong and act as a centrifugal force, whose potentially divisive effects central governments seek to minimize.[6] The corollary is that cross-border collaboration has not evolved as smoothly as in some other parts of the world.

The reluctance to compromise, let alone surrender, sovereign authority manifests itself most vividly in regional organizational settings. Asian members of institutions such as the Association of Southeast Asian Nations (ASEAN) and Asia-Pacific Economic Cooperation (APEC) have

---

and Environment in Asia' in Harris (ed.), above note 1; Michael C. Howard (ed.), *Asia's Environmental Crisis* (Boulder: Colorado, 1993).

[4] See Mark Beeson, 'Sovereignty under Siege: Globalisation and the State in Southeast Asia', *Third World Quarterly* 24 (2003): 357–74; Allen Carlson, *Unifying China, Integrating with the World: Securing Chinese Sovereignty in the Reform Era* (Stanford: Stanford University Press, 2005); Amitav Acharya, *Whose Ideas Matter? Agency and Power in Asian Regionalism* (Ithaca: Cornell University Press, 2009).

[5] See Amitav Acharya and Evelyn Goh (eds), *Reassessing Security Cooperation in the Asia-Pacific: Competition, Congruence and Transformation* (Cambridge: MIT Press, 2007); Ralf Emmers, *Geopolitics and Maritime Territorial Disputes in East Asia* (London: Routledge, 2009); Min Gyo Koo, *Island Disputes and Maritime Regime Building in East Asia: Between a Rock and a Hard Place* (Berlin: Springer, 2009); Jacob Berkovitch and Mikio Oishi, *International Conflict in the Asia-Pacific: Patterns, Consequences and Management* (London: Routledge, 2010).

[6] See Shaun Narine, 'Sovereignty, Political Legitimacy and Regional Institutionalism in the Asia-Pacific', *Pacific Review* 17 (2005): 423–50; Shale Horowitz, U.K. Heo and Alexander C. Tan (eds), *Identity and Change in East Asian Conflicts: The Cases of China, Taiwan and the Koreas* (Basingstoke: Palgrave Macmillan, 2007).

gone to considerable lengths to ensure that their powers are not eroded. The fundamental norms, rules, structures and modes of operation of these organizations largely reflect sensitivities over sovereignty due to a conflu- ence of external and internal factors that are deep-rooted and unlikely to recede into the background in the foreseeable future.[7]

The sluggish development and fragility of mechanisms for managing transboundary pollution is indicative of the underlying cross-currents. Pollution is looming increasingly large on the policy agenda, both domes- tic and regional (as well as international), but addressing it earnestly is an intricate issue. In industrializing countries where standards of living are yet to be lifted to a satisfactory level, abject poverty to be mostly eradicated, unemployment to be materially reduced and the threat of overpopulation to be meaningfully curtailed, the inherent tension between economic progress and ecological sustainability continues to fester. An examination of transboundary pollution in Hong Kong, the subject of this chapter, may help bring some of the basic imbalances, particularly those between economic dynamism/integration and institutional brittleness/ drift, into focus.

BROAD RELEVANCE OF THE TOPIC

The capitalist enclave at China's southern tip is not a typical participant in macro-level Asian politico-economic processes. Unlike the other actors intimately involved, it is not a sovereign entity. At no historical juncture has it enjoyed complete policy discretion, although in certain spheres of government activity it has functioned virtually unencumbered by external constraints. Hong Kong had matured into a sophisticated manufactur- ing and service centre (initially the first, latterly the second) under British colonial rule and is currently operating as an integral, yet separate (Special Administrative Region/SAR), part of the Chinese body politic.[8]

This configuration notwithstanding, there is considerable analytical leeway for treating Hong Kong as a largely autonomous player within

---

[7]   See Narine, above note 6.

[8]   For a detailed account see Roda Mushkat, *One Country, Two International Legal Personalities: The Case of Hong Kong* (Hong Kong: Hong Kong University Press, 1997); Yash Ghai, *Hong Kong's New Constitutional Order: The Resumption of Chinese Sovereignty and the Basic Law*, 2nd edn (Hong Kong: Hong Kong University Press, 1999); Roda Mushkat, 'Hong Kong's Exercise of External Autonomy: A Multi-Faceted Appraisal', *International and Comparative Law Quarterly* 55 (2006): 945–62.

the 'one country–two systems' framework in matters not pertaining to defence and foreign affairs. Economic and ecological management are two policy domains where the impediments to local initiative are conspicuous by their absence. Unless stipulated otherwise, multilateral environmental treaties signed or acceded to by China extend to the entire country, including Hong Kong, but this leaves the territory with substantial room for maneuver to pursue its own ecological agenda. Risk aversion stemming from the ambiguities inherent in the delicate relationship with the Chinese authorities at both the national and provincial levels may lead to an overly narrow reading of powers granted by the 'mini constitution'/Basic Law drafted jointly with China, and consistent with the letter and the spirit of the Sino-British Declaration regarding the future of Hong Kong, yet this should be regarded as a self-imposed constraint rather than an exogenous one.[9]

The SAR status bestowed on Hong Kong is unique in the Chinese context. Definitely in theory, and most probably in practice, no other sub-national unit is free to enjoy policy discretion on a scale comparable to that of Hong Kong. Even the special economic zones that have proliferated during the post-1978 reform era are considerably more circumscribed than Hong Kong in terms of their ability to shape their own destiny in a strategic fashion. Nevertheless, their existence attests to the degree of administrative decentralization that China has undergone since the curtain descended on the revolutionary period shortly following the death of Mao Zedong.[10]

The policy influence exerted by Chinese sub-national units, particularly provinces, can be so substantial that they may be in a position to thwart central government initiatives and inflict material damage on each other through adversarial measures of a defensive nature.[11] This phenomenon may be discerned beyond the country's confines, where the units promote their interests and compete, as well as within them. Its prevalence has prompted some researchers to portray the People's Republic of China (PRC) as a State with perforated sovereignty.[12] To the extent that this

---

[9] See Mushkat, 'Hong Kong's Exercise of External Autonomy: A Multi-Faceted Appraisal', ibid.

[10] See Jinglian Wu, *Understanding and Interpreting Chinese Economic Reform* (Mason: Thomson Higher Education, 2005), 44–71.

[11] See Andrew Hall Wedeman, *From Mao to Market: Rent Seeking, Local Protectionism and Marketization* (Cambridge: Cambridge University Press, 2003).

[12] See Samuel S. Kim, 'Sovereignty in the Chinese Image of World Order' in Ronald S.J. Macdonald (ed.), *Essays in Honour of Wang Tieya* (Dordrecht: Martinus Nijhoff, 1994), 442–5; Zheng Yongnian, 'Perforated Sovereignty:

depiction is valid, semi-autonomous Hong Kong may be viewed as the tip, albeit a highly significant one, of a loosely structured iceberg whose component parts are endowed with sufficient capabilities to affect outcomes in the regional/international arena.

The social science literature suggests that there is a relationship, although not necessarily deterministic or irreversible, between economic integration and political fragmentation.[13] The opening up of the Chinese economy, and the decentralization accompanying the process, thus may undermine to some extent central government power. Paradoxically, it may be easier, in the era of globalization, to resist pressures from outside than those originating internally. Evidence from other parts of Asia is sparse at this juncture, but it tentatively indicates that China may not be altogether atypical.[14] The corollary is that Hong Kong's experience as an essentially freewheeling component of a perforated system may hold broader lessons.

A disjoined political structure is not the sole manifestation of dysfunctional segmentation across the Chinese institutional landscape. The country's bureaucratic machinery is fractured as well. It consists of tenuously integrated organizational units whose energies are directed inwards and whose activities defy coordination efforts aimed at enhancing both

---

Provincial Dynamism of China's Foreign Trade', *Pacific Review* 7 (1994): 309–21. For additional insights see Ivo D. Duchacek, Daniel Latouche and Garth Stevenson (eds), *Perforated Sovereignties and International Relations: Trans-Sovereign Contacts of Subnational Governments* (New York: Greenwood Press, 1988); Hans H.J. Michelmann and Panayotis Soldatos (eds), *Federalism and International Relations: The Role of Subnational Units* (Oxford: Clarendon Press, 1990).

[13]   See Alessandra Casella, 'Trade as an Engine of Political Change: A Parable', *Economica* 61 (1994): 267–84; Marc Holitscher and Roy Suter, 'The Paradox of Globalisation and Political Fragmentation: Secessionist Movements in Quebec and Scotland', *Global Society* 13 (1999): 257–86; Alberto Alesina, Enrico Spolaore and Romain Wacziarg, 'Economic Integration and Political Disintegration', *American Economic Review* 90 (2000): 1276–96; Alessandra Casella, 'The Role of Market Size in the Formation of Jurisdictions', *Review of Economic Studies* 61 (2001): 83–108; Alessandra Casella and Jonathan S. Feinstein, 'Public Goods in Trade: On the Formation of Markets and Jurisdictions', *International Economic Review* 43 (2002): 437–62; Manuel Leita-Monteiro and Motohiro Sato, 'Economic Integration and Fiscal Devolution', *Journal of Public Economics* 87 (2003): 2507–25; Mehrad Vahabi, *The Political Economy of Destructive Power* (Cheltenham: Edward Elgar, 2004); Gregoire Rota-Graziosi, 'Economic Integration and Political Fragmentation', accessed 15 December 2009, http://publi.cerdi.org/ed/2006/2006.28.pdf.

[14]   See generally Dennis Rondinelli and John Hefron (eds), *Globalization and Change in Asia* (Boulder: Lynne Rienner, 2007).

horizontal and vertical organizational alignment. Synchronized collective action in such an institutional milieu requires laborious and protracted bargaining. The combination of political and bureaucratic disconnectedness results in an overall pattern whose essence has been captured by terms such as 'fragmented authoritarianism' (or, alternatively, 'negotiated State').[15]

Pervasive organizational segmentation raises the issue of policy capacity to address effectively the adverse impacts of economic integration. This question has been accorded considerable attention by researchers exploring institutional performance in China. While the findings vary from one case to another, it may be legitimately argued that they lend support to the assertion that State capacity poses a serious challenge in key areas of government initiative, including the environment, even if the authorities somehow typically manage to find the will and mobilize the resources to confront crises when they erupt.[16] Again,

---

[15] This phenomenon is dissected painstakingly in Kenneth G. Lieberthal and Michel Oksenberg, *Bureaucratic Politics and Chinese Energy Development* (Washington: U.S. Government Printing Office, 1986); David M. Lampton (ed.), *Policy Implementation in Post-Mao China* (Berkeley: University of California Press, 1987); David M. Lampton, 'Chinese Politics: The Bargaining Treadmill', *Issues and Studies* 23 (1987): 11–41; Kenneth G. Lieberthal and Michel Oksenberg, *Policymaking in China: Leaders, Structures and Processes* (Princeton: Princeton University Press, 1988); David M. Lampton and Kenneth G. Lieberthal (eds), *Bureaucracy, Politics and Decision Making in Post-Mao China* (Berkeley: University of California Press, 1992); Shaun G. Breslin, 'Sustainable Development in China', *Sustainable Development* 4 (1996): 103–8; Gorild Heggelund, *Environment and Resettlement Politics in China: The Three Gorges Project* (Aldershot: Ashgate, 2004).

[16] See Vivienne Shue, *The Reach of the State: Sketches of the Chinese Body Politic* (Stanford: Stanford University Press, 1988); Wang Shaoguang and Hu Angang, *The Chinese Economy in Crisis: State Capacity and Tax Reform* (Armonk: M.E. Sharpe, 2001); Jonathan Schwartz, 'The Impact of State Capacity on Enforcement of Environmental Policies', *Journal of Environment and Development* 12 (2003): 50–81; Wang Shaoguang, 'The Problem of State Weakness', *Journal of Democracy* 14 (2003): 36–42; Dali L. Yang, 'Population Control and State Coercion in China', *Journal of Democracy* 14 (2003): 43–50; Barry J. Naughton and Dali L. Yang (eds), *Holding China Together: Diversity and National Integration in the Post-Deng Era* (Cambridge: Cambridge University Press, 2004); Wang Shaoguang, 'Regulating Death at Coalmines: Changing Mode of Governance in China', *Journal of Contemporary China* 15 (2006): 1–30; Tim Wright, 'State Capacity in Contemporary China: Closing the Pits and Reducing Coal Production', *Journal of Contemporary China* 16 (2007): 173–94; Jonathan Schwartz and Gregory Evans, 'Causes of Effective Policy Implementation: China's Public Response to SARS', *Journal of Contemporary China* 16 (2007): 195–213.

there is no reason to assume that such problems are not encountered elsewhere in Asia.[17]

Regulatory, rather than fiscal or monetary, policy is arguably the most appropriate instrument for minimizing the negative consequences of economic integration. The effectiveness of this tool in the Chinese context however is severely compromised by widespread politicization. Like other countries in the region, China has embraced the Japanese development model of regulation, rather than its independent regulator counterpart. The former entails a direct and substantial government involvement in private sector activities.[18] The Chinese variant may give 'the initial *appearance* of independent regulators, [but] the actual *function* of an independent regulatory structure is far from established'.[19] Indeed,

> the relationship between regulators, the rest of the [S]tate, and (though, to a lesser degree) the regulated firms remains bound in a Gordian knot. Regulatory independence is constrained by the broader political-institutional context in which the new regulatory bodies are situated, a context that possesses four salient features: continued [S]tate ownership of strategic assets; continued dominance of [S]tate and party 'comprehensive' institutions with authority over economic development; the bureaucratic origins of regulators in the former line industries; and the fragmented, ambiguous authority of the regulator.[20]

On the Hong Kong side of the regulatory divide the picture is fundamentally different. The territory has shunned Japanese-style economic control and has practised, by international standards, an ultra-pure version of Anglo-Saxon capitalism. 'Big market, small government' has traditionally

---

[17] See Joel Migdal, Atul Kohli and Vivienne Shue (eds), *State Power and Social Forces: Domination and Transformation in the Third World* (Cambridge: Cambridge University Press, 1994); Kield E. Brodsgaard and Susan Young (eds), *State Capacity in East Asia: China, Taiwan, Vietnam and Japan* (Oxford: Oxford University Press, 2001); Ka Ho Mok and Ray Yep, 'Globalization and State Capacity in Asia', *Pacific Review* 21 (2008): 109–20.

[18] See Margaret M. Pearson, 'The Business of Governing Business in China: Institutions and Norms of the Emerging Regulatory State', *World Politics* 57 (2005): 296–322.

[19] See ibid.

[20] Ibid., 297–8. For additional insights see Takatoshi Ito and Anne O. Krueger (eds), *Deregulation and Interdependence in the Asia-Pacific Region* (Chicago: Chicago University Press, 2000); Takatoshi Ito and Anne O. Krueger (eds), *Governance, Regulation and Privatization in the Asia-Pacific Region* (Chicago: University of Chicago Press, 2004); Khai Leong Ho (ed.), *Reforming Corporate Governance in Southeast Asia: Economics, Politics and Regulations* (Singapore: Institute of Southeast Asian Studies, 2005).

been the principle guiding the local authorities.[21] Unambiguous restraint, or unqualified non-interventionism, may have given way to greater policy activism, or positive non-interventionism, as structural transformation and exogenous crises have compelled the government to provide a wider range of services and resort periodically in earnest to counter-cyclical stabilization. The underlying policy tenets (fiscal moderation, high transparency, incentive compatibility, institutional minimalism, preference for rules over discretion, procedural predictability and systematic openness) have nevertheless remained largely intact.[22]

However, a less competitive/Anglo-Saxon characteristic of the organizational facade has also proved resistant to the forces of change. Despite halting progress towards representative and accountable government, the business community has continued to function as key pillar of the political system. It would be inappropriate to suggest that it has effectively captured key layers of the bureaucratic pyramid because there has been no compelling reason to do so. Throughout the territory's history, the Hong Kong government has pursued policies geared towards maximizing business advantages and its strategy vis-à-vis the sector has been underpinned by institutional arrangements reflecting this stance.[23] The form may have

---

[21]　See Alvin Rabushka, *The Changing Face of Hong Kong* (Washington DC: American Enterprise Institute, 1973); Alvin Rabushka, *Hong Kong: A Study in Economic Freedom* (Chicago: Graduate School of Business, University of Chicago, 1979); Alwyn Young, *Hong Kong and the Art of Landing on One's Feet: A Case Study of a Structurally Flexible Economy* (Medford: Fletcher School of Law and Diplomacy, Tufts University, 1989); Miron Mushkat, *The Economic Future of Hong Kong* (Boulder: Lynne Rienner, 1990), 4–10; David Mole, 'Introduction' in David Mole (ed.), *The New Hong Kong Economy* (Hong Kong: Oxford University Press, 1996), 1–17; Kui-wai Li, *The Hong Kong Economy: Recovery and Restructuring* (Singapore: McGraw-Hill Education, 2006), 5–10, 17–24; Miron Mushkat and Roda Mushkat, 'The Transfer of Property Rights from the Public to the Private Sector in Hong Kong: A Critical Assessment', *Global Economic Review* 35 (2006): 445–61.

[22]　See Li, above note 21, 17–24.

[23]　See Benjamin K.P. Leung, *Perspectives on Hong Kong Society* (Hong Kong: Oxford University Press, 1996); David G. Lethbridge and Ng Sek Hong (eds), *The Business Environment of Hong Kong* (Oxford: Oxford University Press, 2000); Leo F. Goodstadt, *Uneasy Partners: The Conflict Between Public Interest and Private Profit in Hong Kong* (Hong Kong: Hong Kong University Press, 2006); Miron Mushkat and Roda Mushkat, 'The Political Economy of Loose Regulation: Modernity Meets Tradition in Hong Kong', *International Journal of Regulation and Governance* 7 (2007): 101–46; Miron Mushkat and Roda Mushkat, 'The Political Economy of Hong Kong's "Open Skies" Legal Regime: An Empirical and Theoretical Exploration', *San Diego International Law Journal* 10 (2009): 381–438.

diverged from those witnessed elsewhere in Asia, but this variant of regulation has had distinct corporatist features with deep roots in the region.[24] Hong Kong may be considerably different from its neighbours, yet it is not entirely unique.

PLATFORM FOR ECONOMIC INTEGRATION

Hong Kong began its historical journey as a fishing village and a modest, albeit lively, channel for supporting entrepot trade. Its fortunes ebbed and waned in the highly turbulent environment of the early twentieth century, but it displayed resilience without turning into a significant actor in the global economic arena. Paradoxically, the imposition of a UN embargo on China during the Korean War, when it allied itself with Pyongyang and plunged into a state of total isolation, provided the catalyst for accelerated industrialization. Hong Kong had no choice but to shift its focus away from mainland-related trade and reinvent itself promptly as a thriving manufacturing centre based on labour-intensive industries.[25]

The adoption of the open-door policy by the post-1978 Chinese leadership has provided the territory with another opportunity to capitalize swiftly on its evolving comparative advantage. The adjacent Guangdong Province was the first sub-national unit across the border to respond to this strategic initiative in earnest, partly because of its inherent locational pull and partly due to its legacy of outward-looking orientation. Hong Kong's light manufacturing industries migrated *en masse* there in order to profit from low wages and the low cost of land in a culturally familiar and welcoming environment. Their modest-skill service counterparts soon followed, allowing the territory to climb up the value-added ladder.[26]

Hong Kong has consequently become a forerunner and an epitome of the 'front shop–back factory' configuration that features prominently in modern-style economic integration processes. Managing its industrial platform in Guangdong Province/Pearl River Delta (PRD) region and operating the foreign trade engine stretching across the whole area

---

[24]   See Howard J. Wiarda, *Corporatism and Comparative Politics: The Other Great 'Ism'* (Armonk: M.E. Sharpe, 1996), 81–8.

[25]   See Li, above note 21, 5–10; Steve Y.S. Tsang, *A Modern History of Hong Kong* (London: I.B. Tauris, 2004); Steven Chiu and Tai-lok Lui, *Hong Kong: Becoming a Global Chinese City* (London: Routledge, 2009); David Clayton, *Hong Kong since 1945: An Economic and Social History* (London: Routledge, 2010).

[26]   See ibid.

was initially the principal focus of the venture. Financial deepening has materialized shortly thereafter as commercial and investment banking has acquired an increasingly regional and international character. Structural transformation has proceeded apace and, by the end of the twentieth century, Hong Kong had evolved into a full-fledged service centre.[27]

The territory has not shed its traditional entrepot identity but, like Singapore, it is currently far more a crucial and multi-dimensional component of the global exchange system. It still specializes in matching sellers and buyers in different markets, yet on a much larger scale than during previous phases of its economic development. Together with Singapore, it presently intermediates a substantial portion of the trade in goods and services within Asia and between the region and the rest of the world. Further, as indicated, the function is performed in a less circumscribed fashion and is even less confined to trade than in the not too distant past.[28]

Strictly speaking, the entrepot role refers primarily to re-export trade, in the course of which Hong Kong firms purchase goods outside the territory for resale elsewhere, and the goods are imported into the territory for re-exporting; such goods clear customs twice, first during importation and later during exportation. The Hong Kong middleman however is also involved in offshore trade, whereby the goods do not go through local customs, either because merchanting is relied upon (in which case, Hong Kong traders purchase goods outside the territory for export elsewhere without clearing them through local customs) or merchandizing is resorted to (in such circumstances, Hong Kong traders arrange on behalf of buyers/

---

[27] See ibid.

[28] See ibid., 380–424; Chiu and Lui, above note 25; Yun-wing Sung, *The China–Hong Kong Connection: The Key to China's Open Door Policy* (Cambridge: Cambridge University Press, 1991); Ronald Findlay and Stanislaw Wellisz, 'Five Small Open Economies: Hong Kong' in Ronald Findlay and Stanislaw Wellisz (eds), *Five Small Open Economies: A World Bank Comparative Study* (Oxford: Oxford University Press, 1993), 16–92; Joseph C.H. Chai, Yak-yeow Kueh and Clement A. Tisdell (eds), *China and the Asian Pacific Economy* (Brisbane: Department of Economics, University of Queensland, 1997); David R. Meyer, *Hong Kong as a Global Metropolis* (Cambridge: Cambridge University Press, 2000); Robert C. Feenstra and Gordon H. Hanson, 'Intermediaries in Entrepot Trade: Hong Kong Re-Exports of Chinese Goods', *Journal of Economics and Management Strategy* 13 (2004): 3–35; Yun-wing Sung, *The Emergence of Greater China: The Economic Integration of Mainland China, Taiwan and Hong Kong* (Basingstoke: Palgrave Macmillan, 2005); Lok Sang Ho and Robert Ash (eds), *China, Hong Kong and the World Economy: Studies on Globalization* (Basingstoke: Palgrave Macmillan, 2006), 152–69.

sellers outside the territory the purchase/sale of goods without assuming ownership and without seeking clearance through local customs).[29]

Offshore trade has expanded dramatically in recent years. This form of intermediation exposes Hong Kong to less intensive competitive pressures than its entrepot counterpart. This is due to the fact that, unlike shipping, pure trading does not require container terminals and cargo areas, which are highly land-intensive. Specifically, trading activities (arbitration, documentation, financing, marketing, negotiation and search) may be undertaken virtually anywhere, including skyscrapers, which allow agents to economize on land use. The shift in this direction is emblematic of the increasing scope of economic integration.[30]

International trade does not flow in an institutional vacuum, certainly not when the magnitudes are on the scale witnessed in Hong Kong. Its enduring growth hinges on the availability of complementary services such as communications, finance, information processing and transportation. These have grown by leaps and bounds as the territory has consolidated its position as a regional/global middleman. A parallel expansion has been seen in connected industries such as professional and corporate services (in the case of the latter, particularly in relation to support for the formation and maintenance of multinational headquarters). Hong Kong's position as a circulator of financial capital (emporium of finance) and corporate management centre (overarching business controller) is especially noteworthy because it highlights the unique contribution of strategically placed intermediaries to economic integration.[31]

Notably, Hong Kong/Singapore-style middlemen lower significantly transaction costs for other parties engaged in mutually beneficial exchanges and reap healthy gains for themselves in the process. The nature of their enterprise is such that they face strong incentives to agglomerate in order to reduce further their operating expenses. They seek close contact, often direct, to coordinate, negotiate, share (complex, confidential and specialized) information and build trust among themselves and service recipients. Economies of agglomeration realized via a highly concentrated hub-

[29]   See Sung, 'The Evolving Role of Hong Kong as China's Middleman' in Ho and Ash (eds), ibid., 155–6.

[30]   See ibid.

[31]   See ibid., 152–69; Sung, *The China–Hong Kong Connection: The Key to China's Open Door Policy,* above note 28; Findlay and Wellisz, above note 28; Chai, Kueh and Tisdell, above note 28; Meyer, above note 28; Feenstra and Hanson, above note 28; Sung, *The Emergence of Greater China: The Economic Integration of Mainland China, Taiwan and Hong Kong,* above note 28; Ho and Ash, above note 28; Chiu and Lui, above note 28.

and-spoke structure, provided by world cities such as Hong Kong and Singapore, are crucial for their effectiveness and success.[32]

Intermediation, and hence integration, is a cultural, rather than merely an economic, phenomenon. Hong Kong is, by virtue of its institutional architecture and long experience of serving as a bridge between East and West, the nerve centre of a vast Overseas (Nanyang) Chinese network capable of linking synergistically its members and their partners. It is underpinned by elaborate family ties and tangible relationships of trust. This edifice is structurally and functionally different from the Western model of business organization, the Japanese *kaisha* (large, industrially specialized corporations) and the Korean *chaebols* (conglomerates). Singapore is a vital component of that network, but Tokyo lies on its periphery.[33]

Hong Kong's connection with Guangdong, or PRD region, features prominently in the literature on economic integration in Asia. Yet, the territory's tentacles extend much further. The Southeast Asian dimension of the process (the formation of a Pan-Pearl River Delta/Pan-PRD zone) is also accorded considerable attention in academic work,[34] but again this falls short of reflecting the scope of the phenomenon. In recent writings, the focus has shifted to portraying Hong Kong-driven economic fusion as an evolutionary enterprise entailing the emergence of three concentric layers of a China Circle and acceleration in the pace of integration into the world economy.[35]

The Hong Kong–Guangdong/PRD nexus, or Greater Hong Kong, acts as the core of this new entity. Greater Southeast China, encompassing Hong Kong, Taiwan and the mainland's south-eastern coastal provinces (Guangdong, Fujian, Shanghai, Jiangsu and Zhejiang), constitutes the inner layer and Greater China/the Chinese Economic Area (CEA) forms its outer ring. Hong Kong operates as the engine of economic integration within the China Circle and a bridge builder vis-à-vis the rest of the world, including (perhaps even particularly) Southeast Asia, but without overshadowing other increasingly close and vital relationships.[36]

As the process of broad-based economic integration has unfolded,

---

[32] See Sung, *The China–Hong Kong Connection: The Key to China's Open Door policy*, above note 28, 30–32; Meyer, above note 28, 21–2; Sung, 'The Evolving Role of Hong Kong as China's Middleman', above note 29, 154–55.

[33] See Meyer, above note 28; Chiu and Lui, above note 28.

[34] See Li, above note 21, 413.

[35] See Sung, *The Emergence of Greater China: The Economic Integration of Mainland China, Taiwan and Hong Kong,* above note 28, 9–10.

[36] See above.

Hong Kong has been transformed into a Chinese global city, or simply a global metropolis.[37] The number of such urban centres is small (London and New York are obvious examples), but social scientists (primarily economists and geographers) posit that they play a crucial role in facilitating economic fusion/globalization (an argument bolstered by invoking the global urban network and hierarchy thesis, the global city function thesis and the dual city thesis).[38] This is another facet of economic integration, within the region and beyond, that Hong Kong's experience helps to illuminate and one that has been a source of substantial benefits for the territory.

COSTS OF ECONOMIC INTEGRATION

The trends charted in the previous section have not been without adverse consequences. The pursuit of economic growth as currently conceptualized and measured involves inevitable trade-offs. Structural transformation is no exception in this respect and may prove selectively highly disruptive in terms of its socio-environmental impact. Overall assessment is a matter of subjective judgment. It is commonly assumed that Hong Kong people's preference set is skewed heavily in favour of the material side of the equation, but surveys carried out in the territory suggest that other concerns are not marginalized.[39] They should not be overlooked, whether in the local or the broader regional context.

Early expressions of disquiet were directed at the supposedly tenuous foundation of the economic middleman paradigm, rather than the socio-environmental implications of accelerated cross-border economic cooperation. After all, as more countries embrace market deregulation and trade liberalization, and the economic integration process broadens and deepens, players in the global arena may be able to interact with each other directly, without relying on the services provided by costly go-betweens. The empirical and theoretical underpinnings of this scenario, however, were never solid and it has not withstood serious academic scrutiny.

In fact, a contrary view is warranted. Economic decentralization (marketization and opening up) boosts significantly the demand for intermediation because of the proliferation of autonomous agents, the

---

[37] See Meyer, above note 28; Chiu and Liu, above note 28.
[38] See Chiu and Lui, above note 28, 6–7.
[39] For example see Timothy K.Y. Wong and P.S. Wan, 'Lingering Environmental Pessimism and the Role of Government in Hong Kong', *Public Administration and Development* 29 (2009): 441–51.

escalation in the volume of information and the heightened specialization that ensues. Greater product heterogeneity, which typically materializes in such an environment, has a similar effect. The more differentiated goods and services (particularly the latter) become, the less able are the numerous decision units occupying well-defined segments of the economy to proceed by targeting their counterparties via the shortest route possible. The transaction costs are excessively heavy.[40]

On the other hand, the mild sense of unease about the negative social ramifications of rapid economic integration, which surfaced subsequently, has turned out to be justified. According to the well-known Stolper–Samuelson theorem, trade liberalization is expected to have an adverse impact on the wages of unskilled workers in high-income countries because of outsourcing to low-income ones. The Hong Kong experience bears this out. The earning gap between skilled and unskilled workers in the territory has widened further as labour-intensive industries have migrated across the border and Hong Kong has climbed up the value-added ladder. This has exacerbated income inequality in a city (now a global metropolis) where disparities between rich and poor were pronounced well before Chinese reforms gained momentum.[41]

The social consequences of economic integration should not be minimized, but they have been attenuated by high individual mobility in a fluid structural setting, a vibrant labour market and worker retraining initiatives.[42] It is legitimate to argue that the adverse ecological implications have been far more serious and less amenable to countervailing influences. Hong Kong's nimble entrepreneurs were quick to seize investment opportunities in manufacturing industries, physical infrastructure and

---

[40]   See Sung, *The China–Hong Kong Connection: The Key to China's Open Door Policy,* above note 28, 30–32; Meyer, above note 28, 235–7; Sung, 'The Evolving Role of Hong Kong as China's Middleman', above note 29, 153–4.

[41]   See, Kui-yin Cheung and C. Simon Fan, 'Economic Integration between Hong Kong and Mainland China: Did Trade Hurt Hong Kong's Unskilled Workers?' in Ho and Ash, above note 28, 186–99.

[42]   See Lok-sang Ho, 'Labour Market in a Changing Political Economy' in Mole (ed.), above note 21, 76–94; Margaret H.Y. Chan, Ng Sek Hong and Elaine Y.Y. Ho, 'Labour and Employment' in Lethbridge and Ng (eds), above note 23, 74–96; Gary S. Fields, 'Changing Labor Market Conditions and Economic Development in Hong Kong, the Republic of Korea, Singapore and Taiwan, China', *World Bank Economic Review* 8 (1994): 395–414; Tak-wing Chan, Tai-lok Lui and Thomas W.P. Wong, 'A Comparative Analysis of Social Mobility in Hong Kong', *European Sociological Review* 11 (1995): 135–55; May M.L. Wong, 'An Evaluation on the Employees' Retraining Programmes in Hong Kong', *Employee Relations* 20 (1998): 404–14.

the property sector across the border. The explosion of economic activity that has followed has led to a severe deterioration in environmental conditions in Guangdong Province/PRD region and, despite triggering de-industrialization at the point where the process has originated, in Hong Kong itself. The territory's air quality and waterways have been the most seriously impacted by the reconfiguration of the southern China economy.[43]

The movement of air masses over long distances is subject to consider-

---

[43] See Peter Hills, Lei Zhang and Jianhua Liu, 'Transboundary Pollution between Guangdong Province and Hong Kong: Threats to Water Quality in the Pearl River Estuary and their Implications for Environmental Policy and Planning', *Journal of Environmental Planning and Management* 41 (1998): 375–96; J.H. Liu, Peter Hills and William Barron, 'Cross-Border Water Pollution and Sustainability in Hong Kong' in Brian Morton (ed.), *The Marine Biology of South China Sea* (Hong Kong: Hong Kong University Press, 1998), 563–78; William Barron and Peter Hills, 'The Issue of Cross-Border Pollution' in Andy T. Chan et al. (eds), *The Air We Breathe: Air Pollution in Hong Kong* (Hong Kong: Hong Kong University Press, 2001), 73–83; Peter Hills and Peter Roberts, 'Political Integration, Transboundary Pollution and Sustainability: Challenges for Environmental Policy in the Pearl River Delta Region', *Journal of Environmental Planning and Management* 44 (2001): 455–73; Johnny C.L. Chan et al., 'Air Pollution Considerations in Town Planning in Hong Kong' in Anthony G.O. Yeh et al. (eds), *Building a Competitive River Delta Region: Cooperation, Coordination and Planning* (Hong Kong: Centre of Urban Planning and Environmental Management, University of Hong Kong, 2002), 165–81; Thomas Chow, 'Fighting Pollution in Hong Kong' in Yeh et al. (eds), *Building a Competitive Pearl River Delta Region: Cooperation, Coordination and Planning*, 153–7; Wang Tao, 'Photochemical Smog: An Air Pollution Problem Requiring Regional Solutions' in Yeh et al. (eds), *Building a Competitive Pearl River Delta Region: Cooperation, Coordination and Planning*, 159–63; Peter Hills, 'Environmental Policy and Planning in Hong Kong: An Emerging Regional Agenda', *Sustainable Development* 10 (2002): 171–8; Yok-shiu F. Lee, 'Tackling Cross-Border Environmental Problems in Hong Kong', *China Quarterly* 172 (2002): 986–1009; Lisa Hopkinson and Rachel Stern, 'One Country, Two Systems, One Smog: Cross-Boundary Air Pollution Policy Challenges for Hong Kong and Guangdong', *China Environment Series* 6 (2003): 19–36; Business Environment Council, *Market-Based Mechanisms to Tackle Air Pollution in Hong Kong and the Pearl River Delta* (Hong Kong: Business Environment Council, 2005); Joyce P.S. Chan et al., *A Study of the Hong Kong–Guangdong Regional Pollution Problem* (Hong Kong: Department of Politics and Public Administration, University of Hong Kong, 2006); Yok-shiu Lee, 'Managing Water Resources in the Delta Border Zone: Challenges and Opportunities' in Anthony G.O. Yeh et al. (eds), *Developing a Competitive Pearl River Delta in South China under One Country–Two Systems* (Hong Kong: Hong Kong University Press, 2006), 357–81; Richard Welford, Peter Hills and Jacqueline Lam, 'Environmental Reform, Technology Policy and Transboundary Pollution in Hong Kong', *Development and Change* 37 (2006): 145–78.

able variations. Some constituent organic substances lack cohesion, and tend to decompose promptly. Others, such as suspended particulates, display greater sturdiness and may travel hundreds of kilometers before settling out of the air. The latter loom large in scientific work on the long-range transport of air pollutants (particularly nitrogen and sulphur). They cross virtually intact from Guangdong Province/PRD region into Hong Kong. Seasonal influences, notably the drop in humidity witnessed during the winter months, which allows some pollutants to linger in air, compound the problem. The strong winds blowing from the mainland reinforce the movement southward, exacerbating it further.[44]

The harmful flow of air pollutants into Hong Kong does not stem exclusively from Guangdong Province/PRD region. The key particulate substances crossing into the territory may travel from as far as central and northern China (although, in such circumstances, they are typically characterized by lower concentrations). Moreover, the monsoon winds and the tropical depressions/typhoons, to which Hong Kong is exposed in one form or another throughout the year, also carry air pollutants into the territory, predominantly (but not solely) through Guangdong Province/ PRD region.[45] The steep rise in vehicle ownership across the border has markedly aggravated the situation. This is an institutional, as well as a technical, issue in that vehicle production on the mainland is not subject to highly stringent environmental standards.[46]

Pollution in Hong Kong is both internally and externally generated and the dire condition of the territory's waterways is no exception to the rule. The local government/populace has long tolerated activities with very deleterious effects on a pivotal resource with a limited carrying capacity and shares responsibility for the damage wrought on it. Notably, a substantial volume of domestic sewage and industrial waste has been allowed to be discharged, largely untreated, into Hong Kong's waterways. These substances have been 'heavily contaminated with bacteria, organic material and other pollutants which seriously affect fish and other marine life by depleting oxygen levels in the water and also cause risks to humans through the marine food chain'.[47]

The Guangdong Province/PRD region connection is reflected in the western waters of Hong Kong, which receive significant inputs from the Pearl River, one of the most gravely contaminated in the world.

---

44 See Barron and Hills, above note 43.
45 See Hills and Roberts, above note 43.
46 See Barron and Hills, above note 43.
47 Liu, Hills and Barron, above note 43, 566.

In this geographical segment, 'levels of organic pollution and nutrient content (nitrogen and phosphorous) are high, mainly due to heavy discharges of livestock wastes, industrial effluents and domestic sewage.'[48] It 'suffers from severe oxygen depletion, with two thirds of water quality samples having less than 50% oxygen saturation and high levels of unionized ammonia. Oyster contamination and algal blooms have also been recorded'.[49]

The PRD region forms the economic and social core of southern China. Although it is industrializing at breakneck pace, its agricultural sector remains a vital component of the economic landscape. Animal and human wastes, effluents, fertilizers and pesticides from its dynamic urban centres and resilient rural hinterland are eventually washed, mostly untreated, into Hong Kong's estuarine waters to the west and an adjacent bay. Two of the territory's principal conservation areas, which are located nearby, are impacted as well and the adverse consequences may be observed farther south.[50]

Water pollution has raised fewer concerns in Hong Kong than the sharp impairment of air quality. The latter's symptoms are easier to observe, the persistent haze that grips the territory during the winter months being a conspicuous example. The tendency to focus more closely on air pollution may also be attributed to the fact that tracking shifts in its level in a fairly reliable manner is a comparatively manageable undertaking. Perhaps more significantly, Hong Kong has seen a number of notorious air pollution episodes that have provoked a strong reaction by eroding its reputation as an international commercial centre and tourist magnet. The profound challenge that transboundary water pollution poses may have thus not been duly acknowledged by the community and the policy establishment.[51]

INSTITUTIONAL RESPONSES

The underlying causes and symptoms of cross-border ecological dislocation may be addressed unilaterally and/or jointly. The potential for effective independent action is better on the Chinese/Guangdong Province/

---

[48]   Ibid.

[49]   Ibid., 567.

[50]   See ibid., 567–78; Hills, Zhang and Liu, above note 43; Barron and Hills, above note 43; Hills and Roberts, above note 43; Welford, Hills and Lam, above note 43.

[51]   See Hills and Roberts, above note 43.

PRD region side because of closer proximity to current sources of the problem, or greater control over presently relevant variables. However, this is the inherently more problematic part of the area-wide embryonic policy architecture in terms of the willingness and ability to undertake initiatives likely to have a meaningful impact, and sooner rather than later, on transboundary pollution in Greater Hong Kong. The picture is fluid, with momentum apparently turning favourable at the margin, but the impediments to progress remain formidable.

China seems to be in the early stages of a fundamental paradigm shift which, if carried out unwaveringly, might lead to a lesser misalignment between the goals of economic prosperity and environmental preservation. Some observers believe that, having undergone a transition from a configuration characterized by State-driven 'catching-up development' to one featuring 'economism/GDPism', it is now on the verge of embracing 'people-centred development'. During this phase, broad human concerns are expected to come to the fore, restoring a modicum of balance between the energies channeled towards the pursuit of economic betterment, social equality and ecological harmony.[52]

Perhaps a more realistic assessment of the evolving policy dynamics would substitute the pragmatic concept of ecological modernization for the lofty notion of people-centred development. The former stops short of espousing sustainability, which may for all intents and purposes imply a steady-state or zero-growth economy in the Chinese context, and seeks to reconcile the imperatives of robust economic expansion and adequate environmental protection in a measured fashion. The goal of raising living standards continues to loom large on the strategic agenda, but is pursued in a restrained manner without inflicting severe damage on the increasingly fragile ecosystem.[53]

A subtle shift in this direction took place, at least in the form of policy signaling, at the 17th Communist Party Congress, held in October 2007. The costs of relentless industrialization were acknowledged openly and specific steps were proposed to address notable institutional shortcomings (such as bureaucratic constraints, insufficient legal capacity, ineffective regulatory mechanisms, perverse environmental incentives and weak local

---

[52] See Kinglun Ngok, 'Redefining Development in China: Towards a New Paradigm for the New Century' in Ka Ho Mok and Ray Forrest (eds), *Changing Governance and Public Policy in East Asia* (London: Routledge, 2009), 49–66.

[53] See Peter Ho, 'Trajectories for Greening in China: Theory and Practice', *Development and Change* 37 (2006): 3–28; Arthur P.J. Mol, 'Environment and Modernity in Transitional China: Frontiers of Ecological Modernization', *Development and Change* 37 (2006): 29–56.

ecological infrastructure) and deepen the impact of strategic initiatives (such as erecting a basic policy framework to confront ecological degradation, which has culminated in the elevation of the State Environmental Protection Administration (SEPA) to a ministerial entity, establishing an elementary legal/regulatory system, intensifying the process of the devolution of environmental responsibility from the national to the local level, implementing the environmental responsibility system, and encouraging non-governmental actors to play a constructive role in the quest for ecological improvement) undertaken during the preceding three decades.[54]

This shift has not gone unnoticed in Guangdong Province/PRD region. Various institutional reforms have been embarked upon in that area with a view to enhancing the effectiveness of environmental management in line with the emerging spirit of ecological modernization. The trend has been reinforced by autonomous (that is, not policy induced) changes in the economic structure (for example, the proliferation of service and skill-intensive industries).[55] There have even been previously unseen bottom-up

---

[54]   See Joshua S.Y. Wu, 'The State of China's Environmental Governance after the 17th Party Congress', *East Asia: An International Quarterly* 26 (2009): 265–84. The long-term evolution of the Chinese ecological management system, including the institutional dimension, which is crucial to understanding the intricate relationship between the national centre (Beijing) and the sub-national periphery (e.g., Guangdong Province, but potentially also Hong Kong), is charted in Barbara J. Sinkule and Leonard Ortolano, *Implementing Environmental Policy in China* (Wesport: Praeger, 1995); Shaun G. Breslin, 'Sustainable Development in China', *Sustainable Development* 4 (1996): 103–8; Kenneth G. Lieberthal, *China's Governing System and its Impact on Environmental Policy Implementation* (Washington: Woodrow Wilson Center, 1997); Richard L. Edmonds, *Managing the Chinese Environment* (Oxford: Oxford University Press, 2000); Xiaoying Ma and Leonard Ortolano, *Environmental Regulation in China: Institutions, Enforcement and Compliance* (Lanham, MD: Rowman and Littlefield, 2000); Geoffrey Murray and Ian G. Cook, *Green China: Seeking Ecological Alternatives* (London: RoutledgeCurzon, 2002); Elizabeth C. Economy, *The River Runs Black: The Environmental Challenge to China's Future* (Ithaca: Cornell University Press, 2004); Gorild Heggelund, *Environment and Resettlement Politics in China: The Three Gorges Project* (Aldershot: Ashgate, 2004); Kristen A. Day (ed.), *China's Environment and the Challenge of Sustainable Development* (New York: M.E.Sharpe, 2005); Benjamin van Rooij, *Regulating Land and Pollution in China: Lawmaking, Compliance and Enforcement* (Leiden: Leiden University Press, 2006); Neil T. Carter and Arthur J. Mol (eds), *Environmental Governance in China* (London: Routledge, 2007); Miron Mushkat and Roda Mushkat, 'The Political Economy of Chinese "Federalism": New Analytical Directions', *Global Economic Review* 38 (2009): 13–28.
[55]   See Carlos W.H. Lo and Shui-yan Tang, 'Institutional Reform, Economic Changes and Local Environmental Management: The Case of Guangdong Province', *Environmental Politics* 15 (2006): 190–210.

moves designed to arrest the downward spiral of environmental destruction. A salient example is a recent attempt by 11 members of the Pan-Pearl River Delta (PPRD) region to forge cooperative links in an effort to combat water pollution and find a viable way to follow a less unbalanced developmental strategy.[56]

It is debatable however whether the policy adjustment has reached a point whereby the cognitive reorientation and noble strategic intentions, coupled with unplanned influences, may translate into a determined reworking of priorities, painstaking redesign of the organizational edifice, ironclad implementation and reshaping of ground-level agent behaviour. As matters stand, the evidence suggests that, although progress is being made gradually and selectively, the deep-rooted institutional shortcomings persist and the capacity to bring about meaningful change remains limited.[57] To assume that Guangdong Province/PRD region will be able to tackle cross-border ecological ills significantly on its own is thus not a realistic expectation. As a sophisticated global metropolis, Hong Kong is in a better position to adopt independent measures, which are of course scarcely sufficient by themselves, and in parallel combine forces with its northern neighbour.

On the domestic front, statutory mechanisms are the foundation underpinning the evolving strategy to enhance environmental quality. The Air Pollution Control Ordinance, the Water Pollution Control Ordinance, the Noise Pollution Control Ordinance and the Waste Disposal Ordinance are the principal legal instruments relied upon for this purpose (the last two, particularly the Waste Disposal statutory management tool, are not entirely relevant in the transboundary context). Their scope has inevitably expanded over time and their procedural and substantive (preventive/corrective/punitive) attributes have also been fine-tuned to reflect rapidly changing physical conditions and political realities.[58]

The legal machinery constitutes a crucial component of the overall policy to stanch ecological deterioration, but it is not the sole control

---

[56]   See Reut Barak, 'Fighting Pollution on the Pearl River', accessed 15 January 2010, http://www.chinadialogue.net/article/show/single/en/326-Fighting-pollution-on-the-Pearl-River-.

[57]   See Wu, above note 54.

[58]   See   http://www.epd.gov.hk/epd/english/environmentinhk/air/guide_ref/guide_apco.html, accessed 15 January 2010; http://www.epd.gov.hk/epd/english/environmentinhk/water/guide_ref/guide_wpc_wpco.html; http://www.epd.gov.hk/epd/english/environmentinhk/noise/guide_ref/files/CG_E_06n.pdf, accessed 15 January 2010; http://www.epd.gov.hk/epd/english/environmentinhk/waste/waste_maincontent.html, accessed 15 January 2010.

apparatus employed to this end. The government also engages in monitoring activities, undertakes research, invests in projects, manages facilities and endeavours to influence attitudes vis-à-vis the environment through educational channels.[59] Most of these efforts, with the exception of monitoring and research (which overlap considerably), do not impinge directly, at least not materially so, on the cross-border situation. The patterns prevailing there are affected to a greater extent, whether actually or potentially, by statutory/regulatory initiatives, even if merely confined to the Hong Kong side.

The impact of unilateral measures should not be overstated, but it might be equally inappropriate to dismiss their efficacy altogether. To illustrate, the volume of vehicular traffic between the territory and the mainland is substantial and growing by leaps and bounds. The imposition of restrictions on vehicle emissions at home is within the purview of Hong Kong laws/regulations. Indeed, it is a prominent (albeit arguably not sufficiently so) element of the Air Pollution Control Ordinance. In principle, there is nothing to prevent the local authorities from tightening the restrictions to a point whereby the environmental consequences are more palatable, although at a significant economic and possibly political cost.

Hong Kong's home-centred ecological strategy cannot be said to have been characterized by timeliness, comprehensiveness and adequacy.[60] Lagged responses partly account for other shortcomings because the unhurried adjustment of the patchwork-like statutory/regulatory regime has often left substantial gaps and areas of tenuous sway over agent behaviour. The evolution of the Air Pollution Control Ordinance is a notable case in point. Its predecessor, the Clean Air Ordinance, enacted in 1959, was aimed at merely fuel combustion emissions. The current piece of legislation, when originally enacted in 1983, broadened the remit of the law to encompass non-combustion processes. Its scope was expanded further in 1991 to include vehicle emission regulation. Additional amendments have

---

[59] See ibid.; http://www.epd.gov.hk/epd/eindex.html, accessed 15 January 2010.

[60] See Wong and Wan, above note 39; Terri Mottershead (ed.), *Sustainable Development in Hong Kong* (Hong Kong: Hong Kong University Press, 2004); Peter Hills, 'Environmental Reform, Ecological Modernization and the Policy Process in Hong Kong: An Exploratory Study of Stakeholder Perspectives', *Journal of Environmental Planning and Management* 48 (2005): 209–40; Andre Gouldson, Peter Hills and Richard Welford, 'Ecological Modernisation and Policy Learning in Hong Kong', *Geoforum* 39 (2008): 319–30; Christine Loh, 'Heading Down an Unsustainable Path?', accessed 15 January 2010, http://www.hkjournal.org/archive/loh.html; Christine Loh, 'None Too Soon: New Air Quality Standards for Hong Kong', accessed 15 January 2010, http://www.hkjournal.org/archive/2009_winter/5.htm.

enhanced control on the emission of asbestos. Tighter restrictions were imposed on the power sector, the principal source of domestic pollution, in 2008, in the form of emission caps for 2010 and beyond (emission trading was also introduced for this purpose).[61]

Similarly, the Water Pollution Control Ordinance has seen long pauses between much needed adjustments since its enactment in 1980. Its most salient feature was the sub-division of the territory's waters into ten separate zones and the setting of quality parameters for each, reflecting economic and environmental considerations. Subsequent amendments, in 1990 and 1993, have brought stricter restrictions on effluent discharge and more effective controls over connections of wastewater to public sewerage systems, as well as proper operation and maintenance of private communal sewage treatment plants.[62] Both the air and water quality standards have been raised materially in recent years, and the statutory/regulatory architecture has been placed on a firmer footing, but it has been a painfully slow process, with the global Hong Kong metropolis just beginning to embrace in earnest its own version of ecological modernization.[63]

The steepening environmental preservation trajectory and mounting sustainability rhetoric notwithstanding,[64] concerns persist about the timeliness, comprehensiveness and adequacy of the strategies adopted and their implementation. It is debatable whether the quality standards are sufficiently stringent and materially complied with.[65] To pinpoint merely the gaps and deficiencies identified in empirical studies reflecting selectively the current state of affairs, the entire legal edifice is based almost exclusively on rigid command-and-control principles, without significant

---

[61] See http://www.epd.gov.hk/epd.gov.hk/epd/english/environmentinhk/air/guide_ref/guide_apco.html, above note 58.

[62] See http://www.epd.gov.hk/epd/english/environmentinhk/water/guide_ref/guide_wpc_wpco.html, above note 58; F.L. Hua, Y.F. Tsang and H.Chua, 'Progress of Water Pollution Control in Hong Kong', *Aquatic Ecosystem Health and Management* 11 (2008): 225–9.

[63] See Mottershead (ed.), above note 60; Hills, 'Environmental Reform, Ecological Modernization and the Policy Process in Hong Kong: An Exploratory Study of Stakeholder Perspectives', above note 60; Welford, Hills and Lam, 'Environmental Reform, Technology Policy and Transboundary Pollution in Hong Kong', above note 43; Gouldson, Hills and Welford, 'Ecological Modernisation and Policy Learning in Hong Kong', above note 60; Loh, 'None Too Soon: New Air Quality Standards for Hong Kong', above note 60.

[64] See http://www.susdev.gov.hk/html/en/sd/index.htm, accessed 15 January 2010.

[65] See Hopkinson and Stern, above note 43; Loh, 'Heading Down an Unsustainable Path?', above note 60; Loh, 'None Too Soon: New Air Quality Standards for Hong Kong', above note 60.

reliance on more subtle regulatory mechanisms;[66] essential statutory terms (such as pollution) are defined ambiguously;[67] and the deterrent effect of key punitive measures is distinctly modest.[68]

This configuration may be attributed to Hong Kong's peculiar brand of economism/GDPism, underpinned by a close government–business alliance and a political system which is evolving but cannot yet be legitimately portrayed as all-inclusive and equitable.[69] The intimate government–business relationship (corporatist structure of power) is an Asia-wide, rather than Hong Kong-specific, phenomenon.[70] However, elsewhere in the region, democratization may have progressed further (since the 1997–98 Asian financial crisis) and, for better or for worse, the policy process may be characterized by a greater degree of interventionism or less pronounced incrementalist inertia/path dependence[71] (reinforced in the post-colonial Hong Kong context by institutional disarticulation).[72]

This is not a static picture. Learning geared towards ecological modernization, or a quest for a healthier economy–environment relationship, may be observed in Hong Kong.[73] One may surmise that it is driven by rising living standards (according to Wagner's law, the demand for serv-

---

[66]   See Hills, 'Environmental Reform, Ecological Modernization and the Policy Process in Hong Kong', above note 60.

[67]   See Amanda Whitfort and David Dudgeon, 'Muddying the Waters? The Water Pollution Control Ordinance and Defining Pollution of Rivers and Streams in Hong Kong', *Hong Kong Law Journal* 34 (2004): 481–94.

[68]   See Chan et al., above note 43.

[69]   See Leung, above note 23; Mole, above note 21; Lethbridge and Ng, above note 23; Goodstadt, above note 23; Mushkat and Mushkat, 'The Political Economy of Loose Regulation: Modernity Meets Tradition in Hong Kong', above note 23; Mushkat and Mushkat, 'The Political Economy of Hong Kong's "Open Skies" Legal Regime', above note 23; Gouldson, Hills and Welford, above note 60; Kwong-leung Tang, 'Planning for the Unknown: Social Policy-Making in Hong Kong, 1990–1997', *International Journal of Sociology and Social Policy* 19 (1999): 27–56; Ma Ngok, *Political Development in Hong Kong: State, Political Society and Civil Society* (Hong Kong: Hong Kong University Press, 2007).

[70]   See Anthony B.L. Cheung, 'Interpreting East Asian Social Policy Development: Paradigm Shifts or Policy "Steadiness"' in Mok and Forrest (eds), above note 52, 25–48.

[71]   See ibid.

[72]   See Ian Scott, 'The Disarticulation of Hong Kong's Post-Handover Political System', *China Journal* 22 (2000): 29–53; Ian Scott, *Public Administration in Hong Kong: Regime Change and its Impact on the Public Sector* (Singapore: Marshall Cavendish, 2005), 216–26, 242–52; Ian Scott, 'Legitimacy, Governance and Public Policy in Post-Handover Hong Kong', *Asia Pacific Journal of Public Administration* 29 (2007): 29–49.

[73]   See Gouldson, Hills and Welford, above note 60.

ices such as ecological preservation is income elastic),[74] the persistent deterioration in environmental conditions and the deep sense of anxiety that it engenders,[75] gradual political liberalization/the emergence of a more polycentric political system[76] and the eruption of ecological crises requiring an effective response.[77] Nevertheless, it is not a wholly smooth process, but one featuring ideological and institutional impediments rooted in the legacy of economism/GDPism, reactive adaptation and top-down governance.[78]

Movement on the cross-border/external front has been equally uneven. Prior to the transfer of power from the United Kingdom to China, there was a rather shallow engagement between Hong Kong and the mainland in relation to the environment. The sole channel of communication regarding this issue was the Hong Kong–Guangdong Environmental Protection Liaison Group (EPLG), established in 1990 to further bilateral cooperation and coordination in the ecological domain, particularly with respect to pollution and its control. It consisted of senior officials from both sides who met annually, alternating between their respective bases, in order to share information and plan activities. A Technical Sub-Group was also formed for implementation purposes, but joint undertakings were largely confined to knowledge-promoting events such as seminars, visits and workshops.[79]

---

[74]   See Mushkat and Mushkat, above note 21.

[75]   See Wong and Wan, above note 39; Wong Tse-wai, 'Socioeconomic Development and Environmental Pollution in Hong Kong – Risks and Opportunities', *Science of the Total Environment* 106 (1991): 137–41; Kara K.W. Chan, 'Environmental Attitudes and the Behaviour of Secondary School Students in Hong Kong', *The Environmentalist* 16 (1996): 297–306; C.L. Wong, W. Chau and L.W. Wong, 'Environmental Noise and Community in Hong Kong', *Noise and Health: A Quarterly Interdisciplinary International Journal* 2 (2002): 65–9.

[76]   See Ma, above note 69.

[77]   See Scott, *Public Administration in Hong Kong – Regime Change and its Impact on the Public Sector*, above note 72, 327–86; Mushkat and Mushkat, above note 21; John P. Burns, *Government Capacity and the Hong Kong Civil Service* (Oxford: Oxford University Press, 2004), 58–104, 336–52; Anthony B.L. Cheung, 'Policy Capacity in Post-1997 Hong Kong: Constrained Institutions Facing a Crowding and Differentiated Polity', *Asia Pacific Journal of Public Administration* 29 (2007): 51–75; Christine Miethe, *A Description and Critical Review of the Policy Making Process in Hong Kong* (Hong Kong: Hong Kong Democratic Foundation, 2007).

[78]   See Gouldson, Hills and Welford, above note 60.

[79]   See Lee, 'Tackling Cross-Border Environmental Problems in Hong Kong: Initial Responses and Institutional Constraints', above note 43; Hopkinson and Stern, above note 43; Chan et al., above note 43.

Environmental problems were also addressed via broader and more strategically oriented organizational vehicles – such as the Sino-British Joint Liaison Group (JLG) and, after 1997, the Hong Kong–Guangdong Cooperation Joint Conference (CJC) – yet inevitably in a selective and tentative fashion. Somewhat closer attention was accorded to them in less diffuse institutional settings, such as the Sino-British Infrastructure Coordination Committee (SBICC), which was succeeded following the handover by the Hong Kong–Mainland Cross Boundary Major Infrastructure Coordinating Committee (ICC), but again in a wider context and thus not consistently in a focused manner.[80]

The feeble foundation underpinning this organizational setup reflected festering tensions between the colonial regime in Hong Kong and the powers that be in Beijing over the appropriate mode of governance for the territory and related matters. Ecological preservation also did not loom large on the public agenda during a period characterized by economic uncertainties and political turbulence. Perhaps more interestingly, concerns were expressed, both covertly and overtly, that deepening cross-border cooperation and coordination might lead to an erosion of Hong Kong's much-cherished autonomy and result in unequal burden-sharing between a prosperous metropolis and a province in the early stages of industrialization.[81]

The scope of bilateral cooperation and coordination increased somewhat after 1997. This was not necessarily because of a shift to a more proactive policy style but rather was due to an escalation in pollution levels that proved problematic for the post-colonial regime given the adverse public reaction and the perception that the deterioration in ecological conditions might turn into an economic liability for a service-oriented metropolis that had shed its manufacturing industries. The formation of the Hong Kong–Guangdong Joint Working Group on Sustainable Development and Environmental Protection (JWG) in 1999 symbolized the newfound willingness to address jointly and less hesitantly spiraling transboundary pollution.[82]

The JWG was hailed by the Hong Kong government as a highly effective organizational platform for confronting constructively cross-border ecological strains. It was headed by the two most senior officials, on both sides, with functional responsibilities in this area. The frequency of meetings (twice a year) was deemed adequate at that juncture, priority domains

[80] See ibid.
[81] See ibid.
[82] See ibid.

(six altogether) were identified and, importantly, several (as many as eight) panels were established to explore methodically various facets of transboundary pollution, enhance monitoring effectiveness, harmonize standards and adopt (short-term) stabilizing measures. This effort was not entirely unprecedented as, slightly earlier, the EPLG had embarked on a number of reasonably well-funded initiatives whose primary purpose was to improve the quality of the data collection mechanisms and the information fed into decision support systems.[83]

The emphasis during the initial phases of the post-handover period continued to be placed on fact finding and knowledge generation, albeit within a broader and more nuanced framework. The highlight of the JWG programme thus was an in-depth study of air quality in the PRD region. This pattern has remained largely intact in subsequent years, although the two parties have begun to combine selectively learning with action. A notable example of the latter was a series of steps (scarcely radical in nature) taken by the PWD Air Quality Management and Monitoring Special Panel (under the auspices of the JWG) to curtail pollution in the industrial, power and transportation sectors. The setting-up of a regional air quality monitoring network, another significant joint undertaking, fell predominantly into the learning category.[84]

Bilateral cooperation and coordination has also been augmented through formal accords, such as the agreement signed in 2005 by China's State Environmental Protection Administration (SEPA) and Hong Kong's Environmental Protection Department (EPD) to combat air pollution.[85] The two parties have even started extending the planning horizon beyond its traditional short/medium-term limits and address jointly the challenge of mapping the contours of a distant ecological configuration (embodied in the vision of the PRD Quality Living Area) inspired by images of a green-like future.[86] A comprehensive accord, the Framework Agreement on Hong Kong/Guangdong Cooperation, purporting to lay a multifaceted foundation for cross-border collaboration, and given national prominence by virtue of being endorsed by the State Council, has also been reached and may potentially prove to be a vital step towards bolstering the institutional

---

[83]   See ibid.
[84]   See ibid.
[85]   See ibid.
[86]   See http://www.epd.gov.hk/epd/eindex.html, above note. The green vision is embodied in the Environmental Cooperation Agreement between Hong Kong SAR and Guangdong signed by the two governments on 19 August 2009. See http://www.hketousa.gov.hk/usa/press/2009/dec09/120709_1.html, accessed 15 January 2010.

channels for region-wide efforts to alleviate the most pernicious forms of pollution.[87] Be that as it may, the realities on the ground remain grim and the prevailing view outside official circles is that the resolve displayed, organizational capabilities created and strategies pursued are not wholly commensurate with the magnitude of the hazards faced.[88]

Institution-building is not a binary phenomenon, featuring a quantum leap from an organizational vacuum to an elaborate and smoothly functioning infrastructure. Rather, it may be likened to a continuum, characterized by stepwise progression from the low to the high end of the scale. Recently, three forms of environmental institutionalism have been highlighted in the academic literature: constitutive, contributory and warranted.[89] The evolving organizational framework erected to curtail transboundary pollution in Hong Kong can be said to have been more solid than not in the not too distant past but it still has modest constitutive (efficiency and effectiveness), contributory (cooperation and coordination competencies) and warranted (authorization, justification and endorsement mechanisms) foundations.

Alternatively, it may be credibly argued that, as matters stand, the gradually expanding organizational edifice does not yet possess the attributes of a full-fledged environmental governance regime (according to two leading researchers in the field of international ecological management, such entities 'are social institutions consisting of agreed upon principles, norms, rules, procedures and programs that govern the interactions of actors in specific areas').[90] In business administration parlance, the strategies espoused by the two sides may imply otherwise, but the enacted and (particularly) the emergent ones are indicative of a considerably lower level of institutional maturity and organizational achievement.

The theoretical literature on the subject of cross-border pollution is

---

[87] See http://www.info.gov..hk/gia/general/20100407113.htm, accessed 15 April 2010.

[88] See Lee, 'Tackling Cross-Border Environmental Problems in Hong Kong: Initial Responses and Institutional Constraints', above note 43; Hopkinson and Stern, above note 43; Chan et al., above note 43; Loh, 'Heading Down an Unsustainable Path?', above note 60; Loh, 'None Too Soon: New Air Quality Standards for Hong Kong', above note 60.

[89] See Ian Thynne, 'Climate Change, Governance and Environmental Services: Institutional Perspectives, Issues and Challenges', *Public Administration and Development* 28 (2008): 327–39.

[90] See Oran R. Young and Marc A. Levi, 'The Effectiveness of International Environmental Regimes: A Framework for Analysis' in Oran R. Young (ed.), *The Effectiveness of International Environmental Regimes: Causal Connections and Behavioral Mechanisms* (Cambridge: MIT Press, 1999), 1.

not well developed. A fairly sophisticated game-theoretic model has been constructed with a view to enhancing the understanding of player behaviour in such situations,[91] yet it is probably too abstract to capture the essence of complex institutional dynamics. Other explanations, conceptually less rigorous but more versatile, have been formulated[92] without however being placed within a broader analytical scheme. They may thus be employed in similar circumstances, and prove to be quite illuminating in such contexts, yet in order to establish the linkages between insights applicable to specific cases and a general theoretical system one may have to seek inspiration elsewhere.

An advanced and relevant field of inquiry is international trade, because an analogy may be drawn between economic protectionism and trade liberalization and environmental isolationism and cooperation/coordination. The explanatory approaches adopted in this domain include neoclassical economic trade theories, business-cycle theories, political power theories and strategic organizational theories.[93] The second perspective, which hypothesizes that protectionist sentiment (and hence isolationism in other forms) ebbs when economic conditions brighten and intensifies when they deteriorate, is not really pertinent here, at least from a long-term viewpoint, as distinct from a short-term angle.

The structure of power is a critical element of the Chinese policy equation and models highlighting its impact on institutional performance are deemed to have high explanatory value.[94] China may have softened, rather than shed, its authoritarian features, but as indicated earlier, with reference to perforated sovereignty, it is a nominally unitary State with a weak centre and a strong periphery. The precise configuration varies from one sphere of government activity to another, yet the pattern is pronounced in the ecological realm.[95] The environmental 'business' is akin to a loosely

---

[91]   See Fanny Missfeldt, 'Game-Theoretic Modelling of Transboundary Pollution', *Journal of Economic Surveys* 13 (1999): 287–321.

[92]   For example see Kim, above note 1.

[93]   See Beth V. Yarborough and Robert M. Yarborough, *Cooperation and Governance in International Trade: The Strategic Organizational Approach* (Princeton: Princeton University Press, 1992), 7–19.

[94]   See Roda Mushkat, 'Implementing Environmental Law in Transitional Settings: The Chinese Experience', *Southern California Interdisciplinary Law Journal* 18 (2008): 45–94; Roda Mushkat, 'Contextualizing Environmental Human Rights: A Relativist Perspective', *Pace Environmental Law Review* 26 (2009): 119–77; Miron Mushkat and Roda Mushkat, 'The Institutional Foundations of Environmental Governance Regimes', *International Journal of Regulation and Governance* 9 (2009): 99–120.

[95]   See ibid.

connected cluster of strategic business units (SBUs) whose corporate parent (the central government in Beijing) is not endowed with sufficient resources and competencies to ensure overall coherence and cohesion.

Hong Kong's status as an autonomous administrative entity within the Chinese body politic, while an organizational necessity on historical grounds and a source of vitality on key policy fronts, compounds at times the problem by rendering horizontal cooperation and coordination even more challenging. Another factor which merits attention in this context is the political influence enjoyed, both directly and indirectly, by business interests on both sides of the border. The corporatist underpinnings of the institutional edifice in the HKSAR were brought into focus previously. The power configuration on the mainland may in fact be more skewed in favour of parochial interests, whether private or public–private, a phenomenon which has prompted one researcher to portray it as an 'entrepreneurial [S]tate in which officials use [S]tate authority to privilege market activity'.[96] And he has proceeded to note that '[t]his creates a set of structural barriers and elicits local [S]tate resistance to the implementation of [top-down strategies].'[97] Specifically, '[S]tate entrepreneurs pursue alternative forms of compliance, disguise [S]tate participation in the market and exploit their control over information, in an effort to resist monitoring and enforcement regimes.'[98]

The pertinence of neoclassical economic trade theories stems from the importance they accord to the self-interest of actors involved in international exchanges. In the case of Hong Kong and Guangdong Province/ PRD region, the strategic thrust continues to be primarily geared towards maximizing material welfare and preserving organizational autonomy. Ecological threats loom increasingly large on the policy agenda and the logic of sustainability is no longer consigned to the institutional periphery. Nevertheless, economic considerations and the desire to minimize external encroachments on regional authority play a significant role in shaping the demand for bilateral cooperation and coordination.[99]

Strategic organizational theories are multi-directional and wide-ranging. It is not possible to do justice to these conceptual approaches here because

---

[96]   Paul Thiers, 'Challenges for WTO Implementation: Lessons from China's Deep Integration into an International Trade Regime', *Journal of Contemporary China* 11 (2002): 413–31.

[97]   Ibid.

[98]   Ibid.

[99]   See Lee, 'Tackling Cross-Border Environmental Problems in Hong Kong: Initial Responses and Institutional Constraints', above note 43; Hopkinson and Stern, above note 43; Chan et al., above note 43.

of space constraints. They demonstrate that both centripetal forces (for example, unilateral withdrawal from the cross-border relationship is a high-cost option and environmental continuity – indeed, close alignment – is essential for both parties) and centrifugal forces are inevitably at work across southern China. At the same time, the loose institutional structure (which may be contrasted with the tighter pattern observed in the European Union)[100] is a decisive factor which leaves limited scope for third-party intervention and considerable room for opportunism. Unattended organizational fragility thus contains the seeds of institutional stagnation, impeding progress on the environmental front.[101]

Scholars who lean towards this type of explanation emphasize the relevance of relation-specific investments (for example, Canadian–US links in the North American car industry) in the international trade context. Such investments are vast in the geographical area examined here, but predominantly in sectors (such as transportation) supporting productive endeavour and the flow of goods and services. Paradoxically, yet unavoidably, more often than not, they trigger pressures that are not conducive to ecological preservation. By contrast, the ecological investments with the potential to induce the participants to deepen their cooperation and to coordinate their activities in a consistent fashion remain distinctly modest.[102]

CONCLUSION

Hong Kong's unique socio-economic characteristics cannot be denied, but they should not be overemphasized. Whereas some of its experiences may not be extrapolated beyond its narrow confines, others offer broader lessons. The territory has witnessed economic integration on an unprecedented scale since the opening-up of the Chinese economy, yet such trends, albeit evolving perhaps at a less hurried pace, have not been absent elsewhere in Asia. Trade liberalization, whether deliberate or unplanned, has unleashed powerful bottom-up impulses which have propelled countries in the region and their partners in other parts of the world towards each other.

---

[100] See Miron Mushkat and Roda Mushkat, 'The Political Economy of Hong Kong's Transboundary Pollution: The Challenge of Effective Governance', *Journal of International Trade Law and Policy* 9 (2010): 175–92.

[101] See Lee, 'Tackling Cross-Border Environmental Problems in Hong Kong: Initial Responses and Institutional Constraints', above note 43; Hopkinson and Stern, above note 43; Chan et al., above note 43.

[102] See ibid.

At the same time, the journey travelled by Hong Kong, and the specific case dissected in this chapter, serves as a poignant reminder that there are two sides to the economic integration ledger, benefits and costs, and that balancing them has not necessarily proved to be an Asian forte. The contrast between emerging economic capabilities and institutional competencies needed to address collectively endemic market failure is particularly striking. This reflects deep-rooted influences which are unlikely to fade away for a considerable period. The picture is changing for the better – as the negative externalities of the relentless movement towards the internationalization of investment, production and trade intensify – but the long lag between ground-level stimulus and policy response persists.

PART II

Trade integration

4. Japan's FTA (EPA) and BIT strategy in the light of competitive dynamics

Junji Nakagawa

JAPAN'S POLICY SHIFT TOWARD FTAS (EPAS) AND BITS: WHY AND HOW?

In the early 2000s, Japan finally caught up with the global boom of free trade agreements (FTAs) and bilateral investment treaties (BITs). The rest of the world had begun to actively look at FTAs as a means of promoting trade liberalization in the early 1990s, when multilateral trade negotiations under the GATT were making little progress. Interest in FTAs increased even after the establishment of the WTO in 1995, especially after the Doha Development Agenda entered into deadlock. Indeed, the cumulative number of FTAs notified to the GATT/WTO since 1949 increased from 86 in 1990 to 165 in 1995, to 251 in 2000, and further to 457 in October 2009.[1] The number of BITs has also been increasing since the 1990s, and rose to 2676 at the end of 2008.[2]

Japan had long preferred multilateral trade liberalization to preferential trade arrangements. It criticized FTAs as discriminatory against non-parties and detrimental to the GATT/WTO-based multilateral trading system from which it had substantially benefited during its post-war growth. However, it finally made a policy shift toward preferential trade arrangements in the early 2000s. Japan signed its first Economic Partnership Agreement (EPA) with Singapore in January 2002,[3] and it has since concluded EPAs with Mexico (2004), Malaysia (2005),

---

[1]   WTO, Regional Trade Agreements, Facts and Figures, accessed 2 September 2010, http://www.wto.org/english/tratop_e/region_e/regfac_e.htm.

[2]   UNCTAD, *World Investment Report* (Geneva: UNCTAD, 2009), 32.

[3]   The text of this and the other EPAs which Japan concluded are available from the website of the Japan Ministry of Foreign Affaires (MOFA), accessed 2 September 2010, http://www.mofa.go.jp/policy/economy/fta/index.html.

the Philippines (2006), Chile (2007), Thailand (2007), Brunei (2007), Indonesia (2007), ASEAN (2008), Viet Nam (2008) and Switzerland (2009). Currently, it is negotiating EPAs with the Gulf Cooperation Council, India, Korea, Peru and Australia.

Japan also accelerated negotiation of BITs in the early 2000s. Before 2000 it had concluded eight BITs.[4] However, since 2000, it has concluded BITs with Mongolia (2001), Korea (2002), Viet Nam (2003), Cambodia (2007), Laos (2008), Uzbekistan (2008) and Peru (2008). These recent BITs provide not only for investment protection but also for investment liberalization and an enhanced investment protection. Japan is currently negotiating BITs with Saudi Arabia and Colombia, and a trilateral investment agreement with China and Korea.

Why did Japan change its policy and join the global boom of FTAs and BITs in the early 2000s?

I argue that competitive dynamics best explain Japan's policy shift toward EPAs and BITs.[5] Japan has used EPAs and BITs to respond to multiple (economic, political and legal) competitive challenges. First of all, Japan had to restore the competitiveness of its businesses abroad which had been deteriorated by the trade/investment diversion caused by preceding FTAs. This was most salient in the case of Mexico after the NAFTA and later the Mexico–EU FTA.[6] Also, Japanese companies became interested in using EPAs to revamp their production networks in East Asia in order to integrate their regional production networks, and to forestall the advances of rival foreign companies in Southeast Asian countries, which in the aftermath of the Asian financial crisis had courted foreign direct investment (FDI) and export production

---

[4]   They were BITs with Egypt (1977), Sri Lanka (1982), China (1988), Turkey (1992), Hong Kong (1995), Bangladesh (1998), Pakistan (1998) and Russia (1998). The texts of these and the other BITs which Japan concluded are available from the website of the Japan Ministry of Economy, Trade and Industry (METI), accessed September 2010, http://www.meti.go.jp/english/policy/external_economy/trade/FTA_EPA/index.html.

[5]   Mireya Solís, 'Japan's Competitive FTA Strategy: Commercial Opportunity versus Political Rivalry', in Mireya Solís, Barbara Stallings and Saori N. Katada (eds), *Competitive Regionalism: FTA Diffusion in the Pacific Rim* (London: Palgrave Macmillan, 2009), 198.

[6]   According to the estimate of the Japan–Mexico Joint Study Group on bilateral economic relationship, the loss of Japan's exports to Mexico caused by the NAFTA would be 395.1 billion yen, or \$3.2 billion, which would result in the loss of employment for 31 824 persons. See Japan–Mexico Joint Study Group on the Strengthening of Bilateral Economic Relationship, *Final Report* (2002) 4, accessed 2 September 2010, http://www.mofa.go.jp/region/latin/mexico/relation0207/part2.pdf.

more aggressively.[7] Finally, the failure of the Multilateral Agreement on Investment (MAI), sponsored by the OECD in 1998, and the failure of the 1999 Seattle Ministerial Conference to incorporate 'trade and investment' into the agenda of the first negotiating round of the WTO led Japanese companies to lobby for investment rule-making at bilateral/regional levels. Keidanren published a policy statement titled *Challenges for the Upcoming WTO Negotiations and Agenda for Future Japanese Trade Policy* in May 1999.[8] While expressing expectations of the upcoming WTO negotiations, it emphasized the importance of strengthening Japan's efforts to develop a network of BITs and EPAs with investment chapters because they were 'extremely important in terms of the foreign business activities of Japanese companies'.[9]

Japan's policy shift toward EPAs and BITs was much influenced by the economic interests of its businesses facing competitive challenges abroad. The Ministry of International Trade and Industry, or MITI (renamed METI in 2001), supported this.[10] On the other hand, the agricultural lobby opposed the substantive liberalization of agricultural trade through bilateral negotiation. This was the major reason for the Japanese government to start negotiation of its first EPA not with Mexico, which had approached Japan to explore a bilateral trade deal as early as the summer of 1998, but with Singapore, as it offered to exclude agriculture from the negotiation.[11] Japan had to deal with the opposition of its agricultural lobby when it negotiated its second EPA with Mexico, which exports a substantive amount of agricultural products to Japan. However, a compromise was made on agriculture by excluding a number of sensitive products from liberalization commitments, and by applying tariff rate quotas

---

[7] Mark Manger, *Investing in Protection: The Politics of Preferential Trade Agreements Between North and South* (Cambridge: Cambridge University Press, 2009), 189.

[8] Keidanren, *Challenges for the Upcoming WTO Negotiations and Agenda for Future Japanese Trade Policy*, 1999, accessed 3 September 2010, http://www.keidanren,or.jp/english/policy/pol102.index.html.

[9] Ibid., Section 3(1).

[10] Solís, above note 5, 201–4; Mireya Solís and Saori Katada, 'The Japan–Mexico FTA: Cross-Regional Step in the Path Towards Asian Regionalism', *Pacific Affairs* 80 (2) (2007): 290–91.

[11] Takashi Terada, 'The Making of Asia's First Bilateral FTA: Origins and Regional Implications for the Japan–Singapore Eocnomic Partnership Agreement', Australia–Japan Research Centre, Pacific Economic Paper No. 354, 2006, 10–12, accessed 2 September 2010, http://www.waseda.jp/asianstudies/news/ias/doc/JSEPA-Terada_pep354.pdf.

on pork, oranges, and so on.[12] This became a precedent for Japan's EPA negotiation with those countries exporting agricultural products to Japan, such as Thailand and Australia.

Japan's policy shift to EPAs and BITs was also influenced by two central concerns of its foreign policy in the early 2000s: the maintenance of the security alliance with the US, and the need to respond to China's rise in the region. As Japan shaped its EPA policy it had to aim for a delicate political compromise between maintaining its key security alliance with the US, displaying a commitment to the construction of Asian regional integration and striking the balance between competition and cooperation with China. These considerations influenced Japanese EPA policy in three important aspects: (1) the selection of EPA partners, notably the bypassing of China in the negotiation of bilateral EPAs by the Koizumi government; (2) the competitive courting of Southeast Asian nations, from the Japan–Singapore EPA to China's November 2001 announcement of its intention to establish an FTA with ASEAN, and to Japan's response in January 2002 with the proposal for a Japan–ASEAN Comprehensive Economic Partnership; and (3) the attempt to define the contours of an East Asian Trade bloc, with China insisting on the ASEAN+3, and Japan calling for ASEAN+6 with Australia, New Zealand and India.[13]

Finally, Japan's policy shift to EPAs and BITs was also influenced by its determination to achieve a high level of legalization[14] through bilateral/ regional channels. The aforementioned failures of multilateral investment rule-making through the MAI and the Doha Development Agenda motivated the Japanese business sector to lobby the government to shift the forum for investment rule-making to EPAs and BITs. The Japanese FDI

---

[12]   Yoshchi Sekizawa, 'Nihon no FTA seisaku: Sono seiji katei no bunseki' (Japan's FTA Policy: An Analysis of its Political Process), Institute of Social Science, University of Tokyo, ISS Research Series No. 26, 2008. Sekizawa notes that by this compromise 'the taboo was broken' that Japan would not negotiate EPAs which cover agricultural products. See ibid., 48.

[13]   Solís, above note 5, 207–11.

[14]   By 'legalization' I mean obligation, precision, and delegation (F.M. Abbott et al., 'The Concept of Legalization' in J. Goldstein, M. Kahler, R.O. Keohane and A.M. Slaughter (eds), *Legalization and World Politics* (Cambridge, MA: MIT Press, 2001),17–18). Obligation means that states are legally bound by a rule or a commitment in the sense that their behavior thereunder is subject to scrutiny under the general rules, procedures, and discourse of international law. Precision means that rules unambiguously define the conduct they require, authorize, or proscribe. Delegation means that third parties have been granted authority to implement, interpret, and apply the rules; to resolve disputes; and possibly to make further rules.

in East Asia rapidly increased in the 1990s. This trend continued after the Asian financial crisis. For Japanese companies investing in the region, protection of investment through clear and transparent rules and their enforcement through investor–state arbitration are of critical importance. As these were not provided through a multilateral forum, they lobbied the government to secure them through BITs and investment chapters of EPAs with the host countries in the region.[15]

The rivalry between multilateral and bilateral rule-making raises the possibility that a new rule adopted and disseminated by several FTAs will later on be incorporated at the multilateral level. Such bottom-up standard setting by bilateral channels is particularly prominent in the areas of trade rules currently under negotiation within the framework of the Doha Development Agenda. The most salient examples are the rules on technical barriers to trade and those on intellectual property protection, about which I will explain further in the next section.

CHARACTERISTICS OF JAPAN'S EPAS AND BITS

Japan's EPAs and BITs have three major characteristics: moderate trade liberalization, relatively aggressive investment liberalization and investment protection, and moderate legalization on rules covered by the WTO. I will explain these in the following subsections.

Moderate Trade Liberalization

GATT Article XXIV.8 provides that the duties and other restrictive regulations of commerce are eliminated on 'substantially all the trade' between the constituent members of free trade areas and customs unions. While neither GATT nor the WTO has been able to agree on what is meant by 'substantially all the trade', the EC set a precedent for excluding sensitive sectors from bilateral agreements by excluding most agricultural products from its FTAs with Mexico and South Africa. These precedents were seized upon by Japan in its EPA negotiations.[16] It made no liberalization commitments on sensitive agricultural products (rice, wheat, starch,

---

[15] Junji Nakagawa, 'Competitive Regionalism through Bilateral and Regional Rule Making: Standard Setting and Locking-in' in Mireya Solís, Barbara Stallings and Saori N. Katada (eds), *Competitive Regionalism: FTA Diffusion in the Pacific Rim* (London: Palgrave Macmillan, 2009), 78–9.

[16] John Ravenhill, 'The New Bilateralism in the Asia Pacific', *Third World Quarterly* 24(2) (2003): 308.

and so on) in any of its EPAs. Even in its EPA with Singapore, whose agricultural exports to Japan are negligible, the few products in the sensitive agricultural sector, principally cut flowers and goldfish, were excluded from the liberalization commitments of Japan.

In addition to the exclusion of sensitive agricultural products from liberalization commitments, Japan has made a significantly low level of commitments in agricultural trade liberalization. First, it made commitments on agricultural products which are mostly imported (tropical fruits, fish, and so on).[17] Secondly, it made limited commitments on some products which are produced domestically (for example, chicken, pork, beef, sugar, wine), mainly through import quotas.[18]

A Japan–Australia EPA may become a touchstone of Japan's policy stance on bilateral agricultural trade liberalization, as agricultural import accounts for more than 20 per cent of Japan's total import from Australia, and Japan imports many sensitive agricultural products (beef, dairy products, wheat, rice, sugar, and so on) from Australia. However, this may not be an insurmountable obstacle to the conclusion of a Japan–Australia EPA. As was suggested by the final report of the Japan–Australia joint study group on Enhancing Economic Relations, there are sensitivities on both sides, and the best way to handle these sensitivities might be through negotiations, with both sides taking a flexible approach, including not only 'phasing' but also 'exclusion' and/or 'deferral for later negotiation'.[19]

In comparison with the low level of agricultural liberalization, Japan's liberalization commitments on manufactured products have been at a high level. First, it abolished tariffs on a wide range of industrial products, whose rates were already low.[20] Secondly, on sensitive manufactured products of its counterparts, Japan has adopted a flexible approach, which corresponds to the aforementioned flexible approaches with respect to the sensitive agricultural products for Japan. For instance, the Japan–Thailand EPA adopted a phasing-out of tariffs on steel products and auto parts. It also provided for the renegotiation of a tariff reduction on

---

[17]   See Japan's commitments in its EPAs with Malaysia, the Philippines, Brunei, Indonesia, ASEAN and Viet Nam.

[18]   See Japan's commitments in its EPAs with Mexico, Chile, Thailand and Switzerland.

[19]   Joint Study for Enhancing Economic Relations between Japan and Australia, including the Feasibility or Pros and Cons of a Free Trade Agreement, *Final Report*, 2006, 19, accessed 2 September 2010, http://www.dfat.gov.au/geo/japan/fta/study_group_report.pdf.

[20]   The simple average MFN concessional rate of Japan's tariffs on non-agricultural products was 2.5 per cent in 2008, and its trade weighted average rate was 1.2 per cent in 2007. See WTO/UNCTAD/ITC, *World Tariff Profiles 2009*, 98.

autos with engines of less than 3000cc. All these were sensitive manufactured products of Thailand. The Japan–Viet Nam EPA adopted a similar phasing-out of tariffs on steel products, auto parts and electronic appliances. On the other hand, Japan maintained high tariff rates on a small number of sensitive manufactured products such as leather products, petroleum products and petrochemical products.

The benefits of trade liberalization through EPAs, however, may be discounted by the complicated rules of origin. For example, Annex II of the Japan–Malaysia EPA provides for product-specific rules of origin for determining substantial transformation, and the 40 per cent regional value content principle and the change in tariff classification (CTC) principle are available on an equal basis for many products. Importers may choose whichever principle they like. Many other EPAs adopt a similar approach, but some use a different principle on some product items. Those Japanese companies who want to avail themselves of the benefits of EPAs will, therefore, have to be familiar with country-specific and product-specific rules of origin, and will have to pay the cost of getting certificates of origin.[21]

Japan's liberalization commitments in services trade have also been moderate. Acceptance of nurses and care workers has been the major area of Japan's liberalization commitments through its EPAs. Japan made such commitments with the Philippines and Indonesia, and made commitments to negotiate on such liberalization at a later time with Thailand[22] and Viet Nam.[23] However, Japan opened the market for these service providers only to a very limited extent. For instance, the Japan–Philippines EPA made the following conditions.[24] First, those who are granted entry as nurse candidates shall be qualified as a nurse with work experience in the Philippines for at least three years. Secondly, after being granted entry as nurse candidates, they will have to pursue a course of training including

---

[21] According to a survey conducted by the Japan Economic Foundation, only about 50 per cent of the Japanese companies exporting products to Mexico have applied for Japan–Mexico EPA tariff rates. See METI, 'On Japan's EPA Policy' [in Japanese], accessed 2 September 2010, http://www.meti.go.jp/policy/trade_policy/epa/html2/1-souron7.html.

[22] Annex 7 to the Japan–Thailand EPA, in its Part 1.C, provides that Japan shall enter into negotiations with Thailand on the possibility of accepting Thai certified care workers within one year, if possible, but not later than two years after the entry into force of the Agreement.

[23] Japan made a commitment to start negotiations with respect to Vietnamese nurses and care workers not later than two years after the entry into force of the Japan–Viet Nam EPA. See Annex 7 to the Agreement, Part 1.B.

[24] See Annex 8 to the Japan–Philippines EPA, Part 1, Section 6.

Japanese language training for six months and, after completion of the training, acquire necessary knowledge and skills at hospitals in Japan by training under the supervision of certified nurses for a maximum period of three years. Thirdly, they shall have to pass the national examination for certified nurses in Japan in order to extend their stay in Japan as nurses. Finally, Japan set the quota of 1000 persons during the first two years after the entry into force of the Agreement. Similar conditions were applied to care worker candidates from the Philippines and to those from Indonesia.[25] Japan accepted 283 nurse and care worker candidates from the Philippines in 2008, and 569 nurse and care worker candidates from Indonesia in 2008 and 2009,[26] both of which were below the quota set by Japan.

Relatively Aggressive Investment Liberalization and Investment Protection

In contrast to the BITs that Japan concluded before the early 2000s, Japan's BITs and investment chapters of its EPAs after the early 2000s (hereinafter referred to as 'new-generation BITs') adopt a relatively aggressive stance toward investment liberalization and investment protection. First, Japan's new-generation BITs provide for national treatment at pre-investment stage. For instance, Article 2, paragraph 1 of the Japan–Korea BIT provides that each Contracting Party shall accord national treatment with respect to the establishment, acquisition and expansion of investments. Investors of Contracting Parties are, thus, secured access to the market of the host country insofar as access is secured to the nationals of the host country, except in the sectors or with respect to the matters specified in the Annex to the Agreement.[27]

Secondly, Japan's new-generation BITs provide for prohibition of performance requirements with respect to investment activities. Prohibition of performance requirements is stipulated under the WTO Agreement on Trade-Related Investment Measures (TRIMs Agreement). However, the

---

[25]   See Annex 10 to the Japan–Indonesia EPA, Part 1, Section 6.

[26]   Japan, Ministry of Health, Labour and Welfare, 'On the Adequate Acceptance of Foreign Candidates of Nurses and Care Workers based on the Economic Partnership Agreements' [in Japanese], 24 November 2009, accessed 2 September 2010, http://www.mhlw.go.jp/bunya/koyou/other22/index.html.

[27]   Annex I to the Japan–Korea BIT enumerates sectors excluded from the application of national treatment under Article 2 for each contracting party. These include the defense industry, broadcasting industry, fisheries and tobacco industry, among others, for Korea, and the nuclear energy industry, space industry and broadcasting industry, among others, for Japan.

prohibition of performance requirements under Japan's new-generation BITs covers a much broader range of investment activities. For instance, Article 9, paragraph 1 of the Japan–Korea BIT prohibits Contracting Parties from imposing any of the following requirements: (a) to export a given level or percentage of goods or services; (b) to achieve a given level or percentage of domestic content; (c) to purchase goods produced or services provided domestically; (d) to relate the volume or value of imports to the volume or value of exports; (e) to restrict sales of goods or services of investors by relating them to the volume or value of its exports or foreign exchange earnings; (f) to transfer technology; (g) to locate the headquarters of the investor in its territory; (h) to achieve a given level or value of research and development in its territory; (i) to hire a given level of its nationals; or (j) to supply one or more of the goods or services that the investor produces or provides to a specific region or the world market exclusively from the territory of the Contracting Party. Activities which fall within the categories (a) to (e) above are also proscribed under the TRIMs Agreement, but the others are not. This gives investors a wider range of freedom in their investment activities than that provided under the TRIMs Agreement.

Thirdly, Japan's new-generation BITs provide enhanced protection to foreign investors at the post-investment stage through (a) an umbrella clause and/or (b) institutional arrangements for the improvement of business environment.

An umbrella clause is a provision of a BIT whereby a host country commits itself to perform the obligations it has assumed for individual investments based on the contracts with foreign investors. Such contracts are often concluded with respect to massive investment projects such as infrastructure building, natural resources development, and so on.[28] As a result of an umbrella clause, a host government's breach of an obligation in an investment contract automatically establishes a breach of obligation under the BIT, and the dispute settlement mechanism under the treaty (including investor–state arbitration) becomes available in addition to the dispute settlement mechanism under the contract.

Japan's new-generation BITs establish institutional arrangements for the improvement of business environment. First, many of them establish a sub-committee on improvement of business environment under the bilateral joint committee for the implementation and operation of the BIT. Such

---

[28]   See, for instance, Article 4, paragraph 2 of the Japan–Cambodia BIT, which provides: 'Each Contracting Party shall observe any obligation it may have entered into with regard to investments of investors of the other Contracting Party.'

sub-committees comprise representatives of government officials and investors of both contracting parties. They meet regularly, discuss a wide range of issues to improve business environment, and make recommendations and advisory opinions for the solution of the issues.[29] Secondly, some of them establish liaison offices or contact points on improvement of business environment within the government, which receive complaints from foreign investors, transmit them to the relevant authorities, and provide the investors with necessary information and advice in collaboration with the relevant authorities.[30] These institutional arrangements enable foreign investors to consult with host governments through low-profile and informal channels for the improvement of business environment, with support from their home governments. They cover a wide range of issues with respect to the improvement of business environment, such as public safety, improvement of infrastructure, labor relations, and intellectual property protection.[31]

Table 4.1 shows the major contents of Japan's BITs and investment chapters of EPAs.

Moderate Legalization on Rules Covered by the WTO

At the end of the first section, I pointed out that Japan's policy shift to EPAs and BITs was partly motivated by its determination to achieve a high level of legalization through bilateral/regional channels. In particular, Japan's EPAs contain provisions which secure a higher level of legal protection than that provided under the WTO Agreements. Such WTO-plus is most salient with respect to (a) technical barriers to trade, (b) protection of intellectual property rights, and (c) competition law and policy.

On technical barriers to trade, many of Japan's EPAs provide for reaffirmation of the rights and obligations under the WTO Agreement on Technical Barriers to Trade (TBT Agreement). However, some provide for mutual recognition, whereby the contracting parties mutually accept the accreditation of the conformity assessment body (CAB) of the exporting country, based on the criteria and procedure provided by the

---

[29] See, for instance, Article 25 of the Japan–Peru BIT on 'Sub-committee on Improvement of Investment Environment'.

[30] See, for instance, Article 109 of the Japan–Indonesia EPA on 'Liaison Office'.

[31] On the achievements of Japan's institutional arrangements for the improvement of business environment under its BITs, see Trade Policy Bureau, METI, *Report on Compliance by Major Trading Partners with Trade Agreements, WTO/ FTA/EDA, BIT*, 2010, 687–97, accessed 2 September 2010, http://www.meti.go.jp/ report/data/g100402a01j.thml.

Table 4.1 BITs and investment chapters of EPAs concluded by Japan (as of June 2010)

No.	Counterpart	Signed	Took effect	preNT	neg/pos	R&D	techtrans	locempl	umbrella	busenv
B1	Egypt	28 Jan. 1977	14 Jan. 1978	no	no	no	no	no	no	no
B2	Sri Lanka	1 Mar. 1982	7 Aug. 1982	no	no	no	no	no	no	no
B3	China	27 Aug. 1988	14 May 1989	no	no	no	no	no	no	no
B4	Turkey	12 Feb. 1992	12 Mar. 1993	no	no	no	no	no	no	no
B5	Hong Kong	15 May 1997	18 Jun. 1997	no	no	no	no	no	yes	no
B6	Pakistan	10 Mar. 1998	29 May 2002	no	no	no	no	no	no	no
B7	Bangladesh	10 Nov. 1998	25 Aug. 1999	no	no	no	no	no	no	no
B8	Russia	13 Nov. 1998	27 May 2000	no	no	no	no	no	yes	no
B9	Mongolia	15 Feb. 2001	24 Mar. 2002	no	no	no	no	no	no	no
E1	Singapore	13 Jan. 2002	30 Nov. 2002	yes	neg	A*1	A*1	no	no	A*2
B10	Korea	22 Mar. 2002	1 Jan. 2003	yes	neg	A*1	A*1	A*1	no	AB*2
B11	Viet Nam	14 Nov. 2003	19 Dec. 2004	yes	neg	A*1	A*1	A*1	no	no
E2	Mexico	17 Sep. 2004	1 Apr. 2005	yes	neg	no	A*1	no	no	A*2
E3	Malaysia	13 Dec. 2005	13 Jul. 2006	yes	neg	no	no	no	no	AB*2
E4	Philippines	9 Sep. 2006	11 Dec. 2008	yes	neg	A*1	A*1	A*1	no	AB*2
E5	Chile	27 Mar. 2007	3 Sep. 2007	yes	pos	no	A*1	no	no	A*2
E6	Thailand	3 Apr. 2007	1 Nov. 2007	yes	neg	no	no	no	no	AB*2
B12	Cambodia	14 Jun. 2007	31 Jul. 2008	yes	neg	A*1	A*1	B*1	yes	no
E7	Brunei	18 Jun. 2007	31 Jul. 2008	yes	neg	no	no	no	no	A*2
E8	Indonesia	10 Aug. 2007	1 Jul. 2008	yes	neg	A*1	no	no	no	AB*2
B13	Laos	16 Jan. 2008	3 Aug. 2008	yes	neg	A*1	AB*1	AB*1	yes	no
B14	Uzbekistan	15 Aug. 2008	24 Sep. 2009	yes	neg	A*1	A*1	AB*1	yes	no
B15	Peru	22 Nov. 2008	10 Dec. 2009	yes	neg	no	A*1	no	yes	C*2

Table 4.1 (continued)

No.	Counterpart	Signed	Took effect	preNT	neg/ pos	R&D	techtrans	locempl	umbrella	busenv
E10	Viet Nam	25 Dec. 2008	1 Oct. 2009	no	no	no	no	no	no	AB*2
E11	Switzerland	19 Feb. 2009	1 Sep. 2009	yes	neg	no	no	no	yes	AB*2

Notes:
*1: A = prohibited unless required as a condition of the receipt of advantage; B = prohibited unless otherwise provided in the Annex.
*2: A = Sub-committee on business environment; B = liaison office/contact point; C = Sub-committee on investment environment.

Source: Made by the author from the texts of the agreements and the annexes thereto.

importing country.[32] This enables exporters to acquire an accreditation on their export products *ex ante* in the exporting country, and thus to save their cost and time.

Some of Japan's EPAs provide for a higher level of intellectual property protection than the WTO Agreement on Trade-Related Aspects of Intellectual Property Rights (TRIPS Agreement). For instance, the Japan–Malaysia EPA provides for the following TRIPS-plus protection: (a) simplified procedure, (b) strengthened protection, and (c) strengthened enforcement. With respect to procedural simplification, it provides for the application of an international classification system on patents under the Strasbourg Agreement and on trademarks under the Nice Agreement (Article 116, paragraph 2), and the publication of a patent application after the expiration of 18 months from the filing date (Article 119, paragraph 5), among other things. With respect to strengthened protection, for instance, it provides for an enhanced protection of well-known trademarks by obliging Parties to refuse or cancel the registration of a trademark, which is identical or similar to a trademark well known in either Party, if use of that trademark is for unfair intentions, *inter alia* the intention to gain an unfair profit (Article 121, paragraph 2). Finally, with respect to strengthened enforcement, for instance, it provides for the prohibition of re-exporting goods infringing trademarks or copyrights or related rights (Article 125, paragraph 3).[33]

Trade and competition policy was among the 'Singapore issues', which were proposed as among the new agenda items of the first negotiating round of the WTO and were later dropped therefrom. Some of Japan's EPAs resuscitate them by incorporating (a) commitment to implement each contracting party's competition law domestically, (b) cooperation on notification and information sharing with respect to the application and enforcement of competition law and policy, and, occasionally, (c) positive comity.[34]

Japan is also seeking WTO-plus commitments from its EPA counterparts in trade facilitation and government procurement. With respect to trade facilitation, some of Japan's EPAs contain the following WTO-plus provisions: (a) cooperation for the promotion of paperless trading,[35]

---

[32] See, for instance, Chapter 6 of the Japan–Singapore EPA on 'Mutual Recognition', in particular Article 46.

[33] Article 59 of the TRIPS Agreement prohibits re-exporting goods infringing trademarks, but it does not prohibit re-exporting goods infringing copyrights.

[34] See, for instance, Articles 103 and 104 of the Japan–Switzerland EPA and Articles 9 to 21 of the Implementing Agreement of the Japan–Switzerland EPA.

[35] See, for instance, Articles 57 to 61 of the Japan–Thailand EPA and Article 8 of the Implementing Agreement of the Japan–Thailand EPA.

(b) cooperation for simplification and harmonization of customs procedures,[36] and (c) cooperation and information exchange between customs authorities of contracting parties.[37]

EPA negotiations with countries not partaking in the WTO's plurilateral Agreement on Government Procurement are frequently the only way in which Japanese companies can gain access to their markets, which was the case in the Japan–Mexico EPA.[38] However, Japan was unable to secure substantial commitment on government procurement in its EPAs with Malaysia and ASEAN.[39]

Table 4.2 shows the major contents of Japan's EPAs including their WTO-plus components.

Japan's legalization strategy through the WTO-plus provisions of its EPAs is located between the NAFTA model and the Chinese FTAs. Compared with the US, Japan has not made binding obligations in such areas as liberalization in financial services, and labor and environmental standards. On the other hand, Japan's EPAs are more comprehensive in terms of issue coverage and more legalistic in terms of defining precise obligations and establishing formal dispute settlement mechanisms than Chinese FTAs, which have been characteristically brief and vague, with an emphasis on conciliation rather than formal dispute settlement. Solís (2009) thus argues that the dissemination of a distinct Japanese approach to preferential trading is a central concern in Japan's competitive FTA strategy, especially toward China.[40]

THE FUTURE OF JAPAN'S POLICY TOWARD EPAS AND BITS

Let me make a few remarks with respect to the prospective direction of Japan's policy toward EPAs and BITs: (a) Will Japan continue to conclude EPAs and BITs, and if so, who will be its counterparts? (b) Will Japan be able to take the initiative in establishing regional integration in the Asia Pacific?

With respect to the first question, the most probable answer is yes, given the prolonged impasse of the Doha Development Agenda. Japan

---

[36]   See, for instance, Article 53 of the Japan–Thailand EPA.
[37]   See, for instance, Articles 55 and 56 of the Japan–Thailand EPA and Articles 1 to 7 of the Implementing Agreement of the Japan–Thailand EPA.
[38]   See Articles 119 to 130 of the Japan–Mexico EPA.
[39]   See Solís, above note 5, 206.
[40]   Ibid., 207.

Table 4.2 *List of FTAs (EPAs) concluded by Japan (as of June 2010)*

No.	Counter-part	Signed	Took effect	agri[1]	biSG	trafac	ROO	SPS[2]	TBT[2]	hummov[3]	govproc[4]	TRIPS+[5]	compe[6]	ecocoop[7]
E1	Singapore	13 Jan. 2002	30 Nov. 2002	A	yes	yes	yes	no	ABCD	ABC	A	ABC	ABCD	ABDEH
E2	Mexico	17 Sep. 2004	1 Apr. 2005	C	yes	yes	yes	AB	ABC	BC	C	none	ABCD	ABDEFGH
E3	Malaysia	13 Dec. 2005	13 Jul. 2006	B	yes	yes	yes	AB	ABCE	ABC	no	ABC	ABD	BDEFGH
E4	Philippines	9 Sep. 2006	11 Dec. 2008	B	yes	yes	yes	no	D	ABCDE	D	AC	AB	ABCDEGH
E5	Chile	27 Mar. 2007	3 Sep. 2007	C	yes	yes	yes	AB	AC	BC	C	ABC	AB	none
E6	Thailand	3 Apr. 2007	1 Nov. 2007	C	yes	yes	yes	no	D	ABCF	D	ABC	AB	ABCDEFGH
E7	Brunei	18 Jun. 2007	31 Jul. 2008	B	yes	yes	yes	no	no	ABC	D	A	no	ABCDEFGH
E8	Indonesia	10 Aug. 2007	1 Jul. 2008	B	yes	yes	yes	no	no	ABCDE	D	ABC	AB	ABCFGH
E9	ASEAN	14 Apr. 2008	1 Dec. 2008	B	yes	yes	yes	AB	ABC	none	no	A	none	ABCEFGH
E10	Viet Nam	25 Dec. 2008	1 Oct. 2009	B	yes	yes	yes	AB	ABC	ABCD	D	ABC	ABD	ABEFGH
E11	Switzerland	19 Feb. 2009	1 Sep. 2009	A	yes	yes	yes	A	ABC	ABC	B	ABC	ABC	none

Table 4.2 (continued)

Notes:
1 A = Japan made (virtually) no commitment; B=Japan made commitments on products which are mostly imported; C=Japan made commitments on products which are produced domestically.
2 A = reaffirmation of rights/obligations under WTO; B=enquiry points; C=cooperation; D=mutual recognition; E=shall start MRA negotiation.
3 A = professional service providers; B=engineers; C=humanities and international service; D=nurses; E=care workers; F=others.
4 A = enhanced GPA rule on another GPA party; B=reaffirming GPA on another GPA Party; C=apply GPA to non-party; D=best effort.
5 A = simplifying procedures; B=enhancing protection; C=enhancing enforcement.
6 A = obligation to control anti-comptetitive activities; B=cooperation in controlling such activities; C=positive comity; D=technical assistance.
7 A = trade and investment promotion; B=human resource development; C=energy; D=science and technology; E=small and medium enterprises; F=agriculture, forestry, fisheries and plantation; G=environment; H=tourism.

will need to conclude new EPAs and BITs for further liberalization of trade and investment. The serious question is the next one: who will be its counterparts? Here it is important to note that Japan has not concluded EPAs with its major trading partners. According to the data of 2008, the following are the top five trading partners of Japan: on exports, the US (with 17.8 per cent share of the total exports), China (16.0 per cent), the EU (14.1 per cent), Korea (7.6 per cent), and Chinese Taipei (5.9 per cent); on imports, China (18.8 per cent), the US (10.4 per cent), the EU (9.2 per cent), Saudi Arabia (6.7 per cent), and Australia (6.2 per cent).[41] However, Japan has not concluded EPAs with most of them.

Although in terms of expected trade gains it would be advisable for Japan to conclude EPAs with these major trading partners, it does not seem likely that Japan can conclude EPAs with them at least in the near future, for various reasons. An FTA with the US would be unfeasible in the light of issues such as the handling of agricultural, forestry and marine products. Japanese businesses have been lobbying for an EPA with the EU, but the EU has been reluctant due to the lack of substantial trade benefits on its side.[42] China, Japan's biggest trading partner of 2008 (exports and imports combined), has so far been bypassed in the negotiation of a bilateral EPA, despite overwhelming business support for such an initiative, due, among other things, to the large portion of agricultural trade and the deterioration of bilateral relations between Japan and China during the Koizumi administration.

As an EPA is a comprehensive agreement, with many subject matters to be negotiated, Japan may opt for lighter agreements such as BITs, tax treaties and/or social security treaties with its major counterparts in trade and investment. Japan's Ministry of Foreign Affairs (MOFA) announced a policy on the strategic utilization of BITs in June 2008. It enumerated several criteria for selecting counterparts for Japan's BITs, including (a) countries where Japan has made a substantial amount of investment or where it is likely to make such investment, (b) countries whose business environments need improvement, and (c) countries which are important to Japan as providers of energy resources and other mineral resources. Based on the criteria (a) and (b) above, it listed Brazil, Poland, the Czech Republic and Hungary. Based on the criterion (c), it enumerated UAE, Oman, Algeria, Nigeria, Bolivia, Ukraine, Bahrain, Kazakhstan, Angola

---

[41] See WTO, Trade Profiles, Japan, accessed 2 September 2010, http://stat. wto.org/CountryProfiles/JP_e.htm.
[42] The regular summit meeting of Japan and the EU in April 2010 could not agree on starting a joint study for the bilateral EPA, due mainly to the opposition of the EU. See *Nihon Keizai Shimbun*, 14 April 2010, morning issue, 5.

and South Africa.[43] Even though this is a 'wish list', it suggests a direction of Japan's BIT policy in the near future.

With respect to the question as to whether Japan will be able to take the initiative in establishing regional integration in the Asia Pacific, I can only suggest a few possible scenarios due to a number of policy options and uncertainties. One possible scenario is the formation of an East Asian Community. Another possible scenario is the formation of a broader regional integration in the Asia Pacific. These two scenarios have different options, which will lead to different results.

The idea of an East Asian Community was first proposed by the then Prime Minister Koizumi in January 2002. It originally meant the formation of a comprehensive economic partnership agreement between Japan and ASEAN.[44] It was intended that the formation of a formal Community in East Asia would strengthen the deeply interdependent business relationship in the region. Japan has since been advocating the idea of an East Asian Community. China also started to promote the idea of an East Asian Community around the same time, soon after its accession to the WTO. However, the two countries have taken different approaches as to the geographical coverage and the subject matter coverage.

China has been promoting the idea of an East Asian Community consisting of ASEAN plus Three (China, Japan and Korea). The coalition government after Prime Minister Koizumi, while endorsing the ASEAN plus Three concept, advocated the idea of a Comprehensive Economic Partnership in East Asia (CEPEA), where ASEAN plus Six (China, Japan, Korea, Australia, New Zealand and India) should be involved.

With respect to the subject matter coverage, as I explained in the previous section, Japan opted for a full-set negotiation, consisting of financial and monetary cooperation, liberalization of trade in goods and services, investment promotion and protection, intellectual property rights, competition and government procurement.[45] On the other hand, China put priority on liberalization of trade in goods, and negotiation on the liberalization of trade in services and investment promotion has been postponed.

---

43   MOFA, 'On the Strategic Utilization of BITs,' June 2008 (in Japanese), accessed 2 September 2010, http://www.mofa.go.jp/mofaj/gaiko/investment/pdfs/bit_katsuyo.pdf.

44   Prime Minister Koizumi, mail magazine, 17 January 2002, accessed 2 September 2010, http://www.kantei.go.jp/jp/m-magazine/backnumber/2002/0117.html.

45   Ministry of Foreign Affairs, 'Japan's EPA Negotiation: Current Status and Challenges', June 2009 [in Japanese], accessed 2 September 2010, http://www.mofa.go.jp/mofaj/gaiko/fta/pdfs/kyotei_0703.pdf.

The rivalry between the two countries has so far been at the level of competition among visions, none of which has gained enough political support for realization. The Democratic Party of Japan won the general election of August 2009. Its Manifesto sets out the formation of an East Asian Community as one of the priority goals in diplomacy.[46] The foreign Ministers of Japan, China and Korea met in Shanghai on 28 September 2009 and agreed to cooperate for the formation of an East Asian Community.[47] However, it is too early to regard this as a major breakthrough. The Manifesto does not specify the geographical coverage and subject matter coverage of the Community, and the agreement of the Foreign Ministers does not specify these contents. As Prime Minister Hatoyama declared that he would not visit Yasukuni Shrine, one of the diplomatic barriers to promoting the idea of an East Asian Community may have been eliminated among the three countries. However, there remain a number of other barriers. First, the Manifesto 2009 of the Democratic Party emphasizes economic cooperation in the Asia Pacific region and does not exclude the possibility of forming an East Asian Community on the basis of open regionalism among ASEAN plus Six, which may not be acceptable to China. Secondly, the Japan–Korea EPA negotiation has been stalled since 2004 due mainly to the reluctance of Korea to eliminate its tariff barriers on manufactured products. This situation has not changed since then,[48] and the incoming Kan administration has done little to change it.[49]

While Japan and China have been competing with their own visions for an East Asia Community, there have appeared a few initiatives for the formation of a broader regional integration in the Asia Pacific: (a) a Free Trade Area of the Asia Pacific (FTAAP), and (b) the Trans-Pacific Partnership (TPP). The idea of an FTAAP was proposed at the APEC

---

[46] Democratic Party of Japan, Manifesto 2009, item 52, accessed 2 September 2010, http://www.dpj.or.jp/english/manifesto/manifesto2009.pdf.

[47] *Nihon Keizai Shimbun*, 29 September 2009.

[48] Political leaders of Japan, China and Korea agreed on 29 May 2010 to promote comprehensive economic cooperation among them, including (a) the achievement of a framework agreement on a trilateral investment agreement by the summer of 2010, and (b) the start of a joint study on the free trade agreement among them, which is scheduled to be finalized by 2012. However, they could not reach agreement on launching the negotiation of a trilateral FTA. See *Nihon Keizai Shimbun*, 30 May 2010.

[49] The Manifesto 2010 of the Democratic Party of Japan, which was released on 17 June 2010, refers to an EPA/FTA, but does not specify the regional scope thereof. See Democratic Party of Japan, Manifesto 2010, 7, accessed 2 September 2010, http://www.dpj.or.jp/english/manifesto/manifesto2010.pdf.

(Asia Pacific Economic Cooperation) summit meeting in November 2006, and has since been discussed within the framework of APEC.[50] Most recently, the meeting of APEC trade ministers held in June 2010 in Sapporo welcomed the progress made to explore possible pathways to achieve an FTAAP.[51] The negotiation to form a Trans-Pacific Partnership was started in 2002 among Chile, New Zealand and Singapore. Brunei joined it at the final round of negotiations in April 2005, and the four countries reached an agreement on a Trans-Pacific Strategic Economic Partnership Agreement in June 2005. Negotiations to expand the TPP to include the US, Australia, Peru and Viet Nam began in March 2010.[52]

Japan needs to decide whether to join these new initiatives in regional integration in the Asia Pacific. With respect to the FTAAP, Japan has no reason to oppose it. The FTAAP is still in the process of discussing ideas and visions. Japan has been a persistent promoter of APEC, and it will host its summit meeting in 2010. Japan is, therefore, likely to endorse the idea of the FTAAP and to promote its realization within the framework of APEC. The situation is different with respect to the TPP. The original agreement on the TPP has already entered into force, and it 'is open to accession on terms to be agreed among the Parties, by any APEC Economy or other State' (Article 20.6.1).[53] Although the original TPP looked a minor trade agreement to Japan, the US's decision to join it dramatically increased the economic and political significance of the TPP. As the eight countries have already started negotiation of the enlarged TPP, Japan will have to decide whether it will be able to negotiate over the wide range of subject matters such as comprehensive tariff eliminations including agricultural products and liberalization of trade in financial services, both of which might pose political challenges to the government of Japan.

Starting in the early 2000s, Japan's FTA (EPA) and BIT policy has

---

[50] See APEC, 'Free Trade Agreements and Regional Trade Agreements', accessed 2 September 2010, http://www.apec.org/apec/apec_groups/other_apec_groups/FTA_RTA.html.

[51] See Meeting of APEC Ministers Responsible for Trade, Sapporo, Japan, 5–6 June 2010, Statement of the Chair, para.7, accessed 2 September 2010, http/www.mofa.go.jp/policy/economy/apec/2010/japan/chairstatement2010.html.

[52] See New Zealand Ministry of Foreign Affairs & Trade, Trans-Pacific Strategic Economic Partnership Agreement (TPP, previously known as P4), 'Overview', accessed 2 September 2010, http://mfat.govt.nz/Trade-and-Economic-Relations/Trade-Agreements/Trans-Pacific/index.php.

[53] The text of the Trans-Pacific Strategic Economic Partnership Agreement is available from the website of the New Zealand Ministry of Foreign Affairs & Trade, accessed 2 September 2010, http://mfat.govt.nz/downloads/trade-agreement/transpacific/main-agreement.pdf.

gone through its first decade fairly successfully, with 11 EPAs and 8 BITs. However, Japan will face a number of serious political challenges in the next decade as to which countries to negotiate EPAs and BITs with and which regional initiative(s) to take.

5. China's strategy for free trade agreements: political battle in the name of trade

Henry Gao

Compared with Europe and America, East Asia is a latecomer in the new gold-rush of free trade agreements (FTAs). In this process, China has played a significant role. This is not only due to the growing economic clout of China but also because China has taken a conscious strategy to push for economic integration in the region. Thus, for the benefit of the countries in the region, it is very important to understand China's FTA strategy. This chapter starts with the evolving picture of China's FTA web, then discusses the key components of China's FTA strategy, and concludes by noting the implications of China's FTA strategy on the region and beyond.

OVERVIEW OF CHINA'S FTAS

While China adopted an export-oriented development model when it started its economic reform in the late 1970s, it did not contemplate the possibility of entering into FTAs until much later for the following reasons.

The first reason is the general hostile attitude towards FTAs. Throughout the 1970s and 1980s, there was little interest in FTAs. It was only in the early 1990s that countries around the world started to engage in FTAs seriously. Indeed, of the most important FTAs existing in the world today, such as the EU, NAFTA, MERCOSUR and ASEAN, most only took their current form in the 1990s. In particular, Asian countries lag behind their European and American counterparts when it comes to FTAs. Thus, even if China had been interested in FTAs then, it would have had difficulty in finding negotiating partners.

The second reason is the different trade structure of China. When China first started its economic reform, most of its exports went to developed countries such as the US, the EC and Japan. As China's export volume was low, these countries provided sufficiently big markets and there was no need to look for export markets elsewhere. For various reasons, however, it is quite difficult for China to negotiate FTAs with these countries. As for other countries, it did not make sense for China to try to negotiate FTAs with them due to the low trade volume with them.

The third reason is the resource constraint. From 1986, the top priority for China was resuming its contracting party status in the GATT. When this proved impossible with the establishment of the WTO in 1995, China tried to step up its accession talks so that it could join the WTO as a founding Member. With most of its resources devoted to one of the most complicated accession processes in the history of the GATT/WTO, China could not afford the luxury of engaging in FTA talks.

The fourth reason is strategic. Even if China had had extra capacity to explore possible FTA deals, it would not have been a good move for China to start FTA negotiations in tandem with its WTO accession negotiation. On the one hand, any interest in FTAs would cast doubt on China's true commitment to the multilateral trading system and make Members more reluctant to negotiate with China at the multilateral level. On the other hand, any serious FTA negotiation would require China to table offers that would go beyond what it is willing to offer at the multilateral level. As China was not a WTO Member yet, however, other WTO Members would almost certainly use China's FTA offers as a benchmark to measure its WTO commitments so as to minimize the possibility of diluting the benefits they might obtain under the WTO. Essentially, by entering into FTA negotiations, China could only make its WTO accession negotiations more difficult for itself.

Important changes came in the early 1990s, however. First, China gradually lost patience with the WTO accession process when faced with a series of setbacks, including first its failure to 'resume' its contracting party status in the GATT, and then the unsuccessful attempt to join the newly established WTO as a founding Member. Frustrated by the slow progress in Geneva, China started to look for opportunities elsewhere, including in FTAs. Second, with the emergence of regionalism in Latin America (MERCOSUR, 1991), Southeast Asia (AFTA, 1992) and North America (NAFTA, 1992) in addition to the further strengthening of European economic integration with the formation of the European Union (Maastricht Treaty, 1992), China did not want to be left out of the new wave of regional integration. Third, with China's growing trade volume, it became increasingly difficult for Chinese firms to find new markets. In this regard, FTAs became a useful tool.

Thus, in the mid-1990s, China started to consider the possibility of entering into FTAs. This is evidenced in 1996 by the publication of the Ninth Five-Year Plan, which is the key blueprint for national economic and social development drafted by the State Council with advice from the Central Committee of the Communist Party of China and adopted by the National People's Congress. According to the Plan, China shall 'actively participate and develop regional economic cooperation', as well as 'strengthen "South–South Cooperation", and promote and develop . . . the economic and trade cooperation with developing countries'. The same Plan, however, also calls for China to '*actively participate in and defend the global multilateral trading system, develop both bilateral and multilateral trade*, so that they can promote each other and the market can be diversified' (emphasis added). Such an equivocal attitude seems to indicate that China took a cautious approach on FTAs initially and tried to hedge its risks by giving equal emphasis to both multilateral and regional/bilateral initiatives. Nonetheless, this is still a very important first step in China's move towards FTAs.

Shortly after, China was presented with the first opportunity for real FTA negotiations when the Southeast Asian countries were hit by the East Asian Financial Crisis in mid-1997. Whatever its cause, one consequence of the crisis was that people have lost faith in global institutions such as the IMF and World Bank, which were allegedly responsible for the crisis with their highly intrusive policy suggestions. Thus, in his speech at the first China–ASEAN summit, held in December 1997, President Jiang Zemin called for the two sides to build a 'Good Neighboring Partnership of Mutual Trust'.[1] In November 2000, the two sides further agreed in another summit to explore ways to further enhance integration and economic cooperation between the two regions, including the possibility of establishing a free trade area.[2] After the summit, an ASEAN–China Expert Group on Economic Cooperation was established to conduct feasibility studies on an ASEAN–China FTA. In October 2001, the Expert Group issued its report and concluded that an FTA would be in the interests of both parties.[3] At the ASEAN–China Summit held a month later, the two sides decided to establish an ASEAN–China Free Trade Area ('ASEAN–China FTA') within ten years.[4] One year later, the Framework

---

[1]   The text of the speech is available at http://news.xinhuanet.com/ziliao/2002-10/28/content_610547.htm, accessed 2 September 2010.

[2]   'Forging Closer ASEAN–China Economic Relations in the Twenty-First Century', A Report Submitted by the ASEAN–China Expert Group on Economic Cooperation, October 2001, 4, accessed 2 September 2010, http://www.aseansec.org/newdata/asean_chi.pdf.

[3]   Ibid.

[4]   Premier Zhu Rongji Attended the Fifth ASEAN–China Leaders Summit and Gave Important Speech, Xinhua Net, 6 November 2001, accessed 2 September 2010, http://news.xinhuanet.com/world/2001-11/06/content_101950.htm.

Agreement on Comprehensive Economic Co-operation between ASEAN and the People's Republic of China was signed, and this marked the start of the tariff-reduction process leading to the eventual elimination of tariffs among the parties.[5]

For a long time, the ASEAN states have viewed China more as a threat than a potential partner. At first, the ASEAN states were concerned mainly with political and military threats from the north.[6] Indeed, one of the primary reasons for the formation of ASEAN in 1967 was to counter the spread of communism in the region.[7] With China's emergence as one of the most competitive producers of many products in the world, ASEAN started to perceive China more as an economic threat. After all, there is remarkable similarity in their industrial structures: both specialize in labor-intensive products, and both have the US, the EU and Japan as their major export markets.[8] To a large extent, the increase in China's exports during the last two decades of the twentieth century was achieved at the expense of its neighbors in Southeast Asia. With China's rise as a major exporter, it also started to suck FDI away from its neighbors to the south: as wage levels in China were much lower, it made sense to invest in China rather than ASEAN states. While before 2001 ASEAN could still take comfort in the idea that China was largely excluded from the many benefits offered by the multilateral trading system, such as MFN, this advantage it enjoyed soon became history with China's accession to the WTO at the end of that year. With its foot into the global trade club, China now enjoys more predictable access to its major export markets with much lower costs, and this means intensified competition against ASEAN.[9] Thus, China's call for an FTA at around the same time as its WTO accession was an offer too good to reject: on the one hand, the ASEAN states could not do much to stop China from replacing them in the major exporting markets; on the other hand, with the growth in the domestic market in China, an FTA deal with China, the first of its kind, could guarantee the ASEAN states a first-mover advantage in the largest emerging market in the whole world.

---

5   The full text of the Agreement, accessed 2 September 2010 http://www.ase
ansec.org/13196.htm.
6   'The Three Ages of ASEAN', Lecture delivered by Rodolfo C. Severino, Secretary-General of ASEAN at the ARCO Forum of Public Affairs, Kennedy School of Government, Harvard University, 3 October 2002, accessed 2 September 2010, http://www.aseansec.org/12310.htm.
7   Ibid.
8   ASEAN–China Expert Group Report, above note 2, 15.
9   Ibid., 24.

The Financial Crisis of 1997 also taught ASEAN states important lessons. First, global institutions such as the IMF and the World Bank are not panaceas, and it is important to have regional cooperation mechanisms as contingency plans. With the growing importance of China as an economic power, however, any regional cooperation mechanism in this part of the world would not be effective without the participation of China. Indeed, China's decision not to devalue its currency was widely appreciated among ASEAN states as an important factor in helping them through the period: should China have decided to float the yuan, the ASEAN states would have had to face more fierce competition from cheaper Chinese products and this could have greatly exacerbated their problems. While Japan is also an important partner in regional cooperation, Japan was having its own problems during the 1990s. Thus, China became the natural choice. Second, it is important for ASEAN states to diversify both their export markets and investment sources. Along with the growth of its domestic market, China has developed an increasingly big appetite for overseas investment. For ASEAN states, investment from China is a good way to make sure that their economic well-being is not tied up with the economic performances of a few economies.

With the ASEAN–China FTA as a starting point, China firmly embarked on the road towards FTAs. The following years witnessed the signing of the two Closer Economic Partnership Arrangements, with Hong Kong, China[10] (June 2003) and Macau, China[11] (October 2003), respectively; the FTAs with Chile[12] (November 2005), Pakistan (November 2006), New Zealand (April 2008), Singapore (October 2008) and Peru (April 2009); and the launch of FTA negotiations with the Gulf Cooperation Council[13] (April 2005), Australia[14] (May 2005), Iceland[15] (April 2008),

---

[10]   The full text of the Arrangement is available at http://www.tid.gov.hk/english/cepa/legaltext/cepa_legaltext.html, accessed 2 September 2010.

[11]   The full text of the Arrangement is available at http://www.economia.gov.mo/page/english/cepa_e.htm, accessed 2 September 2010.

[12]   The full text of the Agreement is available at http://www.direcon.cl/documentos/China2/tlc_chile_china_ing_junio_2006.pdf, accessed 2 September 2010.

[13]   See 'China Completed First Round of FTA Negotiations with Six Gulf States', available at http://gjs.mofcom.gov.cn/aarticle/af/ak/200505/20050500088391.html, accessed 2 September 2010.

[14]   Australia–China FTA Negotiations, Subscriber Update, 26 May 2005, available at http://www.dfat.gov.au/geo/china/fta/050526_subscriber_update.html, accessed 2 September 2010.

[15]   http://fta.mofcom.gov.cn/article/iceland/200809/49_1.html, accessed 2 September 2010.

Norway[16] (September 2008), and Costa Rica[17] (January 2009); with the negotiations with the South African Customs Union to be started soon.[18] Also, China has been quite eager to sign an FTA with India, while India has given China the cold shoulder over concerns such as the lack of competitiveness of Indian firms,[19] the mismatch between the trade patterns[20] and industrial structures[21] of the two economies, and security concerns.[22] That probably explains why, despite the joint feasibility study report on an FTA being concluded more than two years ago,[23] there are still no signs that the actual negotiations will pick up any time soon. Last but certainly

---

[16]   http://fta.mofcom.gov.cn/article/norway/200809/93_1.html.   accessed   2 September 2010.

[17]   http://fta.mofcom.gov.cn/article/costarica/200902/465_1.html, accessed   2 September 2010.

[18]   http://fta.mofcom.gov.cn/article/southafrica/200809/48_1.html, accessed   2 September 2010.

[19]   See P. Vaidyanathan Iyer and Amiti Sen, 'India Yes to Bipa, no to FTA/ RTA', *Financial Express*, 11 April 2005, accessed 2 September 2010, http://www.bilaterals.org/article.php3?id_article=1636.

[20]   As one article argues, '[India's] exports to China are basically raw materials, ores and steel (accounting for roughly 57% of exports), while China's exports to India are primarily manufactured goods (like electric machinery, electronic and audio-video equipment). Since manufactured goods have a much higher level of duty compared to raw materials, free trade will mean we give away our advantage more than gaining from them. Besides, unless our exports become more diversified, trade will not be sustainable in the long term', http://www.bilaterals.org/article.php3?id_article=1701. See Anjan Joy, 'The Journey Has Begun, But It'll Take Long to Arrive', *Financial Express* (India) 20 April 2005, accessed 2 September 2010, http://www.bilaterals.org/article.php3?id_article=1701.

[21]   As noted by one article, '[o]ver 50% of China's GDP comes from manufacturing and construction, over 30% from services and just under 15% from agriculture. . . . In contrast, over half of India's GDP comes from services with industry and agriculture sharing the remaining less than 50% in roughly equal proportions. . . . That's where the rub lies. For the Chinese, an FTA focused on trade in goods would enable them to best leverage their comparative advantage. For India, on the other hand, an agreement restricted to or focused on merely free movement of goods across borders would be one that gives Chinese manufacturers ready access to Indian markets without a corresponding benefit for India in its area of strength.' See Shankar Raghuraman, 'Why an FTA Gives Us Cold Feet', *Times of India*, 9 April 2005, accessed 2 September 2010, http://www.bilaterals.org/article.php3?id_article=1629.

[22]   See Monica Gupta, 'Trade Pact with China Stuck Over Security', *Business Standard* (India), 8 August 2006, accessed 2 September 2010, http://www.bilaterals.org/article.php3?id_article=5455.

[23]   http://fta.mofcom.gov.cn/article/india/200809/68_1.html,   accessed   2 September 2010.

not least, China has reached an advanced stage in its joint feasibility study with Korea, with five rounds of working group meetings concluded.[24]

With eight FTAs under its belt and more to come, it is time now to review China's FTA negotiating approach. In the following sections, we will discuss the following key issues in China's FTA strategy: choice of FTA model, criteria for the selection of partners, and negotiating objectives.

CHOICE OF FTA MODEL

If we look around the world, FTAs can be broadly divided into two models. One is the EU model, which includes both economic and political integration. The other is the NAFTA model, which focuses on economic integration only. Within the NAFTA model, there are two sub-categories. The first is the Economic Partnership Agreement (EPA) approach advocated by Japan, which seeks to conclude comprehensive agreements that include trade in goods, services, and sometimes even environment protection and intellectual property rights. The other approach is narrower and focuses mainly on trade in goods.

China has chosen to adopt the narrower model. Normally, China would start with an agreement on trade in goods only and would only expand to trade in services and investment after the commitments on goods have been substantially implemented. Take the FTA with Pakistan, for example; while the liberalization of trade in goods dates back to the signing of the Agreement on the Early Harvest Program in April 2005, the Agreement on Trade in Services was only signed in February 2009. Similarly, in the FTA with ASEAN, the agreement on trade in goods was signed in November 2004, while the agreement on services was only signed in January 2007. A counter-example is the FTA negotiation with Australia, which has languished for years partly due to the fact that Australia insists on dealing with services liberalization first while China wishes to proceed with the usual 'goods and then services' order.

With regard to the issues which are not traditionally trade-related, such as environment protection, competition policy, and labor standards, China has been reluctant to include them as part of the FTA package. Recently, however, China has shown some willingness to include these issues as part of the FTA package. Nonetheless, in line with its cautious

---

[24]   http://fta.mofcom.gov.cn/article/ftanews/200909/988_1.html.   accessed   2 September 2010.

approach, China has largely chosen not to include these issues in the main agreement of the FTA, but preferred to address them in stand-alone side agreements or MOUs.

CRITERIA FOR THE SELECTION OF NEGOTIATING PARTNERS

When we take a look at the list of countries/regions which have negotiated or are negotiating FTAs with China, it seems to be quite random. To start with, the top three trading partners of China, namely the EU, the US and Japan, are not on the list. Furthermore, even when we expand the scope to include the top ten trade partners of China, only three, ASEAN, Singapore and Hong Kong, have concluded FTAs with China. Among the remaining seven countries/regions, only another two, Australia and Korea, have started or are about to start negotiations with China. However, for one reason or another, these two negotiations are not going to proceed on a smooth basis. Among the other countries/regions which have concluded or are negotiating FTAs with China, many only have negligible trade volume.

One tentative conclusion that we can draw from the facts above is that trade volume does not seem to be an important factor for China in selecting its negotiating partners, otherwise we would not have so few of the important trade partners in the list. How, then, does China decide which countries shall be graced with the honor of becoming a member of the coveted FTA club with China? In an interview done in May 2007, Vice Minister Yi Xiaozhun of MOFCOM suggested the following criteria: first, the country has a good political and diplomatic relationship with China; second, the country has complementary economic structures and trade patterns with China; third, the country either has a substantial domestic market or serves as an FTA hub in a particular region; and fourth, the country shares common intentions on building FTAs with China.[25]

While these criteria combined seem to explain most of China's FTA activities so far, as the examination of these factors below reveals, some seem to have more importance than others.

First, a political and diplomatic relationship seems to carry most weight, as almost all the countries do have good political and diplomatic relationships with China. Among them, Pakistan has been a very close

---

[25] Yi Xiaozhun, 'China's Four Criterion in Selecting FTA Partners', 29 May 2007, available at http://finance.sina.com.cn/roll/20070529/20571438980.shtml

ally of China for a long time. As to the others, they have also generally maintained good relationships with China. For example, Chile is the first country to establish a diplomatic relationship with China in South America.[26] Similarly, New Zealand was the first WTO Member to conclude the bilateral talks in China's accession process and the first developed country to recognize China's market economy status, as well as the first developed country to propose FTA negotiations with China.[27] As to Singapore, while it was rather late in establishing a formal diplomatic relationship with China, its support of China came with perfect timing – 1990 – when China faced one of the worst sanctions from developed countries around the world after its crackdown on student movements in June 1989. With regard to the other countries in ASEAN, most of them historically were not really on friendly terms with China. In recent years, however, their relationships with China have become increasingly warm as China has tried to maintain peace and security in an area that it views as its geopolitical backyard. The strongest case of political undertone can be found in the FTA negotiation with Costa Rica, which was formally kicked off only one year after the tiny Latin American country switched alliances to China by breaking up with Taiwan, its friend for nearly 60 years.[28]

Second, while economic and trade complementarities are important, they do not seem to be major factors. It is true that several of the partners do complement China economically. For example, Singapore and Hong Kong are highly competitive in services exports, while New Zealand, Chile and Peru, as Cairns Group members, are quite competitive in agricultural exports. Both services and agriculture are sectors in which China is relatively uncompetitive. On the other hand, several FTA partners specialize in industries that compete with, rather than complement, China. For example, most of the ASEAN countries actually share with China an industrial structure that relies heavily on export-oriented labor-intensive manufacturing sectors. Their exports are also mostly in electronics and textile products, similar to those from China.

Third, between domestic market size and hubbing effect, the latter seems to be more important. Measured by most standards, the domestic markets of many partners are rather small. On the other hand, almost all of them are important FTA hubs. For example, Singapore has FTAs with a dozen countries, including the US, Japan, Korea and Australia; Chile is

---

[26]   http://www.fmprc.gov.cn/chn/gxh/cgb/zcgmzysx/nmz/1206_11/1206x1/t80 19.htm, accessed 2 September 2010.

[27]   http://gov.people.com.cn/GB/7093066.html, accessed 2 September 2010.

[28]   http://www.msnbc.msn.com/id/19080068/, accessed 2 September 2010.

an associate member of both MERCOSUR and the Andean Community; Iceland and Norway are members of the European Free Trade Association (EFTA), which has a free trade relationship with the EU via the European Economic Area (EEA); while India and Pakistan are both members of the South Asian Association for Regional Cooperation (SAARC). By entering FTAs with these partners, China could potentially tap into the bigger markets created by the FTA arrangements that are already in place. This is a highly cost-effective way of exploring new markets.

Fourth, the existence of common intentions on forming FTAs seems to play little part. While such common intentions can be found in FTA negotiations with Pakistan, Chile and Peru, the other negotiations seem to have started in a one-sided manner. The FTA negotiations with Singapore and New Zealand seem to have resulted from the heavy lobbying of these two countries respectively. As to the FTA negotiations with ASEAN and India, China invested heavily in trying to court these countries during the initial phase. Of course, as the Chinese are not very good at saying no, even if an FTA is first proposed by another party, China generally will try to accommodate such a request. This is in marked contrast to the approach taken by some other countries, especially the US and the EU, where the selection of FTA partners seems to be mostly a one-way process.

NEGOTIATING OBJECTIVES

What does China try to achieve with its growing list of concluded FTAs and those currently under negotiation? Has China managed to achieve the intended objectives? A review of China's growing FTA network reveals the following common features.

First, in terms of the geographical distribution of FTA partners, China has tried to strike a balance. So far, China has concluded FTAs, or entered into negotiations, with almost every major region in the world, including Europe (Iceland and Norway), America (Chile, Peru and Costa Rica), the Middle East (GCC), Africa (SACU), East Asia (Korea, Hong Kong and Macau), Southeast Asia (ASEAN and Singapore), South Asia (Pakistan and India), and Oceania (New Zealand and Australia). In each region, China usually selects one trade partner to start the negotiations. In the author's view, this seems to indicate that China has some really clever strategy in structuring FTA deals to suit its best interest. One thing all these FTA partners share in common is that they are either FTAs themselves, such as ASEAN and the Gulf Cooperation Council, or are members of another FTA deal.

Second, with the exception of ASEAN, Singapore and Australia, none of China's existing FTA partners are major markets for China's exports. At the same time, however, China is always one of the top five markets for these nations' exports. Thus, while China could afford to ignore these economies, none of them could afford to ignore China. With such asymmetric trade relationships, China could have more bargaining power in the FTA setting than at the multilateral level. This is very important for China as it does not have much experience in trade negotiations. By focusing on FTAs with those economies which are of minor importance to China, China could divert some of the trade with its major trading partners, so that it could further balance and diversify its import sources and export markets and would not be over-reliant on one or several economies. At the same time, these FTA partners would have a lot of their trade diverted to China. This would further increase their reliance on China and further strengthen China's bargaining power and political clout.

Third, all economies that have entered or are about to enter FTAs with China have recognized the market economy status of China. This is mainly concerned with a provision in China's Accession Protocol. As China is an economy with a long history of government planning in economic development, during its accession process many WTO Members suspected that the Chinese government still interferes with micro-economic activities and thus doubted that the market data in China is really reliable. Thus, Section 15(a) of the Accession Protocol allows WTO Members to deem China a non-market economy in anti-dumping investigations. The first step in anti-dumping investigations involves the determination of the existence of dumping, which is derived by comparing the export price and normal value. Normal value is usually the sale price of the product in the exporting economy. This provision, however, would allow WTO Members to disregard the domestic sales price in China and use the prices from some surrogate economies or a constructed price. Because the comparative advantages of China mostly come from the low costs of its factors of production, this provision makes it more likely for other WTO Members to arrive at a higher normal value and thus easier for them to find the existence of dumping.

This mechanism is available to WTO Members for up to 15 years after China's accession. As this provision is highly technical, it was hardly noticed before and in the first couple of years after China's accession. In recent years, however, as more and more Chinese firms are subject to anti-dumping investigations abroad, people have started to realize the damaging effect of this provision. Indeed, it was largely because of this provision, along with several other discriminatory provisions in China's accession package, that Mr Long Yongtu, the outspoken former chief negotiator in China's WTO accession, was called a 'traitor' and likened to Li Hongzhang, the nineteenth-century diplomat who allegedly sold China out by signing unequal treaties with Western imperialist powers on behalf of the late Qing government. The Chinese government was embarrassed by such criticism and tried to get rid of this provision. Theoretically, they could have the Accession Protocol amended by the WTO General Council, but this would be highly unlikely given that the General Council works on the basis of consensus and so far the only instance where consensus has been achieved was when the Members decided in July 2006 to suspend the Doha negotiations.

The remaining option is for China to negotiate with each of its trade partners to recognize China's market economy status. As China has much more bargaining power at the bilateral/regional level, this strategy seems to be working. As of 11 January 2010, 80 economies have recognized the market economy status of China.[29] As more and more economies recognize China's market economy status, there will be mounting pressures on those who still deem China to be a non-market economy to accept China's market economy status as an established precedent.

Fourth, in terms of the trade pattern, these FTA partners mostly export raw materials, energy products or agricultural products to China, while they import mainly textile products and electronic products from China. In order to maintain its position as the 'World Factory', China needs a steady supply of raw materials and energy; also, as most of the agricultural sector in China is not very competitive due to its low per capita land ratio, China needs to ensure the supply of agricultural products in order to free up its labor from agriculture to go into manufacturing. Thus, the FTA partners are probably chosen with these considerations in mind. Moreover, many of the FTAs also include investment provisions, which is another way for China to make sure that it can invest in and subsequently control strategic resources.

Fifth, in the grand scheme of things, FTAs also provide a way for China to build up mutual trust with countries around the world and improve its image as a benign emerging power. With China's growing importance on the world stage, many countries started to feel the 'China threat' with concerns that originate from China's ideological difference and political, military and economic weight. In East Asia, in particular, the United States–Japan coalition has historically exerted considerable political influence. Indeed, such influence has dragged China into quite a few conflicts and clashes with several ASEAN states during the second half of the twentieth century. With the amazing development in its economy, China

---

[29]   http://smc.hunancom.gov.cn/zxdt/137112.htm, accessed 2 September 2010.

once again has the opportunity to rise as a world power. China has maintained that it will adopt a course of 'peaceful rise', which is interpreted by Professor Zheng Bijian, the senior advisor to President Hu Jintao, to mean that:

> China will not follow the path of Germany leading up to World War I or those of Germany and Japan leading up to World War II, when these countries violently plundered resources and pursued hegemony. Neither will China follow the path of the great powers vying for global domination during the Cold War. Instead, China will transcend ideological differences to strive for peace, development, and cooperation with all countries of the world.[30]

However, the opportunity to seize the leadership role in Asia is too good for China to pass. As it would take quite some time before China could challenge the military dominance of the US in Asia, economic integration with ASEAN and other economies in Asia will be the way to achieve political ends using economic means. When the ASEAN states are dependent on China for their economic well-being, they can hardly ignore the political message from Beijing. Therefore, even though many commentators have doubted the economic benefit to China from an ASEAN–China FTA as the two are competitors on many products, China has adopted the guideline of 'give a lot while demanding little'[31] in the FTA negotiations as the political significance of such an FTA greatly outweighs economic considerations.

Sixth is the Taiwan factor. Since the Nationalist government retreated to Taiwan 60 years ago, cross-strait reunification has become one of the most important political problems facing the Mainland government. At first the Mainland government tried military and political means, which have largely been unsuccessful. In recent decades, with the growing economic ties between the two sides, the Mainland government has switched to FTAs in an effort to lure back the renegade province. Such strategy includes several components.

The first is to use FTAs to entice the small and already dwindling group of countries that maintain diplomatic relationships with Taiwan to switch sides. For example, in June 2007, Costa Rica ended its ties of over six decades with Taiwan and instead established a formal diplomatic

---

[30] 'China's "Peaceful Rise" to Great-Power Status, Zheng Bijian', *Foreign Affairs* 84 (5) (Sep/Oct 2005): 18.

[31] Remarks on the China–ASEAN FTA by Mr Bo Xilai, the Minister of Commerce of China, 21 July 2006, accessed 2 September 2010, http://boxilai. mofcom.gov.cn/column/print.shtml?/speeches/200607/20060702702431.

relationship with China. One may argue that Costa Rica's main motivation was political, that is, to gain the support of China to be elected a non-permanent member of the UN Security Council.[32] At the same time, however, fostering stronger economic ties with China was probably another important consideration, as Costa Rica was soon selected by China as its first FTA partner in Central America. In a way, the Costa Rica FTA is also China's fight-back against Taiwan in Central America, one of the island's few remaining spheres of influence in the world. In the four years before Costa Rica's 'betrayal', Taiwan had signed a flurry of FTAs, all with Central American countries: Panama (signed August 2003), Guatemala (signed September 2005), Nicaragua (signed June 2006), El Salvador and Honduras (signed November 2006).[33] In addition, Taiwan has started FTA negotiations with the Dominican Republic, while the negotiations with Paraguay have been stalled over the approval of other MERCOSUR member countries.[34] Once Costa Rica concludes the FTA with China and starts to reap considerable economic benefits, the other Central American countries will probably have to reconsider the costs and benefits in maintaining diplomatic ties with Taiwan.

The second component is to use the Closer Economic Partnership Arrangements (CEPA) with Hong Kong and Macau as a model for a future deal with Taiwan. In terms of both the breadth of the coverage and the depth of the concessions, the two CEPAs far exceed the FTAs China has concluded.[35] This is understandable as Hong Kong and Macau are both regions of China, even though they each are separate Members of the WTO in their own right. By offering Hong Kong and Macau a better deal than other FTA partners, China is also signaling to Taiwan that the same level of access to the largest market in the world could be extended to the island. Of course, there is no free lunch in the world. Hong Kong and Macau were able to get such a good deal because they are both sub-central regions in the People's Republic. Initially, it seems that Beijing would insist on Taiwan accepting the same status rather than holding on

---

32 http://goliath.ecnext.com/coms2/gi_0199-7140637/COSTA-RICA-S-SOPHISTICATED-AND.html, accessed 2 September 2010.

33 Bureau of Foreign Trade of Taiwan, 'Pushing for FTAs', http://cweb.trade.gov.tw/kmi.asp?xdurl=kmif.asp&cat=CAT514, accessed 2 September 2010.

34 http://www.bilaterals.org/article.php3?id_article=266, accessed 2 September 2010.

35 For a discussion of the coverage of the China–Hong Kong, China CEPA, see Henry Gao, 'The Closer Economic Partnership Arrangement (CEPA) between Mainland China and Hong Kong – Legal and Economic Analyses', in *Trading Arrangements in the Pacific Rim: ASEAN and APEC* (New York: Oceana, 2004), Chapter 6.

to its claim of being an independent sovereign state. This is reflected in the careful selection of the name of the agreements with Hong Kong and Macau. During the negotiations leading to the conclusion of the CEPAs, it had been suggested that they should be called FTAs. In the end, however, they were named 'Closer Economic Partnership Arrangements' instead. In substance, the two CEPAs are no different from the other FTAs around the world. Moreover, legally speaking, China, Hong Kong and Macau would run the risk of violating their MFN obligations unless they treat the CEPAs as FTAs, which allow them to invoke the exception provided for under Article XXIV of the GATT.[36] By calling them 'arrangements' rather than 'agreements', however, the Mainland authorities were trying to avoid the impression that China was signing 'international agreements'. Instead, they are just some 'arrangements' offered by the Central Government to local governments. Initially, China insisted on using the same name for the deal with Taiwan. Recently, however, China has softened its position by agreeing to accept the more neutral-sounding ECFA (Economic Cooperation Framework Agreement) as the name for the future agreement.

The third component of the strategy is to use the proposed ECFA with Taiwan to further integrate Taiwan into the economy of the Mainland. Whatever its name, the ECFA will significantly boost the already substantial Taiwanese investment in the Mainland, legalizing cross-strait direct trade which has so far been prohibited by Taiwan's age-old Act Governing Relations between Peoples of the Taiwan Area and the Mainland Area. The deeper the economic integration between the two sides, the more difficult it will be for Taiwan to be politically separate from China. Eventually, the economic ties between the two sides will be so strong that Taiwan will probably become even more dependent on China than Hong Kong and Macau.

Seventh, FTAs also provide an effective way for China to push for trade liberalization in selected markets even though the multilateral negotiations have been moving only at a disappointing pace. With the slow progress in the Doha Round, FTAs have become the only feasible option to achieve trade liberalization. While this holds true for all WTO Members, China in particular has more to gain from bilateral/regional negotiations as it is placed in an awkward position in the current multilateral negotiations. First of all, as a newly acceded Member, China is required to undertake

---

[36]   Indeed, China and Hong Kong, China and Macau, China have effectively conceded that the CEPAs are FTAs by notifying them to the Committee on Free Trade Agreements of the WTO (CFTA) for review.

a lot of commitments, many of which are higher than those of existing WTO Members. It is already a huge challenge for China to try to implement these commitments. After having been in the spotlight for 15 years, what China needs now is some quiet breathing space, which it can only get at the bilateral/regional level as China had to face the annual transitional review and biennial trade policy review in the WTO. Second, with most of its exports concentrated in labour-intensive or resource-intensive products, China would compete with rather than complement the industrial structure of other developing economies. It is no wonder that other developing economies view China as a competitor rather than a friend. Indeed, notwithstanding that the Chinese government has repeatedly held that China is, and always will be, a developing economy, and in spite of the fact that the per capita GDP in China is comparable to that of many LDCs, China is also the third largest trading power in the world and the only one among all developing economies to be among the top five traders worldwide. Thus, on many issues, China's interests are actually closer to those of major developed economies than those of developing economies. Agriculture is one such example: as China imports a large quantity of agricultural products, it is actually not in China's interests to adopt the position of most developing economies and demand the elimination of export subsidies. Trade facilitation, one of the four 'Singapore issues', is another such example: as China exports a lot, it is actually in the interest of China to push for the inclusion of trade facilitation in the WTO framework to make the customs process more efficient and cheaper. However, as China has formally joined the G-20,[37] the major developing country grouping in the WTO, it would be embarrassing for China to publicly depart from the G-20 party-line in the Doha negotiations. At the bilateral/regional level, China would have more flexibility in asserting its true interests.

Eighth, FTA negotiations have also provided a good opportunity for China to build up its trade negotiation capacity. Compared with other regions which have long been active in trade negotiations at both multilateral and regional levels, East Asia lagged behind. By engaging in

---

[37] The G-20 is the coalition of developing countries pressing for ambitious reforms of agriculture in developed countries with some flexibility for developing countries (not to be confused with the G-20 group of finance ministers and central bank governors, and its recent summit meetings). It currently has 23 members: Argentina, the Bolivarian Republic of Venezuela, Bolivia, Brazil, Chile, China, Cuba, Ecuador, Egypt, Guatemala, India, Indonesia, Mexico, Nigeria, Pakistan, Paraguay, Peru, the Philippines, South Africa, Tanzania, Thailand, Uruguay, Zimbabwe. See http://www.wto.org/english/tratop_e/agric_e/negoti_groups_e.htm, accessed 2 September 2010.

FTA negotiations, these countries could develop the necessary negotiating expertise. Of course, it would not be good policy to risk FTAs with economically significant partners for the sake of honing the negotiating skills of the officials. This also explains why China chose to start the FTA negotiations with some countries that are less important economically. It is interesting to note that other countries in the region, such as Korea, also adopted the same strategy in their FTA negotiations.[38]

CONCLUSION

While initially reluctant to engage in FTA negotiations, China has gradually become an active player in the global rush to FTAs. While the number of China's FTAs still lags behind those of other major players, it is rapidly growing. As one of the most important trading nations in the world, China's decision to pursue an active path of FTA negotiation will undoubtedly have implications for all countries in the world. Before they can decide how to respond to China's FTA shopping spree, they must first understand China's FTA strategy. This chapter provides a critical analysis of this issue from economic, geo-political and legal perspectives. The chapter argues that, while economic considerations might be an important factor in China's decision to pursue FTAs, the main motivation so far seems to have been political considerations. In essence, China has been trying to use its FTA network to foster and reward strategic allies as part of its strategy to build an international environment conducive to China's goal of 'peaceful rise'. This presents challenges and opportunities for different countries. While some countries could be chosen as FTA partners due to their strategic importance, other countries might be left out for lack of strategic value. Thus, paradoxically, it seems that the best way for a country to jump on China's FTA bandwagon is to enhance its political significance to China rather than strengthen its economic ties with China. In a way, this is another tale of how politics has gone global with the help of trade, and hijacked trade into becoming its handmaiden during the process.

---

[38] See Sung-Hoon Park and Min Gyo Koo, 'Forming a Cross-regional Partnership: the South Korea–Chile FTA and its Implications', *Pacific Affairs*, 80 (2) (2007): 270, noting that Korea selected Chile as its first FTA partner with the explicit goal of capacity building.

6. Bilateral and regional trade agreements in Asia: a skeptic's view

Bryan Mercurio

INTRODUCTION

The per capita gross domestic product (GDP) of almost every Asian nation has rapidly risen throughout the last three decades.[1] During this time, intra-Asian regional trade has also grown at a brisk rate – in large part due to the enhanced specialization among regional industries and the interlinking of regional production networks which facilitate production sharing among and between companies.[2] Without doubt, liberalization commitments at the multilateral level have greatly assisted the process of deeper regional integration. So too has the corresponding expansion of bilateral and regional trade agreements (RTAs)[3] between and among Asian nations.[4] In some areas, liberalization commitments made as part of intra-Asian RTAs have been critical to the process of increased regional trade. Some commentators even go as far as saying that RTAs deserve the credit for increasing regional trade and increasing per capita GDP. It is the contention of this chapter, however, that the role of RTAs in expanding

---

[1] Statistics can be viewed at http://unstats.un.org/unsd/databases.htm, accessed 2 September 2010.

[2] See generally Prema-chandra Athukorala and Archanun Kohpaiboon, 'Intra-Regional Trade in East Asia: The Decoupling Fallacy, Crisis, and Policy Challenges', (2009) ADBI Working Paper Series No. 177, accessed 2 September 2010, http://www.adbi.org/files/2009.12.11.wp177.intra.regional.trade.east.asia.pdf.

[3] This chapter uses the abbreviation 'RTA' when generally referencing bilateral and regional trade agreements, and 'FTA' when referring to a specific agreement, regardless of the official moniker (e.g. Free Trade Agreement, Closer Economic Relations, Economic Partnership Agreement).

[4] For discussion, see Richard Baldwin, 'Multilateralizing Regionalism: Spaghetti Bowls as Building Blocks on the Path to Global Free Trade', *World Economy* 29 (11) (2009): 1451; Siow Yue Chia, 'Regional Trade Policy Cooperation and Architecture in East Asia' (2010) ADBI Working Paper Series No. 191, accessed 2 September 2010, http://www.adbi.org/files/2010.02.02.wp191.regional.trade.policy.east.asia.pdf.

regional trade in Asia has been overstated and exaggerated. Put simply, this chapter intends to demonstrate that most of the increased regional trade and per capita GDP growth in Asia occurred despite and not as a result of the growth of intra-regional RTAs. In other words, while it is true that the growth of RTAs occurred in the same time period as increased regional trade and per capita GDP growth, there is no significant causal relationship between the events. Taken further, this chapter asserts that intra-regional trade and per capita GDP in Asia would be far higher with the broadening of scope and coverage in Asian RTAs.

At present, Asian RTAs suffer from two main impediments which limit the effectiveness of intra-Asian RTAs. First, regional integration in Asia almost exclusively focuses on liberalization of market access for goods to the exclusion of other trade sectors and 'beyond the border' issues. These issues, which include non-tariff barriers, services, investment, intellectual property, government procurement and competition policy, are becoming increasingly important not only to world trade but also to the significance of trading relationships. The gradual reduction of tariff rates over the last 60 years resulting from membership in the GATT/WTO means that trade in other sectors and 'beyond the border' issues are becoming an important determining factor of trade volumes between countries. Second, Asian regional integration suffers from a low level of ambition; liberalization commitments are often not deep enough to be meaningful or are otherwise stymied by the presence of significant exclusions and non-tariff barriers which reduce the impact of the RTA. Taken together, the presence of these two impediments means that the coverage, depth and scope of Asian RTAs are simply not large enough to have a meaningful impact on the business community or broader economy.

As a result of the focus on trade in goods and the corresponding low level of ambition, the business community in Asia has essentially ignored the intra-regional RTAs. The utilization rates of intra-Asian RTAs, that is, the percentage of businesses which actually make use of the RTAs, are appallingly low when compared with those of other regions. Thus, while it is true that intra-Asian trade has increased throughout the last three decades, and particularly in the last decade, the low utilization rates demonstrate that the increased regional trade has not directly occurred as a result of the trade agreements. This also leads one to question how much more intra-Asian trade could have occurred had the trade agreements been more ambitious in their scope and coverage. Perhaps more importantly, the business community (and others) in Asia should question why almost all governments continue expending monetary and political capital negotiating multiple RTAs if the agreements are not even being utilized by the intended beneficiaries.

The end goal, for some, is the creation of an Asian Economic Community.[5] At this stage, the exact form this will take is uncertain, as is whether it is even politically feasible to do so. Such discussion is presently premature given the low levels of ambition of existing Asian RTAs. In order for any incarnation of an Asian Economic Community to be economically meaningful, Asian nations must raise their ambition and ensure that trade and community considerations take precedence (or at least compete with) internal political ones.

The next section elaborates on the two main factors which limit effective regional economic integration – a heavy focus on goods and low ambition. In large part, the section examines a select group of 16 existing intra-Asian trade agreements and contrasts their scope and coverage with five selected RTAs between a non-Asian developed country and an Asian country (whether developed or developing) in order to demonstrate the lack of ambition among intra-Asian RTAs.[6] In so doing, the section demonstrates how the low ambition and the focus on goods rather than other trade-related issues prevents effective regional integration. The third section surveys the utilization rates of several intra-Asian RTAs and evaluates the reasons why intra-Asian utilization rates are far lower than such rates in other regions for the purpose of demonstrating a link between low ambition and low utilization rates. The final section offers some recommendations on improving the make-up and utilization rates of intra-Asian RTAs.

TRADE LIBERALIZATION IN ASIAN RTAS

The biggest drawbacks to intra-Asian RTAs are the connected issues of focusing almost exclusively on the liberalization of goods while at the same time providing for only modest liberalization in the sector. In this regard, liberalization efforts are severely hampered and potential gains from the RTA curtailed. This section analyzes both issues in turn.

---

5   For discussion of the issues, see Chia, above note 4; Siow Yue Chia, 'Whither East Asian Regionalism? An ASEAN Perspective', *Asian Economic Papers* 6 (2007): 1; Nicholas Thomas, 'Developing an East Asian Economic Community', paper presented at the annual meeting of the International Studies Association, Hawaii, 5 March 2005, accessed 2 September 2010, available at http://www.allacademic.com/meta/p70707_index.html.

6   In order to demonstrate the heavy focus on goods in most intra-Asian RTAs, the section evaluates the differences in scope, coverage and level of commitments in three sectors: services, intellectual property and government procurement.

Focus on Goods

To date, the primary focus of intra-Asian RTAs is the liberalization of goods, with many such RTAs virtually ignoring issues such as non-tariff barriers, intellectual property, investment, services, government procurement and competition policy. This can be accomplished in one of two ways. First, the agreement could simply not include a particular trade sector within the scope of the RTA (for example, the agreement could have no provisions on services). Second, when a particular trade sector is included in the RTA, these provisions could simply reference, mirror or contain only slightly more detailed or comprehensive rules than the relevant WTO agreement. Both are particularly common in intra-Asian RTAs. Entire trade sectors are often excluded, and when they are included there is often little more than a re-affirmation of WTO norms. In some cases, certain sectors are included within the scope of a particular RTA merely through the parties agreeing to abide by existing obligations under a particular WTO agreement. Thus, intra-Asian RTAs neglect non-tariff issues either by failing to include chapters/provisions covering such issues in the RTA itself or by covering such issues in a cursory fashion.

Table 6.1 provides a listing of the coverage of 16 separate intra-Asian RTAs. Even a perfunctory inspection of the table reveals significant gaps in coverage of non-tariff-related issues. Such treatment of non-tariff issues is in distinct contrast to RTAs involving a non-Asian developed country, whether it be an RTA between non-Asian countries or even an RTA between a non-Asian developed country and an Asian country (whether developed or developing). Table 6.2 provides a similar analysis of the coverage of five RTAs between Asian countries and non-Asian developed countries. Again, even a perfunctory inspection reveals the significantly expanded coverage of this group of RTAs in comparison with the intra-Asian RTAs.

In order to demonstrate the disparity in scope and coverage between intra-Asian RTAs and RTAs between an Asian nation and a non-Asian developed country, this section evaluates the differences in scope, coverage and level of commitments in three sectors: services, intellectual property and government procurement. These three sectors represent a large and important share of international trade. They also represent three sectors of increasing importance to the business community. Liberalization and/or disciplines and commitments in these three sectors bring real benefits to employment levels and the growth of a nation. It follows that liberalization of these three sectors would be an important issue, if not a priority, for the business community. A large percentage of intra-Asian RTAs exclude these important issues from their scope. This is in

Table 6.1 Select intra-Asian RTAs

	Tariff reduction	Services	Contingency measures (AD, CVD and SG)[1]	Standard related measures (TBT, SPS)[2]	Intellectual property rights	Trade facilitation	Investment	Government procurement	Dispute settlement	Labour standards	Environment standards	Labour mobility	Technology transfer	Capacity building
ASEAN–South Korea	Yes	Yes	Yes: AD, CVD & SG	Yes	Yes	No	Yes	No	Yes	No	No	Yes	Yes	Yes
ASEAN–Japan	Yes	Yes	Yes: SG, AD	Yes	Yes	Yes	Yes	No	Yes	No	Yes	No	Yes	No
China–ASEAN	Yes	Yes	Yes: SG	No	Yes	No	Yes	No	No	No	No	No	No	No
China–Singapore	Yes	Yes	Yes: AD, CVD & SG	Yes	No	Yes	Yes	No	Yes	No	No	Yes	No	No
Pakistan–China	Yes	No	Yes: AD, CVD & SG	Yes: TBT, SPS	No	Yes	Yes	No	Yes	No	No	No	No	No
China–Hong Kong	Yes	Yes	Yes: AD, CVD & SG	No	No	Yes	No	No	No	No	No	No	No	No

Table 6.1 (continued)

	Tariff reduction	Services	Contingency measures (AD, CVD and SG)	Standard related measures (TBT, SPS)	Intellectual property rights	Trade facilitation	Investment	Government procurement	Dispute settlement	Labour standards	Environment standards	Labour mobility	Technology transfer	Capacity building
Japan–Philippines	Yes	Yes	Yes: AD, CVD & SG	No	Yes	No	Yes	Yes	Yes	Yes	Yes	No	No	No
Japan–Thailand	Yes	Yes	Yes: AD, CVD & SG	No	Yes	No	Yes	Yes	Yes	No	Yes	No	No	No
India–Singapore	Yes	Yes	Yes: AD, CVD & SG	Yes: TBT, SPS	Yes	Yes	Yes	No	Yes	No	No	Yes	No	No
Japan–Malaysia	Yes	Yes	No	No	Yes	No	Yes	No	Yes	Yes	Yes	No	No	No
South Korea–Singapore	Yes	Yes	Yes: AD, CVD & SG	Yes: TBT, SPS	Yes	Yes	Yes	Yes	Yes	No	Yes	No	No	Yes
Pakistan–Malaysia	Yes	No	No	No	No	No	No	No	No	No	No	No	No	No
Pakistan–Sir Lanka	Yes	No	Yes: SG	No	No	No	No	No	Yes	No	No	No	No	No

SAPTA (South Asian Preferential Trade Agreement)	Yes	No	Yes: SG	No	No	Yes	No	No	No	Yes	No	No
ASEAN Free Trade Agreement	Yes	Yes	Yes: SG	Yes	Yes	Yes	No	Yes	No	No	No	No
South Korea–India	Yes	Yes	Yes: AD, CVD & SG	Yes	Yes	Yes	Yes	Yes	No	Yes	No	No

Notes:
1   AD: anti-dumping; CVD: countervailing duties; SG: safeguards.
2   TBT: technical barriers to trade; SPS: sanitary and phytosanitary standards.
Yes: covered to some degree.
No: no coverage, completely excluded from the scope of the agreement.

Source: The table uses the template and format established in the UNCTAD–Japan External Trade Organization (JETRO), *South–South Trade in Asia: the Role of Regional Trade Agreements* (2008), 50–52.

Table 6.2 *Select RTAs between an Asian and a non-Asian developed country*

	Tariff reduction	Services	Contingency measures (AD, CVD and SG)[1]	Standard related measures (TBT, SPS)[2]	Intellectual property rights	Trade facilitation	Investment	Government procurement	Dispute settlement	Labour standards	Environment standards	Labour mobility	Technology transfer	Capacity building
Singapore–United States	Yes	Yes	Yes: AD, CVD & SG	Yes	Yes	Yes	Yes	Yes	Yes	Yes	Yes	Yes	No	No
Singapore–New Zealand	Yes	Yes	Yes: AD, CVD & SG	Yes	Yes	Yes	Yes	Yes	Yes	No	No	No	No	Yes
South Korea–EFTA	Yes	Yes	Yes: AD, CVD & SG	Yes	Yes	Yes	Yes	Yes	Yes	No	No	No	Yes	No
Trans-Pacific Partnership (P4)[3]	Yes	Yes	Yes: AD, CVD & SG	Yes	Yes	Yes	No	Yes	Yes	Yes	Yes	No	No	Yes
ASEAN–Australia–New Zealand	Yes	Yes	Yes: AD, CVD & SG	Yes	Yes	Yes	Yes	No	Yes	No	No	Yes	No	No

Notes:
1 AD: anti-dumping; CVD: countervailing duties; SG: safeguards.
2 TBT: technical barriers to trade; SPS: sanitary and phytosanitary standards.
3 Parties to the P4 are Brunei, Chile, New Zealand and Singapore.
Yes: covered to some degree.
No: no coverage, completely excluded from the scope of the agreement.

Source: The table uses the template and format established in the UNCTAD–Japan External Trade Organization (JETRO), *South–South Trade in Asia: the Role of Regional Trade Agreements* (2008), 50–52.

contradistinction to RTAs involving an Asian nation and a non-Asian developed nation. Moreover, as will be shown in the analysis below, the intra-Asian RTAs which do include such issues in their scope more often than not fail to provide meaningful commitments and liberalization so as to make a positive impact.

Services

Included into the multilateral trading system as part of the Uruguay Round of trade negotiations, services is 'the main sector of activity in high-income countries (both in terms of GDP and employment) and its importance is growing in lower-income countries'.[7]

In fact, trade in services represents more than two-thirds of world GDP, with the share of services constituting on average 71 per cent of total GDP in high-income countries, 55 per cent in middle-income countries and 47 per cent in low-income countries.[8] Services has been rising at a rate of over 10 per cent a year for the last decade (including 19 per cent growth in 2007 and 12 per cent growth in 2008)[9] and now accounts for 19 per cent of global trade.[10] The importance of services in the world economy, however, 'greatly exceeds its share in world trade . . . in part because these statistics only count cross-border transactions and not services provided through affiliates'.[11]

The growing economic importance of services has also had an effect on the structure of modern RTAs. For instance, only 11 RTAs contained provisions on services in 1999, a figure which had risen to 82 agreements by March 2010 (out of 202 RTAs in force).[12] Moreover, 39 of the 62 RTAs coming into force since 1 January 2006 include services.[13]

Owing to the structure and rules contained in the WTO General Agreement on Trade in Services (GATS) and the level of commitments

---

[7]   WTO, *Annual Report 2002*, 37, accessed 2 September 2010, http://www.wto.org/english/res_e/booksp_e/anrep_e/anrep02_e.pdf.

[8]   Simon Lester and Bryan Mercurio, *World Trade Law: Text, Materials and Commentary* (Oxford: Hart Publishing, 2008), 597.

[9]   WTO International Trade Statistics 2009, accessed 2 September 2010, http://www.wto.org/english/res_e/statis_e/its2009_e/its09_toc_e.htm.

[10]   Federico Ortino, 'Services' in Simon Lester and Bryan Mercurio (eds), *Bilateral and Regional Trade Agreements: Commentary and Analysis* (Cambridge University Press, 2009), 184. See also Lester and Mercurio, above note 8, 597.

[11]   WTO, *Annual Report 2002*, above note 7, 37.

[12]   Statistics compiled by the author using the WTO RTA Database, accessed 2 September 2010, http://rtais.wto.org/UI/PublicMaintainRTAHome.aspx.

[13]   Ibid.

made by Member States in their individual Schedules, there is significant scope for deep and meaningful liberalization in services through RTAs.[14] Developed countries usually take advantage of these opportunities by negotiating comprehensive chapters on services in their RTAs.[15] In fact, liberalization of services accounts for a greater percentage of total gains than trade in goods in some RTAs.[16]

Thirteen of the 16 intra-Asian RTAs surveyed include provisions on trade in services.[17] For the most part, intra-Asian RTAs that include services follow a positive list approach (whereby services are liberalized only to the extent that they are positively included and mentioned) as opposed to the generally more liberalizing negative list approach (all sectors are liberalized except those specifically excluded) favoured by many non-Asian developed countries.[18] Moreover, the majority of intra-Asian RTAs do not provide for most favoured nation treatment. In some agreements, commitments in certain sectors and sub-sectors are unquestionably GATS-Plus, those which include more detailed rules or a higher level of commitments than those contained in the GATS. This is particularly the case with Mode 4 (natural movements of persons) commitments in intra-Asian RTAs. On the whole, however, liberalization commitments do not significantly go further than existing GATS commitments.

---

[14] For the background of the GATS, see Markus Krajewski, *National Regulation and Trade Liberalization in Services: The Legal Impact of the General Agreement on Trade in Services* (The Hague: Kluwer Law International, 2003). See also the groundbreaking research of Fink and Molinuevo: Carsten Fink and Martin Molinuevo, 'East Asian Free Trade Agreements in Services: Key Architectural Elements', *Journal of International Economic Law* 11 (2008): 263.

[15] For the types of commitments made in RTAs, see Federico Ortino, above note 10; Markus Krajewski, 'Services Liberalization in Regional Trade Agreements: Lessons for GATS "Unfinished Business"?' in Lorand Bartels and Federico Ortino (eds), *Regional Trade Agreements and the WTO Legal System* (Oxford: Oxford University Press, 2006).

[16] See generally Carsten Fink and Marion Jansen, 'Services Provisions in Regional Trade Agreements: Stumbling Blocks or Building Blocks for Multilateral Liberalization?' in Richard Baldwin and Patrick Low (eds), *Multilateralizing Regionalism: Challenges for the Global Trading System* (Cambridge: Cambridge University Press, 2009).

[17] Those excluding services include: Pakistan–China, Pakistan–Malaysia and Pakistan–Sri Lanka. Broadly speaking, South Asian counties (less India) are generally averse to including services in RTAs.

[18] See Sherry Stephenson, 'Regional versus Multilateral Liberalization of Services', *World Trade Review* 1 (2002): 187. It should be noted that the negative list approach does not always result in more liberalization than the positive list approach. See, for example, http://www.rieti.go.jp/jp/publications/dp/07e015.pdf, accessed 2 September 2010; Fink and Molinuevo, above note 14, 275–9.

In most respects, intra-Asian RTAs are closely modeled on the GATS structure, rules and approach to liberalization.[19] As mentioned, very few agreements contain GATS-Plus provisions. That being said, ASEAN (in its internal agreement but less so in its RTAs with other countries),[20] South Korea, Japan and Singapore have used their RTAs to provide for greater transparency, openness and liberalization.[21] The latter three countries are willing to embrace a negative list approach in their RTAs and consistently attempt to make improved or new commitments in all sub-sectors and modes.[22]

Generally speaking, intra-Asian RTAs do little to substantially liberalize the services sector beyond that which is agreed in the GATS. This has led numerous studies to conclude that intra-Asian services commitments produce very little actual liberalization and, correspondingly, very little economic benefit.[23] While this is understandable given the GATS commitment levels of most Asian countries, it is undesirable from an economic standpoint and severely detrimental to efforts to promote regional integration.

Intellectual Property

Intellectual property rights became directly incorporated into the multilateral trading regime in 1995 with the creation of the WTO. Negotiated as part of the Uruguay Round of trade negotiations, the Agreement on Trade-Related Aspects of Intellectual Property Rights (TRIPS) establishes the intellectual property rules, standards and disciplines at the multilateral level. Building from existing IP-related treaties, most notably the Paris Convention and the Berne Convention, the TRIPS Agreement expands

---

[19]   This is not the case with all other agreements. See Ryo Ochiai, Philippa Dee and Christopher Findlay, 'Services in Free Trade Agreements' (2007), RIETI Discussion Paper Series 07-E -015, accessed 2 September 2010, http://www.rieti. go.jp/jp/publications/dp/07e015.pdf.

[20]   Although it must be noted that several countries have in certain sectors made deeper GATS commitments than in the ASEAN series agreement.

[21]   See further Carsten Fink and Martin Molinuevo, 'East Asian Free Trade Agreements in Services: Roaring Tigers or Timid Pandas?' (2007) World Bank Policy Research Paper, 66–7.

[22]   See, for example, Korea–Singapore FTA, Japan–Mexico FTA. See Fink and Molinuevo, above note 21, 65–6.

[23]   See, for example, Ray Trewin et al., 'East Asian FTAs: Facilitating Free Flow of Services in ASEAN?' (2008) REPSF II Project No. 07/004 (calling intra-Asian RTA commitments in services 'generally weak in their liberalisation both relative to the WTO and unilateral liberalisations'), 3.

topical coverage, standards and procedures by which Member States must abide. Trade agreements also commonly contain some additional level of commitments in the IP sector. These commitments, known as 'TRIPS-Plus' provisions, add both in scope and topical coverage to existing levels of commitments within the TRIPS Agreement. Several TRIPS-Plus provisions are controversial, and it is not the intent of this chapter to discuss the worthiness, appropriateness or effect of such provisions. These issues are thoroughly discussed elsewhere in existing literature;[24] instead, the intent of this section is merely to demonstrate that the coverage of intra-Asian RTAs is significantly less than that of most RTAs, including RTAs between Asian and non-Asian developed countries.

Seventy-nine of the 202 agreements in force contain provisions on IPRs, including 34 of the 75 agreements coming into force since 1 January 2005. The inclusion of IPRs in RTAs is clearly the result of a strategy by developed countries to increase standards – almost all agreements involving at least one developed country partner include a chapter or provisions on IPRs (including all five of the surveyed agreements between an Asian country and a non-Asian developed country). By contrast, five of the intra-Asian agreements surveyed do not contain any provisions on IPRs.

More meaningfully, RTAs involving a non-Asian developed country provide for substantial commitments in all areas of IPRs, such as the broadening of criminal procedures and penalties relating to the enforcement of IPRs, term extensions and technical protection measures in the area of copyright, the extension of the scope and coverage of protection of geographical indications, and term extensions, the protection of test data and limits on compulsory licensing in the area of patents.[25] By contrast, most intra-Asian agreements including provisions on IPRs do little

---

[24] See, for example, Jayashree Watal, *Intellectual Property Rights in the WTO and Developing Countries* (Oxford: Oxford University Press, 2001); Peter Drahos, 'Expanding Intellectual Property's Empire: the Role of FTAs' (2003), accessed 2 September 2010, http://www.grain.org; Sisule Musungu and Cecilia Oh, *The Use of Flexibilities in TRIPS by Developing Countries: Can They Promote Access to Medicine?*, Commission on Intellectual Property Rights, Innovation and Public Health, Study 4C (2005), accessed 2 September 2010, http://www.who.int/intellectualproperty/studies/TRIPSFLEXI.pdf; Bryan Mercurio, 'TRIPS-Plus Provisions in FTAs: Recent Trends' in L. Bartels and F. Ortino (eds), *Regional Trade Agreements and the WTO Legal System* (Oxford: Oxford University Press, 2006); and Michael Handler and Bryan Mercurio, 'Intellectual Property' in Simon Lester and Bryan Mercurio (eds), *Bilateral and Regional Trade Agreements: Commentary and Analysis* (Cambridge: Cambridge University Press, 2009).

[25] For an overview, see Handler and Mercurio, above note 24.

(or even no) more than reaffirm existing rights and obligations under the TRIPS Agreement.[26]

Chapter 12 of the India–South Korea FTA is typical of most intra-Asian provisions on IPRs. The chapter is limited and does not provide for any real commitments.[27] Instead, the chapter simply reaffirms existing rights under the TRIPS Agreement (including the right to provide more extensive protection of IPRs than accorded under the TRIPS Agreement and the right to enforce IPRs in a manner consistent with the TRIPS Agreement)[28] and provides for cooperation in the field of intellectual property.[29] Moreover, Article 12.6 explicitly states that the chapter is not subject to the Agreement's dispute settlement provisions.

Likewise, the South Korea–Singapore FTA merely reaffirms existing obligations under the TRIPS Agreement, provides for the enforcement of IPRs, allows the Parties to implement more extensive protection of intellectual property rights than required by the Agreement[30] and establishes a Joint Sub-Committee on IPRs.[31] In addition, the Parties endeavour to enhance cooperation in the protection of plant varieties.[32] Of note, Singapore did agree to designate the Korean Intellectual Property Office as a prescribed patent office to facilitate processing of patent applications in Singapore that correspond to patent applications in South Korea.[33]

Chapter 11 of the India–Singapore FTA contains even fewer provisions and merely calls for cooperation, including the organization of symposia, seminars, workshops and other training programmes and joint

---

[26]   See, for example, Chapter 10 of the Pakistan–Malaysia FTA.

[27]   Another provision, Article 5.9.3(f), commits both parties in the areas of customs to 'promot[e] a strong and efficient regime of intellectual property rights in accordance with their laws and regulations'.

[28]   See Article 12.2, 12.3 and 12.4.

[29]   Article 12.5 provides that the parties endeavour to enhance cooperation in the field of intellectual property through (a) education, workshops, fairs, etc., in the field of intellectual property for the purposes of contributing to a better understanding of each other's intellectual property policies and experiences; (b) international search and international preliminary examination under PCT, and facilitation of international patenting process; (c) joint prior art search, including exchanging prior art search result, comparing search result, and reviewing differences of search result; (d) licensing of intellectual property, and market intelligence for intellectual property protection; (e) plant variety protection; (f) personnel interchange, including examiners; and (g) information systems on intellectual property. The parties may also promote cooperation through separate arrangements as mutually agreed.

[30]   See Articles 17.1–17.4.

[31]   Article 17.9.

[32]   Article 17.5.

[33]   Article 17.7.

consideration of collaboration in projects including the development of programmes, platforms, tools and other infrastructure to promote the effective use and application of intellectual property rights.[34] The ASEAN–China FTA contains only one 'commitment' – that both parties abide by their existing obligations under the TRIPS Agreement.[35]

By contrast, a few intra-Asian RTAs provide TRIPS-Plus provisions in certain areas. For instance, Article 127 of the Japan–Philippines FTA directs the Parties to endeavour to increase the number of plant genera and species that can be protected under their laws and regulations. This can be distinguished from Article 27.3(b) of the TRIPS Agreement, which provides for the possibility of Members to exclude from patentability plants other than micro-organisms. The Agreement also goes beyond the TRIPS Agreement by expanding the scope of eligible criminal procedures and penalties to be applied for the infringement of rights relating to new varieties of plants or infringement or repetition of infringement of patents, utility models, industrial designs or layout-designs of integrated circuits on a 'commercial scale'.[36]

On the whole, parties to intra-Asian agreements do little more than merely recognize and agree to abide by existing obligations in the TRIPS Agreement in a number of ways. This is in contradistinction to recent RTAs involving a non-Asian developed country, which provide for meaningful commitments in almost all areas of IPRs.[37]

Government Procurement

Government procurement can be defined as:

> the process by which a government obtains the use of or acquires goods or services, or any combination thereof, for governmental purposes and not with a view to commercial sale or resale or use in the production or supply of goods or services for commercial sale or resale.[38]

---

[34] Article 11.1 and 11.2.
[35] Article 7 of the ASEAN–China FTA, entitled 'WTO Disciplines', simply states: '[T]he Parties hereby agree and reaffirm their commitments to abide by the provisions of the WTO disciplines on, among others, non-tariff measures, technical barriers to trade, sanitary and phytosanitary measures, subsidies and countervailing measures, anti-dumping measures and intellectual property rights'.
[36] Article 129.3 states: 'Remedies available shall include imprisonment and/or monetary fines sufficient to provide a deterrent, consistently with the level of penalties applied for crimes of a corresponding gravity as may be provided for in the laws and regulations of each Party'.
[37] See Handler and Mercurio, above note 24.
[38] Article 1.3 of the Korea–India FTA.

Underestimated and virtually ignored until recently, businesses and governments are now fully aware of the opportunities presented by public procurement. In fact, it is estimated that in developed countries government procurement represents 7–14 per cent of GDP.[39] For this reason, the WTO's Agreement on Government Procurement (GPA) promotes open, transparent and non-discriminatory procurement practices.[40] Originally negotiated as part of the Tokyo Round (and coming into force on 1 January 1981) and revised during the Uruguay Round, the GPA remains one of a few plurilateral agreements (meaning Members are not obligated to be signatories to the agreement) within the WTO. Counting members of the European Union as individual WTO Members, a total of 40 nations have signed the GPA. Included among the signatories are five Asian WTO Members: Hong Kong, South Korea, Japan, Singapore and Taiwan. With such a low take-up rate among nations, significant gains could be made by opening up government bidding and tender processes among and between RTA partner countries.

Several governments are taking advantage of the opportunities to benefit from government procurement provisions/chapters in RTAs. In total, 64 RTAs in force meaningfully include government procurement (out of 202 RTAs in force),[41] with the vast majority of RTAs having some government procurement content or references to procurement.[42] Similarly to the situation of services, the percentage of RTAs including government procurement is rising. In fact, almost half of all RTAs containing government procurement have come into force since January 2005. In total, 29 of the 75 RTAs coming into force from 1 January 2005 contain government procurement content.[43]

For a country that is not a signatory to the GPA, including provisions in an RTA allows for its businesses to bid on and win government procurement contracts in its partner countries.[44] It also means that the country opens its procurement market only to businesses from its partner countries

---

[39]   Sue Arrowsmith, *Government Procurement in the WTO* (London: Kluwer Law International, 2003), 3.

[40]   For a brief introduction to the GPA, see http://www.wto.org/english/ tratop_e/gproc_e/gpa_overview_e.htm.

[41]   WTO   RTA   Database,   available   at   http://rtais.wto.org/UI/ PublicMaintainRTAHome.aspx, accessed 2 September 2010.

[42]   See Arwel Davies, 'Government Procurement' in Simon Lester and Bryan Mercurio (eds), *Bilateral and Regional Trade Agreements: Commentary and Analysis* (Cambridge: Cambridge University Press, 2009), 274.

[43]   Twenty-one of the total 62 RTAs coming in force from 1 January 2006 contain provisions on government procurement.

[44]   For the type of commitments made in RTAs, see Davies, above note 42.

as opposed to all WTO Members. Recent history shows that economic benefits can be gained from such a situation. For instance, Australia is not a signatory to the GPA but has included provisions on government procurement (essentially mirroring in most respects provisions of the GPA) in several of its recent RTAs. As a result, Australian businesses have bid for and won several lucrative supply contracts (most notably in the United States) which they would not have been permitted to bid for without the RTA (or in some cases, bids from non-signatory countries are subject to a penalty – that is, 10 per cent additional costs).[45]

Unfortunately, most Asian nations have ignored the potential opportunities and gains from including provisions on government procurement in their RTAs. Only 4 of 16 intra-Asian RTAs surveyed contain provisions relating to government procurement.[46] By contrast, the majority of RTAs negotiated by developed countries and even four of the five surveyed RTAs between an Asian country and a non-Asian developed country include government procurement.[47] Among the five intra-Asian RTAs that include government procurement, it is clear that only Japan and South Korea promote the insertion of such provisions. Conversely, ASEAN and China oppose the inclusion of procurement in their agreements. Other nations, such as Singapore, will include such provisions but do not actively lobby for their inclusion in RTAs.[48]

Even where included in an intra-Asian RTA, most government procurement provisions are quite weak and contribute little to the liberalization of the sector. For example, Article 13.12 of the South Korea–India FTA

---

[45] For instance, the Buy American Act (1933, 41 USC 10) imposes a 6 per cent penalty on foreign goods; this penalty can be waived as a result of provisions in the various US RTAs.

[46] Agreements with provisions on government procurement include: Japan–Philippines, Japan–Thailand, Korea–Singapore and Korea–India. One additional agreement, the SAPTA, allows for negotiations in the public procurement sector but at present provides no rules or commitments. See SAPTA, definition of 'direct trade measures' and Articles 4 and 5.

[47] The ASEAN–Australia–New Zealand FTA excludes government procurement, which is not surprising given ASEAN's reluctance to include the sector in any of its RTAs (and even in the ASEAN AFTA) and the fact that none of the parties to the agreement are signatories to the GPA.

[48] Singapore includes provisions on government procurement in its RTAs with EFTA, Japan, Jordan, Korea, New Zealand, Panama, Peru, Australia, the TPP and the United States. Singaporean agreements which do not include provisions on government procurement include those with ASEAN, China and India. Thus, Singapore includes provisions on government procurement in its agreements with non-Asian countries (and Korea and Japan) but excludes such provisions in its RTAs with Asian countries.

simply recognizes the importance of government procurement and states that each party will 'endeavour to promote cooperative activities between the Parties in the field of government procurement'. The Article then provides a non-exhaustive list of four items which 'may' be included in such cooperation:

(a)   promoting the exchange of information and views on government procurement policies and regulatory framework;
(b)   providing each other with accumulated knowledge, experience and information;
(c)   facilitating the exchange of knowledge, experience and information on e-Procurement;
(d)   designating contact points for information exchange.

The Agreement, therefore, contains no binding commitments and will provide no economic benefit to either party.

While likewise not requiring any commitments or providing any tangible economic benefit, the Japan–Thailand FTA goes one step farther in providing for (1) the exchange of information on laws, regulations, policies, practices and reforms on government procurement; and (2) the establishment of a Sub-Committee on Government Procurement to discuss, *inter alia*, 'ways to enhance cooperation for mutual benefit of the Parties in the field of government procurement'.[49]

Chapter 11 of the Japan–Philippines FTA (which contains four Articles) is similar to the provisions of the Japan–Thailand FTA but is potentially more useful in several respects. First, the Agreement offers potential gains to both parties by 'recogniz[ing] that it is important for a Party to accord national treatment and most-favored-nation treatment to goods, services and suppliers of the other Party with respect to the measures regarding government procurement, with a view to achieving greater liberalization and expansion of trade between the Parties'.[50] The Agreement further provides that where one partner country offers a non-partner country 'any advantages of access to its government procurement market or any advantageous treatment concerning the measures regarding government procurement' that country must enter into negotiations with the other partner 'with a view to extending these advantages or advantageous treatment to the other Party'.[51] Next, the Chapter establishes what could

---

[49]   Japan–Thailand FTA, Articles 145 and 146.
[50]   Article 131.
[51]   Article 132.

become quite a meaningful Sub-Committee on Government Procurement as the parties have included in its mandate the authority to discuss, *inter alia*, the possibility of according national and MFN treatments to goods, services, and suppliers of the other Party and consistency of each Party's government procurement measures with international principles on government procurement, such as the GPA.[52] Finally, Article 134 requires the parties to enter further negotiations with a view to liberalizing procurement practices in each country.

By contrast, the South Korea–Singapore FTA includes a more extensive chapter on government procurement (Chapter 16). Both signatories to the GPA, Chapter 16 of the agreement begins by explicitly reaffirming the rights and obligations under the WTO GPA[53] before stating that the procurement procedures under the agreement are to be applied in accordance with GPA Articles II–IV, VI–XV, XVI:1, XVIII, XIX:1–4, XX, XXIII; Notes; and Appendices II–IV.[54] Moreover, Article 16(1)(4) contains a statement of commitment to transparency and non-discriminatory treatment in the sector by stating that the parties desire to apply the APEC (Asia-Pacific Economic Cooperation) Non-Binding Principles on Government Procurement for government procurement that is not covered by the GPA or Chapter 16 of the agreement. However, the immediate economic effect of the agreement is limited. The only tangible gains for either party are the lowering of certain thresholds. For instance, the thresholds for procurement of goods and services (at the central government level) have been decreased to SDR100 000 compared with SDR130 000 under the GPA (whereas threshold levels for construction services remain the same as those under the GPA).[55] With respect to all other entities (except the sub-central level),[56] the thresholds are set at SDR400 000 (which represents a decrease for South Korea compared with its GPA threshold of SDR450 000). Thresholds on services and construction services for both parties remain the same.

The above review of government procurement provisions contained in intra-Asian RTAs clearly demonstrates the lack of desire to liberalize

---

[52] Article 133.

[53] Korea–Singapore FTA, Article 16.1.1

[54] Ibid., at Article 16.3. Article 16.3.4 also provides for the possibility of amending the agreement if the GPA is amended or superseded by another agreement.

[55] The GPA thresholds are contained in document WT/Let/543 (23 May 2006) for Korea and WT/Let/429 (11 August 2002) for Singapore.

[56] At the sub-central level, Korea offered no decrease in threshold level. Singapore does not have any sub-central levels.

this increasingly important sector. The vast majority of intra-Asian RTAs exclude the sector entirely. When it is included in intra-Asian RTAs, liberalization commitments are either non-existent or minimal at best. This, of course, is unfortunate from an economic viewpoint as liberalization of the sector not only provides clear rules and transparency to the bidding process but also lowers government purchasing costs while providing opportunities for domestic companies to bid for contracts with partner governments.

Too Few Commitments, Too Many Exceptions and Exclusions

While many of the recent intra-Asian RTAs go beyond the mere liberalization of trade in goods in some fashion, the focus of intra-Asian RTAs remains on trade in goods. This is perhaps not surprising given the manufacturing and agricultural bases of most Asian countries. What is surprising, however, is the disappointingly modest level of ambition among intra-Asian RTAs. Simply stated, most intra-Asian agreements combine low levels of tariff line coverage with low levels of preferential margins. As such, few intra-Asian RTAs would meet any meaningful 'substantially all trade' test.[57] In other words, it is a stretch even to call most intra-Asian RTAs legitimate 'free trade agreements'.[58] Other intra-Asian RTAs ostensibly liberalize a large percentage of trade between the parties, but contain long lists of Sensitive or Highly Sensitive products (usually of great interest to the exporters of the trading partner) subject to lesser cuts, longer implementation periods or no liberalization.[59] Such

---

[57]   Article XXIV of the GATT provides the legal basis for RTAs, including the 'substantially all trade' test. It is generally thought that a quantitative figure of 80–90 per cent of tariff lines or a qualitative method based on broad sectoral coverage is needed to meet the test. Note, RTAs between developing countries can still be in accordance with the GATT via the Enabling Clause. For more on Article XXIV's requirements and its relationship to RTAs, see Andrew D. Mitchell and Nicholas J.S. Lockhart, 'Legal Requirements for PTAs under the WTO' in Simon Lester and Bryan Mercurio (eds), *Bilateral and Regional Trade Agreements: Commentary and Analysis* (Cambridge: Cambridge University Press, 2009).

[58]   See also UNCTAD–Japan External Trade Organization (JETRO), 'South–South Trade in Asia: the Role of Regional Trade Agreements' (2008), xvi, accessed 2 September 2010, http://www.unctad.org/en/docs/ditctabmisc20082_en.pdf ('only a limited number of [South–South] RTAs can be regarded as genuine "free trade agreements" at this stage').

[59]   For examples of such issues in relation to ASEAN, see Ludo Cuyvers, Philippe De Lombaerde and Stijn Verherstraeten, 'From AFTA Towards an ASEAN Economic Community . . . and Beyond' (2005) CAS Discussion Paper No. 46, accessed September 2010, http://webh01.ua.ac.be/cas/PDF/CAS46.pdf.

exceptions significantly detract from the economic benefits of the RTAs. Furthermore, intra-Asian RTAs contain several 'pullbacks' which allow countries to halt or pull back trade preferences granted to the other party under certain circumstances. In combination these factors undoubtedly minimize actual liberalization and stymie potential gains and prospective growth. Every intra-Asian RTA also contains complex rules of origin requirements which complicate compliance and can detract from the usefulness of the agreements.

It is not an exaggeration to state that the majority of intra-Asian RTAs suffer from low levels of tariff line coverage. For instance, using RTAs negotiated by China as an example, the majority of Chinese RTAs would fail the 'substantially all trade' test of Article XXIV of the GATT. For instance, the China–Pakistan FTA makes extensive use of phase-ins and exclusions and, at best, will cover only 85 per cent of tariff lines for China and 83.6 per cent for Pakistan in 2012. In other words, China has made no commitments on 15 per cent of tariff lines, including in the agriculture, chemical and electronics sectors. For its part, Pakistan has made no commitments on 16.4 per cent of tariff lines, including in the agriculture and energy sectors and some manufacturing sectors. If liberalization occurs at the fullest extent possible under the agreement (a very doubtful proposition), 70 per cent of Pakistani goods and 55.5 per cent of Chinese exports will eventually receive duty free treatment in the other market.[60] The recently agreed China–Taiwan FTA is even less comprehensive, with Taiwan only reducing or eliminating tariff rates on a total of 267 goods and China reducing or eliminating duties on 539 items.

The Malaysia–Pakistan FTA is another example of an intra-Asian agreement with low ambition. In fact, the agreement contains far more exceptions and exclusions than it does liberalization commitments. Under an Early Harvest Programme which came into force in 2007, MFN tariffs of less than 5 per cent are scheduled to be eliminated while tariffs of 10 per cent are to be reduced by 50 per cent. However, the Programme only

---

[60] The China–Hong Kong EPA is also illustrative of the point. Although special in the sense that Hong Kong has technically been returned to China, Hong Kong maintains its own customs regime and has the ability to negotiate RTAs with other countries. Under the CEPA, China initially granted effective preferential tariffs on below 15 per cent of Hong Kong exports to China. The agreement, however, was updated to expand coverage from 273 items in 2004 to an additional 529 items in 2005. Updates in subsequent years have significantly expanded the scope of the agreement. The China–Macao EPA is similar, with the agreement effectively only covering 8.6 per cent of Macanese exports to China in 2005. In both the Hong Kong and the Macao CEPA, there are no transparent, predetermined phase-ins, merely occasional updates which expand topical coverage.

applies to a very limited number of tariff lines for each party – Malaysia agreed to liberalize 114 tariff lines (yarn, clothing and textile products) and Pakistan agreed to liberalize 125 tariff lines (electrical appliances and machinery, plastics, chemicals, rubber and timber products).[61] That the agreement contains liberalization commitments in so few sectors prompts the question of whether it can indeed be called a free trade agreement. Instead, it seems to be the type of agreement that Article XXIV of the GATT seeks to prevent, a commodities arrangement or liberalization of merely a few sectors.

Perhaps the most egregious example of low ambition levels in an RTA can be seen in the SAPTA, where the preferential margin is less than 3 per cent for all members and the coverage rates of effective preferential tariffs in 2006 were: Sri Lanka 3.4 per cent, Pakistan 5.5 per cent, Bangladesh 7.1 per cent, the Maldives 7.1 per cent, India 15.3 per cent and Nepal 42.2 per cent. Moreover, party lists of sensitive products total 16–23 per cent for all LDCs, and 16.3 per cent for India (Bhutan's sensitive product list admirably totals only 3.0 per cent of its lines). While tariff reductions are scheduled for 2013 and 2016, many parties will still cover less than 80 per cent of tariff lines in 2016 (namely Bangladesh (76 per cent), Nepal (75.5 per cent), Pakistan (77.4 per cent) and Sri Lanka (79.7 per cent)). By combining low tariff preferences, low sectoral coverage and a high number of exceptions and exclusions, the parties to the SAPTA have almost guaranteed that the agreement will produce minimal, if any, economic benefit.

While the SAPTA is overtly low in ambition, the ASEAN–China FTA at first glance gives the appearance of being a full-scale RTA; for instance, approximately 90 per cent of ASEAN and 93 per cent of Chinese goods were scheduled to be cut to zero per cent in 2010 (so-called 'Normal Track' goods). The tariff reduction/elimination schedule and tariff line coverage for the ASEAN+6 (Brunei Darussalam, Indonesia, Malaysia, the Philippines, Singapore and Thailand) are comprehensive and should elicit some gains. However, 'Sensitive' and 'Highly Sensitive' Lists of products are extensive for each partner country and in certain instances will severely curtail potential gains from the agreement. In fact, these lists cover a significant portion of actual trade flows between the two countries. This is especially the case with ASEAN exports to China, which managed to place 139 items on the Sensitive List and 138 items on the Highly Sensitive List, including important ASEAN export sectors such as agriculture, automobiles, chemicals and electronics. In total, all automobiles, over 400 agricultural tariff lines, over 300 tariff lines for plastic and rubber, almost 300 tariff lines

---

[61]   References to tariff line commitments are at the six-digit level.

for transport machinery, over 250 tariff lines for steel and steel products, over 200 tariff lines for garments, and hundreds of other tariff lines (including textiles, paper products, footwear, heavy machinery, air conditioners, refrigerators, washing machines and other household electrical appliances) appear on the Sensitive or Highly Sensitive List for China and the various ASEAN countries.[62] Moreover, trade between China and the four LDC members of ASEAN (Cambodia, Lao PDR, Myanmar and Vietnam) is barely liberalized – Sensitive and Highly Sensitive Lists are extensive (for example, 67.3 per cent of Chinese exports to Cambodia are on the Sensitive or Highly Sensitive List) and phase-in periods remain until 2020.

Perhaps more importantly, the agreement includes a principle of reciprocity whereby preferential tariff rates are offered only on goods designated as in the Normal Track by both trading partners; in other words, even if a country designates a certain good as in the Normal Track, that country is under no obligation to offer the preferential rate to an ASEAN trading partner if that country lists the same good as Sensitive or Highly Sensitive. For this reason, the amount of actual Normal Track liberalization is likely to be far less than the number of goods listed as Normal Track.

Even the relatively comprehensive RTA between South Korea and Singapore contains long phase-ins and a long list of exclusions of 'sensitive products' for Singaporean exports to South Korea. In fact, even though almost 60 per cent of tariff lines are granted duty-free access to Singaporean exports, it is estimated that only 75 per cent of actual Singaporean exports receive any preferential tariff treatment into South Korea. While tariff rates on most items are to be reduced and/or eliminated within a ten-year phase-in period (by 2016), exclusions will remain on such 'sensitive products' (that is, hundreds of agricultural, fishery and chemical products). Likewise, the India–Singapore FTA provided for immediate duty-free access to the Indian market for less than 10 per cent of product lines (506 products in total), with an additional 2202 products benefiting from phased elimination and 2407 products receiving phased tariff reductions of up to 50 per cent by 2009. Even then, the agreement excludes 6551 Singaporean goods from its scope. Thus, a greater percentage of Singaporean goods receive no tariff reduction or elimination than those that benefit under the agreement.[63]

---

[62]   For a brief analysis, see 'Free Trade Agreements in Asia: A Progress Report' (October 2009) 4 (6) (Bank of Tokyo-Mitsubishi UFJ, Ltd, Economic Research Office) *Economic Review* 1, accessed 2 September 2010, http://www.bk.mufg.jp/report/ecorev2009e/ecoreview_e20091014.pdf.

[63]   For a list of the 6551 excluded items, see http://www.fta.gov.sg/ceca/annex%202a%20-%20tariff%20schedule%20of%20india.pdf, accessed 2 September 2010.

In addition to low coverage and extensive Sensitive and Highly Sensitive Product Lists, intra-Asian RTAs also limit liberalization commitments through the use of pullbacks. Pullbacks halt liberalization by either suspending future preferential commitments or removing preferences granted under the agreement. The pullback of choice for most intra-Asian RTAs is the use of safeguards. All 16 surveyed intra-Asian RTAs provide for the use of safeguards if increased imports from an RTA partner constitute a substantial cause of serious injury (or threat of injury) to a domestic industry. In most instances, intra-Asian RTAs authorize both global and bilateral safeguards. In global safeguards, the parties to an agreement retain the right to apply a safeguard measure (in accordance with Article XIX of the GATT 1994 and the WTO Agreement on Safeguards, or Article 5 of the WTO Agreement on Agriculture).[64] In such cases, imports originating from the RTA partner country would be included in the application of a safeguard measure pursuant to Article XXIX of the GATT 1994 and the WTO Agreement on Safeguards. By contrast, bilateral safeguards allow a country to impose safeguards against goods originating in an RTA partner country provided they are imported in such increased quantities (either in absolute terms or relative to domestic production) and under such conditions that the imports constitute a substantial cause of serious injury or threat thereof to the domestic industry of the importing party.[65] In such cases, the aggrieved party can either suspend further reductions under the RTA or increase the relevant tariff rate to the MFN applied rate.

The impact of safeguards in RTAs, of course, varies between and among agreements depending upon, *inter alia*, the text of the agreements, the nature of the trading relationship among the RTA partner countries and the importance of political and policy determinations made in each country. Finally, the definition and determination of the threshold which triggers the right to implement the safeguard is a key determinant in whether the RTA will truly be trade liberalizing or whether protectionist instincts prevail. For instance, Article 23 of the Japan–Malaysia FTA uses the traditional definition of an increase in imports in absolute or relative terms, causing or threatening to cause serious injury. It further defines 'serious injury' as 'a significant overall impairment in the position of a domestic industry' and 'threat of serious injury' as 'serious injury that, on the basis of facts and not merely on allegation, conjecture or remote possibility, is clearly imminent'.[66] The incorporation of such definitions

---

[64]   See, for example, Article 23.6 of the Japan–Malaysia FTA.
[65]   See, for example, Article 23 of the Japan–Malaysia FTA.
[66]   Article 16.

provides little predictability, as they allow for a wide range of local determinations. The incorporation of actual quantitative triggers provides
for absolute certainty but explicitly limits the liberalizing effect of the
agreement.

Most intra-Asian RTAs fail to meet any 'substantially all trade' test
and some appear to merely be sectoral arrangements. Too often, intra-
Asian RTAs contain too few commitments, provide too little tariff rate
reduction, and contain too many exclusions and sensitive/highly sensitive
products, and provide for considerable preferential pullbacks (mostly in
the form of safeguards). Perhaps most damning, an UNCTAD study published in 2008 found only one 'genuine free trade agreement' negotiated
between two Asian countries, the India–Sri Lanka FTA.[67] Unsurprisingly,
therefore, the Asian business community has been slow to embrace and
make use of the RTAs. The next section evaluates the evidence on the
utilization rates of intra-Asian RTAs.

UTILIZATION RATES IN ASIAN RTAS

As this volume clearly shows, RTAs have recently flourished in the Asian
region. As of 1 August 2010, East Asia alone had negotiated 16 agreements within the region, with an additional 30 agreements negotiated
between East Asian nations and nations in other regions. In addition,
West Asia had negotiated six RTAs within the region and a further 11
inter-regional agreements. It goes without saying that considerable energy,
time, effort and monetary resources have gone into the negotiations of
those agreements. It also goes without saying that both the governments
negotiating these agreements and business groups, industries and workers
reasonably expect to benefit from the negotiation of the agreements. Yet,
while it is true that the growth rates of most Asian nations have risen
alongside the increase in RTAs, the evidence suggests that there is at best
only a minimal causal link. Instead, the specialization and production
networks between and among industries in the region pre-date the rise in
intra-Asian RTAs and continue to flourish even though regional RTAs do
not provide ambitious scope or coverage.

The ambivalence towards intra-Asian RTAs in the business community is perhaps the most damning assessment of the agreements. Trade
agreements are generally seen to be in large part negotiated in order to
assist local industries and businesses to grow and develop (that is, expand

---

[67]   UNCTAD–JETRO, above note 58, 70.

market access). But if RTAs provide minimal preferences, low coverage and high compliance costs, the regional business community will realize there is no value in utilizing the agreements. This is indeed occurring with the business community in Asia, as utilization rates of most intra-Asian RTAs remain at appallingly low levels.

A study by the Asian Development Bank (ADB) revealed the low utilization rates in intra-Asian RTAs. By comprehensively surveying 841 manufacturing firms covering a wide range of key industries and sectors, the ADB found RTA utilization rates to be as follows: China 45.1 per cent, Japan 29 per cent, South Korea 20.8 per cent, the Philippines 20 per cent, Singapore 17.3 per cent and Thailand 24.9 per cent.[68] Thus, only approximately 28 per cent of all firms surveyed actually utilize RTA preferences.[69]

A related survey of Japanese-affiliated firms across Asia similarly found low utilization rates (in terms of both importing and exporting), from a high of 31.8 per cent of firms in Singapore making use of the ASEAN agreement to a low of 5.0 per cent of firms in Malaysia making use of its preferences with China.[70] In a survey of 16 country agreements, seven had utilization rates under 10 per cent, another seven had utilization rates of 10–20 per cent, one had a utilization rate of 20–30 per cent and one had a utilization rate of over 30 per cent.[71] Utilization rates of imports were even lower, from a high of 17 per cent of Indonesian-based Japanese firms making use of the RTA preferences with Japan to a low of 7.4 per cent of Indonesian-based Japanese firms making use of the ASEAN agreement.[72]

---

[68]   Masahiro Kawai and Ganeshan Wignaraja, 'Asian FTAs: Trends and Challenges' (August 2009) ADBI Working Paper Series No. 144, accessed 2 September 2010, http://www.adbi.org/files/2009.08.04.wp144.asian.fta.trends. challenges.pdf. See also Masahiro Kawai and Ganeshan Wignaraja, 'Free Trade Agreements in East Asia: A Way toward Trade Liberalization' (June 2010) ADB Briefs No. 1, accessed 2 September 2010, http://www.adb.org/documents/briefs/ ADB-Briefs-2010-1-Free-Trade-Agreements.pdf.
[69]   Ibid. Interestingly, an additional 25 per cent stated that they planned to make use of RTA preferences.
[70]   See UNCTAD–JETRO, above note 58, 157–72 (citing a study conducted by JETRO).
[71]   Kazaunbou Hayakwa, Daisuke Hiratsuka, Kohei Shiino and Seiyo Sukegawa, 'Who Uses FTAs?' (July 2009) IDE Discussion Paper No. 207, accessed 2 September 2010, http://ir.ide.go.jp/dspace/bitstream/2344/851/1/207_ hhss.pdf; Ganeshan Wignaraja, Rosechin Olfindo, Wisarn Pupphavesa, Jirawat Panpiemras and Sumet Ongkittikul, 'How Do FTAs Affect Exporting Firms in Thailand?' (January 2010) ADBI Working Paper Series No. 190, accessed 2 September 2010, http://www.adbi.org/files/2010.01.29.wp190.fta.affect.exporting. firms.thailand.pdf.
[72]   Ibid.

These statistics on utilization rates compare negatively with those of other RTAs. For instance, utilization rates among the NAFTA partner countries are as follows: US imports from Canada equal 54 per cent, while exports from the US to Canada equal 50 per cent utilization and Mexican exports to the US equal 62 per cent utilization.[73] While these rates do not seem exceedingly high, it must be noted that due to the high number of tariff lines receiving duty-free treatment under MFN an additional 45 per cent of Canadian exports and 37 per cent of Mexican exports to the US essentially entered duty free (and thus there is no need to utilize the NAFTA for preferential treatment).[74] The same is true in Australia's RTAs. While utilization rates are not remarkably high (ranging from nearly 51 per cent of imports in its RTA with New Zealand to a low of under 7 per cent in the recent agreement with Chile), the actual percentage of trade entering at preferential or duty-free rates is over 90 per cent for most of Australia's agreements (including over 95 per cent of New Zealand exports and 96 per cent of Chilean exports to Australia).[75] Moreover, the applied tariff rate on imports to Australia from its RTA partners is exceedingly low, ranging from a high of 6.12 per cent on New Zealand goods to a low of 0.13 per cent on goods from Pacific Island trading partners. Goods from other RTA partner countries – Chile (0.16 per cent), Thailand (0.43 per cent), Singapore (1.25 per cent) and the US (2.85 per cent) – also entered at a low average applied tariff rate. Such statistics are in contradistinction to trade statistics in Asia, where countries generally have higher average applied tariff rates and fewer imports entering duty free.[76]

When the Asian firms were asked why they did not make use of RTAs, the most common reasons were as follows: lack of awareness of RTA benefits (45 per cent) and low preference rates (26 per cent); and delays and administrative costs associated with complex rules of origin requirements

---

[73] Government of Canada, 'NAFTA Rules of Origin' (June 2005) Policy Research Initiative Discussion Paper. See also Daniel Lederman, William F. Maloney and Luis Servén, *Lessons from NAFTA for Latin America and the Caribbean Countries* (World Bank, 2003), 86–95, accessed 2 September 2010, http://ctrc.sice.oas.org/geograph/north/lessonsNAFTA_e.pdf.

[74] For detailed information including product and sector breakdowns, see Government of Canada, above note 73.

[75] Richard Pomfret, Uwe Kaufmann and Christopher Findlay, 'Are Preferential Tariffs Utilized? Evidence from Australian Imports, 2000–9' (July 2010), University of Adelaide Research Paper No. 2010-13, 15.

[76] See, for example, World Bank, 'Trends in Average Applied Tariff Rates in Developing and Industrial Countries, 1981–2007', accessed 2 September 2010, http://siteresources.worldbank.org/INTRES/Resources/469232-1107449512766/tar2007.xls.

(25 per cent).[77] While country-level reasons did not usually significantly vary with most options, a high of 37.5 per cent of firms in Singapore (and 31 per cent of Japanese firms) saw multiple rules of origin as a significant burden whereas only 6.3 per cent of Chinese firms agreed.[78] Interestingly, the study also found that large firms utilize RTAs more often than small firms; that foreign-owned firms utilize RTAs more often than wholly domestic firms; and that established firms utilize RTAs more often than newer firms.[79]

It can thus be concluded that while less than half of the low rate of utilization can be associated with a lack of information (with a likely concentration towards SMEs), more than half is associated with the dual problem of minimal preferential benefits provided by intra-Asian RTAs and multiple rules of origin requirements in the various agreements.

CONCLUSION

While some believe that an East Asian Economic Community is only a few short years away, this chapter demonstrates that meaningful, economically beneficial economic integration in the region is still but a distant dream. Trade among regional partners has grown steadily over the past three decades and the region is undoubtedly more integrated and inter-reliant than it ever has been, but the failure to negotiate important and consequential RTAs holds back further integration. Economic communities are built on liberalization as the rule, subject to minor exceptions (for instance, the European Union and NAFTA). By contrast, while regional trade integration over the years has liberalized some sectors, all too often intra-Asian RTAs focus almost exclusively on goods to the detriment of other sectors and even then contain too few liberalization commitments and too much protectionism in the form of exclusions and pullbacks. Almost without exception, countries in the region are simply not ready to embrace full-scale, legally binding regional integration. Thus, while much has been accomplished over the past few decades in strengthening the relationships between Asian countries, much more could have been accomplished during the last decade had the regional RTAs been more comprehensive in scope and coverage.

This chapter demonstrates the reservedness of the region in embracing

---

[77]   Kawai and Wignaraja, above note 68, 12.
[78]   Ibid.
[79]   Ibid.

regional integration by evaluating the scope and coverage in a broad range of 16 intra-Asian RTAs, with commitments in goods contrasted with those in other sectors, namely services, intellectual property and government procurement. Too often, intra-Asian RTAs exclude or only marginally include these and other economically important sectors. Moreover, liberalization commitments in the goods sector are also sometimes lacking in depth, with Sensitive and Highly Sensitive Lists and liberalization pullbacks providing protection to domestic markets.

The statistics presented in the previous section of this chapter clearly show that the problems revealed in the second section are real detriments to meaningful Asian regional integration in the goods sector. Liberalization resulting from the multilateral tariff reductions has unquestionably assisted in improving intra-regional trade flows, but more meaningful integration cannot occur without RTAs which require actual commitments and deliver real gains. At present, less than 30 per cent of Asian firms utilize RTA preferences with over half the firms identifying low preference rates and rules of origin as the reasons for the lack of utilization. These statistics are damning and prompt the question: why are governments expending resources negotiating RTAs when the vast majority of the business community does not even utilize the resulting preferences?

The aim of this chapter is not to provide the answer to the posed question. The answer is undoubtedly multi-faceted and perhaps would differ depending upon the country and firm in question. The need does exist, however, for governments to set clear aims and objectives before entering into RTA negotiations. Governments should also extensively consult with business and industry leaders prior to entering into negotiations to ascertain what they would like liberalized and what they need protected. Finally, and most importantly, RTAs should provide tangible economic benefits for partner countries through meaningful preferential benefits (in goods and other sectors) and not negatively affect trade through complex and costly administrative procedures.

7. When 'failure' indicates success: understanding trade disputes between ASEAN members

Lisa Toohey

In Southeast Asia, economic integration into global and regional trade institutions has proceeded at a remarkable pace. Within just 15 years, most of the states in the region have integrated into both the World Trade Organization (WTO) and, at a regional level, AFTA, the Free Trade Area of the Association of Southeast Asian Nations (ASEAN). While these arrangements are also supplemented by a web of bilateral and preferential trade arrangements, the ASEAN members have chosen to keep ASEAN as the centerpiece of their trading relationships. The ASEAN Economic Community Blueprint, contained in the 2009–2015 Roadmap for an ASEAN Community, sets out an ambitious program of economic integration that will see the creation of an integrated production base and a single market by 2015.

From the perspective of a trade lawyer, one of the most interesting aspects of ASEAN's development is the expansion of its dispute settlement mechanisms. In 2004 the ASEAN Protocol on Enhanced Dispute Settlement Mechanism ('the 2004 Protocol')[1] was enacted to replace a more basic instrument for the settlement of trade disputes, the 1996 Protocol on Dispute Settlement Mechanism ('the 1996 Protocol').[2] The most recent Protocol to the ASEAN Charter on Dispute Settlement Mechanisms ('the 2010 Protocol'),[3] while of general application rather than a replacement for the 2004 Protocol, is nonetheless considered

---

[1] Adopted in Vientiane, Laos, on 29 November 2004, accessed 2 September 2010, http://www.aseansec.org/16754.htm.

[2] Adopted in Manila, the Philippines, on 20 November 1996, accessed 2 September 2010, http://www.aseansec.org/16654.htm.

[3] Adopted in Hanoi, Vietnam on 8 April 2010, accessed 2 September 2010, http://cil.nus.edu.sg/2010/2010-protocol-to-the-asean-charter-on-dispute-settlement-mechanisms/.

by ASEAN and its constituent members to be important evidence of ASEAN's commitment to creating a rules-based organization.[4]

The existing literature on ASEAN's trade disputes focuses on whether the organization will indeed develop into a rules-based association, or whether political methods will continue to be used in preference to legal principle.[5] The conclusion, generally from outside observers, is that if ASEAN seeks to prioritize economic integration and increased cooperation on trade liberalization, it will probably be forced to become more 'legalized'.[6] The discussion thus tends to revolve around legal mechanisms that will best achieve this end-point.[7] The assumption that underpins the existing literature is that it is an inevitability, or perhaps simply a matter of time, that the available dispute settlement mechanisms will be used by the ASEAN members. However, now approaching fifteen years of operation of the 1996 Protocol and six years of the 2004 Protocol, it seems that the questions should be framed differently.

Accordingly, this chapter considers whether the ASEAN mechanisms are likely to be accepted and the organization used as a forum of choice for trade disputes between ASEAN members. Across the range of major ASEAN disputes – those concerning trade and territory – the ASEAN members have shown a clear preference for quiet self-resolution or external adjudication rather than internal adjudication, not just in relation to trade disputes but also in relation to territorial disputes. Legalism, within the ASEAN context, does not mean referring disputes to institutionalized and procedurally sophisticated adjudicatory mechanisms, but rather

---

[4] See the preamble to the 2010 Protocol, in which member states affirm their desire to '[transform] ASEAN into a rules-based organisation with practical, efficient and credible mechanisms in place to resolve disputes in an effective and timely manner'.

[5] For a range of viewpoints, see P. Davidson, 'The ASEAN Way and the Role of Law in ASEAN Economic Cooperation', *Singapore Year Book of International Law* 8 (2004): 165–76; M. Kahler, 'Legalization as Strategy: The Asia-Pacific Case', *International Organization* 54 (3) (2000): 549–71.

[6] See G. Maggi, 'The Role of Multilateral Institutions in International Trade Cooperation', *American Economic Review* 89 (1) (1996): 190–214; J.M. Smith, 'The Politics of Dispute Settlement Design: Explaining Legalism in Regional Trade Pacts', *International Organization* 54 (1) (2000): 137–80; cf. J. Ravenhill, 'East Asian Regionalism: Much Ado About Nothing?', *Review of International Studies* 35 (2009): 215–315.

[7] See P. Davidson, 'ASEAN: The Legal Framework for Its Trade Relations', *International Journal* 49 (3) (1994): 592; H.C. Rieger, 'The Treaty of Rome and its Relevance for ASEAN', *ASEAN Economic Bulletin* 8 (1991): 160–72; L.H. Tan, 'Will ASEAN Economic Integration Progress Beyond a Free Trade Area?', *International and Comparative Law Quarterly* 53 (4) (2004): 935–67.

relying on the legal rights and obligations established by the ASEAN agreements in a substantive sense. Another, and equally compelling, reason that ASEAN is unlikely to ever become a forum of choice for trade disputes lies in the broad nature of the institution's objectives. ASEAN is first and foremost a security community, and while economic integration is increasingly important, it is only one of three pillars on which the community rests. There are a large number of unresolved territorial disputes amongst the ASEAN members, and there seems to be a sense amongst the ASEAN membership that the so-called 'ASEAN Way' of behind-the-scenes diplomacy and public non-confrontation best preserves peaceful ongoing relations within the region.

This chapter commences with an overview of ASEAN's economic integration and the pathways offered by ASEAN and the WTO for the resolution of trade disputes. The chapter then provides analysis of the emerging trends in the settlement of trade disputes, both in a general sense and in selected examples. The remainder of the chapter examines the inevitable questions that arise from a study of ASEAN's apparent reluctance to utilize its own dispute settlement mechanisms. To what can we attribute the fairly distinct disputing patterns of the ASEAN states? Does it demonstrate a lack of efficacy of the ASEAN system? Is it attributable to superior qualities of the WTO system? There is clearly some type of forum-shopping involved, but is it the type of regulatory arbitrage that gives rise to systemic concerns about the fragmentation of international law?

'RULES-BASED' TRADE INTEGRATION IN ASEAN

ASEAN was originally a five-member organization, established in Bangkok on 8 August 1967 by Indonesia, Malaysia, Thailand, Singapore and the Philippines. The founding document, the ASEAN Declaration (known also as the Bangkok Declaration), was a short and largely aspirational document that established an organization to enhance 'regional solidarity and cooperation', 'promote regional peace and stability through abiding respect for justice and the rule of law', provide mutual technical assistance and collaboration, and secure 'for posterity the blessings of peace, freedom and prosperity'.[8] Membership has doubled to also include Brunei Darussalam since 1984, Viet Nam since 1995, the Lao People's Democratic Republic and Myanmar since 1997, and Cambodia since 1999.

---

[8] 'Bangkok Declaration', 8 August 1967, 6 *International Legal Materials* 1233 (1967).

Modern ASEAN describes itself as a multi-focus community based on 'three pillars' – a Political-Security Community, a Socio-Cultural Community, and an Economic Community – but, as Leifer has observed, the fundamental concern of ASEAN's founders was regional security, and the organization was created primarily to reduce the risk of internal security threats to states in the region.[9] While economic integration is now an important part of ASEAN's identity, the organization is not, and never has been, an exclusively trade-focused organization. The fact that trade is a subsidiary, albeit important, focus of ASEAN relations is a significant factor in the method of handling disputes, as the following parts of this chapter will explain.

Early trade initiatives included a 1977 Preferential Trade Arrangements Agreement ('PTA Agreement')[10] that offered preferential tariffs, but this was ultimately of limited effect due to a broad exclusion list that tended to cover a large proportion of traded products.[11] The PTA Agreement has been described, in derisive terms, as 'a rather comical free trade in snow plows and other Southeast Asian essentials'.[12] Attempts at deeper and more effective trade integration occurred only fairly recently in ASEAN's history, with the ASEAN Free Trade Area (AFTA) being created out of the Framework Agreement on Enhancing ASEAN Cooperation ('the Framework Agreement on Cooperation')[13] and implemented through the Common Effective Preferential Tariff Scheme ('the CEPT Scheme'),[14] which became effective on 1 January 1993. Some observers argued that the creation of AFTA was mainly a reaction to the creation of trade blocs in Europe and North America,[15] with others viewing AFTA more as a

---

[9]   Michael Leifer, *ASEAN and the Security of South-East Asia* (London and New York: Routledge, 1989): 2–3.

[10]   Adopted in Manila, the Philippines, on 24 February 1977, accessed 2 September 2010, http://www.aseansec.org/1376.htm.

[11]   For a detailed early history of trade and integration within ASEAN, see Shaun Narine, *Explaining ASEAN: Regionalism in Southeast Asia* (Boulder, CO: Lynne Rienner Publishers, 2002) 24–31.

[12]   P. Kenevan and A. Winden, 'Flexible Free Trade: The ASEAN Free Trade Area', *Harvard International Law Journal* 34 (1) (1993): 225.

[13]   Singapore Declaration, 28 January 1992, 31 *International Law Materials* 498 (1992)

[14]   Agreement on the Common Effective Preferential Tariff Scheme for the ASEAN Free Trade Area, 28 January 1992, 31 *International Law Materials* 513 (1992).

[15]   See, for example, J.I. Garvey, 'AFTA After NAFTA: Regional Trade Blocs and the Propagation of Environmental and Labor Standards', *Berkeley Journal of International Law* 15 (1997): 245–74; D.A. Haas, 'Out of Others' Shadows: ASEAN Moves toward Greater Regional Cooperation in the Face of

means of improving the attractiveness of the region for foreign investors, as opposed to merely generating increased internal trade.[16]

The ASEAN aspiration of an economic community has slowly been articulated in a series of 'roadmap' documents such as the ASEAN Vision 2020,[17] the 2007 ASEAN Economic Community Blueprint,[18] and the more recent Roadmap for an ASEAN Community 2009–2015.[19] This 'vision' of an ASEAN Economic Community includes a single market and production base that incorporates free flow of goods, services, investment and skilled labor and the liberalization of capital. Since the mid-1990s, these high-level agreements, community visions and roadmaps have been slowly transformed into a series of framework agreements on investment,[20] trade in services,[21] intellectual property[22] and information and communications technology.[23] The framework agreements are quite formulaic, and largely expressed in aspirational terms that require the signatories to 'enhance cooperation', 'undertake the joint development of programmes' and undertake further negotiations. The framework agreements have now been fleshed out into more comprehensive agreements containing detailed commitments. The most recent round was in Thailand in 2009, resulting in the ASEAN Comprehensive Investment Agreement ('Comprehensive Investment Agreement'),[24] a Seventh Package of Commitments under the ASEAN Framework Agreements on Trade in Services,[25] and the harmo-

---

the EC and NAFTA', *American University Journal of International Law and Policy* 9 (3) (1994): 809–10.

[16] See P. Bowles and B. MacLean, 'Understanding Trade Bloc Formation: The Case of the ASEAN Free Trade Area', *Review of International Political Economy* 3 (2) (1996): 319–48.

[17] Adopted in Kuala Lumpur, Malaysia, on 15 December 1997, accessed 2 September 2010, http://www.aseansec.org/1814.htm.

[18] Adopted in Singapore on 20 November 2007, accessed 2 September 2010, http://www.aseansec.org/5187-10.pdf.

[19] Adopted in Cha-Am, Thailand, on 1 March 2009, accessed 2 September 2010, http://www.aseansec.org/publications/RoadmapASEANCommunity.pdf

[20] Framework Agreement on the ASEAN Investment Area, adopted in Makati, the Philippines, on 7 October 1998, accessed 2 September 2010, http://www.aseansec.org/7994.pdf.

[21] ASEAN Framework Agreement on Services, 15 December 1995, 35 *International Legal Materials* 1072 (1996).

[22] ASEAN Framework Agreement on Intellectual Property Cooperation, 15 December 1995, 35 *International Legal Materials* 1072 (1996).

[23] e-ASEAN Framework Agreement, 24 November 2000, 40 *International Legal Materials* 515 (2001).

[24] Adopted in Cha-am, Thailand, on 26 February 2009, accessed 2 September 2010, http://www.aseansec.org/documents/FINAL-SIGNED-ACIA.pdf.

[25] The Protocol to Implement the Seventh Package of Commitments under the

nization or mutual recognition of standards and certification and professional qualifications.[26]

ASEAN has also rapidly expanded its range of external relationships. The enhancement of ASEAN's economic community creates a powerful bloc through which the ASEAN members can advance and consolidate their interests in international negotiations and continue to pursue broader regional integration. In addition to the regular ASEAN+3 summits involving ASEAN, China, Japan and the Republic of Korea, ASEAN has engaged with the broader Asia-Pacific region by pursuing Closer Economic Relations (CER) with Australia and New Zealand and engaging at various levels with the United States, Russia, and India. ASEAN has now entered into four quite comprehensive free trade agreements with China,[27] the Republic of Korea,[28] Japan,[29] and Australia and New Zealand.[30] It has also partnered with China, Hong Kong, Japan and the Republic of Korea to form the Chiang Mai Initiative,[31] a multilateral currency swap agreement designed to minimize short-term liquidity problems and regional balance of payment issues. Finally, ASEAN is continuing to

---

ASEAN Framework Agreement on Services, adopted in Cha-am, Thailand, on 26 February 2009, accessed 2 September 2010, http://www.aseansec.org/22221.htm.

[26]   To date, agreements establishing mutual recognition of professional qualifications have been established for medical practitioners, dentists, and accountants (2009), architects and surveyors (2007), nurses (2006) and engineers (2005). For a comprehensive list of these agreements, see http://www.aseansec.org/19087.htm, accessed 2 September 2010.

[27]   The ASEAN–China Free Trade Area is established pursuant to the Framework Agreement on Comprehensive Economic Cooperation between ASEAN and the People's Republic of China, 4 November 2002, 43 *International Legal Materials* 23 (2004), and implemented through a series of sectoral agreements between 2004 and 2009. ASEAN–China obligations in relation to goods are phased in during 2010 for China and six of the ASEAN states (Brunei Darussalam, Indonesia, Malaysia, the Philippines, Singapore and Thailand) and China, and during 2015 for Cambodia, Laos, Myanmar and Vietnam.

[28]   Cooperation with Korea has taken place pursuant to the Framework Agreement on Comprehensive Economic Cooperation Among the Governments of the Member Countries of the Association of Southeast Asian Nations and the Republic of Korea, adopted in Kuala Lumpur on 13 December 2005 and, like the Chinese arrangement, implemented through various sectoral agreements.

[29]   ASEAN and Japan have entered into the Agreement on Comprehensive Economic Partnership among Member States of the Association of Southeast Asian Nations and Japan, adoption of which was completed on 14 April 2008.

[30]   Agreement Establishing the ASEAN–Australia–New Zealand Free Trade Area, Cha-am, Thailand, 27 February 2009.

[31]   Chiang Mai Initiative Multilateralization Agreement, adopted on 28 December 2009, entered into effect on 14 March 2010.

extend its trade integration in the greater region by seeking a free trade agreement with another major regional power, India.[32] While the plethora of regional trade agreements creates, in the words of Baldwin, a series of 'fuzzy, leaky trade blocs',[33] it also serves to enhance the legitimacy of ASEAN as a cohesive force within the region and at an international level. There is near-universal membership of the WTO within ASEAN, with the exception of Laos, which is currently in the process of acceding to the WTO,[34] and the ASEAN name is being increasingly used as a negotiating bloc within WTO fora.[35]

The picture painted above is of a regional organization that is rapidly expanding its formal trade arrangements, in terms of both external engagement and internal integration. This is part of ASEAN's drive towards becoming a rules-based institution. The other part, in ASEAN's words, is having 'practical, efficient and credible mechanisms in place to resolve disputes in an effective and timely manner'.[36] The following section of this chapter explains the various options for the resolution of ASEAN disputes, describes the evolving patterns of behaviour of ASEAN members when confronted with an intramural dispute, and considers how such mechanisms really operate in the ASEAN context.

SETTLEMENT PATHWAYS FOR ASEAN DISPUTES

As indicated above, the vast majority of ASEAN members are also members of the WTO, which means that in the event of a trade dispute there is the potential for a choice of forum. To date, however, none of the ASEAN dispute settlement mechanisms have been formally invoked.

---

[32] For an overview of ASEAN–Indian relations, see http://www.aseansec. org/5738.htm, accessed 2 September 2010.

[33] A phrase coined by R.E. Baldwin, 'Multilateralising Regionalism: Spaghetti Bowls as Building Blocs on the Path to Global Free Trade', *The World Economy* 29 (11) (2006): 1451–1518.

[34] The Lao PDR made its application for accession to the WTO in July 1997.

[35] See, for example, statements made by Singapore on behalf of ASEAN countries in response to a European proposal to review the Information Technology Agreement in December 2009 (WTO Document G/IT/M/50) and on behalf of ASEAN countries in discussions concerning the status of work undertaken in relation to the Trade-Related Aspects of Intellectual Property Rights (WTO Document TN/IP/M/19). Other ASEAN member states have spoken on behalf of the Association, such as Malaysia in relation to negotiations under the Doha Development Agenda on Trade in Services (WTO Document TN/S/M/28).

[36] Paragraph 2 of the Preamble of the 2010 Protocol.

Instead, in the limited number of situations in which a dispute has escalated to the point of initiation of legal proceedings (discussed below), the complaint has been made in the WTO. As this chapter also discusses, similar trends towards external adjudication are seen in other areas of ASEAN activity, including territorial and human rights disputes. There are, of course, various reasons as to why this is the case. Critics of ASEAN cite this trend as evidence of the organization being stagnant or irrelevant. Others may simply argue the 'culture card', saying that formal adjudicatory processes such as the DSU or the ASEAN protocols are inconsistent with the conciliatory approaches typically preferred in Asian cultures. The reality, however, is more complex. After briefly explaining how the WTO and ASEAN dispute settlement systems operate, the remainder of this chapter deals in detail with the reasons why ASEAN members appear to eschew their formal regional options for dispute settlement.

The WTO Dispute Settlement Understanding

If, as the WTO asserts, the success of a dispute settlement mechanism can be measured by the frequency of its use, then the WTO's Dispute Settlement Understanding (DSU) is a success.[37] Ten years after the establishment of the WTO, the Sutherland Report commented that '[b]y most accounts, and most measures, the operation of the dispute settlement system in the WTO has been a remarkable success', and cited as its primary piece of evidence the very high rates of use of the dispute settlement processes.[38] Bacchus observes that within only seven years of the WTO's establishment, its dispute settlement mechanism had become 'the busiest international system for resolving international disputes in the history of the world'.[39] In the 15 years since its inception, over 400 disputes have been submitted for determination by a panel, and a large body of literature has emerged that deals in detail with the pros and cons of the WTO's dispute settlement system.[40]

---

[37]   World Trade Organization (2004), *A Handbook on the WTO Dispute Settlement System* (Geneva: World Trade Organization) 116–17.

[38]   Peter Sutherland, *The Future of the WTO – Addressing Institutional Challenges of the New Millennium,* A report by the Consultative Board to the Director-General Supachai Panitchpakdi (Geneva: World Trade Organization, 2004), paragraphs 221–5.

[39]   J. Bacchus, 'Groping Toward Grotius: The WTO and the International Rule of Law', Speech at Harvard Law School Cambridge, MA, 1 October 2002, 8.

[40]   See, for example, K. Lida, 'Is WTO Dispute Settlement Effective?', *Global Governance* 10 (2) (2004): 207–25; Rufus H. Yerxa and Bruce Wilson, *Key Issues in*

Article 3(2) of the DSU describes the WTO's dispute settlement process as a 'central element in providing security and predictability to the multilateral trading system'. While the DSU's predecessor, Articles XXII and XXIII of the General Agreement on Tariffs and Trade (GATT) had similar objectives, the more basic infrastructure and procedures became inadequate to deal with the disputes that emerged. The DSU was created in order to clarify and amplify the operation of Articles XXII and XXIII of the GATT, and to correct some of the procedural mechanisms that had hampered its effective operation. Improvements included the addition of an appeals process that had been absent under the GATT, and the removal of the capacity of individual members to veto the creation of a panel or the adoption of a decision.[41]

Equally importantly, the transition from the GATT to the WTO brought about an attitudinal shift that ultimately led to the DSU being more heavily used than its predecessor. Jackson has observed of the GATT era that there was a view 'that invocation of the [dispute settlement] procedure would be deemed an "unfriendly act"'.[42] In the WTO era, it seems that the conduct of DSU proceedings is merely one part of the very robust and often combative milieu of trading relationships. Other commentators have pointed to a larger paradigmatic shift from the GATT being dominated by economists and politicians to the WTO as an organization dominated by lawyers,[43] a change that flows through to the disputing culture of an organization.

Surely a good indicator of the true success of the DSU would seem to be the fact that its processes are utilized by less powerful members of the WTO. In particular, small and developing states are using the DSU.

WTO Dispute Settlement: The First Ten Years (New York: Cambridge University Press, 2005).

[41]   For further information, see 'Weaknesses of the GATT Dispute Settlement System', accessed 2 September 2010, http://www.wto.org/english/tratop_e/dispu_e/disp_settlement_cbt_e/c2s1p1_e.htm.

[42]   John H. Jackson, *The World Trading System: Law and Policy of International Economic Relations* (Cambridge, MA: MIT Press, 1997), 114.

[43]   See, for example, Robert Hudec's consternation just three years after the creation of the WTO that the Secretariat was already 'lawyer-ridden'. R.E. Hudec, 'The Role of the GATT Secretariat in the Evolution of the WTO Dispute Settlement Procedure' in Jagdish Bhagwati and Mathias Hirsch (eds), *The Uruguay Round and Beyond: Essays in Honour of Arthur Dunkel* (Ann Arbor, MI: University of Michigan Press, 1998) 117. See also J.H.H. Weiler, 'The Rule of Lawyers and the Ethos of Diplomats: Reflections on the Internal and External Legitimacy of WTO Dispute Settlement', Jean Monnet Working Paper 09/00 (2000), accessed 2 September 2010, http://centers.law.nyu.edu/jeanmonnet/papers/00/000901.html.

Examples include Thailand, which has brought 13 cases, and Brazil, which has brought 25 cases, and even very small island states such as Antigua and Barbuda, which successfully took action against the United States in the *Gambling* case.[44] While these statistics are vastly outnumbered by the European Union's initiation of 82 cases and the United States' 94 cases, they do demonstrate that even politically vulnerable WTO members have a certain amount of confidence that a trade dispute brought to the WTO will not significantly impact upon other aspects of the diplomatic relationship with the protagonist.[45] In contrast, McRae characterizes as a 'great achievement' of the DSU the fact that it 'depoliticizes disputes between countries. It downplays the diplomatic importance of the dispute and provides a practical means of resolving it.'[46] When compared with the ASEAN processes (below), it appears to have been a great advantage that, as Weiler observes, the GATT (and WTO) process 'tended to treat [trade disputes] as discrete eruptions between members requiring "settlement"'.[47]

The DSU sets out a multi-stage procedure to enable WTO member states to resolve trade disputes at a state–state level. The dispute settlement process begins with consultation, reflecting the commitment in Article 3(7) that a mutually agreed solution is to be preferred to any adjudicated outcome. Throughout the dispute settlement process, a variety of facilitated settlement options are available to the disputing states, including conciliation, mediation, and good offices, pursuant to Article 5 of the DSU. However, if settlement efforts are unsuccessful, there are three stages of adjudicatory processes available to determine whether a party's measure is inconsistent with WTO principles, and to place pressure on

---

[44]   Appellate Body Report, *United States – Measures Affecting the Cross-Border Supply of Gambling and Betting Services*, WT/DS285/AB/R, adopted 20 April 2005, DSR 2005:XII, 5663 (Corr.1, DSR 2006:XII, 5475). Admittedly, at the time of writing, the United States has failed to bring its impugned measures into conformity, but Antigua and Barbuda are at least authorized to suspend US\$21 million per annum worth of concessions under the TRIPS Agreement.

[45]   See generally R. Abbott, 'Are Developing Countries Deterred from Using the WTO Dispute Settlement System?', ECIPE Working Paper No. 01/2007, accessed 2 September 2010, http://www.ecipe.org/publications/ecipe-working-papers/are-developing-countries-deterred-from-using-the-wto-dispute-settlement-system/PDF, at 4.

[46]   D. McRae, 'Measuring the Effectiveness of the WTO Dispute Settlement System', *Asian Journal of WTO & International Health Law and Policy* 3 (1) (2008): 13.

[47]   J.H.H Weiler, 'The Rule of Lawyers and the Ethos of Diplomats: Reflections on the Internal and External Legitimacy of WTO Dispute Settlement', Jean Monnet Working Paper 09/2000, accessed 2 September 2010, http://centers.law.nyu.edu/jeanmonnet/papers/00/000901.html.

parties to bring WTO-inconsistent measures into conformity. The initial
panel process is essentially one of arbitration, with a panel of three or
five panelists being called upon to examine the consistency of the dis-
puted measure with the WTO Agreements.[48] A standing Appellate Body
is available, as its name suggests, to hear appeals on questions of law,[49]
and has jurisdiction to uphold, modify, or reverse the legal findings and
conclusions of a panel. In correcting any legal errors made by panels, the
Appellate Body helps to ensure the consistency of decisions and the WTO
jurisprudence.[50] Arbitration procedures are available to assist with the
process of bringing impugned measures into conformity, with Article 21.3
providing for arbitration if the parties are unable to establish a timetable
for implementation, and Article 22.6 utilizing arbitration to assess the
extent to which concessions can be suspended in retaliation against a recalcitrant party that refuses to bring its measures into conformity. Finally,
Article 21.5 provides a mechanism (sometimes referred to as a 'compliance' panel procedure) to review compliance with previous decisions of
a panel or the Appellate Body and determine whether an implementing
measure has remedied the violation, nullification or impairment of WTO
obligations.

ASEAN'S General Dispute Settlement Mechanisms

Like the WTO, ASEAN's dispute settlement system combines facilitated
and adjudicated processes, but contains general as well as trade-specific
agreements. The fact that ASEAN is a community that needs to deal
with security interests has a significant bearing on how trade disputes
are conducted – see the sixth section in this chapter. Initial attempts at a
dispute settlement mechanism were incorporated into Chapter IV of the

---

[48]   See Article 11 of the DSU.

[49]   In reality, however, the distinction between 'law' and 'facts' is problematic
and difficult to discern. For example, a panel's factual examination is still subject
to legal rules and therefore can be reviewed on appeal on the basis that the panel
has not made an objective assessment of the facts as required under Article 11 of
the DSU. See Appellate Body Report, *EC Measures Concerning Meat and Meat
Products (Hormones)*, WT/DS26/AB/R, WT/DS48/AB/R, adopted 13 February
1998, DSR 1998:I, 135, paragraphs 115–17.

[50]   See further J.M Smith, 'WTO Dispute Settlement: the Politics of Procedure
in Appellate Body Rulings', *World Trade Review* 2 (1) (2003): 65; P.V. Bossche,
'From Afterthought to Centerpiece: The WTO Appellate Body and its Rise to
Prominence in the World Trading System' in Giorgio Sacerdoti, Giorgio, Alan
Yanovich and Jan Bohanes (eds), *The WTO at Ten: The Contribution of the Dispute
Settlement System* (Cambridge: Cambridge University Press, 2005), 289–325.

Treaty of Amity and Cooperation in Southeast Asia,[51] and provided for consensual submission of disputes to the ASEAN High Council, comprising a ministerial representative from each member state. Similarly, the ASEAN Charter, adopted on 20 November 2007, clearly sets out the obligation of members to resolve disputes peacefully, and the need for dispute settlement mechanisms in all fields of ASEAN cooperation. The 2010 Protocol represents the organization's latest commitment to a formalized process to settle disputes that arise in relation to the interpretation of the ASEAN Charter, creating a further mechanism based on legal rules and a process of principled adjudication.

The 2010 Protocol is not intended to replace the trade-specific dispute settlement mechanisms. It could, however, still be used indirectly in relation to the interpretation of constitutional-type trade-related issues arising from the Charter and its interpretation, or as an alternative as the trade mechanisms do not claim exclusive jurisdiction over the disputes to which they apply.[52] It of course remains to be seen whether such a challenge is made, and how the 2010 Protocol would be interpreted in that event.

ASEAN's Trade-Specific Dispute Mechanisms

Early trade-specific dispute settlement mechanisms were incorporated into agreements such as the Framework Agreement on Cooperation. This foreshadowed the creation of a more formal dispute settlement structure, and in 1996 ASEAN's first discrete dispute settlement mechanism protocol was implemented. The 1996 Protocol was, in many ways, a hybrid of political and legal mechanisms. While it created a panel process for the adjudication of disputes based on legal principle and 'objective determination', the Senior Economic Officials Meeting (SEOM) retained almost total control over the carriage of the dispute. Not only was the SEOM to convene the panel, and some of its number actually comprise the panel, but it also had discretion to decline to establish a panel at all, and instead, pursuant to Article 4, 'decide to deal with the dispute to achieve an amicable settlement without appointing a panel'. An appeal was available under Article 8 of the 1996 Protocol from a SEOM decision to the ASEAN Economic Ministers (AEM), the peak body within ASEAN's economic community. It seems that the bureaucratic approach to dispute settlement, with determinative powers vested in the two major political bodies of the economic community,

---

[51] Adopted in Denpasar, Bali, Indonesia, on 24 February 1976, accessed 2 September 2010, http://www.aseansec.org/1217.htm.

[52] Article 1 of the 2004 Protocol.

offered few advantages over informal dispute settlement options. In any event, the 1996 Protocol was never invoked, and no reports exist to suggest that invocation was ever threatened by an ASEAN member.

The 2004 Protocol was enacted on 29 November 2004. Appendix 1 of the 2004 Protocol sets out the 46 covered agreements to which its provisions apply. A second appendix contains the working procedures for the panel, which bear a strong resemblance to the WTO requirements for composition of panels and the conduct of party proceedings. As in the DSU procedure, the ASEAN Secretariat is required to maintain an Indicative List of Panelists, who should preferably (but need not) be ASEAN nationals. At the time of writing, and based on information available on the ASEAN website, it does not appear that such a list has ever been created.

The skeleton of the 1996 Protocol remains intact, maintaining a focus on self-resolution and facilitated settlement through consultative mechanisms. However the enhancements to the 2004 Protocol are significant. The Enhanced Protocol expands on the administrative side of the dispute settlement process by lessening the responsibilities of the SEOM. In the 2004 Protocol, the SEOM acts somewhat more as an oversight body than as an adjudicator. The SEOM administers the dispute mechanism, not just in terms of receiving and distributing information but also in terms of deciding whether a dispute should be referred to a panel. Nonetheless, Article 5 of the Enhanced Protocol still allows the SEOM by consensus to decide not to establish a panel, and it likewise is able to accept or reject a panel report (Article 9). The Enhanced Protocol also introduced procedures, frequently used in the WTO system, for the consolidation of multiple complaints (Article 10 of the 2004 Protocol), and the representation of third parties. It has also provided in Article 12 for the establishment of a permanent Appellate Body selected by the Meeting of the AEM. This is a change to the original protocol, in which any appeal would have been dealt with directly by the AEM. Like the WTO's Appellate Body, the ASEAN body is to be composed of recognized authorities in trade and international law, irrespective of nationality, and professionally engaged as members of the Appellate Body.

In addition to the purely state–state mechanisms described above, two mechanisms are available through which individuals and corporations can address grievances. Firstly, the ASEAN Consultation to Solve Trade and Investment Issues (ACT)[53] is an internet-based dispute settlement network

---

[53]   See http://act.aseansec.org/, accessed 2 September 2010; see also http://www.aseansec.org/Fact%20Sheet/AEC/2007-AEC-006.pdf, accessed 2 September 2010.

that is modeled on the European SOLVIT scheme.[54] The scheme operates somewhat like an inter-state ombudsman, offering non-binding resolutions of disputes between businesses and ASEAN member states, and also extends to China by virtue of the ASEAN–China Free Trade Area. An individual or enterprise is able to lodge a complaint online to their home government, which conveys the dispute to the government of the state in which the dispute has occurred. The two governments can then liaise to resolve the dispute. As an individual researcher it seems impossible to access any detailed information about how frequently the ACT process is utilized, the types of complaints which commonly arise, or how the process is used in practice.[55]

The other mechanism that is available as a means of direct redress for investors, without the involvement of their home government, is investor–state arbitration. The original basis for this mechanism can be found in Article X of the 1987 ASEAN Agreement on the Promotion and Protection of Investments,[56] and subsequently in the Comprehensive Investment Agreement.[57] Both agreements provided for arbitration under either ICSID (provided the jurisdictional requirements are satisfied), UNCITRAL Arbitration Rules, or ASEAN regional centres for arbitration. Article 33 of the Comprehensive Investment Agreement now gives the choice of these forums to the investor, but requires the agreement of all disputants if they wish to choose an alternative forum. Article 33 also makes it clear that the investor can select the disputing state's own courts or tribunals, should they wish to do so. Only one arbitral decision has been rendered to date, pursuant to the 1987 Agreement, and it is discussed briefly in the next section.

Finally, for the sake of completeness it is also worth observing that ASEAN now appears to routinely conclude individual dispute settlement protocols as part of the suite of agreements that establish free trade areas with its neighbours. Since 2004, ASEAN has included mechanisms for a

---

[54] See http://ec.europa.eu/solvit/site/index_en.htm, accessed 2 September 2010.

[55] There is extremely limited information available on the operation of the ACT, other than the fact sheet referred to in note 53 above. Enquiries by email and letter to the ASEAN Secretariat from the author about the operation of the ACT mechanism went unanswered, and to the author's surprise, even telephone calls were not answered during office hours.

[56] Adopted in Manila, the Philippines, on 6 February 2009, accessed 2 September 2010, http://www.aseansec.org/12812.htm.

[57] ASEAN Comprehensive Investment Agreement, Cha-am, Thailand, 26 February 2009.

type of state–state arbitration in agreements with China,[58] the Republic of Korea[59] and India.[60] These are also based loosely on the WTO consultation-adjudication process, but without an appellate mechanism. Other notable features of these processes are the inclusion of a third-party process and retaliation measures based on Article 22 of the DSU. The agreements have fairly minor differences – such as a lack of reference to good offices in the ASEAN–China document, which also contains detailed confidentiality provisions.

FORUM SELECTION – REGIONAL AND GLOBAL TRENDS

While the WTO and ASEAN have dispute settlement mechanisms of very similar age and structure, as well as a considerable number of common members, the patterns of disputing within the two organizations are quite different. Whereas the WTO has dealt with a large number of disputes since its inception, ASEAN has not had any disputes referred to adjudication. For a variety of reasons (discussed below), ASEAN members are generally less litigious than their counterparts in other regions, but it is instructive that in the limited number of situations in which a dispute between ASEAN members has been brought to adjudication, the parties appear to have deliberately selected to bring the dispute to the WTO in preference to their own, self-designed, regional architecture for dispute settlement.

Intra-ASEAN Disputes

The subject of intra-ASEAN trade disputes is a difficult one to study. The distinctive culture of ASEAN leads to disputes being handled quietly, as

---

[58] Agreement on Dispute Settlement Mechanism of the Framework Agreement on Comprehensive Economic Co-Operation Between the Association of Southeast Asian Nations and the People's Republic of China, adopted in Vientiane, Laos, on 29 November 2004.

[59] Agreement on Dispute Settlement Mechanism Under the Framework Agreement on Comprehensive Economic Cooperation Among the Governments of the Member Countries of the Association of Southeast Asian Nations and the Republic of Korea, adopted in Kuala Lumpur, Malaysia, on 13 December 2005.

[60] Agreement on Dispute Settlement Mechanism under the Framework Agreement on Comprehensive Economic Cooperation between the Association of Southeast Asian Nations and the Republic of India, adopted in Bangkok, Thailand, on 13 August 2009.

far away as possible from public attention. The keen observer, without government connections, can at best observe glimpses of trade spats from newspaper reports. There is, however, no doubt that disputes exist amongst ASEAN members, including disputes about the implementation of ASEAN agreements.

For example, Hsu reports that in 2003 Singapore sought compensation from the Philippines due to measures affecting the importation of petrochemical products.[61] The Philippine Government issued an Executive Order in 2003 that suspended agreed tariff reductions on certain resin and plastic products, in order to protect a proposed domestic production facility. The case was settled with a US$8 million compensation arrangement.[62] However, materials publicly available from ASEAN devote only a few lines to this quite substantial conflict. A press statement from the sixteenth meeting of the AFTA Council merely says, 'The Ministers noted Philippines' intention to possibly invoke the Protocol regarding the CEPT Temporary Exclusion List with respect to its petrochemical industry. No consensus was reached, and further discussions will be carried out.'[63] In this particular case, Article 9 of the 1996 Protocol was never invoked, as a mutually satisfactory compensation arrangement was reached.

One single arbitration decision has been rendered under ASEAN's investor–state arbitration regime: in the 2003 case of *Yaung Chi Oo Trading Pte Ltd v. Myanmar*, in which a Singaporean entity brought ultimately unsuccessful proceedings relating to the seizure of its brewery and the freezing of bank accounts.[64] While extensive discussion of the case is outside the scope of this chapter, it is interesting to reflect on the dynamics by which the corporation pursued the case on its own behalf, without apparent support or lobbying from its own government. The private party nature of investor–state arbitration keeps the dispute functionally separate from the ASEAN processes, which has the advantage of distancing the complainant's government from the dispute, avoiding the perception that the state is being confrontational.

---

[61] L. Hsu, 'WTO and Regional Trade Liberalization: Implications for ASEAN', paper presented at the 9th General Assembly of the ASEAN Law Association (2004), accessed 2 September 2010, http://www.aseanlawassociation. org/9GAdocs/w3_Singapore.pdf.

[62] *Plastics News*, 'Singapore Agrees to Compensation Package in Petrochem Dispute with Philippines', 5 December 2006, accessed 2 September 2010, http:// www.plastemart.com/Plasticnews_desc.asp?news_id=8689#.

[63] ASEAN, 'The Sixteenth Meeting of the ASEAN Free Trade Area (AFTA) Council', Joint Press Statement, 11 September 2002, Bandar Seri Begawan, Brunei Darussalam, accessed 2 September 2010, http://www.aseansec.org/12412.htm.

[64] 42 *International Legal Materials* 540 (2003).

There are numerous other trade tensions simmering amongst the ASEAN members, but if they are ever resolved, they are resolved almost without a visible trace. For example, during 2006 Malaysia and Thailand disagreed over Malaysian import permit requirements, and over Thailand maintaining a retaliatory 20 per cent import duty. The Malaysian Trade Minister, while defending Malaysia's measures, downplayed the dispute as merely one of interpretation, and maintained that the disagreement was a bilateral issue that would not impact upon the greater ASEAN relationship.[65] Disagreements regularly emerge about the treatment of sensitive products, particularly rice. Rice is one of the most emotive issues within trade in goods, due less to its economic value and more to its role in food security and its deeply imbedded cultural significance for all ASEAN members. Another simmering grievance with cultural significance is Vietnamese concerns about the misappropriation by Thai enterprises of the geographical indicator 'Phu Quoc' in relation to fish sauce.[66]

Two further disputes between ASEAN members stand out, because they were not contained within the ASEAN forum but have resulted instead in the invocation of the WTO's DSU procedure. The first was the 1995 dispute between Singapore and Malaysia concerning Malaysian import prohibitions on two types of mid-stream plastic products. Up until the import restriction was put in place, Singapore had been a major exporter of the products to Malaysia. The measure was implemented in order to protect the development of a new factory to create a major ingredient required for the production of plastic products. The details of the very short-lived WTO dispute are set out below, but for present purposes it is interesting to note the responses of ASEAN media and the other ASEAN members to the dispute being brought to the WTO. While there is no record in the online ASEAN archives about the dispute, specialist media reports from the time questioned the 'note of acerbity injected into the quarrel between two members of the six-nation ASEAN subregional grouping' and the 'puzzlement' of observers. The same article reported the suggestion by Indonesia, on behalf of the other ASEAN members, that consultations be facilitated by the Chairman of the Goods Council.[67]

---

[65] 'Malaysia: Spat over ASEAN Autos Free Trade', (2006), accessed 2 September 2010, http://www.just-auto.com/news/spat-over-asean-autos-free-trade_id88766.aspx.

[66] 'Fish Sauce Makers Seek to Protect Name', *VietNamNet/Viet Nam News,* 7 May 2009, accessed 2 September 2010, http://english.vietnamnet.vn/biz/2009/05/846292/.

[67] C. Raghavan, 'Singapore–Malaysia Dispute Takes an Edge at WTO', *South-North Development Monitor,* 21 February 1995, accessed 2 September 2010,

The second, and still ongoing, dispute between ASEAN members in the WTO is the dispute between the Philippines and Thailand concerning Thai treatment of cigarettes. The matters in dispute are extensive and involve allegations by the Philippines of 'partial and unreasonable' application of 'valuation practices, excise tax, health tax, TV tax, VAT regime, retail licensing requirements and import guarantees imposed upon cigarette importers'.[68] Once again, the WTO aspects of the dispute are discussed below, but the broader context of the dispute seems to revolve around the treatment of subsidiaries of the US tobacco giant Philip Morris International Inc. Philippine trade ministry officials commented that the Philippine government had raised the issue firstly within ASEAN, but had 'decided to elevate the issue before the WTO after [meetings] among ASEAN officials in Baguio City yielded no results'.[69] The dispute is just one manifestation of ongoing disputes involving the Thai government, which is effectively the owner of the dominant producer of cigarettes in Thailand, the state-owned enterprise aptly named the Thailand Tobacco Monopoly.[70] Industry news reports have chronicled ongoing difficulties between the Philip Morris Thai subsidiary and Thai authorities. These reports state that the Thai subsidiary has been prosecuted by the Thai government for tax violations resulting from understated import values.[71] The Thai government has also given different treatment of different types of tobacco products, particularly pre-rolled cigarettes as opposed to loose tobacco.[72] The differential tax treatment was the subject of a 1990 decision of a GATT dispute settlement panel, which held that the internal tax treatment of tobacco products was inconsistent with Articles III(2) and XI(1) of the GATT, and furthermore could not be supported by the health

---

http://www.sunsonline.org/trade/process/followup/1995/02210095.htm.

[68]   World Trade Organization, 'Current Status – Thailand – Customs and Fiscal Measures on Cigarettes from the Philippines' (2010), accessed 2 September 2010, http://www.wto.org/english/tratop_e/dispu_e/cases_e/ds371_e.htm.

[69]   'Thailand Cigarette Tax Row Worsens' (undated), accessed 2 September 2010, http://www.topcigshop.com/News/17765.aspx.

[70]   'Philippines–Thai Cigarette Import Rules', (2008), accessed 2 September 2010,   http://snus-news.blogspot.com/2008/11/philippines-thai-cigarette-import-rules.html.

[71]   'Thailand Unit of Philip Morris International Faces Charges that it Violated Custom Tax Rules', (2009), accessed 2 September 2010, http://snus-news.blogspot.com/2009/09/in-process-thailand-unit-of-philip.html.

[72]   'Thailand: Cigarette Maker Phillip Morris Asks Thai Government for Fair Treatment on Taxation', *Thai News Service*, 23 May 2006, 36, accessed 2 September 2010, http://au.nielsen.com/pubs/documents/MarketWatch_FMCG_June_2006.pdf.

exception provided for in Article XX(b).[73] It is interesting to note that underlying the entire, ongoing set of Thai cigarette disputes is the fact that the main protagonist in the Philippines is a US multinational corporation, rather than a locally owned enterprise.[74]

ASEAN and Asian Trends in WTO Dispute Settlement

As indicated above, two disputes between ASEAN members have been raised for consultation under the DSU. The *Polyethylene and Polypropylene products* dispute[75] was the first case brought before the WTO Dispute Settlement Body just after its creation in January 1995. The primary complaint by Singapore concerned the inconsistency of the measures with Articles X and XI of the GATT 1994, and Article 3 of the WTO Agreement on Import Licensing Procedures. Singapore requested consultations with Malaysia on 10 January 1995,[76] and subsequently sought the establishment of a panel in March 1995. While it is not apparent from the official WTO documents, there were newspaper reports of the pressure placed on Singapore by Indonesia to engage in consultation, in order to preserve the international reputation of ASEAN.[77] The establishment of a panel was delayed to allow for further consultations, and ultimately the dispute was withdrawn in July 1995.[78]

The second WTO dispute between ASEAN members is, at the time of writing, still active in the WTO, with a panel report expected to be issued

---

[73]   Report of the Panel, *Thailand – Restrictions on Importation of and Internal Taxes of Cigarettes,* DS10/R – 37S/200, adopted on 7 November 1990.

[74]   This is of course not an unusual feature of WTO disputes. For example, the EC–Bananas disputes (mentioned below), while brought by the developing countries of Colombia, Panama, Guatemala, Honduras and Mexico, were motivated in a large part (although not exclusively) by US-owned interests in those countries. See C. Raghavan, 'The "Banana Heat" in US Political Debate', *South-North Development Monitor*, 28 January 1997, accessed 2 September 2010, http://www.sunsonline.org/trade/areas/commodit/01280097.htm.

[75]   'Malaysia and Lion City Trade Row Simmers', *South China Morning Post*, 6 March 1995.

[76]   'Malaysia – Prohibition of Imports of Polyethylene and Polypropylene – Request for Consultations under Article XXIII.1 of the GATT 1994 by Singapore', WTO Document WT/DS1/1, 10 January 1995.

[77]   C. Raghavan, 'Singapore–Malaysia Dispute Takes an Edge at WTO', *South-North Development Monitor,* 21 February 1995, accessed 2 September 2010, http://www.sunsonline.org/trade/process/followup/1995/02210095.htm.

[78]   See further S Jayasankaran, 'Plastic Explosive', *Far Eastern Economic Review* 158 (4) (1995), 44.

Table 7.1   *Participation in WTO dispute settlement by ASEAN members (as at April 2010)*

Country	Total WTO disputes	Disputes involving ASEAN members	Disputes involving ASEAN+3/AANZFTA partners (other than as 3rd parties)
Indonesia	5 as complainant; 4 as respondent; 4 as a 3rd party	None	1 complaint against the Republic of Korea ; 2 disputes brought by Japan
Philippines	5 as complainant; 5 as respondent; 5 as a 3rd party	1 complaint against Thailand	1 complaint against the Republic of Korea; 2 cases brought against Australia
Thailand	13 as complainant; 3 as respondent; 41 as a 3rd party	1 complaint brought by the Philippines	None
Malaysia	1 as complainant; 1 as respondent; 2 as a 3rd party	1 complaint brought by Singapore	None
Singapore	1 as complainant; 4 as a 3rd party	1 case against Malaysia	None
Vietnam	1 as complainant; 3 as a 3rd party	None	None
Cambodia	None	None	None
Myanmar	None	None	None
Brunei	None	None	None

around June 2010.[79] It is not the first time that the Philippines has brought a WTO complaint, and within ASEAN Thailand is by far the most experienced litigant, albeit as a complainant rather than a respondent. Table 7.1 summarizes the experience that the ASEAN members have had in WTO disputes, and the level of disputing in which they have engaged with ASEAN's external trade area partners (China, Japan, the Republic of Korea, Australia and New Zealand).

While the table excludes the activities of the ASEAN members as third parties in disputes involving the '+3' and AANZFTA signatories, it is

[79]   See World Trade Organization, 'Current Status – Thailand – Customs and Fiscal Measures on Cigarettes from the Philippines' (2010), accessed 2 September 2010, http://www.wto.org/english/tratop_e/dispu_e/cases_e/ds371_e.htm.

interesting to note only Thailand has engaged as a third party in disputes against China. While this is largely consistent with the ASEAN members' overall patterns of engagement, it is interesting that Vietnam has nominated its interest as a third party in the Chinese dispute against the United States[80] but appears to have been unwilling to do so in the eight cases in which China is (or was) the respondent. A review of broader regional engagement with the WTO shows the proximity of the ASEAN members to some of the more frequent users of the WTO system. China rapidly assumed the role of a heavy user of the DSU system, as a complainant in five cases and respondent in seventeen. It has become involved as a third party in the majority of cases that have been initiated since its accession to the WTO, in part because of the breadth of its trade interests but also as a mechanism for gaining experience in the operation of the DSU. Japan and the Republic of Korea have similar records, in the sense that they have a balance of cases as complainant and respondent, and like Thailand they frequently engage as third parties in selected disputes (up to one quarter of the disputes that have occurred).

Regional Dispute Settlement Mechanisms – a Comparative Perspective

While zero-use by ASEAN members of the ASEAN dispute settlement procedures is a striking statistic, it should be placed in a global context. The lack of visible 'forum shopping' is less remarkable when ASEAN's track record is contrasted with other regional trade areas such as that established by the North American Free Trade Agreement (NAFTA)[81] and MERCOSUR, the South American regional organization.[82]

NAFTA offers a variety of dispute settlement mechanisms, including a Free Trade Commission under Chapter Twenty that resolves state–state disputes in a manner broadly similar to the WTO Dispute Settlement

[80] 'United States – Measures Affecting Imports of Certain Passenger Vehicle and Light Truck Tyres from China – Request for Consultations by China', WTO Document WT/DS399/1, 14 September 2009.

[81] The North American Free Trade Agreement (NAFTA), adopted in Ottawa, Mexico DF and Washington DC on 17 December 1992.

[82] MERCOSUR (Mercado Común del Sur) was established pursuant to the Treaty Establishing a Common Market between the Argentine Republic, the Federal Republic of Brazil, the Republic of Paraguay and the Eastern Republic of Uruguay, Asunción, adopted on 26 March 1991. Its dispute settlement mechanism is contained in the Protocol of Olivos for the Settlement of Disputes in MERCOSUR, 18 February 2002. MERCOSUR's dispute settlement reports can be accessed online at http://www.sice.oas.org/Dispute/dispute_e.asp, accessed 2 September 2010.

Understanding. Other chapters of the NAFTA have specific dispute set-tlement mechanisms, including a frequently used process under Chapter Nineteen for a bi-national panel review of decisions relating to anti-dumping and countervailing duties. NAFTA members seeking to initiate a formal complaint may often have to choose in which forum they will bring their dispute, and be able to exploit the differences in substantive and procedural law to select the forum that they believe will offer the best prospects of success.[83] NAFTA and the WTO process receive a steady, substantial caseload of disputes from NAFTA members, although in the case of NAFTA the vast majority of cases are Chapter Nineteen Cases and only three Chapter Twenty Cases have been brought.[84] On the other hand, in the WTO, Canada and the United States have initiated 20 proceedings against one another (including one case against the United States jointly issued by Canada and Mexico) and Mexico and the United States have initiated a total of 15 cases against one another.[85] Mexico and the United States, with other WTO members, have also initiated complaints against the European Communities in the interminable *Bananas* disputes.[86] While not every NAFTA dispute will fall within the WTO's jurisdiction, nor every WTO dispute between NAFTA members be within NAFTA's jurisdiction, there is the potential for forum shopping in many cases. The capacity to select a forum has led to 'forum shopping' even in relation to a single set of contentious national measures, and the use of both fora in disputes such as the *Softwood Lumber* and *Sweetener* cases epitomizes the weaknesses of parallel trade regimes and dispute settlement systems.[87]

---

[83]   Note that this will not be possible in all instances, as the NAFTA and the WTO Agreements do not mirror one another in terms of the commitments required.

[84]   For a full list of NAFTA decisions, see http://www.nafta-sec-alena.org/en/DecisionsAndReports.aspx?x=312, accessed 2 September 2010.

[85]   There are too many cases to list individually; however for a list online see http://www.wto.org/english/tratop_e/dispu_e/dispu_by_country_e.htm, accessed 2 September 2010.

[86]   'European Communities – Regime for the Importation, Sale and Distribution of Bananas – Request for Consultations by Guatemala, Honduras, Mexico, and the United States', WTO Document WT/DS16/1, 28 September 1995; 'European Communities – Regime for the Importation, Sale and Distribution of Bananas – Request for Consultations by Ecuador, Guatemala, Honduras, Mexico, and the United States', WTO Document WT/DS27/1, 5 February 1996; and 'European Communities – Regime for the Importation, Sale and Distribution of Bananas – Request for Consultations by Honduras, Mexico, Guatemala, Panama, and the United States', WTO Document WT/DS158/1, 20 January 1999.

[87]   Elaboration of these disputes is outside the scope of this chapter; however for a detailed explanation see M.L. Busch, 'Overlapping Institutions, Forum Shopping,

Internal dispute settlement processes for MERCOSUR, the South American regional trade area established in 1991, have resulted in 16 decisions,[88] and in the WTO Argentina and Brazil have initiated three WTO disputes against one another.[89] While Article 1.2 of the Protocol of Olivos prevents the same dispute being submitted to both a MERCOSUR and a WTO process, the *Retreaded Tyres* cases are examples of the way in which different jurisprudence can still arise from the two bodies on the same issue,[90] again giving rise to the possibility of forum shopping in subsequent cases.

A general survey of WTO disputes shows that neighbouring states bring comparatively fewer disputes against one another, regardless of whether or not those neighbours coexist in a formal RTA. The two exceptions to this trend are Argentina, which has brought eight complaints against its South American neighbours (out of a total of 15 complaints) and Norway, which has brought three of its four complaints against the European Communities. All other disputants have brought at least half of their total volume of disputes outside their own geographical region.[91]

---

and Dispute Settlement in International Trade', *International Organization* 61 (2007): 735–61; J. Pauwelyn, 'Adding Sweeteners to Softwood Lumber: The WTO–NAFTA "Spaghetti Bowl" is Cooking', *Journal of International Economic Law* 9 (1) (2006): 197–206; D. Gantz, 'Dispute Settlement Under the NAFTA and the WTO: Choice of Forum Opportunities and Risks for the NAFTA Parties', *American University International Law Review* 14 (1) (1999): 1025–1106.

88 Note however that due to the system for designating cases (which allocates each decision a new number, including cases on appeal to the Permanent Review Tribunal, the number of individual cases quoted exceeds the number of discrete disputes. MERCOSUR's dispute settlement reports can be accessed online (in Portuguese and Spanish) at http://www.sice.oas.org/Dispute/dispute_e.asp, accessed 2 September 2010.

89 The three disputes were 'Argentina – Transitional Safeguard Measures on Certain Imports of Woven Fabric Products of Cotton and Cotton Mixtures Originating in Brazil – Request for the Establishment of a Panel by Brazil', WTO Document WT/DS190/1, 11 February 2000; 'Argentina – Definitive Anti-Dumping Duties on Poultry from Brazil – Request for Consultations by Brazil', WTO Document WT/DS241, 7 November 2001; and 'Brazil – Anti-dumping Measures on Imports of Certain Resins from Argentina – Request for Consultations by Argentina', WTO Document WT/DS355/1, 26 December 2006.

90 See further K.R. Gray, 'Brazil – Measures Affecting Imports of Retreaded Tyres [decisions]', *American Journal of International Law* 102 (3) (2008): 610–16; and F.C. Morosini, 'The MERCOSUR and WTO Retreaded Tires Dispute: Rehabilitating Regulatory Competition in International Trade and Environmental Regulation', paper presented at the Society of International Economic Law (SIEL) Inaugural Conference, 2 July 2008.

91 See the map of WTO disputes, available at http://www.wto.org/english/

Placed in a global context, ASEAN's failure to use the 2004 Protocol is fairly consistent with the trends in other regions. Put simply, neighbours will usually contest disputes as a last resort when other conciliatory attempts have failed, and this maxim applies in ASEAN, the WTO, trade politics and human relations generally. This global trend is also interesting in view of recent attention given to the concept of international law's 'fragmentation', the contention that regionalism will exacerbate the fragmentation, and that 'how the WTO treats issues of competing jurisdiction is crucial to the problem of the potential for duplicated or fragmented jurisprudence, and the effectiveness of the dispute settlement process for member states.'[92] While there is certainly no doubt that divergent decisions can have a harmful effect on the overall cohesion of the law, it seems that this phenomenon is manifested in only a handful of 'difficult' cases. It needs also to be acknowledged that it is far easier to point to these cases as problems than to undertake the near-impossible task of calculating how many times choice of forum was unproblematic – where none of the parties objected to the selection of one forum over another, or indeed effectively used the conciliatory mechanisms of the WTO or the RTA and hence never formalized their dispute. There are certainly other aspects of RTAs that are unsatisfactory (and well documented), such as their questionable economic benefits, but it seems doubtful that the proliferation of RTAs of itself will meaningfully impact upon the WTO as a dispute settlement forum.

Structural Differences Between ASEAN and the WTO

Despite the broad similarities of the dispute settlement processes, there are several differences between the WTO and ASEAN in how the organizations manage (or would manage) disputes at an operational level. While it is difficult to gauge the extent to which these features impact upon a choice of forum, they are significant capacity constraints within ASEAN that warrant some investigation.

---

tratop_e/dispu_e/dispu_maps_e.htm?country_selected=ARG&sense=e, accessed 2 September 2010.

[92] C. Henckels, 'Overcoming Jurisdictional Isolationism at the WTO–FTA Nexus: A Potential Approach for the WTO', *European Journal of International Law* 19 (3) (2008): 575. See also Study Group of the International Law Commission (finalized by Martti Koskeniemmi), 'Fragmentation of International Law: Difficulties Arising from the Diversification and Expansion of International Law', UN Doc. A/CN.4/L.682 (2006), 102–10; and H. Gao and C.L. Lim, 'Saving the WTO from the Risk of Irrelevance: The WTO Dispute Settlement Mechanism as a "Common Good" for RTA Disputes', *Journal of International Economic Law* 11 (2008): 899–925.

Role and Capacity of the Secretariat

An often-overlooked aspect of the WTO's operation is the role of the Secretariat, particularly in relation to the dispute settlement process. The WTO Secretariat employs well over 600 staff, the vast majority of whom have highly specialized technical expertise in specific aspects of WTO law.[93] The Secretariat provides quite extensive administrative, technical and legal support for the panelists and members of the Appellate Body from divisions within the WTO Secretariat, particularly from the Legal Affairs Division but also from the Rules Division and the Appellate Body Secretariat. There is also an extensive Dispute Settlement Registry maintained by the Legal Affairs Division, and a considerable amount of outreach in the form of technical assistance and training to developing country members.[94] The Secretariat maintains databases of legal decisions, analytical indices of the WTO Agreements, and comprehensive archives of WTO documents, and makes these available publicly through a sophisticated website.

By way of contrast, the capacity of the ASEAN Secretariat is limited – the organization has only around 175 staff, and according to one estimate, only around 42 of those staff are engaged in a professional capacity.[95] Reports by private consulting firm McKinsey & Company and the Asian Development Bank have identified structural inadequacies of the ASEAN Secretariat, noting that the Secretariat lacks the capacity to effectively manage ASEAN economic integration or deliver the necessary research support for the members.[96] In response, the Asian Development Bank has initiated two technical assistance projects aimed at improving, amongst other things, the development of ASEAN's dispute settlement system.[97] The 2009–10 project has specifically nominated as a performance target

---

[93] 'Overview of the WTO Secretariat', accessed 2 September 2010, http://www.wto.org/english/thewto_e/secre_e/intro_e.htm.

[94] 'Divisions', accessed 2 September 2010, http://www.wto.org/english/thewto_e/secre_e/div_e.htm.

[95] L. Henry, 'The ASEAN Way and Community Integration: Two Different Models of Regionalism', *European Law Journal* 13 (6) (2007): 862–3.

[96] A. Schwarz and R. Villinger, 'Integrating Southeast Asian Economies', *The McKinsey Quarterly,* February 2004, 1; and 'Strengthening Capacity of the ASEAN Secretariat in Regional Economic Integration and Policy Dialogue', April 2007, 2, accessed 2 September 2010, http://www.adb.org/Documents/TARs/REG/40566-REG-TAR.pdf.

[97] The two projects were: *Technical Assistance for Strengthening Capacity of the ASEAN Secretariat in Regional Economic Integration and Policy Dialogue,* Manila (TA 6393-REG) from 2007 to 2008; and *Strengthening the Capacity of the*

the production of 'better-quality policy briefs and notes, background papers, surveillance reports' from the ASEAN Secretariat.[98] While aspects of these technical assistance projects will certainly enhance the capacity of the Secretariat, it is likely to be some time before sufficient technical expertise exists to properly support the dispute settlement process.

The Dispute Settlement Body and the Senior Economic Officials Meeting

A second structural feature of the DSU that presents an interesting contrast to the ASEAN mechanism is the role of the WTO Dispute Settlement Body (DSB). The DSB, created pursuant to Article IV(3) of the Marrakesh Agreement Establishing the World Trade Organization, is in reality the WTO General Council sitting in session under a different name. It is therefore a political body that is comprised of delegates to the WTO, usually diplomatic officers from a foreign affairs or trade ministry. The actual qualifications of the delegates vary from state to state. Large states may have a permanent mission in which the dedicated WTO diplomats specialize in specific areas of the WTO's operation, whereas small members may have only a part-time delegate who may fly in from their home capital. Article 2 of the DSU authorizes the DSB to approve the establishment of a panel, the adoption of reports, and the taking of retaliatory measures in the event of non-compliance. The DSB receives administrative support and legal advice from the WTO Secretariat.[99]

Within ASEAN, the composition of the Senior Economic Officials Meeting is less apparent (as the information is not publicly available) but it appears from secondary sources that delegates are usually around the level of deputy-directors of international relations departments within trade or commerce ministries. Thus the SEOM members tend to lack a legal background, and have work portfolios that focus on many issues other than ASEAN. A number of sources suggest that, as a whole, ASEAN is overburdened with meetings – over 600 per year – which spreads more thin the resources of the members.[100]

ASEAN Secretariat in Regional Economic Integration and Policy Dialogue – Phase 2 (R-CDTA 41534) from 2009 to 2010.

[98] See 'Technical Assistance Report', February 2009, 5, accessed 2 September 2010, http://www.adb.org/Documents/TARS/REG/41534-REG-TAR.pdf.

[99] 'Divisions', accessed 2 September 2010, http://www.wto.org/english/thewto_e/secre_e/div_e.htm.

[100] 'ASEAN Raps Key Trade Partners for Skipping Meetings', *Asian Economic News*, 3 October 2005, accessed 2 September 2010, http://findarticles.com/p/articles/mi_m0WDP/is_2005_Oct_3/ai_n15662844/?tag=content;col1; see also the

Jurisprudence and Other Sources of Information and Assistance

One consideration for a state commencing a formal dispute process is the availability of information about the way in which the dispute will be handled. It is necessary to have an appreciation of the substantive law applicable to the dispute, with some capacity to apply the existing law to predict (within a certain margin) the likely outcome of the dispute. It is also necessary to be aware of the procedural aspects of the dispute mechanism – and preferably to have previous experience of the process as a participant or a trusted advisor. In all of these respects, the WTO DSU offers superior information-gathering potential compared with that of ASEAN, and it must be assumed that the ready availability of information is at least a minor factor in a selection of forum. While the ASEAN members may not agree with individual cases decided by WTO panels or the Appellate Body, there is at least the benefit of a degree of certainty and predictability as to how a future case might be decided.

CULTURAL DIFFERENCES – LEGALISM AND THE 'ASEAN WAY'

ASEAN is very different from other regional trade institutions in its structure and *modus operandi*. The structure of ASEAN was in no way intended to replicate the strongly legalistic approaches of either NAFTA or the European model, or to create strong supranational executive, legislative or judicial functions. The former Secretary-General of ASEAN, Rodolfo Severino, was adamant that ASEAN would have no aspirations 'to be a supranational entity acting independently of its members'.[101] Although the Charter does purport to give ASEAN international personality, ASEAN still retains a unique institutional character. The Charter instead upholds a highly fragmented and decentralized organization composed of various advisory bodies, including various Meetings of heads of government and ministers, over twenty-five fixed and rotating committees and more than one hundred technical advisory groups, and is perhaps described more

---

Report of the Asian Development Bank, 'Strengthening Capacity of the ASEAN Secretariat in Regional Economic Integration and Policy Dialogue', April 2007, 1, accessed 2 September 2010, http://www.adb.org/Documents/TARs/REG/40566-REG-TAR.pdf.

[101] Rudolfo Severino, 'What ASEAN Is and What It Stands For', speech delivered at the Research Institute for Asia and the Pacific, University of Sydney, 22 October 1998, accessed 2 September 2010, http://www.aseansec.org/3399.htm.

appropriately as a framework than a system or structure. As Alagappa observes of this institutional arrangement, 'the loose framework, although making for ambiguity and inefficiency, provides opportunities for "face saving" which is considered vital for ASEAN solidarity and cohesion.'[102]

It is important to emphasize that there is no single culture common to all ASEAN members. While many Westerners tend to associate Asia (and by extension ASEAN) with exclusively Confucian values, ASEAN contains a very rich cross-section of cultural and religious influences. Despite being one of the most long-standing regional arrangements, it is also cultur-ally the most complex. Confucian, Islamic, Hindu and Buddhist cultures extensively shape the legal cultures of most of the ASEAN states, and these influences often co-exist (with varying degrees of harmony) within individual states.[103] According to another former Secretary-General, despite this cultural diversity there are

> behavioural inclinations that cut across societies of Southeast Asia . . . that have been shaped through the centuries by common geography, climate and shared historical experiences with each other and with countries outside the region. Generally speaking, an ASEAN citizen is family-oriented, tradition-minded, respectful of authority, consensus-seeking and tolerant . . . These common qualities in attitudes and predispositions are clearly reflected in the Bali Concord II . . . This important document has stressed shared responsibil-ity, shared prosperity and shared identity.[104]

The concept of consensus is one that ASEAN recognizes as key to the ASEAN identity, and the centrality of this approach to negotiations and disagreements has become known as the 'ASEAN Way'.[105] Two traditional Malay approaches to disputing and negotiation embody the ASEAN Way – the first, *musyawarah*, involves discussion and consultation and the second, *mufakat*, refers to the idea of consensus.[106]

---

[102]   M. Alagappa, 'Institutional Framework – Recommendations for Change', in Kernial Singh Sandhu (ed.), *The ASEAN Reader* (Singapore: Institute of Southeast Asian Studies, 1992), 64.

[103]   See, for example, M. Mastura, 'Legal Pluralism in the Philippines', *Law & Society Review* 28 (3) (1994): 461–76.

[104]   H.E. Ong Keng Yong, 'ASEAN Cultural Connection: ASEAN Values and its Relevance to the Modern World', speech delivered at the Public Relations Academy of Singapore, 12 November 2003, accessed 2 September 2010, http://www.aseansec.org/15988.htm.

[105]   P.J. Davidson, 'The ASEAN Way and the Role of Law in ASEAN Economic Cooperation', *Singapore Year Book of International Law* 8 (2004): 166.

[106]   For a detailed discussion of these concepts and their impact upon ASEAN negotiating styles, see Pushpa Thambipillai, *ASEAN Negotiations: Two Insights* (Singapore: Institute of Southeast Asian Studies, 200) 37.

ASEAN members are known for their rejection of strict negotiation timetables in favour of 'action agendas',[107] and negotiation in informal rather than formal settings – 'sports shirt diplomacy' as opposed to 'business shirt diplomacy'. In a more critical tone, Soesastro reports that the ASEAN Way has also been (accurately) described as 'agree first, talk after',[108] and other commentators argue that ASEAN's norms and mores actually inhibit genuine economic liberalization.[109] In the context of disputes, 'finessing' and 'defusing' are preferred to adversarialism and confrontation.[110] The effect of this approach is summarized by Leifer in the following terms:

> Over the years, ASEAN has achieved its regional standing through an ability to manage problems rather than solving them. For ASEAN governments, a personalized process of consultation and cooperation has become more important than formal procedures for problem-solving. Indeed, ASEAN is not directly about problem-solving, but about creating the milieu in which they either do not arise or can be readily managed. . . . This approach is often hard for Westerners to understand, but a range of intra-mural tensions has been contained in this way as a clear alternative to forms of security arrangement more familiar in the West.[111]

It is interesting to contrast this type of statement with the more routine advice to formalize dispute settlement mechanisms. For example, speaking generally about regional trade agreements in Asia, Davey cautions 'that attention should be paid to creating a robust dispute settlement system as without one, the limited benefits of an RTA are even less likely to materialize.'[112] In some senses, application of the ASEAN Way to

---

[107] See, for example, S. Sugawara, 'Lingering Trade Disputes Cloud Asia-Pacific Summit; With APEC Leaders Due in Osaka, Hopes Dim for Progress on Resolving Difference', *The Washington Post*, 12 November 1995, 24.

[108] H. Soesastro, 'On ASEAN Community', *Indonesian Economic Journal* (2005): 69.

[109] See, for example, V.K. Aggarwal and J.T. Chow, 'The Perils of Consensus: How ASEAN's Meta-Regime Undermines Economic and Environmental Cooperation', S. Rajaratnam School of International Studies Working Paper Series, Paper 177, April 2009, accessed 2 September 2010, http://www.rsis.edu.sg/publications/WorkingPapers/WP177.pdf.

[110] See, for example, R. Pura, 'ASEAN Defuses Trade Dispute with Jakarta Prior to Summit', *The Wall Street Journal Europe*, 11 December 1995, 16.

[111] M. Leifer, 'The Issue Is ASEAN', *Far Eastern Economic Review*, 30 November 1995, 34.

[112] W.J. Davey, 'Regional Trade Agreements and the WTO: General Observations and NAFTA Lessons for Asia', Illinois Public Law Research Paper No. 05-18 (2005), 24.

disputes has proven to be as robust a mechanism as the formal adjudicatory processes offered by the 2004 Protocol. Another way to view the 2004 Protocol is that it ensures that there will be an end-point to disputes should the ASEAN Way fail to resolve them.

THE WTO AS A 'SILO' AND ASEAN AS A COMMUNITY

While ASEAN and the WTO now have very similar dispute settlement mechanisms, the organizations themselves differ markedly from one another. ASEAN differs markedly from the WTO, and indeed from many other regional trade organizations, in the scope of its endeavours. The WTO is an organization focused solely on trade and trade-related issues, and often receives criticism for failing to take account of broader issues.[113] ASEAN, as this chapter has discussed above, is a community that has three pillars, with security issues being of particular importance. While this statement seems self-evident to a political scientist, it is a consideration that is at best on the periphery for a trade lawyer who is accustomed to the politics of the WTO.

At the heart of ASEAN, and the cause of many of its most deep tensions, are traditional security concerns regarding territory. As Abad has observed, '[f]irst, foremost in the minds of the founding members of ASEAN was self preservation.'[114] A clear but generally unstated objective of ASEAN is to deter external threats to regional security. In particular, the individual states use ASEAN as a collective security mechanism acting as a counter-weight to the larger state powers of China, Japan and India. In order to maintain a sense of collective security against these external threats, ASEAN needs to maintain internal peace in spite of a fairly large number of intense territorial disputes. While it is certainly possible to criticize ASEAN for not finding comprehensive settlements to any of these disputes, or even preventing minor outbreaks of violence,[115] the tradition

---

[113] For example, it has often been said that the WTO should pay greater attention to issues such as trade and the environment, labor issues, and human rights and development more generally.

[114] M.C. Abad Jr (2007), 'Constructing the Social ASEAN', paper presented at the 21st Asia Pacific Roundtable of ISIS Malaysia, Kuala Lumpur, 4–8 June 2007, accessed 2 September 2010, http://www.aseansec.org/21224.htm.

[115] C. Bajpaee, 'The Price of Asian Conflict', *Asia Times Online*, 24 May 2005, accessed 2 September 2010, http://www.atimes.com/atimes/Asian_Economy/ GE24Dk01.html.

of maintaining communication through all types of dispute has stood ASEAN in good stead.

While a comprehensive survey of ASEAN territorial disputes is outside the scope of this chapter, it suffices to say that they are quite extensive.[116] For example, Malaysia and the Philippines are in dispute over the Eastern part of the Sabah, Indonesia and Malaysia disagree over control of the Ligitan and Sipadan Islands, Singapore and Malaysia have had extensive disagreements over Middle Rock and Pedra Branca, Brunei has maritime disputes with Vietnam and Malaysia, Thailand and Cambodia dispute ownership of the Preah Vihear Temple, Thailand and Myanmar dispute their borders and there have been low-level incursions by Myanmar into Thai territory, and territorial disputes between Cambodia and Vietnam led to armed conflict in the earlier part of ASEAN's history. Further tensions simmer between the ASEAN members about the treatment of Muslims in the Southern Thai provinces and on the Philippine island of Mindanao, and, most recently, there has been annoyance from the Thai regime at friendly overtures made by Cambodia towards former Thai premier Thaksin Shinawatra.

The way in which ASEAN has generally dealt with the disputes is explained by Acharya in the context of the Sabah dispute:

> ASEAN did not and could not *resolve* the Sabah dispute, which continues to elude a decisive settlement. Neither did ASEAN play the role of conflict mediator/ manager in a formal and legalistic sense. But ASEAN members, through direct and indirect measures of restraint, pressure, diplomacy, communication and trade-offs, did succeed in *preventing* any further escalation of the crisis, which might have led to armed hostilities and destroyed the organization. Thus, the Sabah dispute is an important milestone in ASEAN's early approach.[117]

In a similar vein to trade disputes, ASEAN members tend to refer disputes that cannot be resolved through internal negotiation to external adjudication rather than use an adjudicatory mechanism within ASEAN. Thus, in territorial conflicts, ASEAN members have brought two cases before the International Court of Justice, rather than use the mechanisms articulated in Chapter IV of the ASEAN Treaty of Amity and Cooperation. A third case, *Temple of Preah Vihear (Cambodia v. Thailand)*, was commenced in 1959 and judgment was issued in June 1962, prior to the introduction

---

[116]   For a comprehensive list, see Rongxing Guo, *The Land and Maritime Boundary Disputes of Asia* (New York: Nova Publishers, 2009).

[117]   Amitav Acharya, *Constructing a Security Community in Southeast Asia: ASEAN and the Problem of Regional Order* (London: Routledge, 2001), 50.

of the Treaty of Amity and Cooperation. Singapore and Malaysia also submitted an encroachment dispute arising from Singaporean land reclamation for arbitration before the International Tribunal for the Law of the Sea.[118] A settlement agreement was reached in April 2005 with the Tribunal having only issued orders on provisional measures.[119]

Overall, the ASEAN region is one in which a large number of serious territorial disputes persist, although at low intensity. ASEAN members also face very substantial external threats to their territory from neighbours, particularly China, which has land border disputes with Vietnam, and extensive disputes over the Paracel and/or Spratley Islands with four of the ten ASEAN members. Chinese construction of dams has caused conflict with the downstream ASEAN Mekong delta states of Vietnam, Cambodia, Thailand and Laos.[120] With nearly every ASEAN member in serious dispute with China, and with the constant threat of these conflicts escalating, maintaining a cohesive ASEAN is of vital importance.[121]

The ASEAN organization gives a fragile stability to an otherwise unstable region where border disputes and other tensions abound. ASEAN's role as an institution to maintain that stability is like an eggshell that protects the fragile embryonic entity within. The South-east Asian region can easily be damaged and risk disintegration into armed conflict. ASEAN has so far held the region together and must be sheltered from unnecessary 'knocks' such as trade disputes. It is therefore with good reason that ASEAN's members have repeatedly avoided adjudicating any disputes in-house and turned only when absolutely necessary to the WTO.

CONCLUSION

The fact that the ASEAN Protocols are unlikely ever to be used should not be interpreted as a 'no confidence' vote by the ASEAN members. ASEAN members, amongst themselves and within the broader Asian region, are not heavy users of any adjudicatory mechanisms, including

---

[118] *Case concerning Land Reclamation by Singapore in and around the Straits of Johor (Malaysia v. Singapore)*.

[119] Order 2003/1 of 10 September 2003 and Order of 8 October 2003, accessed 2 September 2010, http://www.itlos.org/start2_en.html.

[120] J. Son, 'Mistrust Lingers over Dams', *Asia Times Online*, 8 April 2010, accessed 2 September 2010, http://www.atimes.com/atimes/China/LD08Ad03.html.

[121] See further Mely Caballero-Anthony, *Regional Security in Southeast Asia: Beyond the ASEAN Way* (Singapore: ISEAS Publications, 2005), 66–9.

those of the WTO. Taking a broader view of regional dispute settlement mechanisms in general, the non-use of the ASEAN mechanism is even less remarkable. Comparable regional trade organizations such as NAFTA and MERCOSUR also have quite low volumes of inter-state dispute settlement, and their members also use the WTO for intractable disputes. The architecture of the DSU, the availability of procedural mechanisms such as third-party processes and retaliation, and the very fact that the organization is global mean that the WTO remains an attractive forum of choice even where regional options are available. In the ASEAN context specifically, there are strong political and cultural incentives to prefer the WTO to ASEAN when negotiation and facilitation has failed. The ongoing use of the consensus mechanism in ASEAN leaves open the possibility of veto, something that was specifically addressed by the WTO when the DSU was created. ASEAN lacks the WTO's well-resourced Secretariat to provide advice to disputants and support to panelists.

Finally, and perhaps most significantly, ASEAN is not solely a trade forum. Whereas the WTO has the benefit of being a self-contained regime for trade, in ASEAN trade must cohabit the same forum as other, more explosive, political concerns such as territorial integrity and the physical security of the state. ASEAN members rely instead on the 'ASEAN Way', which holds that progress can be made through consensus and discussion, not confrontation. Paradoxical as it may sound to the adversarially inclined Western trade lawyer, the absence of ASEAN trade law cases may actually be an indicator of the system's success.

8. East Asian investment treaties in the integration process: quo vadis?

Trinh Hai Yen

INTRODUCTION

Investment treaties are instruments of international law by which states undertake commitments to other states with regard to international investors and investments and they provide enforcement mechanisms for those commitments.[1] Investment treaties in this chapter include bilateral investment treaties (BITs) and bilateral or multilateral economic agreements with investment provisions such as free trade agreements. The ten ASEAN nations and China, Japan and South Korea have made 67 investment treaties. Given this large number, these treaties provide prospects for the development of a common legal investment instrument.

Efforts to regionalize the legal framework for intra-East Asia investment were first undertaken in the East Asia Study Group (EASG) report published at the ASEAN+3 Summit in 2002. The report contained proposals for an East Asia Free Trade Area and an East Asia Investment Area.[2] A Joint Expert Group from ASEAN+3 countries suggested that the economic benefits from an East Asian Free Trade Area (EAFTA) exceed those of AFTA (ASEAN Free Trade Area), any ASEAN+1 Free Trade Area (FTA), or any other bilateral or sub-regional arrangements.[3]

---

[1] Jeswald W. Salacuse, *The Law of Investment Treaties* (New York: Oxford University Press, 2010), 1.

[2] Final Report of the East Asia Study Group (EASG), ASEAN+3 Summit, 4 November 2002, accessed 2 September 2010, http://www.mofa.go.jp/region/asia-paci/asean/pmv0211/report.pdf.

[3] 'Towards an East Asian FTA: modality and roadmap', A Report by Joint Expert Group for Feasibility Study on EAFTA, September 2006, accessed 2 September 2010, http://www.thaifta.com/thaifta/Portals/0/eafta_report.pdf.

ASEAN+3 leaders had already affirmed their 'common resolve to realize an East Asian community as a long-term objective that would contribute to the maintenance of regional and global peace, security, progress and prosperity'.[4]

Nonetheless, regional investment treatification has currently resulted in the evolution of different sub-regional investment regimes. Historic legacies and political and economic considerations of the states involved are obstructing the path to a regionally integrated legal framework for investment. While connected through bilateral investment treaties, China, Japan and South Korea have not achieved a tripartite investment treaty. This is in contrast to the fact that ASEAN, China and South Korea have separately concluded investment treaties and that Japan has pursued FTAs containing a chapter on investment with six ASEAN countries and BITs with the three others. These strategies coincided with ASEAN's intention to make the Northeast Asian (NEA) countries compete with each other. ASEAN will not encourage an East Asia investment treaty project until it has achieved sufficient intra-ASEAN cohesion to compete with all the three NEA countries. As a matter of law, the impression of consistency in regional investment treaties from such condensed investment treaty development is misleading because they bear many specifically negotiated discrepancies irrespective of some similarity in the language and structures of the contemporary treaties. Like fragmented jigsaw puzzles they are difficult to fit together in an integrated framework.

This chapter examines East Asian investment treaties and assesses the necessity and possibility of integrating these treaties to achieve a common East Asia investment treaty framework. The first part explores the strategies of East Asian nations in advancing regional investment treaty making. It also analyzes the investment treaty web, its content discrepancies and bilateralism, which are legal challenges in forming a single East Asia-based investment treaty. The second part considers the necessity for, and explores two possible ways to achieve, an East Asia-based investment treaty.

---

4 Chairman's Statement of the Ninth ASEAN Plus Three Summit, Kuala Lumpur, 12 December 2005, accessed 2 September 2010, http://www.aseansec.org/18042.htm.

THE FRAGMENTATION OF EAST ASIAN INVESTMENT TREATIES

Efforts to Multilateralize East Asian Investment Treaties

ASEAN investment legal framework

Regional cooperation generally starts from a nucleus. The only institutionalized group in East Asia is ASEAN. However, the ASEAN way of non-interference, consultation and consensus keeps integration progressing at a modest pace. The current ASEAN investment legal framework is in transition from the old regime to a newly signed treaty, which has not been effective yet. Applicable ASEAN legal documents regulating intra-investments include:

- the 1987 ASEAN Agreement for the Promotion and Protection of Investments and its 1996 Protocol
- the 1998 Framework Agreement on the ASEAN Investment Area and its 2001 Protocol
- the 2004 Enhanced Protocol on Dispute Settlement Mechanism.[5]

The 1987 Agreement contains the generally defined standards of protection in line with many other investment treaties such as full protection, fair and equitable treatment, an umbrella clause, repatriation of capital and earnings, and dispute settlement. National treatment and most-favored-nation treatment for ASEAN foreign investors were not provided for under the 1987 Agreement; instead, they were introduced 11 years later in the 1998 Framework Agreement.

Both Agreements need improving since their language is in some places very general and vague, which might create too much room for interpretation. Additionally, the provision on settlement of ASEAN investor–state disputes in the 1987 Agreement might raise some concerns about the actual practical force of the substantive principles. Under investment treaties, investors generally have the choice of arbitration after failing to resolve investor–state disputes by negotiation or diplomatic means. This is not true in the 1987 Agreement if the host state opts for conciliation.[6]

---

[5] This Protocol shall replace the 1996 Protocol on Dispute Settlement Mechanism and shall not apply to any dispute which has arisen before its entry into force. Such dispute shall continue to be governed by the 1996 Protocol on Dispute Settlement Mechanism. Both govern state–state investment disputes.

[6] Article X(2) of the 1987 Agreement provides that: 'if such a dispute cannot thus be settled within six months of its being raised, then either party can elect to

Moreover, the 1987 Agreement leaves many issues of investor–state dispute settlement ambiguous.[7]

The 2007 ASEAN Charter[8] clearly provided for the association's legal personality and it provides a more sophisticated structure,[9] launching a platform for intensive integration efforts in building ASEAN security, economic, social and cultural communities. If ASEAN countries are truly committed to moving toward closer economic integration, they must build a strong and efficient legal foundation. The legal framework for ASEAN investment needs renegotiating in order to develop an ASEAN economic community. Such a process has been driven not only by integration but also by ASEAN's desire to be seen as an attractive location for foreign investment.[10]

ASEAN launched negotiations on a new treaty to upgrade the 1987 and 1998 Agreements and concluded the ASEAN Comprehensive Investment Agreement (ACIA) on 26 February 2009. It aims to create a free and open investment regime by fostering progressive liberalization of the investment regimes of ASEAN member states and enhanced protection for intra-ASEAN investors. The ACIA will replace the 1987 and 1998 Agreements when it enters into force.[11] Participants in investments covered by all the three Agreements, however, may invoke one of them for a period of three years after the termination of the 1987 and 1998 Agreements. The ACIA has not been effective yet because not all ten ASEAN countries have ratified it.[12]

---

submit the dispute *for conciliation or arbitration* and such election shall be binding on the other party' (emphasis added).

[7] For instance, if the host state submits the dispute to conciliation and no satisfactory solution is produced, can investors then resort to arbitration? If the first choice is arbitration, is it final or after that may either disputing party resort to domestic courts, administrative tribunals or even conciliation? See Article X of the 1987 Agreement.

[8] See ASEAN Charter, accessed 2 September 2010, http://www.aseansec.org/21861.htm.

[9] Making a breakthrough with the 1967 Bangkok Declaration, ASEAN functions with only one institutional body, the Secretariat, facilitating discussions between representatives of the member states. See the 1967 Bangkok Declaration, accessed 2 September 2010, http://www.aseansec.org/1212.htm.

[10] Paul J. Davidson, 'The ASEAN Way and the Role of Law in ASEAN Economic Cooperation', 8 *Singapore Year Book of International Law* (2004).

[11] See Article 47 of the ACIA.

[12] As of April 2010, eight ASEAN countries, namely Brunei, Cambodia, Lao, Malaysia, Myanmar, the Philippines, Singapore and Vietnam, have ratified the treaty. See Table of ASEAN treaties/agreements and ratification, accessed 2 September 2010, http://www.aseansec.org/Ratification.pdf.

Agreements on investments between NEA countries and ASEAN

ASEAN strategy   ASEAN was believed to be the driving force,[13] or to play a leading role, in East Asian community building and ASEAN's 'unique way' was 'to bring all countries in SEA together gradually and to turn the region into a united and integrated one'.[14] However, in the role that ASEAN is playing in the process of investment integration, it does not speak with the same confident voice. Firstly, it was not ASEAN but NEA countries that initiated the investment treaties and determined how to proceed with them. Secondly, the terms of the treaties do not reflect a shared position but one that is markedly different from country to country. ASEAN countries have made different individual clauses to customize their treaty obligations and their adherence to the treaties with NEA countries is independent of each other.[15]

The reason behind ASEAN's seemingly passive and divided approach lies first of all in the strategies of the NEA countries as analyzed above. Moreover, ASEAN prioritized its own integration for better competitiveness. Since the economic size of China, Japan and South Korea together is much larger than that of the ASEAN economies combined, as Singapore's Trade and Industry Minister George Yeo reportedly said, ASEAN preferred '10 + 1, in a position to deal with Japan, China and South Korea separately' and keep them competing for relations with ASEAN.[16] ASEAN did not push the idea of an East Asia Free Trade Area or Investment Area proposed under the feasibility study of the joint expert group.[17] It will probably be more interested in such broad-based regional integration when its internal integration is successful, resulting in sufficient competitiveness with external powers.

Last but not least, currently ASEAN lacks internal cohesive strength. Although as a bloc it has had FTAs projects with NEA partners, ASEAN does not act as a ten-country organization. Instead, ASEAN has simply served as a convenient negotiation forum, gathering a group of countries

---

[13]   Chairman's Statement of the Eleventh ASEAN Plus Three Summit, accessed 2 September 2010, http://www.aseansec.org/21096.htm.

[14]   Zhang Yunling, *China and Asian Regionalism* (Singapore: World Scientific, 2010), 3.

[15]   See 'Specific "reservations" in the main text of treaties' below.

[16]   Information was from an observer at the joint press conference after the AEM+3 meeting, 14 September 2002, quoted in Naoko Munakata, *Transforming East Asia: The Evolution of Regional Economic Integration* (Washington, DC: Brookings Institution Press, 2006), 122.

[17]   'Towards an East Asian FTA: modality and roadmap', above note 3.

with mutual interests in an FTA with an East Asian partner. The intra-ASEAN integration is still way ahead and ASEAN needs to simultaneously strengthen economic linkages with non-ASEAN powers for its own development. Its robust external relations will have a reverse catalyst effect for ASEAN integration activities. For example, ASEAN's new investment treaty, the ASEAN Comprehensive Investment Agreement, has been acknowledged to absorb the results from negotiations of external treaties.[18]

NEA approaches   NEA countries have made active moves to formulate separate investment agreements with ASEAN. China was the first of the three NEA countries to propose a Framework Agreement for a free trade area with ASEAN which would include an agreement on investment.[19] Instead of Japan or South Korea, China offered ASEAN an FTA possibly because, when facing difficulty in agreeing upon concessions, China and ASEAN could maintain trade barriers without violating WTO rules. This is because, under the 'enabling clause' of WTO rules, developing countries do not have to cover 'substantially all the trade' in their FTAs.[20] Therefore, tying with ASEAN first will make it easier for China to quickly catch up with the regional trend towards FTAs.[21]

China and ASEAN signed the Framework Agreement on Comprehensive Economic Cooperation (ACFA) at the ASEAN–China Summit in 2002, laying down the objectives and principles for subsequent negotiations on investment.[22] The ASEAN–China Investment Agreement was concluded during the 41st ASEAN Economic Ministers Meeting on 15 August 2009.

China's move quickly triggered other Northeast Asian responses in the regional economic competition. Investment cooperation between ASEAN

---

[18]   *Highlights of the ACIA,* accessed 2 September 2010, http://www.aseansec.org/20632.htm. Official information from the ASEAN Secretariat website acknowledged the influence of the negotiations of investment treaties with extra-regional partners on the ASEAN internal investment treaty.

[19]   See Framework Agreement on Comprehensive Economic Cooperation between the Association of South East Asian Nations and the People's Republic of China, accessed 2 September 2010, http://www.aseansec.org/13196.htm.

[20]   Ibid.

[21]   Naoko Munakata, above note 16, 117.

[22]   Article 5 of the ACFA provides that '[t]o promote investments and to create a liberal, facilitative, transparent and competitive investment regime, the Parties agree to: (a) enter into negotiations in order to progressively liberalize the investment regime; (b) strengthen co-operation in investment, facilitate investment and improve transparency of investment rules and regulations; and (c) provide for the protection of investments.'

and South Korea followed the same path as that of ASEAN and China. They signed the Framework Agreement on Comprehensive Economic Cooperation (AKFA) in 2005. Investment negotiations which were conducted under the AKFA resulted in the Agreement on Investment in June 2009. Japan, however, adopted a bilateral approach, which will be discussed below.

Bilateralism in East Asian Investment Treaties

Bilateral investment agreements

BITs between NEA countries   Intra-Northeast Asian investments are currently governed by the three BITs binding upon all the three NEA countries. The fact that China, Japan and South Korea have made commitments towards each other's investors and investments indicated the possibility of merging the BITs into an NEA trilateral investment treaty. The idea of economic cooperation among China, Japan and South Korea was raised in November 1999 by the South Korea President with a joint study proposal.[23] Unfortunately, the process of making a trilateral treaty has been moving very slowly. It had been postponed[24] until 2007 when the official first round of negotiations on the draft articles of the future trilateral investment treaty was not launched.[25] The project is still under cautious consideration by these countries. In addition to research undertaken

---

[23]   Naoko Munakata, above note 16, 128.

[24]   China postponed the trilateral investment deal with Japan and South Korea in January 2005 perhaps because of disagreement over the model BIT on which their negotiations should be based. While China wanted to build upon the 1992 BIT between South Korea and China, South Korea representatives compared the South Korea–China BIT and the South Korea–Japan BIT and chose the latter because of more pro-investment provisions. See *Investment Law and Policy Weekly News Bulletin*, 10 January 2005, published by the International Institute for Sustainable Development, accessed 2 September 2010, http://www.iisd.org/investment. See also Japan's Ministry of Foreign Affairs, 'The Joint Study on Trilateral Investment Arrangements among China, Japan, and the Republic of Korea' (in Japanese), quoted in Naoko Munakata, above note 16, 129.

[25]   See Announcement on the website of Japan's Ministry of Foreign Affairs, accessed 2 September 2010, http://www.mofa.go.jp/announce/event/2007/3/1172855_844.html. See also the Sixth Round of the Negotiation on the Trilateral Investment Agreement and the Twelfth Meeting of the Government Mechanism for the Improvement of Business Environment for Investment among the People's Republic of China, Japan and the Republic of Korea, 10 April 2009, accessed 2 September 2010, http://www.mofa.go.jp/announce/event/2009/4/1190357_1156.html.

between 2003 and 2009 by Korean, Chinese and Japanese research institutions discussing possible improvements in the investment environment and the elements of a possible trilateral investment treaty,[26] the three countries started a joint study of a trilateral FTA involving government officials, industrialists and academics in May 2010.[27]

Compared with ASEAN–NEA investment treaty making, NEA trilateral cooperation has made modest progress, for two reasons. First, some argued that the NEA countries lack the political trust to push integration forward. Unresolved historic issues of World War II still loom large.[28] Regional hegemonic rivalry between Japan and China results in major differences.[29] Notwithstanding, some positive signals on enhanced mutual understanding have been given in their joint statements.[30]

Second, currently the NEA countries have a network of three BITs which bind the three countries together but on different levels of commitments.[31] As an importer of private capital from Japan and South Korea, China has been consistently prudent and restrictive in its commitments in treatment of these investors and investments, as opposed to the Japan–South Korea BIT containing much more pro-investor provisions. The increase in the number of arbitrations brought by foreign investors against host states is also a warning for enthusiastic commitments towards

---

[26]   Ibid.

[27]   News on South Korea's Ministry of Foreign Affairs and Trade, website accessed 2 September 2010, http://www.mofat.go.kr/english/econtrade/fta/consideration/KCJ/index.jsp.

[28]   Christopher M. Dent, *East Asian Regionalism* (London and New York: Routledge, 2008), 172. See also Zhang Yunling, above note 14, 59.

[29]   Christopher M. Dent, above note 28, 172. See also Zhang Yunling, above note 14, 45.

[30]   Japan and China jointly stated that '[t]he two sides resolved to face history squarely, advance toward the future, and endeavor with persistence to create a new era of a "mutually beneficial relationship based on common strategic interests" between Japan and China.' See Joint Statement between the Government of Japan and the Government of the People's Republic of China on Comprehensive Promotion of a 'Mutually Beneficial Relationship Based on Common Strategic Interests', 7 May 2008, accessed 2 September 2010, http://www.mofa.go.jp/region/asia-paci/china/joint0805.html. The three countries consider each other important partners and 'will facilitate negotiations to conclude a trilateral agreement for the promotion, facilitation, and protection of investment as soon as possible'. See Joint Statement on the Tenth Anniversary of Trilateral Cooperation among the People's Republic of China, Japan and the Republic of Korea, 10 October 2009, accessed 2 September 2010, http://www.mofa.go.jp/region/asia-paci/jck/meet0910/joint-1.pdf.

[31]   See the BITs between China and Japan (1988), China and South Korea (2007) and Japan and South Korea (2003).

foreign investments.[32] Reconciling competing approaches in NEA countries' existing BITs would require significant compromise, and thus might take a long time.

Japan's BITs and FTAs with ASEAN   Unlike China and South Korea, Japan did not negotiate an investment agreement with ASEAN as a whole; instead, it concluded three BITs and six bilateral FTAs with individual ASEAN member states. Japan's different strategy might have resulted from considerations of its obligation under WTO rules as a developed country to eliminate trade barriers for substantially all trade with its FTA partners, which is more difficult to achieve in multilateral negotiations than in bilateral dialogues. It adopted a 'one-by-one approach'[33] and started FTA projects with Singapore, Malaysia, Thailand, the Philippines, Brunei and Indonesia in parallel with China and South Korea's integration moves.

At a multilateral level, Japan concluded formal negotiations for the ASEAN–Japan Comprehensive Economic Partnership (AJCEP) in 2008.[34] Under this framework, however, negotiations on a Japan–ASEAN investment agreement have not yet been launched. Given the existing FTAs and BITs that Japan has with all individual ASEAN member states, except for Myanmar, Japan might not be in a hurry to secure a comprehensive Japan–ASEAN investment treaty.

Multilateral investment agreements with bilateral operation schemes
Over one-third of the investment treaty web is bilaterally connected. The remaining part *prima facie* is based on multilateral treaties. However, their multilateral form operates essentially on a bilateral basis reflected in their entry-into-force and 'reservations' provisions.

Entry-into-force clauses   Out of the three multilateral investment treaties in East Asia, only the ACIA requires full ratification to be effective. The China–ASEAN Agreement on Investment does not bind the ten

---

[32]   The total number of known treaty-based cases was 357 by the end of 2009. Of those, 57 per cent (202 cases) were initiated during the last five years (starting in 2005). UN Conference on Trade and Development, *Latest Developments in Investor–State Dispute Settlement*, 1 (2010), accessed 2 September 2010, http://www.unctad.org/en/docs/webdiaeia20103_en.pdf.

[33]   Naoko Munakata, above note 16, 121.

[34]   ASEAN–Japan Comprehensive Economic Partnership Agreement, 14 April 2008, accessed 2 September 2010, http://www.mofa.go.jp/policy/economy/fta/asean/agreement.html.

members of ASEAN together with China and in principle individual ASEAN members can opt out of it. This signifies fragmentation and not the usual form of the ASEAN way – consensus. As of April 2010, it has been effective for China and three ASEAN countries, namely Brunei, Malaysia and the Philippines.[35] The entry into force of the South Korea–ASEAN Agreement on Investment followed the same bilateral adoption scheme.[36]

Specific 'reservations' in the main text of treaties   Even assuming that ASEAN countries will all ratify the ACIA and the Agreements on Investment with NEA countries, these treaties are still bilateral in nature. States may make reservations in a unilateral declaration when signing, ratifying, accepting, approving or acceding to a treaty where they are satisfied with most of the terms of a treaty but want 'to exclude or to modify the legal effect of certain provisions of the treaty in their application' to them.[37] East Asian countries have introduced reservation-like provisions during the drafting phase and recorded them in the main text of their investment treaties.[38]

On the one hand, this legal technique reflects bilateralism. While generally in treaty practice most reservations do not deal with the substantive provisions of the treaties,[39] 'reservations' in East Asian investment treaties have deliberately tailored the core treaty provisions. On the other hand, in an innovative way, ASEAN countries and their NEA partners transform reservations into treaty provisions. Contracting parties have customized the general provisions for themselves by adding paragraphs or footnotes excluding or modifying different rules applicable to them in the treaties. As a part of the negotiated deal, these 'unilateral' provisions have the effect of reservations without objection. In other words, the modifications in the treaty provisions will be applied reciprocally between a 'reserving'

---

[35]   Article 27 of the China–ASEAN Agreement on Investment. See also Table of ASEAN treaties/agreements and ratification, accessed 2 September 2010, http://www.aseansec.org/Ratification.pdf.

[36]   For example, Article 31 of the South Korea–ASEAN Agreement on Investment provides: 'This Agreement shall enter into force on the first day of the second month following the latter date on which at least one ASEAN Member Country and Korea have notified all the other parties in writing of the completion of their internal procedures.'

[37]   Ibid.

[38]   See Article 2(1)(d) of the 1969 Vienna Convention on the Law of Treaties (VCLT).

[39]   Lori F. Damrosch et al., *International Law: Cases and Materials* (St Paul, MN.: West Group, 2001), 488.

party and other parties.[40] For example, if in the South Korea–ASEAN Agreement on Investment Vietnam and Singapore determine the compensation for expropriation relating to land in accordance with their laws, regulations and policies instead of the treaty general standard of 'prompt, adequate and effective', other parties to this agreement will also use the same method to compensate Vietnamese or Singaporean investors in their territories.[41]

The treaties, therefore, create a complex matrix of obligations among parties. They are actually the combination of BITs between ASEAN individual member states and China or South Korea. Making BITs in the form of a multilateral investment treaty might save expenditure in economic diplomacy efforts. Instead of multiple negotiations with ten ASEAN member states which would result in BITs with similar structures and provisions, an East Asian partner and ten ASEAN countries simply need to gather together to discuss the same subject matter. Another motivation for a multilateral investment treaty is the symbolic impression of an organization with an increasing integration trend. If the goal is an ASEAN economic community, its member states should act collectively even in a nominal sense. Notwithstanding the bilateral features of East Asian investment treaties, given the high concentration of the investment treaties in the region, the question is whether a regional investment treaty is needed and, if so, whether it could be deduced from the existing treaties.

POSSIBILITY OF REGIONALIZING EAST ASIAN INVESTMENT TREATIES

Rationale of a Common East Asia Investment Treaty

All over the world, foreign investments are now primarily regulated by bilateral instruments since various multilateral efforts, both official and non-governmental, have failed to produce a broad-based investment treaty. Several efforts after the World War II were unsuccessful due to the competing positions of developing countries and developed countries, with the former trying to retain regulatory powers and the latter asking for stronger commitments on foreign investment protection. These included

---

[40] Article 21 of the VLCT.
[41] See Article 12(4) of the Agreement on Investment with South Korea.

the Havana Charter (1948),[42] the International Chamber of Commerce's International Code of Fair Treatment of Foreign Investment (1949), the International Convention for the Mutual Protection of Private Property Rights in Foreign Countries (1957), the Abs-Shawcross Convention, the OECD Draft Convention on the Protection of Foreign Property (1967) and the OECD Multilateral Agreement on Investment (MAI).[43] A successful project from 1945 to 1980 was the 1965 Convention on the Settlement of Investment Disputes between States and Nationals of Other States (ICSID Convention) initiated by the World Bank.

In the 1980s when developing countries changed from being hostile to foreign investment to actively seeking foreign capital to finance their development,[44] multilateral investment treaty projects resulted in the 1980 Unified Agreement for the Investment of Arab Capital in the Arab States, the 1985 Convention Establishing the Multilateral Investment Guarantee Agency (MIGA Convention), the 1992 North American Free Trade Agreement (involving Canada, Mexico and the United States), two Agreements of the World Trade Organization with limited provisions on investment,[45] and the 1994 Energy Charter Treaty (governing only the energy sector).

In East Asia, no regional investment treaty has been entered into. With 67 investment treaties in the region, every East Asian country has one or two investment treaties with all the other East Asian countries, except Myanmar, which has been left out of the treaty relationship with Japan and South Korea.

The multilateral investment treaties between China, South Korea and ASEAN and that among ASEAN countries coexist with bilateral treaties. They do not specify which will prevail when both are applicable. If they provide the same level of investment protection, the application of either treaty will produce the same effect. In the case of inconsistencies, the multilateral treaties might prevail for three reasons. First, they were signed more recently and, according to the later-in-time rule (*lex posteris*) in treaty law, they will trump the earlier treaties given no contrary intention

---

[42]   Havana Charter for an International Trade Organization, 24 March 1948, U.N. Doc. E/CONF.2/78.

[43]   Jeswald W. Salacuse, 'Towards a Global Treaty on Foreign Investment: the Search for a Grand Bargain', in Norbet Horn (ed.), *Arbitrating Foreign Investment Disputes: Procedural and Substantive Legal Aspects* (The Hague: Kluwer Law International, 2004), 56.

[44]   Ibid., 58.

[45]   See the Agreement on Trade-Related Investment Measures (TRIMs) and the General Agreement on Trade in Services (GATS)

in these treaties.[46] Second, in the relationships with other treaties, the multilateral investment treaties provide that they shall not be construed to derogate from any rights or obligations of a party under its other international agreements.[47] Investment protection standards in the multilateral investment treaties are higher and do not defeat the obligations under bilateral ones; therefore, the above provision does not prevent the application of multilateral investment treaties. Thirdly, the purpose of the later multilateral investment treaties is to promote investment and create a liberal, facilitative, transparent and competitive investment regime.[48] To forgo the better offers for investment protection in the multilateral agreements and continue the application of the bilateral ones would defeat their negotiation goals of promoting foreign investment.

Although having been protected by one or two investment treaties (except in the Japan–Myanmar and South Korea–Myanmar investment relationship), East Asian investors would be better off with a single regional treaty. Sub-regional investment treaties in East Asia were made in response to the desire of investors to invest safely and securely abroad. Furthermore, the treaties helped tackle a lack of consensus on the customary international law applicable to foreign investments which created uncertainty in the minds of investors about the degree of protection they could expect under international law.[49] The complicated matrix of East Asian investment treaties has made it difficult to identify and understand applicable rules especially with the existence of discrepancies across the treaties. An all-in-one treaty would provide more transparency and predictability about investment protection standards. Additionally, the negotiation process of such treaty might lead to a more equal playing field for investors and even better level of protection for East Asian investors in general since the countries having the less favorable terms for their investors would try to grasp this opportunity to improve existing treaty incentives.

For East Asian nations, a single treaty would bring greater benefits for investors in the region, and it would presumably promote more investment than separate contemporary investment treaties, thus helping to

---

[46]   Article 30(2) of the VCLT. See also Anthony Aust, *Modern Treaty Law and Practice* (Cambridge: Cambridge University Press, 2000), 175–9.

[47]   Article 23 of the China–ASEAN Agreement on Investment and Article 23 of the South Korea–ASEAN Agreement on Investment.

[48]   See the Preambles of both the China–ASEAN and the South Korea–ASEAN Agreements on Investment.

[49]   See also Jeswald W. Salacuse, 'The Treatification of International Investment Law', *Law and Business Review of the Americas* (Winter 2007).

realize ASEAN+3's objective of regional prosperity. This treaty would contribute to facilitating intra-region investments and promoting a competitive investment region, not to mention a broader long-term impact in 'extending and intensifying the parties' mutual economic relations' among them.[50]

One might argue that investment treaties cause some counter-effects to the host states. Some developing countries have terminated their BITs or withdrawn from the ICSID Convention, which provides the most widely utilized arbitration service of investors.[51] The language of these treaties is criticized as vague and indeterminate, and 'intended to capture or threaten to capture a wide range of state activities' and 'governments thereby are legally constrained from pursuing a range of legislative strategies that significantly impair investment interests.'[52] Some critics are concerned about expansionary interpretations of investment treaties[53] and the failure to provide environmental and human right interests in investment treaties.[54]

On the other hand, proponents consider that investment treaties contribute to establishing and maintaining an appropriate legal, administrative and regulatory framework for inducing investment which includes an 'efficient and legally restrained bureaucracy'[55] and provisions to remedy the deficiencies in the host states' governance institutions and enforcement

---

[50] See *Saluka Investment BV v. The Czech Republic*, UNCITRAL, Partial Award, 17 March 2006, para. 300.

[51] For example, in April 2007 Bolivia submitted a letter to ICSID under Article 71 announcing its decision to withdraw from the ICSID Convention. See http://www.worldbank.org.libproxy1.nus.edu.sg/icsid/, accessed 2 September 2010. Peru notified ICSID in December 2007 that it was withdrawing its consent for investment arbitrations in the mining and energy sectors. In 2008, Venezuela communicated to the Netherlands its intention to terminate the Dutch–Venezuela BIT by 1 November 2008. Similarly Ecuador has denounced 9 of its 25 investment treaties and announced the renegotiation of the remaining 16. See UNCTAD, *Recent Developments in International Investment Agreements (2007–June 2008)* (New York and Geneva: United Nations, 2008), 4–6.

[52] David Schneiderman, *Constitutionalizing Economic Globalization* (Cambridge: Cambridge University Press, 2008), 34, 37–8.

[53] See Jan Paulsson, *The Denial of Justice in International Law* (Cambridge: Cambridge University Press, 2005), 228–62; M. Sornarajah, 'The Retreat of Neo-Liberalism in Investment Treaty Arbitration', in Catherine A. Rogers and Roger P. Alford (eds), *The Future of Investment Arbitration* (New York: Oxford University Press, 2009), 291.

[54] M. Sornarajah, *The International Law on Foreign Investment* (Cambridge: Cambridge University Press, 2004), 259.

[55] W. Michael Reisman and Robert D. Sloane, 'Indirect Expropriation and its Valuation in the BIT Generation', 74 *British Year Book of International Law* (2003), 117.

of the rule of law.[56] The prevailing trend in investment treaty making is still optimistic. Recently, some countries have started the revision of their model BITs to achieve an 'appropriate balance between protection of the rights of foreign investors on the one hand, and recognition of the legitimate sphere of operation of the host State on the other'.[57] East Asian investment treaties, especially the multilateral ones with broad coverage of states involved, were negotiated in this context and thus reflected the efforts to reach such balance between the rights of investors and host states. They contain provisions for host states to maintain legitimate regulatory powers when other public interests need to be prioritized over investor protection[58] and provide greater clarification of the general investment law terms, such as fair and equitable treatment, full protection and security and expropriation, to guide the interpretation of arbitral tribunals when disputes are brought before them. Negotiating a new East Asia-based treaty would be a good chance for the countries in the region to address inconsistencies, overlapping provisions and imbalance in the existing treaties.

The East Asian treaties should be examined to assess the feasibility of two options to regionalize them: (i) merging all the treaties into a new one by direct negotiations among all East Asian countries and (ii) using most-favored-nation clauses to import the most favorable provisions which would indirectly constitute a combined East Asia treaty. Since the China–ASEAN and South Korea–ASEAN Agreements on Investment and the ACIA are likely to enter into force soon and thus exclude the application of their BITs, their BITs will not be considered. Instead, these Agreements, Japan's BITs or FTAs with ASEAN and NEA countries' BITs will be analyzed to evaluate the two possibilities.

The first option could materialize if the similarities of the treaties are sufficient to persuade East Asian countries to overcome the bilateral schemes of their investment treaties and embark on a project of a regional investment treaty. In the second option, owing to the MFN clause in a basic

---

[56]   Jeswald W. Salacuse, *The Law of Investment Treaties*, above note 1, 127.

[57]   Campbell McLachlan QC, Laurence Shore and Matthew Weiniger, *International Investment Arbitration* (New York: Oxford University Press, 2007), 21. See also the recent model BITs of the US, Norway, Germany and France, accessed 2 September 2010, http://ita.law.uvic.ca/investmenttreaties.htm.

[58]   Many East Asian treaties explicitly permit host states to deal with security, health, environment and labor rights issues without having to give primacy to investment protection provisions. See for example, provisions on general exceptions and security exceptions in the ACIA, the China–ASEAN Agreement on Investment, the South Korea–ASEAN Agreement on Investment and the Vietnam–Japan BIT.

treaty, the beneficiary in that treaty is entitled to the most favorable provisions chosen among the other treaties. Therefore, presumably investors in East Asia would enjoy most favorable rights deduced from the applicable treaties just like those from a most pro-investment East Asia-based treaty.

Negotiation of a New Treaty Reconciling Discrepancies in Treaty Terms

Given that the region of 13 countries has concluded 67 investment treaties, it seems likely that they could be integrated into a single treaty. This is based on the assumption that the contents of the treaties are similar. McLachlan observed that the 'interlocking but separate treaties – each the product of its own negotiation – in fact betray a surprising pattern of common features'.[59] Duprey stated that 'whilst these treaties are signed during different periods of time and with different states, they remain similar in content. Numerous provisions of these treaties are identical.'[60] On the other hand, it is also argued that the treaty content actually shows diversity because each negotiation was based on a different model text and produced a unique treaty text, and especially in the case of developing countries because they have no model language to guide their negotiations.[61] However, the texts of the East Asian investment treaties in question, most of which were concluded recently, share some common approaches, possibly because their negotiations were influenced by the revised or recently developed model treaties used by their external partners in their treaty negotiations.

'Reservation' provisions made in the treaty texts, as stated above, might have been necessary to reconcile different legal, regulatory and administrative structures provided that they would not defeat the general standards of treatment. Inconsistency, however, still exists. For example, the Philippines modified the denial-of-benefits provisions in the three East Asian investment treaties to which it is a party so that it may deny treaty benefits to an investor making an investment 'in breach of the provisions of Commonwealth Act No. 108 (An Act to Punish Acts of

---

[59]   Campbell McLachlan QC, Laurence Shore and Matthew Weiniger, *International Investment Arbitration* (New York: Oxford University Press, 2007), 5.

[60]   Pierre Duprey, 'Do Arbitral Awards Constitute Precedents? Should Commercial Arbitration be Distinguished from Arbitration Based on Investment Treaties?', in Emmanuel Gaillard (ed.), *Towards a Uniform International Arbitration Law?* (Huntington: Juris Publishing, 2005).

[61]   Anna Joubin-Bret, 'BITs of the Last Decade: A Ticking Bomb for States', in Catherine A. Rogers and Roger P. Alford (eds), *The Future of Investment Arbitration* (New York: Oxford University Press, 2009).

Evasion of Laws on the Nationalization of Certain Rights, Franchises or Privileges) as amended by Presidential Decree No. 715, otherwise known as "the Anti-Dummy Law", as may be amended'.[62] Its fourth treaty, the Philippines–Japan FTA, imposes no such requirement. Discrepancies are evident in East Asian investment treaties, not to mention the clauses permitting contracting parties to maintain various non-conforming measures to national treatment, MFN, senior management and boards of directors.[63] So long as they are reconcilable, that is co-existent in a common treaty, it would not be very difficult for East Asian nations to start negotiations on an integrated treaty from existing treaties.

Notwithstanding this, one aspect that would differentiate the seemingly similar substantive rights of East Asian investors is their enforcement mechanisms. When negotiating investment treaties, China might consider itself a capital-importing country in relation to Japan and South Korea but a capital-exporting country in relation to ASEAN. Although investment treaties impose equal obligations on contracting parties, in practice the majority of contemporary investment treaties are one-sided and target poor capital-importing countries.[64] Therefore, the truth behind the treaty benefits is not that China offers generous commitments of protection to ASEAN investors but mainly that ASEAN would be obligated to ensure Chinese investors such treatment. For example, protected investors under the ASEAN–China Agreement on Investment may initiate arbitration to vindicate their rights from Article 4 (National Treatment), Article 5 (Most-Favored-Nation Treatment), Article 7 (Treatment of Investment), Article 8 (Expropriation), Article 9 (Compensation for Losses) and Article 10 (Transfers and Repatriation of Profits). Investors covered under the China–Japan or China–Korea BIT cannot enforce the same broad category of rights. Given the likelihood that China will have to bear the

---

[62]   See Article 17(5) of the ASEAN–South Korea Agreement on Investment and Article 15(3) of the ASEAN–China Agreement on Investment. Article 19(2) of the ACIA has different wording but the same effect, providing that 'a Member State may deny the benefits of this Agreement to investors of another Member State and to investments of that investor, where it establishes that such investor has made an investment in breach of the domestic laws of the denying Member State by misrepresenting its ownership in those areas of investment which are reserved for natural or juridical persons of the denying Member State.'

[63]   See for example Article 9 of the ACIA, Article 6 of the China–ASEAN Agreement on Investment, and Article 9 of the South Korea–ASEAN Agreement on Investment,

[64]   At the end of 2008, only 26 per cent of all the BITs were South–South treaties and 9 per cent were North–North treaties. See United Nations Conference on Trade and Development (UNCTAD), *World Investment Report 2009*, 33.

obligations of the host state because Japan and Korea are among the
top ten economies investing in China,[65] investors from Japan and South
Korea may only sue China in arbitration with respect to disputes on the
amount of compensation. In addition, the latter group of investors may
only resort to ad hoc arbitrations with treaty-specified rules while the
former has a wider range of choices including the International Centre for
Settlement of Investment Disputes (ICSID) Convention, ad hoc arbitrations under ICSID Additional Facility Rules, UNCITRAL Arbitration
Rules and other agreed rules. Except for these two BITs, all East Asian
treaties grant investors multiple-choice access to arbitration.

An East Asia-based treaty could be flexible to the extent that it permits
China's possible 'reservation' paragraphs in dispute settlement mechanisms. However, once agreeing to negotiate an East Asia treaty, China
would appear to be too pragmatic to differentiate between its capital-
importing and capital-exporting partners in a common treaty. At the same
time Japan and South Korea might have a chance to push for common
standards which would mean a change in China's more restrictive position towards their investors. This is the biggest challenge to the option of
negotiating a new regional investment treaty.

MFN Clauses: Is it Possible to Absorb Differences and Produce a Most Favored Integrated Treaty?

The wording of MFN clauses might contain some dissimilarities but it is
argued that their overall efficacy in providing non-discriminatory treatment to investments and investors is not affected.[66] Furthermore an
MFN clause should be applied broadly to incorporate any more favorable
treatment to multilateralize the bilateral treaty relationships and harmonize the protection of foreign investments of a host state, unless it indicates
clear indications to the contrary.[67]

Could a common treaty indirectly be formed by the importation of
most-favored provisions from all East Asian investment treaties? Thailand
tailored the ASEAN–China Agreement on Investment to suit its needs by
adding a paragraph to allow its discretionary determination of 'owned'
and 'controlled' by 'natural persons or juridical persons of a non-Party' in

---

[65]   Statistics on the Chinese Ministry of Commerce website, accessed 2
September   2010,   http://english.mofcom.gov.cn/aarticle/statistic/foreigninvest
ment/201001/20100106726891.html.
[66]   Stephan W. Schill, *The Multilateralization of International Investment Law*
(New York: Cambridge University Press, 2009), 122–3.
[67]   Ibid., 194.

order to deny treaty benefits. In the ASEAN–South Korea Agreement on Investment, Thailand specified the definition that 'a juridical person is (a) owned by investors of a Party if more than 50 per cent of the equity interest in it is beneficially owned by such investors; and (b) controlled by investors of a Party if such investors have the power to name a majority of its directors or otherwise to legally direct its actions.'[68] Would the MFN clause in these treaties reconcile the differences for the most favorable rules to be applicable to investors from the parties to both treaties? To answer this question, specific formulas of MFN clauses in the Agreements need to be examined.

Restrictive formulas of MFN clauses can be used in a treaty with a view to triggering more competition for signing new treaties with each party of the treaty. It would be unnecessary for country B to persuade country A to sign a new treaty if B can import provisions of the A–C treaty. Perhaps because of the strategy of restraining and maintaining competition for closer sub-regional partnerships in the course of integration, many East Asian investment treaties demonstrate clear intentions on the part of the parties to keep their specific bargains from being applied across the board. Two types of MFN clause can be identified in these treaties: (i) discretionary MFN clause and (ii) automatic MFN clause.

Discretionary MFN clause
The MFN clause is the most surprising in the China–ASEAN Agreement on Investment and the South Korea–ASEAN Agreement on Investment because of its self-contradictory content. While the first paragraph(s) sets out the MFN principle, the following paragraphs might render that treatment meaningless because they allow a completely discretionary application of the MFN clause regarding any future agreements or arrangements, providing a hortatory obligation to 'accord adequate opportunity to negotiate the benefits therein'.[69] The party may foreclose all the opportunities of investors to invoke the clause with regard to 'any existing bilateral, regional and/or international agreements or any forms of economic or regional cooperation'. After these paragraphs, perhaps being overcautious, the ASEAN–China Agreement rejects any possible MFN invocation in dispute settlement issues that could already be rendered impermissible under previous paragraphs. The reason might lie in a hotly debated question in investment arbitrations – whether MFN clauses apply only to

---

[68]   See Article 17(4) of the ASEAN–South Korea Agreement on Investment and Article 15(2) of the ASEAN–China Agreement on Investment.
[69]   See Article 5 of the China–ASEAN Agreement on Investment and Article 4 of the South Korea–ASEAN Agreement on Investment.

substantive rights of foreign investors or to their procedural rights as well. China and ASEAN seem to agree with many arbitral tribunals[70] upon the application of MFN clauses to substantive rights, but protest against their invocation in procedural matters, as seen in the *Maffezini* case,[71] and thus explicitly prevent their future arbitrations from following such ruling.

Other East Asian treaties also provide some discretion for parties to grant MFN treatment. Under the Japan–Singapore FTA and the Japan–Thailand FTA, if a party has entered into an international agreement on investment with a non-Party, or entered into such an agreement after the FTAs come into force, that party shall favorably consider according, but is not obliged to accord, no less preferential treatment to investors of the other FTA Party and their investment than it accords, in like circumstances, to investors of that non-Party and their investments.[72]

Automatic MFN clause
The treaties in this category include the ACIA, the BITs between NEA nations,[73] and the FTAs and BITs between Japan and Malaysia, the Philippines, Brunei, Indonesia, Cambodia, Laos and Vietnam.[74] An automatic MFN clause typically allows an unconditional importation of more favorable treatment from existing or future agreements of a party to the

---

[70]   See, e.g., *MTD Equity Sdn, Bhd. & MTD Chile S.A v. Chile,* ICSID Case No. ARB/01/7, Award, 25 May 2004; *Tecnicas Medioambientales Tecmed S.A v. Mexico*, ICSID Case No. ARB(AF)/00/2, Award, 29 May 2003; *ADF Group, Inc. v. U.S.*, ICSID Case No. ARB(AF)/00/1, Final Award, 9 January 2003; *Plama Consortium Ltd. v. Bulgaria*, ICSID Case No. ARBITRATION/03/24, Decision on Jurisdiction, 8 February 2005; *Wintershall v. Argentina,* Award, 8 December 2008.
[71]   See *Maffezini v. Spain,* ICSID Case No. ARB/97/7, Decision on Objection to Jurisdiction, 25 January 2000. In this case, a Spanish investor invoked the MFN clause of the Argentina–Spain BIT to deviate from the obligation to litigate in local courts for 18 months prior to any submission to arbitration by benefiting from a dispute settlement provision in the Chile–Spain BIT, which imposed no such exhaustion requirement. The arbitral tribunal in this case agreed with the investor and applied the MFN clause to his procedural rights. Some other tribunals applied MFN treatment in procedural issues when the clauses do not explicitly prohibit it. See, e.g., *Siemens v. Argentina*, Decision on Jurisdiction, 3 August 2004; *Gas Natural v. Argentina*, Decision on Jurisdiction, 17 June 2005.
[72]   See Article 89 of the Japan–Singapore FTA and Article 96 of the Japan–Thailand FTA.
[73]   See Articles 2 and 3 of the China–South Korea BIT, the China–Japan BIT and the South Korea–Japan BIT.
[74]   See Article 76 of the Japan–Malaysia FTA, Article 90 of the Japan–Philippines FTA, Article 58 of the Japan–Brunei FTA, Article 60 of the Japan–Indonesia FTA, Article 2 of the Japan–Vietnam BIT, Article 3 of the Japan–Laos BIT and Article 3 of the Japan–Cambodia BIT.

relationship, between that party and investors of the other parties. Since automatic MFN clauses are included in investment treaties involving all the 13 East Asian countries, it could be presumed that investment treaties with discretionary MFN clauses could not produce actual barriers to the indirect compilation of most favorable treatment for an East Asia common treaty. Although protected investors under the treaties with a discretionary MFN clause might not be able to invoke it, they can invoke automatic MFN clauses in their other treaties. For example, South Korean investors can use the MFN clause of the South Korea–China BIT to import more favorable rights from the China–ASEAN Agreement on Investment. Nonetheless, there exists another obstacle to the regionalization effect of MFN clauses, which is the exclusion of these clauses through exceptions.

Exclusion of MFN clauses: exceptional matters and sectors
Notwithstanding the possibility of importing more favorable rights from other East Asian treaties, the protected investors under the treaties with automatic MFN clauses actually have limited choice, since the application of such clauses is prevented in exceptional matters and sectors identified by each party. Annexes of many East Asian investment treaties provide long lists of exceptions to the MFN clause.[75] Furthermore, even in the most liberal MFN clause, exceptions regarding separate free trade agreements or sub-regional arrangements are included to keep them untouched or unable to compete.[76]

In summary, MFN clauses provided in East Asian treaties with different wording produce different effects. It would be difficult to achieve an across-the-board importation of most-favored-nation treatment in these treaties. Unless amendments to permit a broader MFN application are made to give such regionalizing effect, we could not expect an indirectly deduced regional treaty.

CONCLUSION

East Asian nations have been active in creating a legal regime to govern international investments. However, it is fragmented and overlapping.

---

[75] See, e.g., the annexes of the South Korea–Japan BIT, the Japan–Laos BIT, the Japan–Vietnam BIT, and the Japan–Cambodia BIT, and Annex 4 of the Japan–Brunei FTA.
[76] See Article 6 of the ACIA or Article 96(3) of the Thailand–Japan FTA.

A common treaty would be beneficial for both East Asian investors and states for practical reasons such as time and resources saving in negotiations and because it would provide a more transparent and predictable legal framework and avoid the search for applicable rules in the matrix of East Asian investment treaties where disputes arise. An all-in-one treaty could be made *de jure* (a new integrated treaty) or *de facto* (through MFN clauses).

The first option would materialize if East Asian nations could accommodate differences in treaty obligations of individual contracting parties or, alternatively, if China changed its dual role approach to accept the same obligations in its relationship with Japan and South Korea as with ASEAN. However, it is more feasible to keep the status quo since other countries have accepted China's different positions in the existing treaties. Moreover, like India and Brazil, China has more negotiating power to resist investment rules restraining its ability to regulate foreign investment.[77]

In the second option, integrating all East Asian investment treaties into a single treaty, the MFN clauses would have to be amended because their wording and structure are not presently consistent and thus do not accommodate such an effect. To avoid prolonged negotiations but at the same time to change the status quo to a better situation, the proposals do not contain extensive substantive modifications to the content of contemporary East Asian investment treaties. Therefore, the new treaty might not be considered a true regional treaty unless a level of integration can be reached. With too many reservations, it would be a combination of BITs in the form of a multilateral investment agreement. However, the bottom line is that it would serve the purpose of enhancing the predictability and transparency of the legal framework for investment and would facilitate the long-term cause of improving the investment environment in the region.

---

[77]   Jeswald W. Salacuse, above note 43, 75. See also E.V.K. FitzGerald, 'Developing Countries and Multilateral Investment Negotiations', in E.C. Nieuwenhuys and M.M.T.A. Brus (eds), *Multilateral Regulation of Investment* (The Hague: Kluwer Law International, 2001), 40.

PART III

Financial integration

9. Global financial regulatory reforms: implications for East Asia

Douglas W. Arner and Cyn-Young Park

INTRODUCTION

The global financial and economic crisis that started in 2007 highlighted gaps and weaknesses in the current international financial architecture as well as national regulatory systems. Two major shortcomings in the modern global financial system have shaped an array of possible regulatory, supervisory, and prudential reforms. First, supervisors failed to limit excessive risk-taking and leverage by financial institutions. Market failures, due in part to rapid financial innovation, discredited the regulatory model that relied on transparency, disclosure, and market discipline to curb inordinate risk. Second, the absence of well-established crisis management mechanisms both locally and internationally – revealed in the failure to quickly address impaired financial institutions – sapped confidence in the system.

Against this backdrop, the objective of global regulatory reform is to build a resilient global financial system that can withstand shocks and dampen, rather than amplify, their effects on the real economy. The goal is to ultimately support vibrant economic activity and growth.[1] There is broad agreement on the key principles of reform – bolstering macroprudential supervision to reduce procyclicality and guard against a build-up of systemic risk, extending the regulatory perimeter to include all systemically important financial institutions, improving international financial standards, and strengthening crisis resolution mechanisms.

Lessons drawn from the recent crisis have led to specific reform proposals with concrete implementation plans at the international level. Leaders

---

[1] See G-20, The G-20 Toronto Summit Declaration (June 2010); G-20, Leaders' Statement: The Pittsburgh Summit (September 2009); G-20, Leaders' Statement – 'The Global Plan for Recovery and Reform' (April 2009); G-20, Declaration: Summit on Financial Markets and the World Economy (November 2008).

of the G-20 have committed to building a stronger, more globally consistent, supervisory and regulatory framework for the financial sector – to
support sustainable growth and serve the needs of business and citizens.
Accordingly, the G-20 has established five main principles to guide the
reforms: (1) strengthen transparency and accountability; (2) enhance
sound regulation; (3) promote integrity in financial markets; (4) reinforce
international cooperation; and (5) reform the financial architecture.[2]

Under the premise of the G-20's guiding principles, the Financial
Stability Board (FSB) and its constituents have identified weaknesses and
are developing reform proposals appropriate to today's global financial
system.[3] In this respect, the G-20 and the FSB have thus far concentrated
on a wide range of issues. The six core aspects are (1) building high-quality
capital and liquidity standards and mitigating procyclicality, (2) reforming compensation practices to support financial stability, (3) improving
regulation of over-the-counter (OTC) derivatives markets, (4) addressing
systemically important financial institutions and cross-border resolutions,
(5) strengthening adherence to international supervisory and regulatory
standards, and (6) strengthening accounting standards.[4]

In addition to these issues, the G-20 and FSB are also working toward
(1) developing macroprudential policy frameworks and tools, (2) addressing the differentiated nature and scope of regulation, (3) establishing
appropriate hedge fund regulations, (4) considering regulation of credit
rating agencies and how credit ratings are used, (5) supporting the development of supervisory colleges for major cross-border financial institutions, and (6) supporting the revival of securitization.[5]

Despite the critical nature of these reforms for developed G-20 members,
concerns are rising among developing economies that these issues tend to
focus on developed economies with advanced financial markets. They
have little direct relevance to the challenges facing emerging economies

---

[2] See G-20, Communiqué: Meeting of Finance Ministers and Central Bank
Governors (June 2010).

[3] For a summary, see FSB, 'Overview of Progress in the Implementation of
the G20 Recommendations for Strengthening Financial Stability: Report of the
Financial Stability Board to G20 Leaders' (June 2010); FSB, 'Ongoing and Recent
Work Relevant to Sound Financial Systems', Cover Note by the Secretariat for the
FSB Meeting on 14 June 2010 (June 2010).

[4] See FSB, 'Overview of Progress in the Implementation of the G20
Recommendations for Strengthening Financial Stability: Report of the Financial
Stability Board to G20 Leaders' (June 2010).

[5] See FSB, 'Progress since the St Andrews meeting in Implementing the G20
Recommendations for Strengthening Financial Stability: Report of the Financial
Stability Board to G20 Finance Ministers and Governors' (April 2010).

and financial systems, especially those with less developed financial systems. As a result, the global financial reform efforts risk ending up being largely seen as irrelevant for developing economies, rather than constructing concrete rules and standards that can be implemented globally.

Moreover, identifying common concerns among East Asia's economies is not simple. In terms of economic development, East Asia has considerable disparities – while the People's Republic of China (PRC) and Japan are the second and third largest economies globally (measured by nominal GDP in mid-2010), Mongolia and Lao PDR remain among the smallest. At the same time, while Japan is a highly developed economy, the PRC, Indonesia, Malaysia, Thailand and the Philippines all remain emerging economies with wide disparities in income levels domestically. However, across the region there is consensus in two areas: first, there is an overriding interest in economic growth and development; and second, there is the drive to create inclusive growth to support social stability and equity. Therefore, when considering issues related to financial regulation and global economic governance, these twin objectives must be central in constructing regional views and strategies related to domestic, regional, and global financial reform.

For East Asia, the key lessons of the crisis are the need to enhance mechanisms to address economic and financial stability, to balance and diversify economies, and to develop more effective domestic, regional, and global financial systems.[6] Such financial systems must support economic growth through financial development and stability.

Based on the above, this chapter evaluates current G-20 proposals for financial regulatory and supervisory reforms, focusing on their potential impact on East Asia's emerging economies and financial systems. The chapter also identifies potential areas of adjustment and improvement in the proposed regulatory guidelines from the FSB and its constituent organizations.[7] In addition, the chapter seeks to identify a basis for the

---

[6] See D. Arner and L. Schou-Zibell, 'Responding to the Global Financial and Economic Crisis: Meeting the Challenges in Asia', ADB Working Paper Series on Regional Economic Integration (September 2010).

[7] The FSB comprises national regulators along with major international and regional financial institutions and regulatory organizations: Bank for International Settlements (BIS), European Central Bank (ECB), European Commission, IMF, Organisation for Economic Co-operation and Development (OECD), World Bank, Basel Committee on Banking Supervision (BCBS), Committee on the Global Financial System (CGFS), Committee on Payment and Settlement Systems (CPSS), International Association of Insurance Supervisors (IAIS), International Accounting Standards Board (IASB), and International Organization of Securities Commissions (IOSCO). The following Asia-Pacific jurisdictions are members of

region's strategic agenda in the G-20 framework for reform of global economic governance – focusing on international arrangements and institutions, including the International Monetary Fund (IMF) and the World
Bank, as well as the role of regional arrangements, especially in East Asia.

KEY ISSUES IN THE CURRENT G-20 REGULATORY REFORM AGENDA

Reforming the regulatory environment for financial systems has been
a key priority of the G-20. G-20 Finance Ministers and Central Bank
Governors met in Busan, South Korea, on 5 June 2010 to affirm their
commitment to intensify efforts and accelerate financial repair and reform
respecting the following regulatory issues: (1) developing stronger capital
and liquidity standards; (2) addressing systemically important financial
institutions (SIFIs); (3) ensuring proper loss allocation; (4) improving
the regulation of hedge funds, credit rating agencies, compensation practices, and OTC derivatives; and (5) strengthening global accounting and
financial standards.[8] Other issues discussed included designing macroprudential supervisory frameworks, developing supervisory colleges for cross-
border institutions, and resuming securitization. G-20 leaders affirmed on
26–27 June 2010 in Toronto, Canada, their focus on these issues in the
context of four 'pillars': (1) a strong regulatory framework and financial
market infrastructure; (2) effective supervision; (3) resolution and addressing systemic institutions; and (4) transparent international assessment
and peer review.[9] Each of these raise specific issues affecting East Asia's
economies. There is also concern over relevance – that East Asia's developing economies and regional economic and financial arrangements are
somewhat different from the European and North American economies
and thus their needs differ.

Developing Stronger Capital and Liquidity Standards

Capital, leverage, and liquidity standards have been a central focus of
G-20 regulatory reform throughout the crisis, with the Basel Committee
on Banking Supervision (BCBS) tasked to develop detailed proposals.

---

the FSB: Australia, the PRC, Hong Kong, India, Indonesia, Japan, South Korea
and Singapore.
   [8]   G-20, Communiqué: Meeting of Finance Ministers and Central Bank
Governors (June 2010).
   [9]   G-20, The G-20 Toronto Summit Declaration (June 2010).

There is broad agreement on the need to strengthen prudential standards for financial institutions that require more capital, higher liquidity, better risk management, and more limited leverage.[10] The emerging focus (Basel III) combines higher and more consistent capital requirements with renewed risk-weighting and assessment requirements, and liquidity and leverage requirements. However, there are currently disagreements over the context of levels and form of capital, and in relation to the nature of liquidity requirements and the level of leverage limitations.

East Asian banking systems must work to meet international standards, although their relatively strong capital positions see them well placed compared with their western counterparts.

On capital, global regulators have agreed to raise the quality, consistency and transparency of the Tier 1 capital base. To do this, it would be advisable for the majority of Tier 1 capital to be in common shares and retained earnings, with deductions and accounting treatment (especially for provisioning) being harmonized internationally. In addition, all components of the capital base need to be fully disclosed.

East Asia's financial institutions would be relatively less affected than US and European financial institutions by new capital, liquidity and leverage requirements. This is due to the relatively mild impact the global financial crisis had on their balance sheets and partly reflects the positive effects of post-1997/98 Asian financial crisis reforms (Table 9.1).[11] Nevertheless, rapidly developing East Asian financial systems will soon find the new prudential requirements relevant as financial innovation and globalization will expose them to similar risks to those underlying the global financial crisis.

Across East Asia, developing economies will benefit from simplified capital standards, focusing largely on core equity (Tier 1) and subordinated debt (Tier 2). The main challenge facing developing East Asia in terms of capital provision, however, is underdeveloped domestic and regional capital markets. As economies across the region grow and banks increase lending, there will be a consequential need to increase capital. As a result, the availability of well-developed equity and debt capital markets to support bank capital will become increasingly important.

---

[10] BCBS, Consultative Document: 'Strengthening the Resilience of the Banking Sector' (December 2009); BCBS, Consultative Document: 'International Framework for Liquidity Risk Measurement, Standards and Monitoring' (December 2009).

[11] See C.S. Lee and C.Y. Park, 'Beyond the Crisis: Financial Regulatory Reform in Emerging Asia', ADB Working Paper Series on Regional Economic Integration No. 34 (August 2009).

Table 9.1   Banking soundness indicators (%)

	Non-perform-ing loans to total loans[1]		Bank regula-tory capital to risk-weighted assets[2]		Bank provi-sions to non-performing loans[3]		Private sector loans to deposit ratio[4]	
	2000	2009	2000	2009	2000	2009	2000	2009
China, People's Rep. of	22.4	1.6	13.5	10.0	4.7	155.0	95.2	72.6
Hong Kong, China	7.3	1.3	17.9	16.8	–	–	66.7	49.1
India	12.8	2.4	11.1	13.2	–	52.6	63.0	71.4
Indonesia	20.1	3.3	21.6	17.4	36.1	127.4	40.6	75.1
Korea, Rep. of	6.6	0.8	6.7	11.4	81.8	125.2	111.5	126.3
Malaysia	8.3	1.8	11.3	13.5	57.2	95.6	109.4	91.6
Philippines	15.1	3.0	16.2	16.0	43.6	112.3	82.0	58.6
Singapore	3.4	2.5	16.4	13.5	87.2	91.0	99.7	77.9
Taipei, China	5.3	1.2	10.8	8.6	24.1	95.7	72.7	60.6
Thailand	17.7	4.8	7.5	11.7	47.2	99.4	101.6	95.2
Average[5]	**11.9**	**2.3**	**13.3**	**13.2**	**47.7**	**106.0**	**84.2**	**77.9**
Median	**10.5**	**2.1**	**12.4**	**13.3**	**45.4**	**99.4**	**88.6**	**73.9**
eurozone	–	2.4	–	8.3	–	–	135.0	134.7
Japan	5.3	1.9	11.7	15.8	35.5	27.1	83.5	70.1
United States	1.1	5.4	9.4	11.7	146.4	58.3	111.5	109.1

Notes:
– = data not available
[1]   Data for commercial banks, except for Hong Kong, China (authorized institutions);
    Rep. of Korea (commercial and specialized banks); Singapore; Taipei, China;
    Eurozone (banking system); Japan (major banks) and United States (all FDIC-insured
    institutions).
[2]   Data for commercial banks, except for People's Rep. of China in 2009 (banking system);
    Hong Kong, China (authorized institutions); India; Singapore; Taipei, China; eurozone
    (banking system); Rep. of Korea (commercial and specialized banks); Japan (major
    banks); and United States (all FDIC-insured institutions). Values for Rep. of Korea,
    Malaysia, Singapore, Taipei, China, Thailand and United States are Tier-1 capital to
    risk-weighted assets; and for the rest, total capital.
[3]   Data for commercial banks, except for India; Indonesia; Rep. of Korea; Singapore;
    Taipei, China (banking system); Japan (major banks); and United States (all FDIC-
    insured institutions). Values for India in 2009 as of end-2008; Indonesia in 2009 as of
    April 2009; and Rep. of Korea and Japan in 2009 as of September 2009.
[4]   Data cover loans of the private sector or non-financial corporations and deposits of
    banking institutions, other depository corporations, or deposit money banks.
[5]   Simple average.

Source: Global Financial Stability Report (various years) and *International Financial
Statistics*, International Monetary Fund; CEIC database; and national sources.

New capital adequacy requirements should also include a leverage ratio to dampen excessive leverage. Clearly, excessive leverage was at the heart of the global financial crisis. Several mechanisms are being considered to supplement the minimum capital adequacy ratio (CAR); for example, requiring an additional capital charge linked to any mismatch in the asset–liability maturity structure. For developing countries, leverage standards are often easier to implement than the usual capital requirements, as they are both simpler and more transparent. In addition, while risk-weighted capital requirements potentially have the greatest impact in improving financial institutions' risk management practices, leverage limits combined with clear requirements for higher levels of equity capital are likely to contribute to financial stability.

Regulators did not pay sufficient attention to the source and maturity structure funding a bank's asset expansion and growth prior to the crisis. In this regard, it is also important to establish a minimum global standard for funding liquidity. This would include requirements for a stressed liquidity coverage ratio – given that the riskiness of a bank's assets is intimately linked to the bank's funding sources and term structure.

Excessive reliance on short-term funding during booms – particularly when interest costs and margins are low – appears to have contributed to the fragility of the financial system. Thus, a capital charge on the maturity mismatch from the funding of asset–liability growth could help dampen banks' reliance on short-term funds and mitigate procyclicality. This means that banks which have medium- to long-term assets that have low market liquidity, and which funded these assets with short-term liabilities, must hold additional capital. The additional capital charge would then force banks to internalize risks from maturity mismatches that give rise to funding liquidity risks. A multiple of CAR set as a function of the months of effective mismatch between asset maturity and funding maturity, for example, could be used for the additional capital charge for maturity mismatches.

For many economies in East Asia, however, largely underdeveloped local currency bond markets pose a major challenge in requiring stronger capital and liquidity standards.[12] New and strong liquidity standards could be problematic for developing economies, especially those with underdeveloped domestic debt markets with limited availability of liquid assets. Continued support for domestic and regional bond market development is key to promoting effective liquidity management. Enhancing

---

[12]   Asian Development Bank, *Asia Capital Markets Monitor* (May 2010).

regional initiatives, for example the Asian Bond Markets Initiative under ASEAN+3, may be useful in this respect.

Overall, developing East Asian economies would benefit from specific guidance from the BCBS in terms of sequencing reforms, especially combined with implementation support through an FSB development committee. Likewise, this is an area for the development of regional arrangements such as the establishment of a high-level Asian Financial Stability Dialogue (AFSD). Regional implementation and monitoring mechanisms, both through independent and peer review processes at the regional level, could add value in the implementation of Basel III capital standards in East Asia.

Addressing Systemically Important Financial Institutions

The crisis demonstrated that non-bank financial institutions, either individually or collectively, can pose risks to financial stability or trigger contagion when (1) they are closely connected to regulated entities and/or (2) they have a concentration of assets giving rise to systemic risks. In dealing with systemically important financial institutions, international attention has focused on, first, how to define which institutions are systemically important; second, how to close gaps and inconsistencies across regulatory systems and approaches; and third, how to regulate cross-border groups through supervisory colleges.[13]

How to define systemically important financial institutions? It is not always clear what constitutes a systemically significant financial institution that could pose systemic risk because of size or market influence. Therefore, a set of criteria for determining systemically important financial institutions would be helpful. Efforts are being made to develop indicators of systemic importance based on size, complexity, and interconnectedness at international as well as national levels, particularly in advanced economies. However, necessary data and methodologies available for thorough assessments remain a challenge to most economies in East Asia.

Although creating a practical definition of systemic importance may still be manageable for an economy, additional challenges remain for developing economies. Most East Asian financial systems are bank-centric, and then often concentrated in a small number of financial institutions (Table 9.2). At the same time, foreign banks may have a strong presence in their

---

[13]   IMF/BIS/FSB, 'Guidance to Assess the Systemic Importance of Financial Institutions, Markets and Instruments: Initial Considerations' – Report to the G-20 Finance Ministers and Central Bank Governors (October 2009).

Table 9.2 Size and composition of financial systems in selected Asian economies (% of GDP)

	Financial Sector Assets[1]				Stock Market Capitalization[2]		Total Bonds Outstanding[3]	
	Deposit-taking Financial Institutions		Non-Bank Financial Institutions					
	2000	2009	2000	2009	2000	2009	2000	2009
China, People's Rep. of	157.5	200.6	5.1	15.8	48.9	82.7	16.9	52.3
Hong Kong, China	505.5	651.7	188.3	459.0	368.6	1093.9	35.8	68.4
India[4]	64.5	103.5	15.6	29.0	69.9	205.2	24.6	48.8
Indonesia	63.6	34.7	8.7	11.4	16.2	39.8	31.9	18.2
Korea, Rep. of	130.5	158.6	41.9	67.3	27.8	100.3	66.6	122.7
Malaysia	154.2	211.5	41.4	99.9	120.6	149.5	73.3	96.5
Philippines	99.2	83.1	23.9	20.0	33.3	53.6	27.6	39.2
Singapore	646.3	643.7	76.6	83.9	167.3	271.7	48.0	84.7
Taipei, China	256.0	295.9	29.4	92.2	75.9	173.5	37.7	57.5
Thailand	132.3	146.6	10.7	41.1	23.8	67.1	25.3	67.0
Average[5]	**221.0**	**253.0**	**44.2**	**92.0**	**95.2**	**223.7**	**38.8**	**65.5**
Median	**143.2**	**179.6**	**26.6**	**54.2**	**59.4**	**124.9**	**33.8**	**62.2**
eurozone	230.9	315.6	157.8	214.5	79.6	56.5	87.9	114.4
Japan	510.8	541.8	274.7	291.3	67.6	69.7	97.4	189.6
United States	79.6	107.9	279.3	314.1	152.1	105.8	138.0	175.8

Notes:

[1]   Financial asset data for Indonesia as of end-2001 and end-2008.
[2]   Figures are computed using US dollar values of stock market capitalization and gross domestic product; except for China, People's Rep. of, and India computed using local currency unit.
[3]   Data covers domestic debt securities. Figures for the United States exclude non-marketable government securities.
[4]   Financial sector assets data for India refers to the end of fiscal year.
[5]   Simple average.

Source: OREI staff calculations using data from national sources, CEIC, AsianBondsOnline, Bank for International Settlements, *World Economic Outlook Database*, International Monetary Fund, and World Federation of Exchanges.

banking systems. Some institutions, while they do not necessarily pose global risks, may pose domestic and in some cases regional risks. As such, countries need to carefully analyze the concentration of their respective financial sectors and provide special regulatory attention to domestic SIFIs. A similar approach should be taken regionally with regional SIFIs. Overall, the more systemically significant an institution is – domestically, regionally and/or internationally – the more regulatory attention it requires, including resolution in case of any failure.

Beyond these issues, recent proposals have covered the questions of whether systemically significant financial institutions should be broken up and whether banks should be allowed to engage in proprietary trading.[14] Because East Asia's economies frequently face the different problem of having locally significant but internationally non-systemic financial institutions, this first approach of breaking up SIFIs is unlikely to find strong support in the region. Clearly, this means that there is a much greater need for regulatory attention to SIFIs together with the development of relevant, appropriate regulatory standards – and this is where technical assistance from international and regional multilateral development banks could be helpful.

Similarly, in terms of limiting banks' proprietary trading, most authorities in East Asian economies will not view this as a priority problem – as their banking systems remain relatively conservative and their activities remain centered on more traditional banking businesses. However, risks from these activities could soon become relevant given the region's rapidly developing banking systems and their demand for greater profitability, growing sophistication, and increasing interaction with global markets.[15] As a result, the region's developing economies would need a set of guidelines for dealing with banks' proprietary trading, carefully calibrated to financial and regulatory development across different economies.

The growing cross-border nature of banking and financial services underscores the need for a coordinated oversight of international banking entities. Financial activity is becoming increasingly global, but regulation remains utterly national. While the institution of a global regulator is realistically difficult, it is important to establish a global framework that will mandate minimum consistency across jurisdictions in regulatory principles that would apply to similar markets, institutions, services, and products.

Even before the crisis, there were discussions on establishing supervisory

---

[14] See Group of Thirty, 'Financial Reform: A Framework for Financial Stability' (January 2009).

[15] Q. Liu, D. Arner and P. Lejot, *Finance in Asia: Institutions, Regulation and Policy* (London: Routledge, 2011).

colleges for major cross-border financial institutions. Such colleges have now been established and are in operation for the largest cross-border financial institutions. They are currently addressing issues related to regulatory cooperation and information sharing (through memoranda of understanding), living wills and contingency planning. Thus far, the focus appropriately has been on major cross-border SIFIs and has not extended to regional SIFIs (except in the context of the European Union). However, as regional banking systems grow in size, regional supervisory colleges for regional SIFIs should be established through the AFSD (and eventually perhaps an Asian Monetary Fund).

Ensuring Proper Loss Allocation

There is growing agreement that the financial sector should assume a fair and substantial share of costs associated with the financial crisis and subsequent government measures to repair banking systems or bail them out. A range of policy options have been discussed. The G-20 is crafting guiding principles to minimize the use of public funds and reduce risks from financial system procyclicality.[16] For developing economies, it recommended that adjusted charges relating to deposit insurance and customer protection arrangements may be more appropriate, combined with appropriate resolution arrangements including mechanisms to claw back to the extent possible the costs of any government assistance.

A capital surcharge on systemically significant financial institutions based on size, complexity and/or interconnectedness has also been proposed with the aim of mitigating systemic risk. A levy on financial institutions is one option. A levy on the size of bank balance sheets could discourage a financial institution from expanding assets beyond a certain level. A levy can be imposed specifically on non-core bank operations, limiting expansion of banking business into non-core and speculative financial activities. Other alternatives include a range of transaction taxes or Tobin taxes. These may achieve similar purposes by reducing the profitability of speculative financial activities. Transaction taxes can be also applied to cross-border transactions associated with financial speculation. The tax revenue from such levies and taxes can be then used for funding resolutions in times of crisis.[17]

---

[16] At the request of the G-20, the IMF analyzed questions relating to financial institution taxes and charges and recommended charges based on size as well as consideration of possible profits taxes. The report was submitted to the G-20 prior to the June 2010 Toronto Summit.

[17] See United Nations, *Report of the Commission of Experts of the President of*

Improving Regulation of Hedge Funds, Credit Rating Agencies, Compensation Practices and OTC Derivatives

Broadening regulatory scope and increasing regulatory consistency are important at global, regional, and national levels.[18] The global financial crisis showed that the overall design and coverage of a regulatory system is vital to its effectiveness. Domestic regulatory reviews are essential, with reform to eliminate gaps and overlaps, avoid regulatory arbitrage, increase transparency, and improve coordination among relevant authorities. The crisis also highlighted the need to extend supervision over a wider set of market segments and institutions – especially those deemed systemically important. Many non-bank financial institutions – non-life insurance, hedge funds, monolines, private equity funds, and special investment vehicles (SIVs) – were either lightly regulated or unregulated.

Given the central role regulatory gaps and regulatory arbitrage played in the global financial crisis, these issues are likely to be central to future IMF and FSB regulatory reviews and thus a key focus for East Asian jurisdictions, especially for G-20 and FSB members. In East Asia, particular concerns arise in the context of complex financial groups, especially those of systemic significance. Lessons from the recent crisis show that regulatory gaps and balkanization can create issues of financial stability. An important aspect of constructing new regulatory regimes is to consider a system in a broad and integrated way. Against this backdrop, all East Asian jurisdictions should undertake an in-depth analysis of the structure and coverage of their respective regulatory systems. Beyond domestic reviews, regional and international reviews would also be of benefit, at the international level through the Financial Stability Assessment Program (FSAP) or the FSB, and perhaps regionally through an AFSD.

Hedge funds and sovereign wealth funds

Reflecting the infant development stage of the hedge fund industry in East Asia, the region's policymakers need to ensure that application of new international regulatory standards and guidelines has proper allowance to support the market development. The hedge fund industry remains limited in most East Asian economies. However, the region is certainly not insulated from the changing global financial landscape, especially the growth

---

the United Nations General Assembly on Reforms of the International Monetary and Financial System (September 2009).

[18] Joint Forum, *Review of the Differentiated Nature and Scope of Financial Regulation: Key Issues and Recommendations* (January 2010).

of hedge funds. Many of the region's economies have consciously promoted regional financial centers, where strict adherence to international norms would be a prerequisite to maintain competitiveness. While hedge funds are often causes of concern in terms of potential speculation and instability, they are also an important element for financial market development. They provide diversity and liquidity to markets. In this regard, international regulatory standards and guidelines should be carefully crafted to support appropriate market development.

Given the increasing significance of sovereign wealth funds in the region, development of international and regional regulatory guidelines could potentially be very valuable. Such funds also have the potential to both significantly benefit economic development in the region and provide a mechanism for achieving some rebalancing of regional financial flows by potentially better channeling regional savings into regional investments. While the focus to date has largely been at the international level,[19] there is a merit in clarifying the role of these funds as well as investment rules and expectations at the regional level in this regard.

Credit ratings and credit rating agencies

Misaligned incentives in credit ratings and credit rating agencies (CRAs) drew major criticism during the global financial crisis. While there had been ongoing global efforts to review and reform the role and use of credit ratings, it was the global financial crisis that prompted the International Organization of Securities Commissions (IOSCO) to revise the Code of Conduct – adding several tighter provisions against structured finance in May 2008. The FSB and global standard setters have repeatedly affirmed since then their commitment to the review and reform of CRA regulations, with the aim of establishing a globally consistent standard.

East Asia has been working to develop domestic and regional institutions for credit rating systems. While the momentum slowed due to the global financial crisis, these efforts should continue. The crisis exposed inherent dangers in relying on credit rating agencies to the detriment of investor and regulatory due diligence. The recent financial instability in several European Union member states again raised real questions about the role of international credit ratings and credit rating agencies – in many ways similar to the Asian financial crisis.

There is also a need for serious discussion of the merits of basing regulation solely on private sector credit ratings – for example, capital and

---

[19]   IWG, 'Sovereign Wealth Funds: Generally Accepted Principles and Practices' (October 2008).

institutional investor investment requirements. A major opportunity exists to strengthen domestic and regional credit rating agencies while removing excessive reliance on international credit rating agencies for regulatory purposes. At the same time, there will be a need to find adequate replacements – a role which regional credit derivatives markets could take up, if the trading becomes exchange based, centrally cleared, and transparent.

Compensation and financial institution corporate governance
Compensation practices have been a central G-20 focus, with the release of principles, implementation guidance and FSB monitoring of compliance.[20] In East Asia, where financial sector compensation is generally much lower than in Europe and the United States economies, this is unlikely to be seen as a major concern. While Asian G-20 members have all taken steps to implement new standards, it could be a potentially difficult issue for some East Asian financial centers, as they have been relatively less affected by the crisis and stand to gain competitive benefits.

However, compensation is only one aspect of the concern over wider corporate governance, particularly in the financial sector. G-20 attention to financial sector corporate governance more generally has greater direct relevance across East Asia. In the crisis aftermath, there has been growing support for shifting the focus of governance of financial institutions from sales to risks. Financial firms have begun strengthening internal risk management by increasing board oversight of risk, changing policies and procedures to evaluate credit and trading decisions, and reforming compensation policies to align employee incentives with a more risk-focused culture. These changes will likely influence the region's corporate governance practices going forward.

OTC derivatives markets
While derivatives have important benefits in risk management and financial asset pricing, the crisis made it clear that they should not be left entirely unregulated. OTC derivatives markets are generally underdeveloped in the region. Most activity takes place in Japan, Singapore and Hong Kong. In many other jurisdictions, OTC markets are embryonic. At this stage, there are real questions as to how much economies in the region should embrace OTC derivatives market development. Reflecting this, the region's developing economies have been rather quiet while the United States and Europe have taken the lead role in regulating OTC derivatives markets, covering regulation, clearing, and settlement.

---

[20] FSB, 'Thematic Review on Compensation: Peer Review Report' (March 2010).

However, this is an area where East Asia needs to take further steps, both domestically and regionally. In East Asia, there are important opportunities to steer the development of the OTC derivatives markets on a more stable and transparent path – for example, building central clearing and exchange trading arrangements, and developing both regional infrastructure and regional standards. Clear international consensus on regulation would be highly beneficial in supporting the stable future development of these markets in the region.

As markets develop, concerns in the region will probably focus on the potential for speculation and thus potentially destabilizing effects on financial and economic conditions – concerns brought into focus by the recent instability in Europe and the region's collective memory of the 1997–98 Asian financial crisis. The region's developed and developing economies are both likely to support mechanisms to reduce volatility arising from these new markets. For example, although credit default swaps should not be banned altogether, they should be subject to appropriate regulation. Measures should include trading them on an exchange where possible, in addition to central clearing, settlement, and disclosure.

Strengthening Global Accounting and Financial Standards

Accounting standards
The G-20 has repeatedly affirmed commitment to developing a single set of international accounting standards. Currently, the focus of discussion is on the scope of fair value – mark-to-market versus a wider fair value based on longer-term historical value. A broad range of issues also exist as to how to harmonize different accounting and regulatory treatments in relation to capital, off-balance-sheet assets, and provisioning.

At the same time, most economies in East Asia have brought or are in the process of bringing their domestic accounting systems into line with International Financial Reporting Standards. Thus, there is a continuing need to build accounting infrastructure across the region in line with international standards. Developing countries in particular can benefit from implementing international accounting standards, with regional support for implementation and related human capital development essential for effectiveness.

Adherence to international supervisory and regulatory standards
Following the Asian financial crisis, the Financial Stability Forum (FSF) was established along with the FSAP to coordinate standard development and implementation. In the wake of the global financial crisis, the FSF was transformed into the FSB and supported by a new G-20/FSB review

process – in addition to the strengthening of the FSAP system.[21] The region actively adopted international standards and financial regulatory reform following the Asian financial crisis.

Looking forward, the FSB process should be strengthened by expanding into a proper international self-regulatory organization. In addition, the IMF should be given a specific mandate under its Articles of Agreement to address financial stability, which would enhance the effectiveness of the FSAP process. At the domestic level, authorities across the region will require technical assistance to implement standards. International standards should be developed further at the regional level, with regional support for implementation and regional monitoring, potentially through an Asian Monetary Fund incorporating the AFSD, the Chiang Mai Initiative Multilateralization and its associated ASEAN+3 Macroeconomic Research Office (AMRO).

Other Issues

Macroprudential supervision

The major objective of macroprudential supervision is to maintain financial stability. This requires a reshaping of regulatory systems so that authorities are able to identify and take account of systemic risks. The scope of regulation and oversight should extend to systemically important financial institutions, instruments, and markets. They should include non-bank financial institutions and credit rating agencies to ensure they meet international codes of good practice, particularly to prevent unacceptable conflicts of interest. In addition, prudential standards must be designed to address both cross-sectional dimensions (how risk is distributed across a financial system) and time dimensions (how aggregate risk evolves over time) to build buffers for use in bad times.

The macroprudential approach to supervision and regulation should also be complemented and reinforced by effective monetary policy. Financial excess is essentially a macroeconomic problem. Maintaining medium- to long-term price stability is usually considered to be the overarching objective of monetary policy. Price stability in general promotes financial stability, and a sound financial system would contribute to price stability and macroeconomic stability. In the aftermath of the global economic crisis, however, many policymakers and commentators have suggested that central banks should pay greater attention to the financial

---

[21]   See FSB, 'Framework for Strengthening Adherence to International Standards' (January 2010).

sector and financial excess, and take financial stability as a statutory objective. For example, monetary policy could put more emphasis on macrofinancial risks. This implies a 'preemptive tightening' to try to reduce procyclicality and to prevent dangerous excesses from building in asset and credit markets, even if inflation appears to be largely under control. This includes an attempt to 'lean against' an upturn of the credit cycle rather than relying on cleaning up after a bubble bursts.

There is an urgent need to design and implement an effective macroprudential supervisory framework. As the global financial crisis demonstrated, there is a complex interplay between monetary policy, fiscal policy, and supervision and regulation, domestically, regionally, and globally. Monetary policy and macroprudential supervision should play complementary roles, with fiscal and structural policies playing their part in mitigating systemic risks. This requires a proper mechanism allowing domestic regulators, central bankers, and policymakers to share information, cooperate and, if necessary, coordinate policies. They also need to effectively communicate with the public with one voice. But finding an appropriate mechanism for a particular economy is not always an easy task.

A key challenge is instituting a macroprudential supervisory framework and developing appropriate tools for supervisors in developing economies. Strengthening international or regional surveillance mechanisms can help by complementing and augmenting relatively weak national monitoring systems in many developing economies across the region.

Supervisory colleges for major cross-border financial institutions
As noted above, while supervisory colleges have now been implemented for major international cross-border financial institutions, there is a need to address major regional financial institutions through similar arrangements, as is now being done in the European Union. In East Asia, as financial institutions become increasingly active regionally, supervisory arrangements will need to be developed in a parallel fashion, with the AFSD potentially playing the coordinating role.

Securitization and bond market development
Securitization remains largely underdeveloped in East Asia, especially compared with the United States or Europe (Figure 9.1).[22] While debt market development remains an important objective regionally and

---

[22] See J.W. Lee and C.Y. Park, 'Global Financial Turmoil: Impact and Challenges for Asia's Financial Systems', 8 (1) *Asian Economic Papers* (2009).

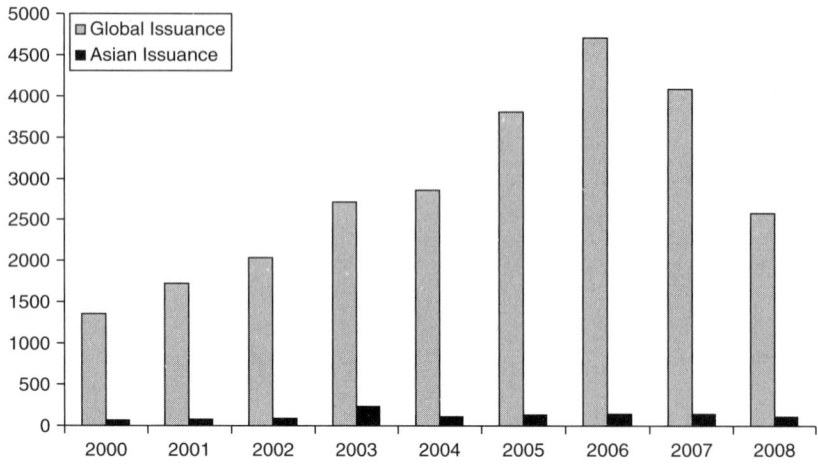

Note: Asian issuance includes Japan and the Republic of Korea.

Source: *Global Financial Stability Report*, October 2009, International Monetary Fund.

Figure 9.1   Private-label securitization issuance (US$ billion)

domestically, the use of securitization has been generally limited for various reasons, including inadequate legal and regulatory support, along with poor market infrastructure.

Vibrant local currency bond markets are essential for efficient allocation of the region's vast resources. The development of local currency bond markets also has the potential to mitigate the global shortage of sound and liquid financial assets; lessen the probability that a currency depreciation will morph into a full-blown financial crisis; and reduce massive inflows into, for example, US debt securities and hence help unwind global imbalances. In addition, developed local currency bond markets can reduce the reliance on foreign currency debt – and its concomitant currency mismatches – thus reducing the burden of having to hold large foreign exchange reserves in many developing economies in the region.

Looking forward, regional and national progress toward more transparency and disclosure, centralized trading, and investor due diligence can support market development, financial stability, and economic growth. Here, regional initiatives have proved most helpful, as seen in the marked progress in the development of local currency bond markets reflecting the efforts under the ASEAN+3 Asian Bond Markets Initiative (Figure 9.2). Despite the progress, however, corporate bond issuance is still lagging, hence requiring further policy attention. Another area with strong

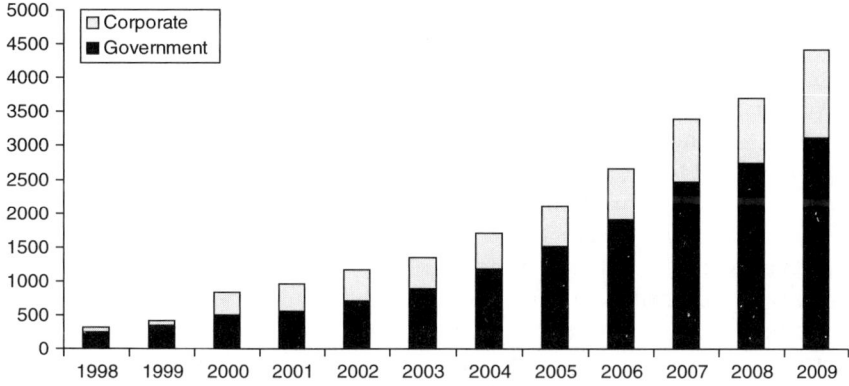

Note: East Asia includes the People's Republic of China; Hong Kong, China; Indonesia; the Republic of Korea; Malaysia; the Philippines; Singapore; Thailand; and Viet Nam.

Source: AsianBondsOnline.

Figure 9.2 *Total government and corporate bonds outstanding – East Asia (US$ billion)*

potential, especially in the context of the region's bank-centric financial systems, is covered bonds.

BALANCING REGULATION AND INNOVATION

The key challenge for regulators in East Asia is how to encourage and manage financial market development without stifling innovation. Ideal regulation leaves space for innovation, although unfettered innovation can generate risks of its own. The experience of past crises suggests caution. But translating caution into regulatory straitjackets stifles innovation. And this has its own costs. Striking the right balance is the challenge, and it is not an easy one.

Crises highlight the importance of adequate monitoring of financial innovation. Regulators should be wary of complex innovations that make the underlying risks of products or services more difficult to assess or trace – whether by bank management, regulators, or investors. Innovative products also lack the historic data needed to apply appropriate stress testing. Regulators need to assess the impact of innovative products on the safety and soundness of financial institutions, risk management, investor protection, and financial stability in general.

An important distinction should be made between the basic elements of financial market development and risky financial innovation. Many economies in the region continue to face the challenge of developing financial markets to efficiently channel domestic savings into productive investment. Moreover, much of the region still lacks essential financial services – authorities need to encourage greater public access to banking, provide credit to promote entrepreneurship, diversify savings instruments, and develop appropriate products to manage risk.

For East Asia, where banks remain the main channel for financial intermediation, building strong banking systems remains paramount. However, authorities must also foster a broader range of markets – including corporate bond markets, securitization, covered bonds, and derivatives – to enhance financial system resilience. Many economies also need to establish, upgrade or reform basic market infrastructure for trading and settlement, all of which will help promote more efficient financial transactions.

ESTABLISHING NATIONAL AND CROSS-BORDER CRISIS MANAGEMENT AND RESOLUTION MECHANISMS

Globally, the financial crisis highlighted that, in addition to effective monetary policy, economies need effective arrangements to ensure financial stability – not only for crisis prevention but also for crisis resolution. Clearly, East Asian economies must review existing liquidity provision arrangements to address coverage, scope (especially relating to collateral availability) and moral hazard. Asian governments had to intervene in 2008 and 2009 to a lesser extent than those in the United States and Europe. But based on the responses to the 1997–98 Asian financial crisis and the recent global crisis, advance planning, especially for resolving major financial institutional failure – whether domestic or foreign – is prudent and necessary.

A comprehensive framework and contingency plan for financial institution failure is needed, including consumer protection measures such as deposit insurance. Clear consensus on building appropriate institutional arrangements and systems would be valuable. Simulations that identify possible consequences of both local and international financial institution failures, as well as market volatility, would help in establishing advance contingency plans.

In reforming crisis management frameworks, remedial or corrective actions need to be harmonized, particularly for large and systemic cross-border financial institutions. In the early stages of the recent crisis, there were issues with cross-border movements of funds and assets to support liquidity or capital requirements of either the parent entity or the subsidiary/branch. To fix this, regulators need to take a broader view of liquidity requirements for cross-border banks and apply a more consistent set of liquidity parameters for them. Disruptive regulatory actions – such as the ring-fencing of liquid assets in the recent crisis – should be used only as a last resort. This requires better knowledge of how cross-border banks conduct business. Complex, large cross-border banks internally manage liquidity in very diverse ways. Host and home supervisory and regulatory authorities need to ensure that these banks hold sufficiently high-quality liquid assets.

The crisis showed that insolvency regimes need to be aligned across economies affected by cross-border bank failures. Delays and uncertainties during the height of the crisis increased uncertainty and exacerbated contagion. For example, measures and processes for managing insolvent banks using close-out netting, managing creditor claims on collateral assets or unwinding financial transactions are often designed for domestic operations. A strengthened resolution framework would also help forestall unilateral actions tantamount to financial protectionism. There is a clear need for better information sharing and cross-border burden sharing on costs – for example, in the case of workout operations, mergers, or liquidation of cross-border banking businesses.

The resolution of cross-border institutions and questions of burden-sharing have different contexts for emerging economies. In particular, foreign banks make up an important portion of the domestic financial system in many developing economies. Any failure of these thus raises real financial stability questions for the host financial system, even when the institution is not necessarily systemically significant internationally or even in its home jurisdiction. In this context, there would be great benefit in building international or at least regional approaches to address issues arising from foreign financial institution participation in developing financial systems. We recognize the need to establish regulations including capital requirements for domestic subsidiaries and branches of foreign banks. However, they should be formulated in a way that they do not give undue advantage or disadvantage to foreign banks over domestic banks.

SUPPORTING GROWTH AND DEVELOPMENT

An appropriately designed institutional framework for finance is needed to achieve the twin objectives of supporting economic growth and financial stability. First, a reliable institutional framework defines the rules of the game for financial transactions and supports financial sector development. Without an appropriate legal and institutional framework, effective finance cannot develop. Second, weak financial sectors have been a significant cause of many financial crises, including the Asian financial crisis and the recent global financial crisis. Well-established legal and regulatory frameworks can strengthen financial intermediaries and help prevent crises. Third, it is necessary to develop an effective framework to help resolve financial distress or crisis. Without a solid structure, crisis resolution is more difficult, time-consuming, and expensive. This again is a primary focus of the G-20.

East Asia's underdeveloped financial systems remain an important hurdle to funding necessary development and ensuring sustained high growth. Financial systems need to be strengthened for more efficient resource allocation. The region's financial needs for infrastructure and for SMEs are particularly significant.

An important issue in bank financing of infrastructure is asset–liability mismatches. While infrastructure typically involves long-term finance, banks rely heavily on deposits as their main source of funds. With banks continuing as the major funding source for the region, this asset–liability mismatch problem becomes especially acute. The relatively limited presence of insurance companies and pension and provident funds also constrains sources of long-term finance in the region.

Financing SMEs is another critical development issue. For most East Asian economies, SMEs are the main pillars of production and job creation. Many SMEs in the region need more effective financial assistance for hedging against foreign exchange volatility and trade finance. At this stage, it is important to encourage simple innovations to provide a better menu of financial services and products catering to the needs of small entrepreneurs and investors.

While more structural reforms are underway to broaden and deepen the region's financial systems, their effect will be gradual given the long-term nature of reform. In addition, policy reforms are needed to improve investment climates across East Asia. Policies that promote SMEs and services also help. Governments should lower entry barriers facing new firms, ensure level playing fields for domestically oriented firms versus export industries, and promote competition including the liberalization of key sectors.

Across East Asia, financial sector development will support growth in the context of financial stability. Efforts should initially focus on developing clear international guidelines for developing effective and efficient finance. These include building the foundations for finance and financial infrastructure, especially effective payment systems, clear and transparent property rights, information infrastructure such as credit information systems and corporate governance, including insolvency arrangements, and dispute resolution.

The BCBS, IOSCO and IAIS are now all revising their respective core principles with a greater focus on 'preconditions' that take into account differing regulatory systems and stages of development. In many East Asian economies, these preconditions (foundations and infrastructure) remain a central development focus. The region's banking systems need to extend their reach to a broader portion of the population, especially to SMEs and through continued development of microfinance. For securities markets, infrastructure, transparency, and corporate governance are central for both development and financial stability, and in both equity and debt markets. In insurance, major opportunities exist for developing pension and contractual savings arrangements to better employ financial savings and build the social safety nets needed to support growth, development and stability across the region.

REFORMING THE INTERNATIONAL AND REGIONAL FINANCIAL ARCHITECTURE

Currently, there is a need to improve and streamline the region's regulatory and supervisory regimes, reinforcing global efforts at revamping the financial architecture to avoid a repeat of the crisis. East Asian banks held up well compared with banks in many advanced economies because of their relatively low exposure to subprime mortgages. Nevertheless, enhancing the strength of the system remains paramount. Capital adequacy requirements must be increased. Regulators need to fully assess the impact of innovative products on both the micro- and macro-prudential soundness of financial institutions, risk management, investor protection, and systemic financial stability.

Reform of International Financial Institutions

Given previous crisis experience, East Asia has a keen interest in reforming international financial institutions – especially the IMF – and the international financial architecture in general. Developing countries face direct financial and economic impact from international economic and financial volatility and are vulnerable to any loss of confidence globally or regionally. IMF reform to keep up with the real challenges of financial globalization is central. Likewise, international support for regional arrangements is extremely valuable, particularly in light of recent crises in Europe and the implications for new regional arrangements such as the CMIM.

Addressing Capital Flows

The potential of speculative capital flows poses policy challenges to most East Asian economies. The links between capital flows, credit expansion – lending booms with capital account liberalization – and adverse macro-economic consequences are not new to the region's emerging economies. A surge in capital inflows could complicate macroeconomic management, especially as many economies are beginning to normalize policies related to crisis response.

Managing capital flows must be done judiciously to ensure that external volatility does not disrupt domestic financial markets. An appropriate policy package includes currency flexibility, a clear and stable monetary and fiscal policy, and enhanced regulatory and supervisory efforts to prevent asset bubbles. Authorities should also communicate clearly and effectively with market participants, which could affect policy outcomes. Regional cooperation and coordination can also be crucial to managing capital flows. The establishment of a regional financial stability dialogue, that is, an AFSD, could help the authorities to address the region's common interests and concerns.

International support and guidance in monitoring and managing capital flows would be helpful for the region's developing economies. This is an area where the IMF and/or other global and regional multilateral developing banks can provide important advice and technical support.

Effective Regional Financial Architecture

East Asia needs to take its rightful place in the new global financial architecture by actively participating and taking on greater responsibility in developing appropriate supervisory and regulatory structures for the region and the world. As such, the region needs to make its voice heard in international forums for debating the future of the global economy and reforming the global financial architecture.

East Asian countries must play their part in ensuring the new financial architecture meets both the challenges of globalized finance and the region's financial development agenda. There are four important areas for regional cooperation: (i) liquidity provision – the Chiang Mai Initiative Multilateralization; (ii) macroeconomic and financial surveillance – the ASEAN+3 Macroeconomic Research Office (AMRO); (iii) regional bond market development – the Asian Bond Markets Initiative; and (iv) a regional financial stability dialogue – the Asian Financial Stability Dialogue.

CONCLUSION

The early crisis response was necessarily reactive, rather than focusing comprehensively on the financial sector role in financial stability, sustainable growth, and economic development. Now it is time to forge a clear agenda to guide longer-term reform domestically, regionally, and globally.

First, the G-20 has thus far focused on a range of specific regulatory issues arising directly from weaknesses identified as a result of the global financial crisis. In terms of supporting financial stability, however, there is merit in taking a more comprehensive approach rather than addressing selected issues on a piecemeal basis.

Second, the crisis presents a real opportunity to redesign the international financial architecture to better address the realities of a global financial system, including the needs of East Asia. It is essential to reform the mandate of the IMF and to design arrangements to support not only financial stability but also financial development at the international level.

Financial systems appear to be inherently subject to periodic financial crises.[23] The international financial architecture (as well as regional financial architectures) should be designed to address the nature of global finance and the characteristics of periodic crises.[24] Likewise, in a world with an increasing range of regional economic and financial arrangements (including in the region), the international architecture should be designed to support both individual domestic economies and financial systems and regional arrangements.

Third, looking forward, East Asia would benefit from the establishment of deeper and more developed mechanisms to support regional economic and financial cooperation, coordination, assistance, and monitoring. In particular, these mechanisms could serve a central role in advocating regional interests in the context of global organizations such as the G-20, the FSB and the IMF. The CMIM and the associated AMRO provide a mechanism for regional economic monitoring, with the ASEAN+3 dialogue process an example of a possible forum for reaching regional consensus on issues being addressed in global forums.

Finally, continuing work to establish an Asian Financial Stability Dialogue to develop a consensus on regulatory concerns has real potential

---

[23] See C. Reinhart and K. Rogoff, *This Time is Different: Eight Centuries of Financial Folly* (Princeton, NJ: Princeton University Press, 2009).

[24] For discussion, see D. Arner and R. Buckley, 'Redesigning the Architecture of the Global Financial System', 11 (3) *Melbourne Journal of International Law* (2010).

value. Support of relevant international institutions such as the IMF, the BIS and the OECD could play a pivotal role in the establishment of an AFSD, with the regional institutions providing technical assistance and other support in furthering these regional initiatives.

10. Legitimacy and power: the political dynamics of East Asian financial regionalism

Injoo Sohn

INTRODUCTION

The international monetary system is in a great flux. A series of international financial crises have significantly undermined the legitimacy and effectiveness of the relatively exclusive decision-making structure of the Group of Seven (G7)-centered international financial architecture. The rise of China and other key emerging economies has reshaped the international power configuration, lending great volatility to the existing international monetary system. At the core of the profoundly evolving international financial architecture are the issues of legitimacy and power. The problems of *legitimacy deficit* and *power shift* have contributed to challenging the post-World War II international financial architecture in general and stimulating East Asian financial cooperation in particular. The perceived deficiency of political legitimacy, even in the post-Asian crisis global financial architecture, and East Asia's growing economic power and power balancing have driven East Asian states to become *rule makers* rather than rule takers through new regional financial arrangements. This chapter will discuss the independent causal effects of legitimacy and power on strategic choices made by East Asian states.

In recent years, clear progress has been made in East Asia's collective efforts to create new regional financial cooperative mechanisms. The main forum for such efforts became one composed exclusively of *East Asian* countries, notably excluding the United States. The Association for Southeast Asian Nations (ASEAN) member countries and China, Japan and the Republic of Korea (ASEAN+3) have transformed the bilateral swap arrangements under the Chiang Mai Initiative (CMI) into a multilateral arrangement. The multilateralization of the CMI is perceived by many Asia watchers as a significant step toward the emergence of an Asian Monetary Fund (AMF), an Asian version of the International Monetary

233

Fund (IMF). East Asian countries also have sought to develop a vibrant regional bond market. The emergence of East Asia's own regional bond market driven by the Asian Bond Fund (and Market) Initiative would possibly complement and constrain the US and Europe-centered global capital markets. Moreover, even the creation of a single Asian currency is now more vigorously studied by East Asian governments.

Such changes have been caused by regional actors' low-key, accommodating and prudent approaches to regional financial cooperation. East Asian countries search for 'counterweight' strategies that will allow them to avoid overdependence even as they maintain cooperative relations with the G7-centered global financial institutions (such as the IMF). East Asian countries do not intend to directly challenge the United States and Europe, given the overwhelming significance of cooperation with these two economic powers to achieve common goals. If East Asia's policy preference diverges significantly from that of the United States and Europe, however, East Asian countries may want to bolster their policy position and bargaining power vis-à-vis the non-Asian economic powers by developing and using regional supplements (or potential alternatives). This pattern of East Asia's counterweight strategy is taking form at the very time that the international financial architecture is profoundly evolving.

In the next section, I discuss the conceptual framework for the problem of legitimacy and power with respect to global financial governance. Then I provide a brief explanation of the causal effect of the legitimacy and power concerns on East Asia's counterweight strategy in international finance. This is followed by an analysis of how East Asia has pursued its counterweight strategy. The last section examines the implications of growing Asian financial regionalism for the post-2008 global financial crisis world.

LEGITIMACY, POWER AND GLOBAL FINANCIAL GOVERNANCE

Legitimacy

Many international relations scholars define legitimacy as the sense of obligation to uphold international laws and contracts and to keep commitments.[1] In this study, the conceptualization of legitimacy goes

---

    [1]   For instance, see Andreas Hasenclever, Peter Mayer and Volker Rittberger, *Theories of International Regimes* (Cambridge: Cambridge University Press,

beyond contractual obligation, which is highlighted by the rational choice approach to politics. In the rational choice framework, obligation is created when parties make agreements. Obligation is thus the outcome of choices made by utility-maximizing actors. However, more culturally and sociologically attuned legal and international relations scholars claim that contractual obligations alone are insufficient to determine behavior.[2] In this view, legitimacy produces obligation and thereby connects obligation to behavior. Here, legitimacy is sticky enough for actors to continue to comply with rules even when the material benefits supplied by the status quo decline.

In order to explore the role of legitimacy in the creation of the new global and regional financial arrangements, I lay out three more specific sources of political legitimacy which are observable in the formal decision-making mechanisms and the explicit policy agenda of the international financial architecture. They are inclusiveness, rule-governance, and fair return.

Inclusiveness refers here to the wider and more meaningful participation of the members of a group in the decision-making process of the global financial system. By participating in the creation of rules, agents better understand why the rules are necessary. Legitimacy also relies on the capacity of actors to gain a genuine stake in the enterprise and to feel that they have an input in the decision-making process. Unless state actors feel a sense of ownership in the decision-making structure of the global financial system, their sense of compliance decreases when material benefits decline or coercion is no longer credible.

Rule-governance refers to policymaking and implementation through a transparent, specific and agreed-upon rule or a process that has been agreed on to interpret such a rule. The absence of an agreed system of rules may increase the uncertainty and ambiguity surrounding governance and thereby expand the room for dominant actors' maneuvering and arbitrary behavior in their favor. Legitimacy can be jeopardized, then, by contradictions and inadequacies in the systems of rules.

The third element of legitimacy is related to the equal sharing of costs and benefits in cooperative efforts – *fair return*. Unless actors can expect

---

1997), and Thomas M. Franck, *The Power of Legitimacy Among Nations* (Oxford: Oxford University Press, 1990).

[2] For the constructivist–rationalist debate over obligation, see Martha Finnemore and Stephen J. Toope, 'Alternative to "Legalization": Richer Views of Law and Politics', *International Organization* 55 (3) (2001): 745–58; and Judith Goldstein, Miles Kahler, Robert Keohane and Ann-Marie Slaughter, 'Response to Finnemore and Toope', *International Organization* 55 (3) (2001): 759–60.

an adequate balance between contributions and rewards, they will not participate or comply.[3] The concept of fair return is different from the neorealist notion of relative gains. The fair return hypothesis challenges the idea that states always base their interaction on the calculations of relative gains or losses vis-à-vis others. Rather, states seek a fair distribution of the costs and benefits of cooperative arrangements. If state actors are confident about the more equal sharing of the costs and benefits, they are more likely to have a sense of compliance with the arrangements.

Power

Realist international political economy scholars emphasize the role of power in global financial governance. International material structure or power configuration is their primary focus.[4] For the most part, power from the realist perspective is concerned with coercion (as opposed to persuasion) and material capability (as opposed to ideational influence), which involves population, economics, military might and resource endowment. Realist approaches trace institutional origin to powerful states that often use institutions as convenient tools of statecraft.[5] While this realist tradition provides a number of distinctive sets of causal claims and predictions, there are at least two prominent realist explanations about the genesis of Asian financial cooperation: *power transition* and *balance of power*.

A power-transition version of realism asserts that East Asia's increasing relative material power allows the region to gain more self-confidence and thereby create regional institutions to shape the rules of international monetary relations in its favor. In other words, its increasing bargaining

---

[3] Wayne Sandholtz, *High-Tech Europe: The Politics of International Cooperation* (Berkeley: University of California Press, 1992), 15.

[4] Unlike the standard political economy approach, which focuses on the domestic politics of national interest formation or state–society interactions, the realist approach assumes that states are primarily concerned about long-term security. Such security concerns are not completely explained by which domestic actors gain more or how.

[5] Andrew Hurrell, 'Regionalism in Theoretical Perspective', in Louise Fawcett and Andrew Hurrell (eds), *Regionalism in World Politics: Regional Organization and International Order* (New York: Oxford University Press, 1995); Joseph M. Grieco, 'Systemic Sources of Variation in Regional Institutionalization in Western Europe, East Asia, and the Americas' in Edward D. Mansfield and Helen V. Milner (eds), *The Political Economy of Regionalism* (New York: Columbia University Press, 1997); Kenneth Waltz, 'Structural Realism after the Cold War', *International Security* 25: 5–41.

power vis-à-vis the G7 could provoke East Asia's multilateral activism.[6] Another variant of the realist explanation is the realist balancing thesis. From this perspective, regional financial cooperation could emerge as regional powers seek to counter either exploitation by hegemonic power or system instability.[7] Asian regional cooperative institutions are an Asian coalition against the aggressive behavior and destructive policies of the dominant player outside the region or a defensive mechanism against (future) international financial crisis.

WHY EAST ASIA COUNTERWEIGHTS

There has been a fundamental shift in the global redistribution of wealth. The Chinese economy, which accounted for about one third of world GDP in the early nineteenth century but significantly declined afterwards, is close to resuming its historical position in the global economy.[8] China and other key Asian economies are increasingly regarded as central rather than peripheral players in the global market, while the developed world's share of world GDP has been shrinking. The decentralizing trend in international economic power has reshaped East Asia's bargaining power not only with the United States and other G7 players

---

[6]   Although I do not deny that the power factor might play a significant role in influencing the regional initiatives, I remain skeptical that increasing power *alone* can explain the rise of regional financial cooperation. It is conceptually plausible that the logic of increasing power can go in two opposite directions. Increasing material power might encourage actors either to value or to disvalue multilateral diplomacy. In my view, only when combined with other factors such as legitimacy and economic interdependence the can power factor provide a convincing explanation of Asian regional cooperation.

[7]   It is the temptation of hegemons to exploit their positions that made the international system unstable. For instance, the United States, the most financially powerful actor in the world economy, was capable of deflecting the costs of macroeconomic adjustment from the early 1970s till the mid-1990s onto Europe and Japan mainly through the use of what C. Randall Henning calls the 'exchange-rate weapon'. C. Randall Henning, 'The Exchange-Rate Weapon and Macroeconomic Conflict', in David Andrews (ed.), *International Monetary Power* (Ithaca: Cornell University Press, 2006).

[8]   Until the mid-nineteenth century, China accounted for over 30 per cent of world GDP, gradually dropping to less than 5 per cent of world GDP in 1950. According to Angus Maddison's calculation, however, China is more likely to reclaim its place as the first world economy in terms of GDP by 2015. See Angus Maddison, *Chinese Economic Performance in the Long Run* (Paris: OECD Development Centre, 2008).

but also with the key international financial institutions such as the IMF and the World Bank.

With their rapid economic ascent, East Asian countries became increasingly aware that their individual and collective positions within the global economy are not fairly reflected in the existing international institutions. For instance, East Asia's quota share and corresponding voting power in the IMF do not represent its relative importance in the world economy. As of the early 2000s, when the East Asian governments began to establish regional financial cooperative mechanisms, ASEAN, China, Japan and the Republic of Korea had about 13 per cent of the total quota but this was much less than their shares of GDP (24 per cent), PPP-based GDP (25 per cent), trade (16 per cent), reserves (28 per cent) and population (33 per cent).[9] The 1997–98 Asian financial crisis brought to the fore East Asian countries' relative positions vis-à-vis the Western countries in the IMF, which deeply intervened in the economic policymaking of the region's crisis-hit countries. From the East Asian countries' perspectives, their ability to influence the IMF conditionality and resist the IMF policies perceived as counterproductive is significantly constrained by their limited quota shares and voting power in the IMF. Although some Asian governments publicly supported the IMF during the Asian financial crisis, their populations harbored strong resentment toward the IMF and the Washington Consensus. There was, and still is, a strong sense that the West in general, and the United States in particular, used the crisis to advance a particular economic agenda that served selfish interests. The crisis-hit countries were also discontent with the perceived unequal sharing of the adjustment costs with private international lenders headquartered in the United States and in other G7 countries.[10]

The dissatisfaction with the IMF's performance in the Asian financial crisis and the discontent with the legitimacy problem with the G7-centered international financial institutions in general left East Asian countries with two primary policy options: global and regional ones. They can seek substantial reforms of the global institutions and/or pursue the creation of regional alternative institutions in order to insulate the region from (future) international financial crisis and counter the destructive policies of dominant players outside the region. However, East Asian countries

---

[9]   David P. Rapkin and Jonathan R. Strand, 'Is East Asia Under-represented in the International Monetary Fund?', *International Relations of the Asia-Pacific* 3 (1) (2003): 1–28.

[10]   Richard Higgott and Nicola Phillips, 'Challenging Triumphalism and Convergence: The Limits of Global Liberalization in Asia and Latin America', *Review of International Studies* 26 (3) (2000).

confront a deep uncertainty about the evolution of both global and regional financial institutions.

At the global level, the prospects for serious reforms in the G7-centered global financial institutions have still been remote in the eyes of many Asian policymakers. Although the G7 finally began to engage more expansively in dialogue with the rest of the world through the Financial Stability Forum (FSF) and the Group of Twenty (G-20) following the Asian financial crisis, such adjustments have not met the expectation of East Asian countries. In the view of many Asian developing countries, the FSF featured heavy G7 representation; the new FSF excluded key emerging Asian economies such as China, Indonesia, South Korea, Malaysia, and Thailand. Even the four new members were not given the same depth of representation held by the G7: the Netherlands, Australia, Hong Kong and Singapore had a single representative rather than the three allocated to their G7 counterparts.

Moreover, the governing rules of the FSF and the G-20 were minimal. The rules guiding membership selection and agenda setting were vague. For example, there were no explicit standards to explain why Indonesia rather than Malaysia was included, or Turkey rather than Thailand, in the G-20. Likewise, it is not clear whether or how the non-FSF members would continue to participate in future FSF working groups. Without a globally agreed system of rules, the FSF and the G-20 appeared to be vulnerable to charges that they were puppet institutions controlled by the G7.

Furthermore, prior to the 2008 global financial crisis, the FSF and the G-20 tended to emphasize the *domestic* aspects of the reforms (in developing countries in particular), as opposed to the *international* aspects of the reforms (such as hedge funds, transnational capital flows, and offshore financial centers), which might entail painful adjustment for the G7 as well as non-G7 countries.[11] Such a perceived unfair sharing of adjustment costs and benefits also contributed to reinforcing East Asia's discontent and skepticism that fundamental changes to the G7-centered global financial institutions would be out of reach.

Deep crisis like the current financial crisis holds great potential for sweeping reform, but financial reform on a global scale is still full of

---

[11]   For example, the FSF working group reviewed but did not recommend direct regulation of unregulated hedge funds, although it keeps the door open to such a possibility. Likewise, even though the FSF emphasized the need for emerging markets to develop sound guidelines for sovereign debt and liquidity management, it was opposed to the idea of them managing or controlling transnational capital flows themselves.

uncertainty and contradiction.[12] The interests of the major G-20 players do not necessarily coincide. Also constraining the pace and scope of reform are the conservative tendencies of the status quo powers and the bureaucratic inertia of existing international institutions. Collective efforts to redesign global institutions are further complicated by the perceived absence of the kind of benign leadership exercised by the United States when the World Trade Organization (WTO) emerged. East Asian states thus recognize the daunting challenges of the fundamental reform of the global institutions, which would reflect the new international power configuration and resolve the legitimacy problems.

At the regional level, skepticism about the feasibility and desirability of Asia's efforts to create more cohesive arrangements or institutions have prevailed both within and outside the region. A series of potential political and economic hurdles seem to overshadow the future of Asian financial cooperation. Among the widely cited obstacles to regional cooperation are economic diversity, interstate political rivalry, and the lack of domestic regulatory capacity.[13] Those skeptical about tight-knit Asian regional institutions thus remain less receptive to the idea of a regional alternative even though they are not sanguine about the sweeping reform of the existing global institutions. Furthermore, Asian policy elites are keenly aware that although East Asia is on the rise, the region is still not capable of creating an *exclusive* regional economic alliance and setting a new global standard on its own, given its growing yet limited power. The ambiguity and uncertainty inherent in reforming global institutions and creating regional institutions has become a central driver of East Asia policy. Against this background, East Asian countries have pursued the risk-averse counterweight strategy, which intends to create new regional financial arrangements and thereby avoid overdependence while sustaining collaborative relations with the G7-dominated global financial institutions.

---

[12]   Following the recent global financial crisis, there is momentum towards greater inclusion of developing countries in international regulatory regimes. For instance, the Financial Stability Board (FSB), which expanded its membership to the G-20, was created in April 2009. The Basel Committee has finally expanded its membership to include all G-20 members. However, the FSB is a relatively powerless body designed to facilitate networks of cooperation among financial officials and regulators. Since the FSB remains a non-decision-making body, the involvement of several Asian countries would make little difference in the actual decision-making process of global financial governance.

[13]   On this point, see, for instance, Natasha Hamilton-Hart, 'Asian New Regionalism: Governance Capacity and Co-operation in the Western Pacific', *Review of International Political Economy*, 10 (2) (2003).

HOW EAST ASIA COUNTERWEIGHTS

A series of initiatives have been launched to increase regional self-sufficiency, ranging from information sharing to financial swap arrangements and a regional bond market. Among the new initiatives are the Chiang Mai Initiative (now CMI Multilateralization) and the Asian Bond Fund Initiative (ABFI), which merit a detailed discussion.

The Chiang Mai Initiative

The CMI is designed to provide liquidity support for member countries that experience short-run balance-of-payment deficits, with the purpose of preventing an extreme crisis or systemic failure in a country and subsequent regional contagion of the kind that occurred in the 1997–98 Asian financial crisis. In the first phase of the CMI, 16 bilateral currency swap arrangements have been negotiated and concluded among ASEAN+3 countries. In May 2005, the size of the CMI stood at US$36.5 billion. Each agreement enabled parties to borrow the equivalent of $1–3 billion in foreign exchange reserves from partners.

The initial amounts (US$36.5 billion) involved under the CMI appeared relatively small and inadequate for single-handedly preventing speculative attacks. Such skepticism is understandable, given the huge amounts of foreign exchange reserves held by ASEAN+3 countries as a whole (which amount to US$2 trillion), as well as the emergency assistance required by the crisis-hit countries in the 1997 crisis, since Thailand alone requested US$17.2 billion. With such small amounts involved, one might expect that assistance via the CMI would have to be supplemented by the IMF and/or additional packages of aid negotiated at the time of crisis.

Recognizing such a weakness, in May 2005 East Asian countries decided to double the amount of emergency funds to be provided to crisis-hit nations to some US$80 billion (the second stage of the CMI). As of early 2010, the size of the CMI (now CMIM) amounted to US$120 billion with the contribution ratio between ASEAN and the Plus Three countries at 20:80 per cent.[14] The recent ongoing efforts to increase the size of the CMI show a clear consensus among East Asian countries that the dependence on an IMF- or US-determined solution to financial crisis in the region

---

[14]   The contribution proportions are China 32 per cent, Japan 32 per cent, Republic of Korea 16 per cent and ASEAN 20 per cent. And the maximum amount that each member country can borrow is determined by its contribution multiplied by its respective borrowing multiplier. For instance, Malaysia's borrowing multiplier is 2.5 and China's borrowing multiplier is 0.5.

is insufficient; East Asia pursues a regional option, as well as the existing global one, to build defenses against future speculative attack.

Another notable feature of the initial CMI is its linkage with the IMF. The initial CMI required its member countries drawing more than 10 per cent from the funds in the CMI to accept an IMF conditionality. This means that East Asia's *preemptive* measure to reduce exchange rate volatility prior to a full-fledged crisis is hindered. In general, IMF programs are not negotiated until a crisis has already occurred. Ten per cent of the swap lines are too small to prevent a significant attack. Some participating countries, particularly Malaysia, opposed the linkage of the CMI with IMF conditionality. Meanwhile, other members such as China and Japan argued for the importance of forging a cooperative relationship with the IMF at an early stage of the CMI development to make it more credible. Eventually East Asian countries agreed to accept the linkage of the CMI to the IMF as a temporary arrangement until a formal surveillance mechanism is put in place.

This compromise can be explained by two factors. First, the IMF possesses better institutionalized surveillance mechanisms that ASEAN+3 lacks. The IMF conducts annual reviews of member country economies via Article 4 consultations, as well as assessments of financial sector vulnerability through the Financial Sector Assessment Program. For some East Asian countries, it would be ineffective and inappropriate to lend funds to countries whose operations were not under this type of regular surveillance. Linking the CMI to the IMF could ensure that funds lent had a better chance of being repaid, even if ASEAN+3 remained critical of IMF conditionality per se.[15] In addition to the 'efficiency' (or 'functional') consideration, the logic of an interstate 'power' structure helped East Asian countries to take an accommodating and prudent approach to the CMI. Many of the East Asian countries worried that the United States and the European Union would oppose a new Asian financial framework which lacked any IMF linkage, as in the case of the aborted Asian Monetary Fund plan in 1997. Given the limited, albeit growing, political power of the East Asian grouping vis-à-vis the US and the EU, East Asian countries needed to water down the independent nature of the CMI at the initial stage of regional financial integration.

At the May 2001 ASEAN+3 Finance Ministers' Meeting in Honolulu, member countries agreed to review the issue of the IMF linkage with the CMI after three years had passed, leaving room for possible revision of

---

[15]   Jennifer Amyx, 'A Regional Bond Market for East Asia?', The Australian National University, Pacific Economic Papers, No. 342, 2004, 6–7.

the linkage requirement. In May 2005, the finance ministers of East Asian governments agreed to double the size of the emergency funds that could be withdrawn without IMF conditionality from 10 per cent to 20 per cent. This revision represents the incremental approach taken by East Asian countries in loosening their adherence to the IMF conditionality. Whether or not the CMI eliminates its IMF linkage in the near future, such a regional liquidity fund clearly intends to complement the role of the IMF in crisis management in the long term. At the moment, the IMF linkage makes the CMI look more inclusive (as opposed to exclusive), thereby helping to deflect suspicions and criticism from non-Asian economic powers. In this sense, the CMI reflects East Asia's strategic behavior to counter the risk of its overdependence on the IMF even as it maintains collaborative relations with the IMF and other G7-centered global financial institutions.

More progress has been made in boosting the CMI recently. ASEAN+3 countries have been increasingly seeking to transform the CMI into a single multilateral framework (CMIM) since 2005. To this end, a collective decision-making procedure for the CMIM activation was adopted. All swap-providing countries can simultaneously and promptly provide liquidity support to any parties involved in swap arrangements at times of emergency. When it comes to the rules of decision-making of the CMIM, any approval and renewal of drawing would be determined by the Executive Level Decision Making Body (ELDMB), composed of representatives from Ministries of Finance of ASEAN+3 and Central Banks of ASEAN+3 countries and the Hong Kong Monetary Authority. The terms, conditions and other key elements of the CMIM are subject to a review very five years by the participating parties.

Moreover, one can find that more concrete steps are being taken by East Asia toward the creation of an independent regional surveillance mechanism, which is crucial for the rise of the CMIM with a regionally tailored conditionality that would fairly reflect Asian circumstances. For example, in May 2006 the ASEAN+3 nations declared the launch of the Group of Experts (GOE) and the Technical Working Group on Economic and Financial Monitoring (ETWG) to explore ways for further strengthening surveillance capacity in East Asia. As of early 2010, the CMIM member countries are still working out details on the surveillance unit, in particular on the governance structure and the location of the unit, to ensure its independence and credibility. Meanwhile, an Interim Surveillance Arrangement, composed of the Asian Development Bank (ADB) and the ASEAN Secretariat, would provide an interim surveillance mechanism. These new efforts will significantly contribute to enhancing East Asia's surveillance capacity, thus increasing the effectiveness of the CMIM.

The Asian Bond Fund Initiative

The Asian Bond Fund Initiative (ABFI) added to the momentum of Asian financial cooperation. The ABFI, along with the CMIM, promised prospects that would contribute to changing the international financial landscape. In June 2003, the Executives' Meeting of East Asia-Pacific Central Banks (EMEAP), the region's central bankers association – which includes representatives from Thailand, Indonesia, Malaysia, Singapore, the Philippines, China, Hong Kong, South Korea, Japan, Australia and New Zealand – announced the creation of the Asian Bond Fund (ABF) with an initial size of about US$1 billion. This first stage of the ABF invested in a basket of US dollar denominated bonds issued by Asian sovereign and quasi-sovereign issuers in EMEAP economies. Building on the success of ABF1, EMEAP launched the second stage of the Asian Bond Fund (ABF2) in July 2005. ABF2 invested in *local*-currency bonds issued by sovereign and quasi-sovereign issuers in the eight EMEAP markets. EMEAP members have invested a total of US$2 billion of seed money in ABF2. ABF2 comprises nine component funds: a Pan-Asian Bond Index Fund (PAIF) and eight single-market funds.

The rationale for broadening and deepening regional bond markets can be two-fold. First, the ultimate aim of the establishment of the Asian Bond Fund is to bring back the huge amount of Asian foreign reserves that were traditionally saved in Europe or in the US to be used in bond investments throughout Asia. In the past decades, Asian savings were largely channeled into international bond markets in the US or Europe due in part to the underdevelopment of the Asian regional bond market. A growing number of Asian policymakers were becoming unhappy about the fact that the wealth of East Asia has been used (in the form of US treasury bonds) to finance the swelling US current account deficit, rather than to create greater prosperity for the region. In his speech advocating substantial regional bond market expansion, Hong Kong Monetary Authority Chief Executive Joseph Yam argued that 'the cost of capital for enterprises in Asia would be lower, if there was a deep and well-functioning corporate bond market in the region to tap the considerable pool of savings, much of which now flows instead to industrial countries.'[16] Such concerns urged Asian governments to accelerate plans for a regional Asian bond market as a counterweight to bond markets in the West.

---

[16] Hong Kong Monetary Authority Chief Executive Joseph Yam, 'A Case for Financial Integration in Asia', 24 February 2006, accessed 2 September 2010, http://aric.adb.org/asianbond/EOS.htm.

Secondly, the ABFI intends to shield the region from external vulner-abilities by building more robust and diversified local capital markets. The dominant view of those supporting Asian bond market expansion is that the Asian financial crisis would have been less severe if local bond markets had been more developed and financial intermediation in the crisis-affected countries had not been so heavily concentrated on banks.[17]

While the ABFI has the potential to challenge the dominance of the US and the EU in the global capital markets, the recent emphasis many Asian leaders have placed on the Asian-Bond–Eurobond linkage and the creation of a Eurobond Market in Asia helped to mobilize EU support for the idea of an Asian Bond Market. In line with Asian–European financial cooperation, for example, 11 Central Bank governors from EMEAP, the president of the European Central Bank, and 12 governors from the Eurosystem National Central Banks held a joint high-level seminar in Singapore in July 2004. The purpose of the seminar was to exchange views on issues that are relevant to both Europe and the East Asia-Pacific region, and to consolidate relations between EMEAP and the Eurosystem. Moreover, East Asian central banks have been working closely with a key international agency, that is, the Bank for International Settlements (BIS), to administer the ABF. The BIS's involvement with the ABF also helped to dispel the non-Asian actors' concern about the possible exclusive nature of Asian bond market development.[18]

Overall, the ABF creates another counterweight enabling East Asia to go beyond the IMF (or the US) support in finance for development and crisis management. East Asian countries now obtain means through which they can push forward their agenda independent of the G7-dominated international institutions, but without antagonizing the G7 and endanger-ing their relationship with the IMF.

---

[17]   Paul Lejot, Douglas Arner, Liu Qiao, Mylene Chan and Marshall Mays, 'Asia's Debt Capital Markets Appraisal and Agenda for Policy Reform', Hong Kong Institute of Economics and Business Strategy Working Paper, No. 1072, October 2003.

[18]   In addition to the CMIM and the ABFI, there are other forums dedicated to dialogue and exchange of information with key players outside the Asia-Pacific region. For example, the APEC (Asia-Pacific Economic Cooperation) Finance Ministers' Process (FMP), which includes the United States, offers an annual forum for APEC member countries to exchange views and information on regional macroeconomic and financial developments. The FMP also works with the Asian Development Bank, the Inter-American Development Bank and the World Bank.

CONCLUSION

The aforementioned Asian financial cooperation shows that legitimacy and power factors have incentivized and conditioned East Asia's strategic behavior in international financial governance. The perceived lack of legitimacy in the existing G7-led global institutions and the changing inter-state power configuration could influence East Asia's policy choice. That is, to develop its own regional supplements (or potential alternatives), thereby better positioning Asian regional actors in the evolution of the international monetary order without antagonizing key players outside the region. My findings also suggest that the scope and pace of future Asian financial cooperation will be determined not merely by actors' consideration of economic interest, efficiency and interdependence, which are the analytical focus of liberal institutionalists and economists, but also by actors' concern about legitimacy and power at the international level. In this sense, unless the existing global financial institutions resolve the legitimacy problems (which involve inclusiveness, rule-governance and fair returns) and reflect today's power shift (in favor of East Asia), Asian emerging economies are unlikely to place whole stock in global solutions in order to deal with international financial issues.

East Asia's collective efforts to craft regional cooperation will acquire new global significance in the post-2008 global financial crisis world. The development of Asian financial cooperation would help to reduce the dependence of East Asia on IMF support in crisis management and finance for development, and thereby increase the autonomy and bargaining power of East Asia vis-à-vis the rest of the world, and the US in particular. This would give Asia an added voice in influencing the shape of new global financial governance in the twenty-first century. However, East Asia's low-key, moderate and prudent approach to Asian financial cooperation would be less likely to generate any sharp confrontation with the G7-centered global institutions or the United States in the near future. Nonetheless, East Asia's strategic behavior may reinforce decentralizing trends in international financial governance. Several leading scholars claim that the international community would face a 'more decentralized and fragmented form of international financial governance',[19] and a new geopolitical reality that comprises a 'variety of regional systems'.[20] East

---

[19] Eric Helleiner, 'Reregulation and Fragmentation in International Financial Governance', *Global Governance* 16 (1) (January–March 2009).

[20] David Calleo, 'Twenty-First Century Geopolitics and the Erosion of the Dollar Order', in Eric Helleiner and Jonathan Kirshner (eds), *The Future of the Dollar* (Ithaca: Cornell University Press, 2009).

Asia's counterweight strategy is more likely to fuel momentum towards the fragmented governance of international finance in the post-crisis world. The world may witness that multiple governance institutions at both regional and global levels will coexist and compete with or complement one another, instead of there being a new super global institution.

11. Institutional completeness in the Chiang Mai Initiatives

Paul Lejot

INTRODUCTION

The Multilateralized Chiang Mai Initiative (CMIM) announced in 2009 is an emergency credit agreement made by ASEAN+3 finance ministers and central bank governors.[1] Their use as counterparties is practical since they often have day-to-day control of foreign currency reserves and domestic monetary policy.[2] It also has tactical value in keeping with accepted practice, by allowing disclosure of no more than the headlines of the agreement. Although rooted in Asia's experience of receiving IMF credit in the regional financial crisis of 1997–98, CMIM is not institutionally developed in consisting of rules of the detail associated with IMF practice for credit, surveillance or the obligations of members. It represents an advance in technical and policy collaboration within the region but of a kind not customary among OECD central banks since 1999.

An agreement to create CMIM was executed on or around 28 December 2009 and took effect on 24 March 2010. The undisclosed document comprises 24 articles and nine schedules but may resemble a commercial heads of agreement,[3] leaving the exact nature of credit and reserve pooling commitments and any single transaction to be agreed and executed later.

---

[1] Including also the head of the Hong Kong Monetary Authority (HKMA); See Table 11.1. See Joint Press Release [of CMIM member central banks], 'Chiang Mai Initiative Multilateralization Comes Into Effect', 24 March 2010, accessed 2 September 2010, http://www.bot.or.th/Thai/PressAndSpeeches/Press/News2553/n1053e.pdf; ASEAN+3 Finance Ministers' statement, 2 May 2010, accessed 2 September 2010, http://www.aseansec.org/documents/JMS_13th_AFMM+3.pdf, and Annex 1, Key Points of CMI Multilateralization Agreement, [Annex] ibid.

[2] Unless stated otherwise, 'reserves' means international reserves, not central banks' reserves, which are their liabilities to the domestic banking sector. International reserves are usually not central bank balance sheet items.

[3] See Annex s.1, above note 1.

This creates an institutional gap, the relevance of which is discussed here in the context of unforeseen systemic shocks. The gap will be shown as both essential to CMIM's functioning and to render the scheme inevitably transitional.

Little of the literature of Asian integration or post-Asian crisis policy deals with the use or utility of the region's evolving collaborative central bank credit lines. Scholars have tended to examine the political economy of the arrangements, citing their value in building confidence among participants or external observers, either as symbols of progress in financial integration or as an indication that a more demanding regional scheme might become feasible.[4] One result is that the purpose and functioning of arrangements created by the 2000 Chiang Mai Initiative (CMI) are commonly accepted as stated by its sponsors, even when the scheme is appraised with some scepticism.[5] Less consideration has been given to the uses to which CMI's lines might be put, or their effectiveness in encouraging systemic financial stability, either in terms of central bank or market practice or the institutional demands of pooling arrangements between members.[6]

While many international financial arrangements are founded in law through overt agreements or adopted custom, Asia's regional financial integration has been less institutional and CMIM shares that characteristic informality. Its effectiveness may in due course be tested, but some informality is necessary, for three main reasons: first, CMIM relies on a non-constituent's currency in its operations; second, the provision of

---

[4] For example, Stephen Grenville, 'Regional and Global Responses to the Asian Crisis', *Asian Economic Policy Review* 2 (2007): 54–70; William Grimes, 'East Asian Financial Regionalism in Support of the Global Financial Architecture? The Political Economy of Regional Nesting', 6 *Journal of East Asian Studies* 361 (2006), asserting that CMIM's forerunner 'significantly supplements the amount of funds that can be mobilized in the event of a crisis as a supplement to IMF lending', ibid., 356; Hyoung-Kyu Chey, 'The Changing Political Dynamics of East Asian Financial Cooperation: The Chiang Mai Initiative', *Asian Survey* 49 (2009): 3; Hadi Soesastro, 'Regional Integration in East Asia: Achievements and Future Prospects', *Asian Economic Policy Review* 1 (2006): 215–34; Fred Bergsten and Yung Chul Park, 'Toward Creating a Regional Monetary Arrangement in East Asia', ADB Institute Research Paper Series No. 50 (2002); T.J. Pempel, 'The Race to Connect East Asia: An Unending Steeplechase', *Asian Economic Policy Review* 1 (2006): 239; Helen Nesadurai, 'The Association of Southeast Asian Nations', *New Political Economy* 13 (2) (2008).

[5] Natasha Hamilton-Hart, 'Co-operation on Money and Finance: How Important? How Likely?', *Third World Quarterly* 24 (2) (2003): 283–97.

[6] Empirical studies on the effectiveness of intervention have not sought to assess the utility of unused lines; see below notes 63 and 66.

credit within CMIM cannot be taken as transparent without the mechanics for appraisal, drawings, taking collateral, and repayments being either revealed in detail or conducted through a new organization that is appropriately capitalized; third, CMIM permits a participant to avoid contributing to a drawing.[7] In addition, there may be doubts as to the uses for which CMIM is suited when they exclude crises that are not purely external liquidity shocks but are as debilitating as in 1997–98. CMIM's design can be questioned in terms of its suitability for acute solvency concerns, with domestic crises that are instigated externally, and whether it can assist only with shocks resembling 1997–98.

This chapter first describes modern uses of short-term lines. It charts the evolution of CMIM and gives an institutional view of how it may function, and shows how CMIM compares with arrangements made by non-Asian central banks. The chapter reviews international lender of last resort (LLR) concepts and the interplay between CMIM and the IMF, and ends with an assessment of the scheme, suggesting that while it lacks formal elements and obligations of the kind associated with the Bretton Woods organizations, its semi-formal, semi-disclosed character is sufficiently robust for it to be regarded as substantive, as an example of regionalism with embedded autonomy. Asian regional financial policy has long operated by consensus without legalization,[8] while traditional thinking is that CMIM must be open and institutionally robust to be effective in the global financial system, both to avoid conflicts with general practice and due to its involvement in bilateral surveillance usually associated with the IMF.[9] An alternative appraisal is that CMIM can succeed only by differing from other collaborations and thus requires a less formal foundation.

---

[7]   See Annex s.9, above note 1.

[8]   See Douglas Arner, Paul Lejot and Wei Wang, 'Assessing East Asian Financial Cooperation & Integration', *SYBIL* 12 (1) (2008); Miles Kahler, 'Legislation as Strategy: the Asia-Pacific Case', *International Organization* 54 (3) (2000): 549.

[9]   Pooling arrangements conventionally require a 'binding arrangement between sovereign states specifying the pooling mechanism and its management', Yves Mersch, Governor, Central Bank of Luxembourg, 'The Framework for Short-term Provision of International Reserve Currencies to Sovereign States and their Central Banks', speech to East Asia-Pacific Region and the Euro Area Central Bank High-Level Seminar, 10 February 2010, *BIS Review* 15/2010, 2, accessed 2 September 2010, http://www.bis.org/review/r100212d.pdf. IMF officials suggest CMIM needs to be institutionally robust but also compliant with IMF practice; see below section on 'Surveillance and competition'.

CREDIT LINES

'Line' denotes an allocation of resources to facilitate subsequently defined transactions. It represents a simple institution that may be formal or informal, born of market practice and influenced by globally harmonized regulation.[10] The allocation is made because of the finite nature of bank resources, whether prudential risk limits or capital-based ceilings. The line is personal to the providing bank and may be withheld from disclosure to its beneficiary, or disclosed to various degrees of detail; that is, the line's existence may be known but not its scale or other conditions. Lines can be reciprocal if they involve similar or matching constructs between two banks, but reciprocal lines need not entail symmetrical commitments.

The simplest line signifies a willingness to consider engaging in transactions from time to time, and its withdrawal for whatever reason is similarly unilateral. In common law terms, no consideration exists to make the line contractual, and more generally it is free of strictly commercial obligation on the part of its provider. Lines can be substantive even when not fully contractual. Disclosure of their existence may create incentives to allow use, including embarrassment or commercial threats, and for central banks a disclosed line may suggest a moral commitment to allow use. In each case these risks encourage mutual confidentiality.

Lines may also be formal, signifying a contractual agreement prior to any transaction being contemplated and allowing compensation for the provider.[11] Documents recording formal lines would not represent fully actionable contracts but contain model terms to be adopted by incorporation into any subsequent such contract. They might include pre-contractual representations or undertakings, the making of which would become conditions precedent to later trades. Lines thus form a spectrum running between five degrees of contractual formality: (i) internal and non-disclosed; (ii) unilateral but disclosed; (iii) bilateral (agreed) but non-committed; (iv) bilateral (agreed) and committed; (v) bilateral and committed according to terms of detail. The contractual spectrum is analogous to the degrees of volition retained by line providers in making advances. Lines of longer duration are more complex, with terms providing a template for contract formation, as with debt issuance programme

---

[10] 'Institution' denotes rules and includes formal laws, regulations and informal but generally accepted practices.
[11] Capital regulation encourages commercial lines to be either unadvised or formal and compensated.

prospectuses or ISDA agreements for derivative contracts.[12] These require the acknowledgment of the counterparty, although lines will be capable of withdrawal in the broadest circumstances without consultation.

Bank lines characterized in this way cover several transaction types and uses, not all of which involve counterparty credit risk. Most are short-term, in that trades made under the line have a life of less than 12 months or shorter than the period remaining prior to the expiry of a non-renewable line.[13] The uses of bank lines are inexhaustible but commonly provide for short-term advances (credit, contingent credit or money market lines), cash and forward dealing in foreign exchange (FX lines), FX swap lines combining currency dealing and short-term credit, securities lending or repurchase (repo) lines, and lines for interest rate, currency or commodity swaps, often of longer terms. Many use a formal umbrella agreement (as with ISDA, ICMA or US money market practice) to allow collateral to be held against a fluctuating net position between counterparties. Lines may be denominated in a major currency or the currency of issue of the bank's domicile but by agreement used in several currencies.

The risks associated with bank lines include credit risk, settlement and liquidity risk, legal risks, and market risks (changes in asset prices, interest rates, FX rates, commodity prices or credit spreads). Contingent credit (guarantee or backup) lines represent an unusual credit risk in that they are drawn *in extremis* or to mitigate market failure, when a rational provider might prefer to avoid commitments that increase its funded risk. Like central bank LLR facilities, these often involve penalty charges and collateral. The assessment of a line's credit risk dictates ordinarily (i) whether to grant a line; (ii) whether to advise its existence and terms, if any; (iii) automaticity of use; (iv) terms for drawings; and (v) collateral requirements. Credit losses sustained under lines are treated as deductions to capital and reserves.

Central bank practice differs from this description only in terms of purpose, although non-commercial factors may influence the granting of central bank lines and credit.[14] This occurred frequently in the 1960s, when

---

[12] The ISDA Master Agreement 2002 provides for novation to allow trades between two counterparties to be treated as a single contract for netting and collateral purposes.

[13] Lines may be renewed but where disclosed or subject to formal agreement will contain triggers allowing the line to lapse upon expiry. Transactions maturing after 12 months usually require separate sanction.

[14] Minutes of the US Federal Reserve's Open Market Committee (FOMC) 1964–95, accessed 2 September 2010, http://www.federalreserve.gov/monetary-policy/fomc_historical.htm; see also the narrative of a Federal Reserve Bank of

external imbalances threatened the global fixed exchange regime and its relationship to gold prices, and in 1997 when US authorities urged Japan not to 'pour money into' Thailand prior to its obtaining IMF credit,[15] the Federal Reserve having refused to grant a line to the Bank of Thailand. Central bank providers of lines concentrate on short-term extension of credit, FX lines for swaps, spot and forward dealing, securities repos, and certain derivative transactions. Many are prolific users of trading lines with commercial counterparties.

Central banks use lines in similar ways to the commercial sector in terms of mechanics and the institutional setting (formal, informal, contractual, disclosed or undisclosed), even if their purposes differ. Their behaviour is analogous, so central banks are concerned with credit and settlement risk, even ignoring LLR operations.[16] Central banks use lines with domestic intermediaries to affect general liquidity or interest rates, and as LLRs to provide tightly collateralized liquidity to single intermediaries.

Lines between central banks may be associated with crises or crisis prevention but are a mechanical feature of the financial architecture introduced with Bretton Woods. They have commonly been of three kinds: short-term credit lines, FX swap lines and (more rarely) repo lines. The first allow short-term advances in a designated currency, notably US dollars as the dominant post-1945 trade currency, or the currency of the provider. These were drawn on occasions prior to the cessation of fixed exchange rates in 1971–73, typically to bridge to IMF or collaborative medium-term credit. Swap lines have been used more frequently since currency convertibility was reintroduced by the industrialized economies

---

New York official responsible for line negotiation in 1961–75, Charles Coombs, *The Arena of International Finance* (New York: Wiley, 1976).

[15] FOMC minutes, 19 August 1997, above note 14, 9–13. A Federal Reserve official told the FOMC that support would create 'two elements of moral hazard' due to the risk of Bank of Thailand defaulting on forward commitments made under FX swap lines, ibid., at 13. A collaborative emergency credit involving *inter alia* the IMF and Japan was announced the following day.

[16] Shown repeatedly in FOMC meetings between 1964 and 1997 when US dollar credit was extended through FX swaps to many central banks; see below section on 'Central bank lines and practice', and see William McChesney Martin, 'Reciprocal Currency Arrangements', *Federal Reserve Bulletin* 53 (1967): 958, referring to US$3.1 billion in swaps conducted in 1962–67 with Canada, France, Italy, Japan, Mexico, the UK and others. Martin saw swap lines solely as 'a first line of defense against disorderly speculation in exchange markets', ibid., with use limited to 'those countries whose financial markets are sufficiently sizable and developed that they may expect from time to time to be the source or the recipient of funds during periods of uncertainty', ibid., 961.

from 1958, and act as a liquidity device by facilitating simultaneous spot and forward FX transactions. As liquidity instruments, FX swaps are effectively repos involving foreign currency rather than securities. In the 1960s, the forward unwinding trade was conducted at the same exchange rate as the opening spot trade but terms became negotiable when the fixed exchange era ended.[17]

In the 2008–09 global crisis, a new use of swap lines involved transnational funding by central banks to allow others to conduct LLR operations in foreign currencies, essentially to help alleviate paralysis in the global interbank markets. This use had not been widely contemplated prior to 2007, nor cited in analyses of CMIM or its predecessor network, nor any ASEAN+3 statement relating to the evolving arrangement notwithstanding its relevance to factors contributing to the 1997–98 Asian crisis.[18]

All central bank lines discussed in this section are bilateral. There are no known modern examples of states fully pooling credit, with conjoint claims against users and theoretical losses apportioned among providers. When credit is provided collaboratively the claims have been channelled through an agent but are several in nature.

IMF facilities are not lines as described here. Although its standby arrangements and other facilities are commercially similar to credit lines, the IMF's status as an international body means that they reflect decisions of the Fund and are not contractual in a legal sense.[19] The final section of this chapter contrasts this with CMIM's probable operations.

---

[17]   In 1978 a weakened US dollar allowed the Bundesbank to win improved terms for cost and revenue sharing on FX swaps with the Federal Reserve; see FOMC minutes 18 July 1978, above note 14.

[18]   Capital flight from East Asia in 1997 included a withdrawal of lending by Japanese banks. It has been suggested that this was effectively a credit run, since they were forced to redirect capital because of domestic loan and accounting losses, and were themselves unable fully to fund their US dollar offshore lending; see Robert McCauley, 'Comment on "Regional & Global Responses to the Asian Crisis"', *Asian Economic and Policy Review* 2 (2007): 71–2. Similar but less severe circumstances arose in late 2008 among Korean banks such that the Bank of Korea used Federal Reserve and Bank of Japan swap lines specifically to provide domestic banks with foreign currency liquidity; see Bank of Korea, *Annual Report* (2008), 32–3.

[19]   See Joseph Gold, 'Stand-by Arrangements', in Jane Evensen and Jai Keun Oh (eds), *Legal and Institutional Aspects of the International Monetary System: Selected Essays by Joseph Gold* (Washington DC: International Monetary Fund, 1979), 462–6.

CHIANG MAI INITIATIVES

Recent Arrangements

ASEAN+3 officials chose a subdued news day on 28 December 2009 to reveal

> the signing of the Chiang Mai Initiative Multilateralization Agreement following the conclusion on all the main components of the CMIM at the ASEAN+3 Finance Ministers' Meeting (AFMM+3) in May 2009. The core objectives of the CMIM are (i) to address balance-of-payments and short-term liquidity difficulties in the region and (ii) to supplement the existing international financial arrangements. The CMIM . . . will provide financial support through currency swap transactions to the CMIM participants facing balance-of-payments and short-term liquidity difficulties. Each CMIM participant is entitled, *in accordance with procedures and conditions set out in the Agreement*, to swap its local currency with United States Dollars.[20]

Most 'procedures and conditions' are withheld. Timing of the announcement was hostage to a declaration seven months earlier that CMIM would take effect by the year-end.[21] That statement of principle revealed more of CMIM's design than December's press release: first, that the arrangement would be governed by a single contract; and second, that decisions on 'fundamental' CMIM issues would be decided by consensus and 'lending issues' by majority voting.[22] Without publication of the agreement, several questions of principle and mechanics are inevitably unanswered. The May 2009 statement suggests three functional interpretations depending upon whether the agreement creates several or partly joint obligations: (i) that no volition is given to participants when swap requests are made and agreed by a majority, unlike in an ASEAN antecedent which allowed members to decline participation;[23] (ii) that members may refuse to join

---

[20] Emphasis added. ASEAN+3 Finance Ministers' statement, 'Establishment of the Chiang Mai Initiative Multilateralization', 28 December 2009, accessed 2 September 2010, http://www.info.gov.hk/hkma/eng/press/2009/20091228e3.htm.

[21] ASEAN+3 Finance Ministers' statement, 3 May 2009, accessed 2 September 2010, http://www.aseansec.org/22536.htm. More accurate is that an agreement was signed in December 2009 allowing CMIM to take effect with a 'step by step approach'; see ASEAN+3 Finance Ministers' statement, 5 May 2007, accessed 2 September 2010, http://www.mof.go.jp/english/if/as3_070505.htm. It did so on 24 March 2010; see above note 1. Timing of these announcements may have been influenced by developments in the Eurozone involving Greece.

[22] ASEAN+3 Finance Ministers' statement, 3 May 2009, above note 21.

[23] The ASEAN Swap Arrangement (ASA), described further in this section.

transactions and the shortfall will be compensated by the willing members; or (iii) that such requests are only partly met. This was partly clarified in May 2010 in a summary of the CMIM agreement. A participant may refrain or 'escape' from contributing to a drawing with the consent of a two-thirds majority of members, and unilaterally in 'exceptional cases such as an extraordinary event or . . . domestic legal circumstances'.[24]

The summary implies that participants in good standing could expect disbursal of funds to follow a swap request, that status being determined by prior 'review of [the requesting party's] economic and financial situation' and there being 'no events of default'.[25] Event of default means a breach of terms on drawings under CMIM and would be determined by a two-thirds majority of members at sub-ministerial level. There is no indication that such an event would include non-payment on other financial obligations. Each member 'is requested to comply with covenants such as submission of the periodic surveillance report and participation in the ASEAN+3 Economic Review and Policy Dialogue'.[26] Members are likely to issue drawing requests only if they are found uncontentious in prior informal discussion.

Neither the conditions for drawing nor the demands of surveillance are explained. ASEAN+3 stated earlier:

> The regional surveillance mechanism *should be further strengthened* into a robust and credible system which will facilitate prompt activation of the CMIM. An independent regional surveillance unit will be established to promote objective economic monitoring [and when this] becomes fully effective in its function, the portion [of the facility not subject to IMF conditions for drawing] may be increased above the current limit of 20 percent.[27]

---

[24] See Annex s.9, above note 1.

[25] Ibid., s.8.

[26] Ibid. The ASEAN+3 Economic Review and Policy Dialogue is a six-monthly exchange of information among senior finance ministry and central bank officials.

[27] Emphasis added; see ASEAN+3 Finance Ministers' statement, 22 February 2009, accessed 2 September 2010, http://www.aseansec.org/22159.htm. No mechanism exists beyond a statement of intent in 2000 by ASEAN+3 finance ministers to 'facilitate the exchange of consistent and timely data and information on capital flows [and] establish a network of contact persons to facilitate regional surveillance in East Asia'; see ASEAN+3 Finance Ministers' statement, 6 May 2000, accessed 2 September 2010, http://www.aseansec.org/635.htm. In 2004 ASEAN+3 commissioned researchers in China, Indonesia, Japan and the Philippines and from the ADB examined economic surveillance and CMI's future, producing seven consensual reports; see ASEAN+3 Research Group Studies, accessed 2 September 2010, http://www.aseansec.org/17880.htm. One report reviewed

The group next agreed to 'enhance the *current surveillance mechanism* in order to lay the surveillance groundwork for the CMIM'.[28] The outcome is an ASEAN+3 Macroeconomic Research Office (AMRO) separate from the ERPD to be established in 2011 in Singapore 'to monitor and analyze regional economies'.[29]

CMIM became a declared objective in 2007 when ASEAN+3 finance ministers agreed 'that a self-managed reserve pooling arrangement governed by a single contractual agreement is an appropriate form of CMI multilateralization, proceeding with a step-by-step approach'.[30] This ambiguity allowed CMIM to be either a contractual arrangement or a substantive organization until the nature of 'pooling' was decided. Two years later, the global crisis had encouraged ASEAN+3 to adopt the larger, more ambitious arrangement shown in Table 11.1 but without legal personality. Participants receive borrowing limits based on fixed multiples of their respective contributions.

CMIM borrowing limits are far smaller than support facilities created in the global financial crisis, and are exceeded by the amounts provided in Asia in 1997–98, when the IMF and the ADB opened credit lines for Indonesia, Korea and Thailand totalling US$25.0 billion, US$35.3 billion and US$6.7 billion respectively, other sources made bilateral commitments to those states of US$54.7 billion,[31] and Hong Kong liquidated

---

institutional and operational matters associated with CMI and its predecessors; see Johnny Roe Ravalo, 'Enhancing the Chiang Mai Initiative to Address the Medium-Term Needs and Vulnerabilities of the Region', February 2005, accessed 2 September 2010, http://www.aseansec.org/17907.pdf. IMF conditionality is neither fixed nor unambiguous, and evolves with the creditworthiness of debtors; see Jacques Polak, 'The Changing Nature of IMF Conditionality', Princeton University Essays in International Finance 184 (1991). This discussion assumes that IMF conditions tie access to its standby facilities as in the Asian crisis, regarded within the region as intrusive demands for domestic policy changes as consideration for access to credit; see Ariel Buira, 'An Analysis of IMF Conditionality', paper prepared for the XVI Technical Group Meeting of the Intergovernmental Group of 24, Port of Spain, February 2003, accessed 2 September 2010, http://www.g24.org/buiratgm.pdf. Since 2009 IMF practice for its Flexible Credit Line (FCL) scheme is less demanding at the point of use, and CMIM may come to resemble this.

[28] Emphasis added; see ASEAN+3 Finance Ministers' statement, 3 May 2009, above note 21.

[29] ASEAN+3 Finance Ministers' statement, 2 May 2010, above note 1.

[30] ASEAN+3 Finance Ministers' statement, 5 May 2007, above note 21.

[31] IMF, 'Commitments and Disbursements of the International Community in Response to the Asian Crisis', accessed 2 September 2010, http://www.imf.org/external/np/exr/ib/2000/062300.htm#table.

Table 11.1   Multilateralized Chiang Mai Initiative (US$ billion)

	Initial commitment	Borrowing multiple	Borrowing limit	Borrowing limit/ short-term external liabilities (%)	Initial commitment/ inter- national reserves, end- 2009 (%)
Japan	38.4	0.5	19.2	4.1	3.8
China	34.2	0.5	17.1	11.7	1.4
Korea	19.2	1.0	19.2	14.8	7.1
Indonesia	4.552	2.5	11.38	37.7	6.9
Malaysia	4.552	2.5	11.38	68.0	4.7
Philippines	4.552	2.5	11.38	121.4	10.3
Singapore	4.552	2.5	11.38	10.7	2.4
Thailand	4.552	2.5	11.38	95.9	3.3
Hong Kong	4.20	2.5	10.5	11.8	1.6
Vietnam	1.0	5.0	5.0	86.7	6.0
Cambodia	0.12	5.0	0.6	689.7	3.6
Myanmar	0.06	5.0	0.3	157.9	NA
Brunei	0.03	5.0	0.15	26.7	2.2
Laos	0.03	5.0	0.15	59.5	4.2
Totals	120.0	NA	129.1	NA	NA

Note: 'ASEAN+3 Finance Ministers' statement, 28 December 2009, above note 20; ASEAN+3 Finance Ministers' statement, 3 May 2009, above note 21; ASEAN+3 Finance Ministers' statement, 2 May 2010, above note 1. 'Short-term external liabilities' means all cross-border bank claims of up to 12 months' maturity. The commitments of Indonesia, Malaysia, Philippines, Singapore and Thailand were altered and made equal in May 2010, the Philippines commitment disclosed in December 2009 having been lower than that of the others. This may have reflected concern that end-2009 Philippines reserves could not support a larger commitment.

Source: BIS Quarterly Review, June 2010, Statistical annex, Table 9A.

over US$15 billion in reserves to support its share and equity derivative markets.[32]

Proponents of collaboration later argued that reserve pooling in 1997 might have induced a recovery in regional confidence; for example,

---

[32]   Joseph Yam, 'Coping With Financial Turmoil', HKMA speech 23 November 1998, accessed 2 September 2010, http://www.info.gov.hk/hkma/eng/speeches/speechs/joseph/speech_231198b.htm. Hong Kong's domestic intervention against external 'speculative attack', ibid., was probably far more costly.

had ASEAN+3 'established a cooperative mechanism in which they could pool their reserves to fend off speculative attacks, they could have managed the Thai crisis and minimized its contagion by supplying a small fraction of their total reserves'.[33] Although this hinted at a future CMIM, it ignored the strain that any such exercise would have placed on regional monetary stability if intended for use rather than as a contingent facility. It also stretches political credibility for when the Thai baht collapsed over 31 per cent of the region's reserves were held by Japan,[34] making pooling irrelevant. A US$17 billion regional emergency credit facility organized by the IMF for Thailand in August 1997 was effectively pre-committed to US$23.4 billion in forward sales of US dollars by the Bank of Thailand,[35] effectively a speculative defence of the currency.[36]

In December 2007 the Federal Reserve created six-month US dollar swap lines with the European Central Bank (ECB) and the Swiss National Bank (SNB). Ten months later the shock to the global interbank market of Lehman Brothers' failure led it to provide lines to 14 central banks in a total nominal amount of US$620 billion.[37] US lines to the Bank of

---

[33]   See Bergsten and Park, above note 4, 16, and Pempel, above note 4, 249. ASEAN+3 aggregate reserves exceeded US$700 billion in mid-1997, far greater than the credit extended to Indonesia, Korea and Thailand. The proposition neglects questions of IMF conditionality needed to trigger drawings. It is also doubtful that confidence would have responded to untried schemes sanctioned in haste.

[34]   Japan Ministry of Finance data, accessed 2 September 2010, http://www.mof.go.jp/english/e1c006.htm.

[35]   Takatoshi Ito, 'Asian Currency Crisis and the International Monetary Fund, 10 Years Later: Overview', *Asian Economic Policy Review* 2 (16) (2007): 25.

[36]   Thai authorities sought to defend the baht's peg to the US dollar, which observers had considered generally valuable; see Michael Hall, *Exchange Rate Crises in Developing Countries: the Political Role of the Banking Sector* (Aldershot: Ashgate, 2005), 55–79. Central bank spot and forward sales of US dollars began in July 1996 and were successful until May 1997, when Thailand's foreign reserves were virtually exhausted; see Jittima Tongurai, 'Bank of Thailand's Swap Operations in 1996–97: Viewpoints of the Bank of Thailand and the Nukul Commission', 16 *Osaka City University Business Review* 16 (2005): 25–40.

[37]   Including central banks in Australia, Brazil, Britain, Canada, Denmark, Japan, Korea, Mexico, New Zealand, Singapore and Sweden; see Linda Goldberg, Craig Kennedy and Jason Miu, 'Central Bank Dollar Swap Lines & Overseas Dollar Funding Costs', Federal Reserve Bank of New York Research Paper No. 429, 2010; and see Federal Reserve press statements, accessed 2 September 2010, http://www.federalreserve.gov/newsevents/press/monetary/2008monetary.htm. The lines were made under standing statutory authority. In the same period the ECB provided lines to non-Eurozone central banks in Denmark, Hungary and Poland; SNB to the ECB and National Bank of Poland; and Norwegian

England, ECB and SNB were made limitless so as to meet any credit-worthy demand for offshore liquidity and allow the Federal Reserve's counterparties to fund the US dollar liabilities of the banks they supervise. Usage peaked at US$583 billion in December 2008.[38] The credit market seizure spread to certain Asian banking sectors; Bank of Korea drew over one third of its new US$30 billion Federal Reserve line in the same month.[39]

Purpose and History

If Asia's experience of the 1997–98 crisis is discounted, the conceptual value of pooling international reserves would be twofold. First, assuming that holding excessive reserves has opportunity costs in domestic output, then collaboration could allow participants each to maintain lesser amounts.[40] This argument has not formed part of headline CMIM discussions, and cannot be addressed without raising nationally sacrosanct questions of currency policy. Without reform of currency policies, reserve accumulation could continue even after the adoption of pooling; indeed the accumulation of excess reserves may be destabilizing since it is related to persistent external imbalances.[41] The second motive is addressed directly by CMIM: that pooling reserves to help a member undergoing external trauma creates resources that would not otherwise be available. However, CMIM's design would allow it to deal with certain but not all such circumstances. Its effective purpose is to create contingent commitments that encourage or forestall market activity, without disclosing how

---

and Swedish central banks to their Icelandic counterpart; see Corrinne Ho and François-Louis Michaud, 'Central Bank Measures to Alleviate Foreign Currency Funding Shortages', *BIS Quarterly Review* December 2008: 14–15. Most of these lines were drawn, ibid.

[38]   Mersch, above note 9.

[39]   Bank of Korea, *Annual Report* (2008), 32–3. Korea exhausted 23.3 per cent of its international reserves in 2008, ibid., 56.

[40]   A suggestion made at intervals by Japanese and Korean officials; see Hidehiko Sogano, 'Foreign Reserve Adequacy from the Asian Perspective', in Age Bakker and Ingmar van Herpt (eds), *Central Bank Reserve Management: New Trends, from Liquidity to Return* (Cheltenham: Edward Elgar, 2007) 72–3.

[41]   Mersch rehearses this long-standing argument, above note 9. The direct costs of maintaining and financing international reserves of East Asia's current scale is examined by Robert McCauley, 'Assessing the Benefits and Costs of Official Foreign Exchange Reserves', in Bakker and Van Herpt, above note 40, 19–36.

those contingencies arise. Seeking to affect sentiment merely by disclosure resembles the original purpose of IMF standby arrangements.[42]

CMIM has two roots, a US$100 million network of bilateral FX swap lines created in 1977 by ASEAN's five founders, and a web of bilateral repo lines initiated by the Executives' Meeting of East Asia-Pacific Central Banks (EMEAP) in 1995–97.[43] ASEAN's lines were drawn by Indonesia, Malaysia, the Philippines and Thailand in 1979–81 and by the Philippines in 1992.[44] Usage required the drawer to be in good standing or have negotiated standby lines with the IMF, a restriction that improbably prevented use of the lines in 1997–98, although their scale was too modest to have been useful.

EMEAP's lines were similarly unused at that time. In common with commercial repo lines, these allow a user with available collateral to raise major currency liquidity for intervention or LLR purposes by discounting with a fellow member a portion of international reserves typically held as US or other sovereign securities. It is assumed that EMEAP repo lines exist among most, if not all, of the group's members in amounts less than or of the same order as the US$5.7 billion nominal aggregate to which the HKMA was party at the end of 2008.[45] Their total is not disclosed.[46] The lines may subsist alongside CMIM for practical and confidentiality reasons.

ASEAN's lines evolved into CMI in 2000, supplemented by Northeast Asian commitments:

---

[42] See Joseph Gold, 'Stand-by Arrangements', above note 19, 463; Rosa Maria Lastra, *Legal Foundations of International Monetary Stability* (Oxford: Oxford University Press, 2006), 409.

[43] Bank of Japan lines were then each of US$1.0 billion; see Ramon Moreno, 'Dealing with Currency Speculation in the Asian Pacific Basin', *Federal Reserve Bank of San Francisco Economic Letter* 97–10 (11 April 1997). EMEAP comprises the Reserve Bank of Australia, People's Bank of China, HKMA, Bank Indonesia, Bank of Japan, Bank of Korea, Bank Negara Malaysia, Reserve Bank of New Zealand, Bangko Sentral ng Pilipinas, MAS and Bank of Thailand.

[44] See Randall Henning, *East Asian Financial Cooperation* (Washington, DC: Institute for International Economics, 2002), 14. An unsubstantiated United Nations Economic and Social Commission for Asia and the Pacific (UNESCAP) report claimed that the lines were 'extensively used'; see Seok-Dong Wang and Lene Andersen, 'Regional Financial Cooperation in East Asia: the Chiang Mai Initiative and Beyond', *Bulletin on Asia-Pacific Perspectives 2002/03* (UNESCAP, 2003), 90.

[45] HKMA, *Annual Report* (2008), 171, and press release, 'HKMA Signs Repurchase Agreement with Reserve Bank of New Zealand', accessed 2 September 2010, http://www.info.gov.hk/hkma/eng/press/1997/970326e.html.

[46] Moreno, above note 43.

In order to strengthen our self-help and support mechanisms in East Asia [ASEAN+3] agreed to strengthen the existing cooperative frameworks among our monetary authorities through the 'Chiang Mai Initiative' [which] involves an expanded ASEAN Swap Arrangement . . . and a network of bilateral swap and repurchase agreement facilities among ASEAN countries, China, Japan and the Republic of Korea.[47]

China, Japan and Korea accordingly created lines between 2001 and 2003 allowing for FX swaps among themselves and with most of the five large ASEAN economies.[48] Their terms adopt traditional IMF conditions for drawings in excess of 20 per cent of each line amount.[49] Most are bilateral asymmetric commitments to swap US dollars for the beneficiary's currency.[50] CMI has remained undrawn since its creation, a period that

---

[47] CMI's bilateral lines could reportedly be drawn for an initial 90 days and renewed up to seven times, with interest accruing at Libor plus an initial credit spread of 1.5 per cent, rising eventually to 3.0 per cent; 1–7 day repos could be transacted under the same lines using as collateral US treasuries of up to five years' remaining life or the provider's local currency sovereign issues, with premiums of 2 per cent and 5 per cent, respectively; and the ASA portion allowed for swaps of up to 180 days, renewable once; see Ravalo, above note 27, 21–3.

[48] ASA later grew to US$2.0 billion. All but ASA consisted of non-ASEAN lines with 49 per cent extended by Japan; see Japan Ministry of Finance, 'Regional Financial Cooperation among ASEAN+3', accessed 2 September 2010, http://www.mof.go.jp/english/if/regional_financial_cooperation.htm; and see Bank of Japan, 'Agreement on the Swap Arrangement under the Chiang Mai Initiative', accessed 2 September 2010, http://www.boj.or.jp/en/type/release/adhoc10/data/un1001a.pdf.

[49] Traditional conditionality refers to terms associated with IMF standby credit lines rather than freer preconditions introduced in March 2009 for FCL, intended for members 'with very strong fundamentals, policies, and track record[s] of policy implementation', IMF statement, 24 March 2009, accessed 2 September 2010, http://www.imf.org/external/np/pdr/fac/2009/pdf/032409.pdf, and above note 27. A narrative of CMI decision making and surveillance appears in William Grimes, *Currency and Contest in East Asia: the Great Power Politics of Financial Regionalism* (Ithaca: Cornell University Press, 2009), 85–9.

[50] Of 17 lines as at 24 July 2010, the bilateral lines made in 2008 between China, Japan and Korea use the currencies of the provider rather than US dollars; China opened a unilateral Renminbi line to the Philippines; Japan has made yen commitments to the Philippines, Singapore and Thailand; and Korea's commitments to ASEAN participants are provided in won in undisclosed circumstances; see Japan Ministry of Finance and Bank of Japan, above note 48. No line exists between Korea and Singapore. China and Singapore established in July 2010 a bilateral yuan/Singapore dollar line of US$22 billion equivalent, the region's largest such continuing line after one of US$30 billion equivalent created in January 2009 between China and Hong Kong and available in their respective currencies.

includes occasions when members experienced demonstrable external instability but certain ASA states may have refused support.[51]

For clarity, CMI comprises ASA and an arrangement of bilateral lines. CMIM is a new arrangement of commitments that are legally separate but similar in nature and may lead to the cancellation of some CMI lines. Lines provided by China, Japan and Korea may not be dismantled even if ASA lapses, reflecting their different utility.[52] When CMIM was announced in May 2009, CMI had grown to the equivalent of US$92 billion, excluding temporary increases made but unused during the global crisis.[53]

Uses and Mechanics

Asia's regional crisis began in 1996 with capital flight that included substantial portfolio shifts by Japanese and European banks. This exposed the fragility of Asia's financial systems in relying on foreign currency borrowings while lacking matching LLR resources, and further stimulated speculative sales of local currencies. For competitive and other reasons related to foreign borrowing approvals, much of the flight capital had funded local banks that used the proceeds to fund domestic assets without fully hedging the resulting currency or interest basis risks. The effect was doubly disruptive: a flight of capital pressured Asian exchange rates and led to exchange losses for cross-border borrowers but also terminally removed their access to funding. Pre-CMI swap lines were ineffectual and were not used in 1997–98. One significant difference between the 1997 and 2008 crises is that in the first no material interbank run took place.[54]

---

[51] Grimes, above note 49.

[52] On 19 January 2010 Bank of Japan and Bank of Korea renewed a crisis-related increase in their bilateral yen/won swap line for three months, and published an updated description of CMI only three weeks after the conclusion of the CMIM agreement; see Bank of Japan, 'Agreement on the Swap Arrangement under the Chiang Mai Initiative', above note 48.

[53] MAS, *Annual Report* (2008–09), 90. No drawings of regional line arrangements were disclosed during the global crisis, despite Bank of Korea using its Federal Reserve line, above note18; above note 39.

[54] By contrast, it has been suggested that in mid-1997 Thailand's foreign currency liquidity and a collaborative credit organized by the IMF were insufficient to prevent a speculative collapse of the baht and ensuing regional contagion; see Ito, above note 35, 24–5. This fails to make clear that Bank of Thailand's forward sales of foreign currency until June 1997 were speculative, in that it knowingly maintained a fixed exchange rate, having exhausted foreign currency resources for later delivery. It claims also that when IMF-arranged credits were announced on 20 August 1997 both 'the IMF and Japan asked and expected that foreign banks would maintain their outstanding loans to Thailand', ibid. at 25 and n. 10, but

Precautionary considerations led to the withdrawal of foreign currency lending, rather than the funding for that lending, which was the core problem in the post-Lehman dislocation.

The workings of central bank FX swaps are simple. If a provider agrees to a swap request, it will sell or repo (that is, sell and repurchase forward) securities assumed to be held to a domestic reserve account and make the proceeds available in exchange for the recipient's currency in the spot transaction through simultaneous crediting of accounts. If the request is for a currency other than the provider's own, then the transaction generally includes a spot sale or repo of foreign securities held as part of the provider's international reserves, a transfer of US dollars to the account of the recipient at the BIS and of the swapped currency to the provider's account with the recipient or the BIS. This model represents CMIM's likely mechanics, with two rotating member central banks substituting for the BIS.[55] The agreement allows a member to decline to contribute to drawings in certain circumstances, as with central bank practice described in the following section.

Other matters of institutional interest are the joint or several nature of the claims created by drawings, and whether arrangements for pooling involve pre-drawing transfers of reserves. It is likely that claims will be several in nature, created simultaneously on identical terms in varying amounts, so that the scheme involves like actions rather than pooling of resources. It is not disclosed whether a participant may decline the renewal of an outstanding swap or what the consequences might be for full or partial liquidation of the amount outstanding, nor whether any provision is made for payment sharing in the event that a drawing is not fully repaid.

For the provider, this constitutes a credit risk choice, for deploying reserves involves a portfolio switch from foreign securities to a claim against the counterparty. When the swap is unwound at maturity, the provider may reinvest in those securities or take delivery of its repo collateral. Each step in the process involves potential balance sheet effects for the two counterparties, with the provider facing a mark-to-market gain or loss on the securities sold or repurchased, and an FX gain or loss that may or may not be compensated by the recipient as part of the swap. Although these effects could be significant when markets are volatile, they are likely to be smaller than the translation of day-to-day balance sheet changes between

---

neglects to state that this was some months after Japanese and other lenders had greatly reduced their foreign currency commitments in Thailand.

[55]   See Annex s.6, above note 1.

the provider state's domestic liabilities and its US dollar reserves. CMIM is contractual rather than substantive, so that, in contrast with IMF practice or the European Financial Stability Facility (EFSF), a member's claim while a drawing is outstanding is recorded against its user.[56]

The use of a commercial agreement allows secrecy and is common among central banks. The Federal Reserve and the Bank of Japan have occasionally revealed specific terms of their respective lines to demonstrate conditionality, but these are exceptions. Establishing CMIM by treaty would create a body of similar legal standing to the IMF and necessitate detailed disclosure for which ASEAN+3 seems unready. While the comprehensiveness of the agreement is undisclosed, certain provisions well established in central bank practice may have been specified; for example, forms of drawing request and basic credit terms.[57] It is known that swaps will extend for 90 days and may be repeatedly renewed for a total period of two years.[58] ASEAN used a similar approach to its US$100 million swap arrangements in 1977, with basic agreement as to mechanics, swap size, maturities and renewals, priorities in disbursements, and appointment of an operational agent chosen by rotation among the members.[59] It also provided for willing members to replace any that were unwilling or unable to accede to swap requests. That members might opt out of swaps was made explicit in ASA's fifth revision.[60] CMIM appears to be less specific.

Members will commit to provide financial resources up to the amounts shown in Table 11.1 but the nature of their respective commitments is withheld. In the spectrum of lines described earlier,[61] CMIM is an example of either the third or fourth type: facilities that are agreed but not wholly

---

[56]   EFSF is a Luxembourg company owned by the 16 Eurozone states created in June 2010 by a framework agreement (available at http://www.efsf.europa.eu/attachment/efsf_framework_agreement_en.pdf, accessed 2 September 2010) to be a conduit for emergency loans to any single Eurozone member. EFSF may borrow in the capital markets with its obligations guaranteed severally by the member states. It is essentially a captive vehicle: the conditions attached to its loans would be negotiated by the European Commission and its borrowing administered by Germany's debt management office.

[57]   Coombs, above note 14, 75–6.

[58]   See Annex s.5, above note 1.

[59]   Memorandum of Understanding on the ASEAN Swap Arrangements, 5 August 1977, accessed 2 September 2010, http://www.aseansec.org/7914.htm.

[60]   Fifth Supplementary Agreement to the Memorandum of Understanding on ASEAN Swap Arrangement (19 September 1992), accessed 2 September 2010, http://www.aseansec.org/6305.htm.

[61]   In the second section of this chapter.

committed, or agreed and committed but not subject to specific preconditions. It may evolve into an example of the fifth variation where terms
for advances are broadly pre-agreed, but without significant institutional
augmentation this would impede external confidence building.

CENTRAL BANK LINES AND PRACTICE

CMIM's contingent permanence differs from the central bank practice
elsewhere of creating emergency liquidity resources only in response to
external shocks, notably 11 September 2001, the 2007 collapse of the US
subprime mortgage market, and Lehman's failure in 2008. Lines were
informal and event driven until the late 1950s, after which the progressive
introduction of currency convertibility for current transactions encouraged leading central banks to establish standing renewable lines. This
period lasted beyond the end of the Bretton Woods and Smithsonian
agreements from the beginning of floating exchange rates until the late
1990s, during which time many OECD central banks engaged in currency
intervention or acted as lenders of last resort with collaborative support.
Almost all lines lapsed after 1999 upon the creation of the single European
currency. Yet ASEAN not only renewed but began increasing its modest
line. During the Asian crisis, Japan was ready to create US$15 billion in
FX swap lines,[62] and in 2000 ASEAN+3 collected its web of lines into the
Chiang Mai Initiative. The region's post-1997 relationship with the IMF
was both an incentive for this and the locus of tension in the succeeding
decade.

Analysis shows that minor currency and emerging market central banks
have more confidence in FX market intervention than their major currency peers,[63] although the results are self-confirming inasmuch as major
currency central banks intervened more seldom after 1995. Most studies
assessed actual use of reserves or credit lines for intervention, rather than

---

[62]   Part of the New Miyazawa Initiative; see Japan Ministry of Finance, 'A
New Initiative to Overcome the Asian Currency Crisis', 3 October 1998, accessed 2
September 2010, http://www.mof.go.jp/english/if/e1e042.htm. Only two unilateral
lines were specifically contemplated in 1999, US$5 billion for Korea and US$2.5
billion for Malaysia, accessed 2 September 2010, http://www.mof.go.jp/english/if/
e1e063.htm and http://www.mof.go.jp/english/if/if005.htm, respectively. Both contemplated swaps using US dollars rather than yen. Drawings would have required
IMF approval and, varying from LLR practice, the lines were to fund trade credit
rather than currency intervention. Malaysia's line is extant.
[63]   'Foreign Exchange Market Intervention in Emerging Markets: Motives,
Techniques & Implications', BIS Papers No. 24, 2005 (hereinafter BIS, *Intervention*).

any effect that the existence of such resources may have on confidence or expectations. There is scant evidence that the existence of networks of lines has a material effect on stability,[64] although central bank cooperation in creating swap lines in the 2007–09 crisis is generally taken to have calmed volatile sentiment.[65] One study found that intervention may be effective in dampening volatility but less useful in correcting exchange misalignments or targeting exchange rates,[66] which accords with the 1967 Federal Reserve's restrictive view.[67] Asia's substantial reserves ironically result in part from intervention to prevent material currency appreciation,[68] as well as being the product of precautionary demand for reserve assets.

History

In the three phases identified above, sporadic crises or threatened instability led central banks to intervene in currency or credit markets or collaborate to improve confidence.[69] Central bank lines were unnecessary in the modern era before 1960 due to the absence of current account convertibility.[70] Its reintroduction led lines to be established among European and

---

[64]   Contrary to one recent narrative claiming CMI's stabilization role as 'essential'; see Tomo Kinoshita and Takayuki, 'Trade, Capital Flows', in John Llewellyn and Lavinia Santonetti (eds), *The Ascent of Asia* (London: Nomura Global Economics, 2010), 56. However, see McCauley, above note 41, 21, for a survey of empirical studies of the effects of holding international reserves in forestalling crises.

[65]   Ho and Michaud, above note 37; and see Committee on the Global Financial System Markets Committee, 'The Functioning and Resilience of Cross-border Funding Markets', CGFS Papers No. 37, 2010, 16–18.

[66]   Piti Disyatat and Gabriele Galatim, 'The Effectiveness of Foreign Exchange Intervention in Emerging Market Countries', in BIS, *Intervention*, above note 63, 97. An earlier analysis suggested that the data period of empirical studies significantly affected the results; see Lucio Sarno and Mark Taylor, 'Official Intervention in the Foreign Exchange Market: Is it Effective and, if so, How does it Work?', *Journal of Economic Literature* 39 (3) (2001): 839. An authoritative study would need to demonstrate the effectiveness of lines in isolation from related factors, such as restrictions on capital flows or the scale of reserves.

[67]   Martin, above note 16.

[68]   New York Federal Reserve analysis shows that during the 2008–09 global crisis the currencies of states maintaining comparatively high levels of reserves were relatively stable against the US dollar while states with lesser reserves experienced currency weakness but the results may not be solely the cause of high reserves; see Goldberg, Kennedy and Miu, above note 37.

[69]   Ignoring general realignments such as the 1985 Plaza Agreement.

[70]   Charles Coombs, 'Treasury and Federal Reserve Foreign Exchange Operations', *Federal Reserve Bulletin* 48 (1962): 1138.

North American banks and Japan according to the precepts described by
the Federal Reserve.[71] Lines were used in considerable volume, not only
for technical reasons associated with lessening FX market or capital flow
volatility but also to alter or defend exchange rates and mitigate capital
outflows when confidence collapsed in a national currency. Britain, France,
Italy, Sweden, the US and others drew extensively on such lines, in some
cases becoming persistent debtors. US dollar credit was extended by the
Federal Reserve through FX swaps to central banks in Europe and Latin
America (less often in East Asia) but refused on occasions to certain Asian
and European states because of solvency concerns, even though advances
were short-term, collateralized and involved the Federal Reserve in minimal
FX risk.[72] These decisions occurred prior to sovereign credit ratings becoming widely used and were wholly subjective, as in the Asian crisis when the
FOMC was reluctant to open swap lines to certain central banks.[73] In the
1970s intervention was largely funded by swap lines, rather than credit lines
as previously, and seen as a substitute for foreign holdings of securities.[74]
The US drew on lines with Germany, and to lesser extents with Switzerland
and Japan, all at times when intervening to support the US dollar.

From being drawn regularly in the 1960s and 1970s, lines became
disused by the mid-1980s and seen as an 'obviously anachronistic setup'.[75]
Prior to the introduction of the euro, permanent or renewable lines
became increasingly abandoned as Neolithic tools imbued with moral
hazard.[76] Regular intervention virtually ceased,[77] and after 1999 the only
remaining disclosed lines were in East Asia, or between Canada, Mexico
and the US as part of the North American Free Trade Agreement (partly
at the wish of Mexico, a confirmed user).[78]

---

[71]   Ibid., and see Martin, above note 16.
[72]   In the absence of defaults, swaps were liquidated at the exchange rate used
for the spot leg of the trade; see Martin, above note 16; and see FOMC minutes,
14 November 1967, 27 December 1967, 17 April 1979, 18 November 1980, 18 May
1981 and 5 October 1981, above note 14.
[73]   FOMC minutes, 19 August and 12 November 1997, above note 14.
[74]   FOMC minutes 17 April 1979, above note 14.
[75]   Federal Reserve chairman Alan Greenspan, FOMC minutes, 19 December
1995, accessed 2 September 2010, http://www.federalreserve.gov/monetarypolicy/
fomc_historical.htm.
[76]   Ibid. Moral hazard fears reflect LLR practice. The FOMC took the view
that conditionality was inappropriate and a line's existence signified its availability.
[77]   Statutory authority for the Federal Reserve to create lines remains in
Section 214.5 of Regulation N: Relations with Foreign Banks and Bankers (12
CFR 2 § 214.5) which dates from 1943 and 1962; see 12 U.S.C. §§ 248, 348a, 358
and 632.
[78]   Board of Governors of the Federal Reserve System, *Annual Report* (1999), 66.

Recent Practice

Leading central banks felt that emergency lines could be created instantly, in most cases under standing authority, so that permanence had no real value given that FX rates were market determined.[79] Lines were extinguished for three reasons: (i) lack of use; (ii) technological growth making permanent lines unnecessary; and (iii) financial innovation and free capital flows eroding the utility of currency intervention.[80] By contrast, CMIM has a simpler purpose of deterrence, given also that the IMF is not an unconditional international LLR. Its utility may result from it being contingent, suited to caution or guide behaviour rather than meet specific tasks. The desire for emerging economies to establish or maintain lines seems clear, so that CMIM reflects not a revival of interest in facilities seen by some as outdated, but a persistent preference.

Major non-Asian central banks withdrew lines certain that replacements could be established upon the occurrence of a shock. September 2001 became the first such event. On 11 and 12 September, the Federal Reserve created 30-day swap lines with the Bank of Canada, Bank of England and ECB in respective amounts of US$10 billion, US$30 billion and US$50 billion.[81] The primary purpose was to allow those counterparties to provide secured LLR facilities in US dollars to local and foreign banks within their jurisdiction, not all such banks being able to seek funds from the New York Federal Reserve for lack of collateral in their US branches or subsidiaries. Importantly, all drawings required prior Federal Reserve approval. These lines eventually expired in October 2009. They were drawn to allow foreign currency to be applied in foreign jurisdictions, not for currency intervention, that is, transnational funding of LLR activity, where foreign intermediaries with currency needs and qualifying collateral could be funded without limit.

---

[79]   But the IMF suggests that 'it is not clear that central bank swap lines would be available on a timely or adequately sized basis in any future period of international market strain'; see John Lipsky, speaking on alternatives to reserve accumulation, Banque de France, 1 March 2010, accessed 2 September 2010, http://www.imf.org/external/np/speeches/2010/030110.htm. The IMF will explore 'whether acceptable multilateral swap-like facilities could be developed that would limit members' perceived need for additional reserves', ibid.

[80]   The BIS noted that in the mid-1990s 'policies designed to influence exchange rates through intervention in foreign exchange markets, without eventually altering interest rates or making broader policy changes, became increasingly ineffective', BIS, *Annual Report* (1997), 144.

[81]   Board of Governors of the Federal Reserve System, *Annual Report* (2001), 4–5.

Swap lines also enable proxy intervention by agents for central banks to influence trading conducted in offshore financial centres. This was common practice in the 1970s and was used, for example, in February 1996 when Bank of Japan funded the HKMA and MAS to intervene on its behalf in their currency markets, and in May 1997 when the HKMA assisted Bank of Thailand.

SURVEILLANCE AND COMPETITION

The global crisis had two effects relevant to this discussion. First, it advanced plans for CMIM so that its announcement in May 2009 was more ambitious than predicted. Second, as if to counter autonomous regional action, it led the G-20 states to propose a broadening of member influence in the IMF.[82] The IMF has responded to strictures on its performance by suggesting cooperation with regional arrangements such as CMIM,[83] confirming a view that practical IMF supremacy among international financial organizations may not be permanent.[84] Credible regional bodies might usurp the position of the IMF, notwithstanding its experience of bilateral surveillance and its hierarchical standing in international law,[85] for the IMF is unable to conduct open surveillance with members that wish not to be examined or have the results disclosed.[86]

Thus the IMF's traditional crisis support function may have been partly replaced by 'self-insurance',[87] and its role in 'rule setting, coordination

---

[82]   The G-20 recommended in April 2009 a shift in IMF quotas and votes to emerging and developing states from over-represented members. CMIM members currently have 14.44 and 14.28 per cent of IMF quotas and votes, respectively, compared to over 30 per cent in each case for the EU and 17.09 per cent and 16.74 per cent, respectively, for the US.

[83]   International Monetary Fund Strategy, Policy, and Review Department, 'The Fund's Mandate: an Overview' (January 2010), accessed 2 September 2010, http://www.imf.org/external/np/pp/eng/2010/012210a.pdf; *idem*, 'The Fund's Mandate: the Legal Framework' (February 2010), available at http://www.imf.org/external/np/pp/eng/2010/022210.pdf.

[84]   Randall Henning, 'Regional Arrangements and the International Monetary Fund', in Edwin Truman (ed.), *Reforming the IMF for the 21st Century* (Washington, DC: Institute for International Economics, 2006), 171.

[85]   See for example Geir Ulfstein, 'Institutions and Competences', in Jan Klabbers, Anne Peters and Geir Ulfstein (eds), *The Constitutionalization of International Law* (Oxford: Oxford University Press, 2009), 45–80.

[86]   Henning, above note 84.

[87]   Robert Wade, 'Feature Review: Ngaire Woods, *The Globalizers: The IMF, the World Bank and Their Borrowers*', *New Political Economy* 12 (2007): 1, 127, 137.

and surveillance . . . marginalised by fora of a more "network" kind'.[88] This refers to financial regulatory groupings like the Basel Committee on Banking Supervision, but might equally include CMIM. The suggestion that the IMF co-exist with regional bodies may require the latter to obey rules to 'create no conflicts, be similarly transparent, lend for liquidity reasons only, and impose sound conditions'.[89] In this view, schemes such as CMIM would be formally notified to the IMF, would refrain from 'undercutting IMF conditionality', and would adopt policies consistent with IMF stabilization.[90] At its most severe, this sees a competing CMIM as eroding IMF sovereignty, for example, by freely providing credit or forgiving defaults, but neglects CMIM's need to act so as to build external confidence. A similar consideration became clear for the Eurozone in 2009–10.

Without mutual CMIM–IMF surveillance it is unclear how detailed cooperation can be agreed. All CMIM states are IMF members and thus undertake to inform and collaborate mutually and with the IMF in macroeconomic policy,[91] but these obligations are confined to exchange rate decisions and operations,[92] or reserve policy,[93] and may be incapable of non-consensual enforcement by the IMF vis-à-vis non-debtor members.[94] Moreover, Asia's participation in IMF standard setting for economic performance and financial regulation is mixed. Table 11.2 shows the dates when members concluded the IMF's Financial Sector Assessment Program (FSAP) and four categories of its Reports on the Observance of Standards and Codes. These are examples of data sharing, economic monitoring, and technical and regulatory assessment.

The reluctance of certain CMIM members to engage in such processes suggests that its own future mechanisms are a practical concern. The ADB's Office of Regional Economic Integration was instructed in May 2009 to develop surveillance mechanisms for CMIM and investigate its needs but the AMRO is an unknown resource that may require IMF intelligence cooperation, a point acknowledged by the IMF in July 2010.[95] ASEAN's

---

88   Ibid.
89   Henning, above note 84, 178.
90   Ibid.
91   IMF Article IV s.1. Laos is the sole CMIM non-signatory to Article IV.
92   Article IV s.3.
93   Article VIII s.7.
94   IMF Legal Department, 'Article IV of the Fund's Articles of Agreement: an Overview of the Legal Framework', June 2006; IMF Legal Department, 'The Fund's Mandate: The Legal Framework', February 2010.
95   Dominique Strauss-Kahn, IMF Managing Director, statement at Asia 21 High-Level Conference, Daejeon, 13 July 2010, accessed 2 September 2010, http://www.imf.org/external/np/sec/pr/2010/pr10290.htm.

Table 11.2 CMIM members concluding FSAP and selected ROSC categories

	FSAP	Data dissemi- nation	Monetary and financial policy trans- parency	Fiscal trans- parency	Banking supervision
Brunei	–	–	–	–	–
Cambodia	–	–	–	–	–
China	–	–	–	–	–
Hong Kong	2003	1999	1999/2003	1999	1999
Indonesia	–	2005	–	2006	–
Japan	2003	2006	2003	2001/04	2003
Korea	2003	2003	2003	2001	2003
Lao PR	–	–	–	–	–
Malaysia	–	–	–	–	–
Myanmar	–	–	–	–	–
Philippines	2004	–	–	2002/04	2004
Singapore	2004	–	2004	–	2004
Thailand	2009	2006	–	2009	–
Vietnam	–	–	–	–	–

Sources: IMF, 'Financial Sector Assessment Program', accessed 2 September 2010, http://www.imf.org/external/np/fsap/fsap.asp; IMF, 'Reports on the Observance of Standards and Codes', accessed 2 September 2010, http://www.imf.org/external/np/rosc/rosc.asp; IMF, 'Fiscal Transparency', accessed 2 September 2010, http://www.imf.org/external/np/fad/trans/index.htm.

Manila Framework for economic surveillance was dissolved in 2004, having been said by its sponsor to be 'losing momentum'.[96] Many observers (including analysts commissioned by ASEAN+3) echo ASEAN+3 finance minister statements that CMIM needs a full-functioning and independent arrangement.[97]

Surveillance is a function to gather and interpret data and issue stress

---

[96] ADB Vice President Liqun Jin, speech, 26 April 2004, accessed 2 September 2010, http://www.adb.org/media/printer.asp?articleID=4849, noting also that the framework 'started as a very serious exercise in the wake of the [1997–98] financial crisis'.

[97] Joshua Aizenman, Yothin Jinjarak and Donghyun Park, 'International Reserves and Swap Lines: Substitutes or Complements?', NBER Working Paper 15804, 2010, 19; and see ASEAN+3 Research Group Studies, above note 27. A

warnings. It will fail as a credible appraisal process that assists confidence building as well as decision making by members if it lacks the means to require policy change. This demands operational independence and a regional outlook so as to consider systemic risks that may induce contagion, as well as traditional bilateral appraisals. An outsourced surveillance function would need arrangements explicit as to how surveillance would impact national policies, while a dedicated resource managed within CMIM could establish its credentials externally and with national governments only over time. Credible surveillance will in time lessen dependence on credit rating agency input for drawings and collateral, which has become controversial in the Eurozone because of its relationship with ECB collateral rules.

As an arrangement among states, it is unclear whether CMIM will challenge its members' adherence to IMF rules. However, it may be a device that increases regional autonomy or the leverage for further changes in IMF practice.[98] Having opposed the creation of an Asian Monetary Fund in 1999, the IMF was initially non-committal on CMI,[99] and no senior IMF official commented publicly on CMI or CMIM between July 2007 and May 2009. A fuller reaction emerged only in late 2009, describing

> various ways to reduce [states' needs] for self-insurance . . . At the regional level, bilateral and multilateral swap arrangements can diversify risks and the extension of the Chiang Mai reserve pool is a welcome development . . . The largest degree of risk diversification could be achieved at the global level.[100]

---

surveillance process initiated earlier by ASEAN+3 was confined to periodic and limited exchanges of information.

[98] The G-20 asked the IMF to engage also in systemic surveillance in cooperation with the new Financial Standards Board; see Carlo Gola and Francesco Spadafora, 'Financial Sector Surveillance and the IMF', IMF Working Paper No. WP/09/247, 2009.

[99] Managing Director Horst Köhler, speech, 2 June 2000, accessed 2 September 2010, http://www.imf.org/external/np/sec/nb/2000/nb0036.htm, a view amplified by his deputy: 'it is important that financing provided under these initiatives be complementary with financial support from the Fund and the associated conditionality', Stanley Fischer, speech, 1 June 2001, accessed 2 September 2010, http://www.imf.org/external/np/speeches/2001/060101.htm.

[100] Deputy Managing Director Takatoshi Kato, speech, 16 October 2009, accessed 2 September 2010, http://www.imf.org/external/np/speeches/2009/101609. htm. This accords with G-20 decisions that the IMF join the FSB in multilateral systemic surveillance; see G-20 Leaders' Statement: The Pittsburgh Summit, 25 September 2009, accessed 2 September 2010, http://www.pittsburghsummit.gov/mediacenter/129639.htm.

IMF interest in reserve demand is not academic but a path to a new function. In November 2009 the IMF managing director described CMIM as providing 'an important complement to IMF financing',[101] and his deputy later stated that 'the IMF is actively exploring ways to strengthen ties with the Chiang Mai initiative . . . that *already provides* an important complement to IMF financing.'[102] The result is a more specific suggestion that tangible cooperation might see the IMF acting as backup to CMIM so as to reduce the global demand for reserves.[103] The implication is that CMIM would replace certain reserves, and the IMF would act as LLR to CMIM, given the unstated assumption that CMIM has no permanent access to US dollar resources. The IMF's suggestion itself relies on CMIM not becoming wholly self-sufficient by adopting one or more currencies of issue of its larger members, without which CMIM and national holdings of reserves are not perfect substitutes, one being facilitated by the other.[104]

ASSESSMENT

Time may show CMIM either remaining a nexus of contracts or becoming an organization that acquires some operational autonomy.[105] The outcome is dictated by and affects the nature of claims created under CMIM, the approach and actionability of CMIM surveillance, and whether pooling

---

[101]   Dominique Strauss-Kahn, speech, 16 November 2009, accessed 2 September 2010, http://www.imf.org/external/np/speeches/2009/111609.htm.

[102]   Emphasis added. John Lipsky, speech, 10 December 2009, accessed 2 September 2010, http://www.imf.org/external/np/speeches/2009/121009.htm.

[103]   The suggestion that IMF resources provide backup to a regional arrangement is directed also at the Eurozone.

[104]   See also Joshua Aizenman, Yothin Jinjarak and Donghyun Park, 'International Reserves and Swap Lines: Substitutes or Complements?', above note 97, stating that '[a]n important issue which arises in connection with the swap deals is the extent to which they can mitigate the precautionary or self-insurance motive underlying the unprecedented reserve accumulation in developing countries', ibid., 17, but asserting that '[i]t is entirely possible that swaps are mutually beneficial not only during crises but also during normal non-crisis periods. Formalizing and institutionalizing swap lines so that they are transformed from temporary anti-crisis measures to more long-term mechanisms for liquidity support may dampen the need for precautionary reserve hoarding', ibid., 20.

[105]   Governance is beyond the scope of this chapter, but only two CMIM central banks have statutory independence (Japan and Korea); two are empowered to act with a high degree of autonomy (Indonesia and Singapore); two must accept the directions of ministers (Hong Kong and the Philippines) and the remainder follow general state policy.

comes to involve a formal transfer of reserves. CMIM's agreement is likely to be a non-actionable contract creating obligations for state bodies to act in certain ways but without sanction, penalty, remedy or mitigation if any should default. CMIM's relationship with other organizations may also be unstated; for example, will CMIM remain open for use if it allows swaps free of conditions and IMF facilities are later withheld from the user?[106]

In addition to allowing members to avoid participating in drawings, CMIM is conditional in that it assumes an availability of US dollars through the application of reserves. There is little chance of US dollars becoming unavailable in general or among CMIM participants, some of which maintain colossal reserves, but this is not wholly impossible due to sudden scarcity, systemic dysfunction or Herstatt failure, thus compounding the shock against which CMIM hopes to guard. It is not unknown for major government bond markets to experience hiatuses in price formation, impeding the sale or repo of securities held as reserves.[107] CMIM is contingent in that its long-term utility may be in deterrence of disruption or contagion rather than to alleviate the realized effects of an exogenous shock. It is substantive because of amassed reserves but those reserves arise partly from common exchange rate policies. CMIM's use of the US dollar as its foundation lessens its full effectiveness as a crisis liquidity facility while justifying an institutional vagueness.[108] This resembles a characterization of certain states as suffering from 'original sin', indicating an inability to borrow overseas in their respective domestic currencies.[109]

---

[106]   This depends partly on the changing nature of IMF conditionality, and the standing of a member with regard to FCL, above notes 27 and 49.

[107]   The October 1987 financial crisis involved seizures in government bond markets. Transactions in 'liquid' US treasury securities for a European central bank client took several days to execute; source, author's recollection from working at a US Treasury primary dealer.

[108]   Bagehot insisted that '[e]ffective lending of last resort requires sufficient resources to reassure markets that the means of payment will remain available in all circumstances. As the ultimate issuers of currencies, central banks are the natural lenders of last resort, which some take to imply that an international financial institution cannot play an analogous role internationally', Patrick McGuire and Götz von Peter, 'The US Dollar Shortage in Global Banking and the International Policy Response', BIS Working Paper No. 291, 2009, 21. The remark would not apply to the ECB, which provided substantial LLR facilities in 2008–09 to Eurozone banks.

[109]   Barry Eichengreen, Ricardo Hausmann and Ugo Panizza, 'Currency Mismatches, Debt Intolerance and Original Sin: Why they are not the Same and Why it Matters', NBER Working Paper No. 10036, 2003. Original sin is not universally accepted, for example since it takes no account of contractual solutions to borrowing obstacles, nor to agglomeration practice in the financial sector.

CMIM is by analogy a constrained LLR arrangement. While Asia's reserves make exhaustion of use or non-availability unlikely, no conditional endowment can eliminate this institutional lacuna. CMIM has a purpose in crisis management but its capacity *in extremis* is limited.[110]

The scheme's purpose is unspecified beyond catering for difficulties in 'balance of payments' or 'short-term liquidity'. This would clearly include enabling a participant to obtain US dollars for external payment purposes, but liquidity has been shown by the global crisis to have both domestic and external manifestations, including interbank access to foreign currency funding.[111] It is unknown whether CMIM would allow participants to obtain US dollars and then act as a domestic LLR, as did Bank of Korea in 2008.[112] To do so would be consistent with recent emergency practice but inevitably involves issues of credit risk and control for CMIM as a whole. For example, is the user central bank required to demand collateral for its domestic facilities, as with LLR practice, or provide for an assignment to CMIM of the value of that collateral in more extreme circumstances? Such questions are linked inevitably to CMIM's appraisal and surveillance functions.

Further, it is incorrect to treat abundant reserves as freely deployable, use of which in CMIM would have no domestic credit or monetary consequences. Reserves are not free resources but investible foreign currency assets and are 'matched' by domestic currency liabilities. Their use by CMIM would represent a potential rise in net domestic debt if a drawer defaulted and the claim was written down. States may decide how reserves are invested but this constitutes a portfolio choice rather than liberty of use.

Unused central bank lines are usually treated as contingent items, becoming assets only as drawn, and CMIM thus represents a new contingent commitment for members. If a drawing occurs, the treatment and mechanics adopted will depend on whether the arrangement is substantive.

---

[110] For Asian and other observers, the IMF's conduct in the 1997–98 financial crisis ended for the foreseeable future the possibility of it being assigned a global LLR function; see notably Martin Feldstein, 'Refocusing the IMF', 77 *Foreign Affairs* (1998): 20. Yet the IMF claimed to have acted as a transnational LLR in the Asian crisis; see Stanley Fischer, 'On the Need for an International Lender of Last Resort', 13 *Journal of Economic Perspectives* (1999): 85. The IMF has more recently accepted that CMIM resulted from hostility to its governance and prior credit practice; see IMF Strategy, Policy and Review Department, 'The Fund's Mandate: an Overview', IMF Policy Paper, January 2010, 8, accessed 2 September 2010, http://www.imf.org/external/np/pp/eng/2010/012210a.pdf.

[111] Above note 18.

[112] Ibid.

As a nexus of contracts CMIM is analogous to ASA, so that drawings are made severally and channelled through an agent. If CMIM is a substantive organization managing pooled reserves, then it must create claims in favour of members that transfer reserves. The same treatment would apply if a substantive CMIM has access to US dollars from members only when meeting a swap request. Thus a substantive CMIM would need to be capitalized or given contingent capital by members in order for the claims it issues to central banks to have value.[113] CMIM will become effective by a nexus of contracts that uses agents for certain functions, even with the imperative for independent surveillance and assuming ongoing access to US dollars, but if it is to be given organizational substance and resources for integral self-management then it can function only with a capital infusion, or by evolving to use one or more currencies of issue of its members.

CMIM could in principle assist in currency management but not with misalignments. It will not of itself protect against a run on domestic parties or credit, as would an LLR. Thailand's US$11.9 billion borrowing limit under CMIM is nominally little more than the reserves spent in buying baht on one May 1997 day.[114] It is clear that CMIM is of insufficient scale to fund similar tactics, but may be of an order to support intervention to prevent disorderly markets, which has been a concern of emerging states in accumulating reserves. The central purpose of CMIM in its present form is to exist, and to help prevent contagion, not to be used, a conclusion reached without considering the politics of regionalism or autonomy. Analysts that suggest that members might make 'greater use' of CMI or CMIM neglect its lack of utility in all but the most trivial circumstances[115] and the fact that institutionalization is unlikely to include automaticity in drawings.

CMIM hopes to provide a remedy to shocks well remembered from 1997–98; unknown threats are less well considered.[116] The global crisis saw an interbank run not previously thought possible. CMI lines provided by

---

[113] True pooling could also be conducted through an organization such as the ADB, which could readily issue claims (currently rated AAA/Aaa) to members.

[114] Nukul Commission, *Analysis and Evaluation on Facts Behind Thailand's Economic Crisis* (Nation Multimedia Group trans., Bangkok: Nation Multimedia Group, 1998), s.180.

[115] See Aizenman et al., above note 97, 19.

[116] Five forms of crises (external and domestic sovereign default, banking and currency crisis, and explosive price inflation plus 'clustering' when an identified crisis alters into a second type) are described in Carmen Reinhart and Kenneth Rogoff, *This Time is Different: Eight Centuries of Financial Folly* (Princeton, NJ: Princeton University Press, 2009), 249, to which might be added securities, commodity and asset price bubbles and rapid deflation.

China, Japan and Korea allow for securities repos but this was given little attention compared with their swap function and was derided for its lack of utility.[117] Repo lines proved essential in 2008–09 in funding LLR facilities. Nonetheless, it has been asserted that swap lines 'can help maintain market confidence even during normal non-crisis periods'.[118]

A detailed CMIM contract would consider requirements for (i) decision making in swap negotiation and operations; (ii) accession and withdrawal of members; (iii) CMIM's standing and its relationship with other organizations; (iv) permitted uses; (v) compliance and remedies; and (vi) relationships with bank claims and other commercial interests.[119] Probably the only aspects of CMIM's functioning that will become subject to greater openness are its credit appraisal and surveillance mechanisms, which external confidence will gradually demand and which will be difficult to conceal if they eventually involve new resources.

CMIM must choose (as with ASA) whether swaps are allowed in requested amounts without the minority participating, or in proportionately reduced amounts, or whether a dissenting minority is compelled to participate in providing credit. This itself has credit risk implications, especially if participants regarded as sophisticated are thought to be in a dissenting minority. An alternative, assuming a surveillance system is seen to be established, would be for CMIM as a whole to make periodic declarations of the good standing of its members, so that outsiders would presume each member had access to funds. If the May 2009 statement is taken literally as to lending being subject to majority voting,[120] then general confidence will rest upon significant non-disclosure, or more informally the willingness of well-resourced members to provide undisclosed credit support to recalcitrant lenders to induce their participation. CMIM may become known not as a precise and formal set of institutions but as a framework for 'commonly agreed action',[121] which is not unknown among central banks.

---

[117] A Bank of Korea official wrote in 2005 that the EMEAP repo system had then 'never been implemented' but this may refer to actual usage, Jee-young Jung, 'Regional Financial Cooperation in Asia: Challenges & Path to Development', BIS Papers No. 42, 2005, 124, adding that 'Under the repo agreements, countries have been able to provide financial support in US dollars, with US Treasury bonds as collateral, during a very short period. Therefore, the agreements have not been so useful as a crisis resolution measure.'

[118] See Aizenman et al., above note 97, 20.

[119] Notably payment priority and whether CMIM activity is a credit event for ISDA protocol purposes.

[120] Above note 21.

[121] Richard Cooper, 'Almost a Century of Central Bank Cooperation', BIS Working Papers No.198, 2006, 2.

CMIM is neither rule nor principle based but aspirational. Its imprecision gives it a paradoxical substance. Agreeing a greater degree of detail in a rule-based pact would require disclosure of terms and a degree of transparency in operations and submission to surveillance that the participants may not countenance, and which would in any event be contrary to many aspects of central bank practice, even among industrialized nations with independent central banks. Developing CMIM into a substantive organization requires a commitment of capital as yet unidentified. From an institutional perspective, these considerations suggest that CMIM can be characterized as an interim arrangement that must in due course either fail if usage is intended or be further developed.

12. Beyond the Multilateralized Chiang Mai Initiative: an Asian monetary fund

Ross P. Buckley

In the preceding chapter, Paul Lejot explained the current state of play of the Multilateralized Chiang Mai Initiative (CMIM) and perspicaciously analysed its institutional incompleteness. Perhaps its greatest inadequacy at the moment is its scale. If the CMIM is to deter contagion and serve to reassure markets, for all the reasons Lejot identifies, its scale needs, in my view, to be increased substantially.

So today the CMIM's potential impact is limited. This is reinforced by the requirement that 80 per cent of the amounts available for drawing thereunder are not available unless a participant has an IMF program in place (because the CMIM has but rudimentary surveillance and technical capacity of its own). Given that the negotiation of IMF programs typically requires months, this further limits the potential of the credit lines to calm panics and deter contagion.

However, another perspective is available on the CMIM when one asks where it might lead. As Lejot has so ably established, the initiative is incomplete and must be developed further or in time will fail. How it might be developed, and where it might lead, are the topics of this chapter. Or, in the words of Lejot, a cautious author, he has built the structure of the high diving platform and left it to me to dive off.

BACKGROUND AND CONTEXT

Before moving on to those two issues, however, some background and contextual analysis might assist. ASEAN comprises ten countries: Brunei, Cambodia, Indonesia, Malaysia, Laos, Myanmar, the Philippines, Singapore, Thailand and Viet Nam. Its people number some 570 million.[1] Its combined GDP is only one-half as much again as Australia's, or about one-third of China's.[2] Yet the grouping has had a real impact, particularly on the trade dynamics of the region. Regional and bilateral trade agreements are both typically initiated by large and powerful nations. Yet in East Asia this grouping of less powerful nations has tended to fulfill the leadership role in the initiation and direction of trade agreements. This is in part because the traditional rivalry for influence between China and Japan has meant it has suited both major powers to allow ASEAN to take the lead. It is also because ASEAN's clunky internal governance processes have paradoxically conferred upon it a somewhat perverse form of negotiating power: it is so difficult for the ASEAN nations to agree among themselves upon issues that, once they have done so, any other nation negotiating with the grouping knows that their position is highly inflexible and unlikely to be able to be adjusted within any reasonable time frame.

Especially with China's rise as 'factory for the world', the region has seen increasing levels of trade and economic integration. Many manufacturing processes today are centered in China but combine inputs from throughout the region in a hub-and-spoke system in which other nations contribute in their areas of comparative advantage to the Chinese production. Trade integration has promoted freer trade and investment particularly through supporting international production networks.[3] As seen in the chapters in Part II of this volume on trade, the region is developing a 'noodle bowl' of regional and bilateral trade agreements. In the interests of trade, and especially administrative, efficiency one can but hope that one day this noodle bowl of different agreements will be replaced by one free trade area extending across the region. One of the preconditions to this being achieved, however, is the emergence of a consensus as to the composition of the region for trade purposes. Does East Asia extend as far south as Australia and New Zealand? Does it extend as far west as India? Or is the region simply the ASEAN+3 nations? These issues are complex and unlikely to admit of resolution any time soon. Some nations want Australia and New Zealand included as their mineral and agricultural resources mean they are complementary economies to those of the region.

---

[1] John McLean, 'Will ASEAN's New Charter Bring Greater Cooperation?', *Development Asia,* April 2009, 20.

[2] ASEAN's 2008 GDP is US$1506 billion, current prices (selected Basic ASEAN Indicators as of June 2009, accessed 2 September 2010, http://www. aseansec.org/13100.htm); Australia's 2008 GDP is US$1011 billion, current prices (*World Economic Outlook*, April 2009); and China's 2008 GDP, current prices, is US$4402 billion (*World Economic Outlook*, April 2009).

[3] Fukunari Kimura, 'Economic Integration in Extended East Asia: Toward a New Trade Regime', paper presented at the JSIE-Kanto Meeting in Otaru, 4 July 2009.

Other nations seek Australia's and New Zealand's inclusion, and that of India also, as a counterweight to Chinese and/or Japanese influence. Yet other nations view East Asia as a region defined more by culture than economics or regional power politics, and coherent cultural considerations point directly to the ASEAN+3 grouping. While we await the emergence of a consensus on these most fundamental of issues, bilateral and regional trade agreements continue to proliferate.

In the field of financial integration, ASEAN has played a role through the establishment, expansion and multilateralization of the Chiang Mai Initiative. However, given that the region has the world's largest foreign exchange reserves, highest savings rates and most dynamic economies, the CMIM is but a very small fraction of the financial cooperation and integration that could be undertaken. Indeed, the financial integration of the region has lagged far behind its economic and trade integration. In the words of an IMF study,

> intraregional financial integration – for example measured directly by cross-border capital flows or indirectly by cross-border correlation of consumption growth – has been more limited than elsewhere. Consequently, Asian economies appear to have become more integrated with countries outside the region than within the region.[4]

This remains the case today.[5]

The seminal event, in terms of East Asian financial integration, was the East Asian financial crisis of 1997–98. It had two immediate consequences. First, because no Asian organization was able to provide support to any Asian state, it led 'to the irony that Indonesia, South Korea and Thailand faced an invasiveness towards national policymaking, especially through credit conditions, that was contrary to all ASEAN precepts'.[6] This experience caused financial cooperation to replace trade cooperation as the number one regional priority. To this day, the changes to domestic policies which the IMF forced upon countries as the price of the bailouts, and the

---

[4]   David Cowen and Ranil Salgado, 'Globalization of Production and Financial Integration in Asia', in David Cowen, Ranil Salgado, Hemant Shah, Leslie Teo and Alessandro Zanello (eds), *Financial Integration in Asia: Recent Developments and Next Steps*, IMF Working Paper No. 06/196, 2006, 4.

[5]   D. Arner, P. Lejot and W. Wang, 'Assessing East Asian Financial Cooperation and Integration', AIIFL Working Paper No. 5, March 2009; J. Ahmed and V. Sundararajan, 'Regional Integration of Capital Markets in ASEAN: Recent Developments, Issues, and Strategies', *Global Journal of Emerging Markets Economies* 1 (2009): 89–90.

[6]   Arner et al., above note 5, 13.

profound extent to which the IMF initially misdiagnosed the causes of the crisis, are deeply resented throughout the region.

Secondly, the crisis brought into being the ASEAN+3 grouping, comprising the ten ASEAN nations plus China, Japan and South Korea. ASEAN+3 had its first summit in Kuala Lumpur in December 1997. In a short time frame, ASEAN+3 supplanted APEC (Asia-Pacific Economic Cooperation) as the principal economic organization within the region.[7] Since then ASEAN+6 (which includes Australia, India and New Zealand) has also developed.

In August 1997, shortly after the onset of the East Asian crisis, Japan lobbied for the establishment of an Asian Monetary Fund, and offered to fund one-half of the cost of the institution.[8] However, the idea met stern opposition from the United States and the IMF, and a lack of support from China, and was dropped.[9] The US had traditionally opposed the development of regional institutions, preferring to promote its network of bilateral arrangements with the region's countries, and the IMF feared the erosion of its influence and role from a competing institution. In place of an AMF, the far less ambitious Chiang Mai Initiative (CMI) was pursued.

Over time the size of the bilateral swap arrangements in the CMI were steadily expanded, while the potentially useful repo arrangements within the CMI were ignored and never really used. This slow growth of the arrangement received a huge boost in February 2009 when the swap agreements were multilateralized and increased by US$40 billion to US$120 billion. China (including Hong Kong), Japan and South Korea are to provide 80 per cent of these commitments, with the balance to come from ASEAN nations. Recent research suggests that the pre-2008 bilateral swap agreements were used in broadly efficient ways.[10] The CMIM should be far more efficient and effective, because the commitments will be multilateral.

---

[7]   Ibid., 23.

[8]   Hyoung-kyu Chey, 'The Changing Political Dynamics of East Asian Financial Cooperation: The Chiang Mai Initiative', *Asian Survey* 44 (3) (May/June 2009): 456.

[9]   Jennifer A. Amyx, *A Regional Bond Market for East Asia? The Evolving Political Dynamics of Regional Financial Cooperation*, Australia–Japan Research Centre, Asia Pacific School of Economics, Pacific Economic Papers, No. 342 (2004); Phillip Lipsey, 'Japan's Asian Monetary Fund Proposal', *Stanford Journal of East Asian Affairs* 3 (2003): 93.

[10]   E. Kohlscheen and M.P. Taylor, 'International Liquidity Swaps: Is the Chiang Mai Initiative Pooling Reserves Efficiently?', *International Journal of Finance & Economics* 13 (2008): 330.

HOW THE CMIM MIGHT DEVELOP

As indicated above, the two pressing needs are to expand the scale of the CMIM and develop a technical surveillance and policy capacity. The scale needs to be expanded, in my view, by a factor of at least three to make the credit lines the size likely to reassure markets and thereby deter contagion. The technical surveillance and policy capacity is needed, otherwise either a substantial majority of the commitments will have to remain conditioned upon there being an IMF program in place for the recipient nation, or the nations in the CMIM will have to accept the possibility of credit lines being extended to a nation without coherent economic policies in place such as to make repayment likely.[11] Neither option is attractive in the longer term. Fortunately, the ASEAN+3 Finance Ministers' Meeting in May 2010 noted that 'consensus has been reached on all the key elements of the regional macroeconomic surveillance unit of the CMIM, called the ASEAN+3 Macroeconomic Research Office (AMRO)'.[12] The AMRO will be located in Singapore 'to monitor and analyze regional economies, which contributes to the early detection of risks, swift implementation of remedial actions, and effective decision-making of the CMIM'.[13] AMRO is to commence operations early in 2011.

So, while work is underway today on developing the surveillance and policy capacity, the full realization of the CMIM commitments is, given ASEAN's track record, likely to take some years. Its success will require a willingness to either share sovereignty or allow one state to design and lead the initiative.[14] There is precious little in the history of ASEAN, in the over four decades since its inception, to suggest either of these paths will be easy or swift. Nonetheless, whatever the institution that arises to discharge these functions is called, in substance it will be close to being a monetary fund.

And this, to me, is where the possible road ahead becomes very interesting. The IMF, the World Bank and (to a more limited extent) the Asian Development Bank have all supported and promoted the Washington Consensus policies. Over the past 25 years, the economic policies of East Asian states have generally been extraordinarily successful, precisely while

---

[11]   C. Randall Henning, 'The Future of the Chiang Mai Initiative: An Asian Monetary Fund?', Peterson Institute for International Economics, Policy Brief, No. PB09-5, February 2009, 8.

[12]   Joint Ministerial Statement of the 13th ASEAN+3 Finance Ministers' Meeting, Tashkent, Uzbekistan, 2 May 2010, at para. 3.

[13]   Ibid., para. 9.

[14]   Arner et al., above note 5, 49.

the Washington Consensus policies have been a conspicuous failure in promoting development. The prospect of an Asian Monetary Fund, or another body discharging the functions of a monetary fund, researching and promoting the policies that have powered East Asia's growth, excites the imagination of those who care about the region, and its potential to chart its own economic course and contribute to global prosperity.

The focus of Washington Consensus policies has been to grow the debtor's economy, so as to alleviate poverty within the country and generate sufficient foreign exchange to service its debts. It has been taken as axiomatic that higher growth rates lead to less poverty, that higher growth rates are only possible once economic stabilization has been achieved through the attainment of a sound macroeconomic profile, and that higher growth is best achieved on the back of exports rather than increases in domestic demand. The policies imposed to achieve these goals have typically included:

- reductions in the budget deficit and limits on domestic credit expansion to control inflation
- exchange rate devaluations to discourage imports and encourage exports
- liberalization of tariff and quota regimes
- a much reduced role for government and a much increased role for markets.

Other Washington Consensus policies imposed on debtors, at times, have included (i) higher income and sales taxes, (ii) higher charges for state-produced goods and services such as electricity and water, (iii) privatization of state-owned companies, and (iv) deregulation of the labour market. These policies have been criticized for their adverse effect on economic growth and their devastating effect upon the living standard of the local people, particularly the poor.[15]

---

[15]   W. Bello, *Dark Victory: The United States, Structural Adjustment and Global Poverty* (London: Pluto Press, 1994); D. Green, *Silent Revolution – The Rise of Market Economics in Latin America* (London: Cassell, 1995) (Green entitled his chapter on the IMF and the World Bank, 'Poverty Brokers', at 32 et seq.). Mark Beeson and Iyanatul Islam, 'Neoliberalism and East Asia: Resisting the Washington Consensus', *Journal of Development Studies* 41 (2) (2005): 197–219; Giovanni Dosi, Mario Imoli and Joseph E. Stiglitz, 'Preface', in Giovanni Dosi, Mario Imoli and Joseph E. Stiglitz, *Industrial Policy and Development: The Political Economy of Capabilities Accumulation* (Oxford: Oxford University Press, 2009).

The focus of the Washington Consensus upon export-led growth has exposed developing countries to the vagaries of demand in foreign markets and to the extreme volatility of global commodity prices. A better policy admits of a larger role for domestic demand, as well as exports, in stimulating growth. In Palley's words, '[t]his is a strategy that lifts all boats since demand growth in one country pulls in exports from others, so that all grow together'.[16]

One way to assess the effectiveness of the Washington Consensus policies is to answer the question, 'How many nations that were developing in 1950 have developed in the 60 years since then?'

The definition of a developed country is not settled. The IMF has identified 34 'advanced economies'[17] and with the recent invitations to join extended to Israel, Estonia and Slovenia, OECD membership will also increase to 34 nations. However, there are significant differences between the two groupings.[18] For instance, Chile and Mexico are OECD members but not considered advanced economies by the IMF.

So there are a range of credible answers to the question of which countries have developed in the past 60 years, but most answers would probably include Hong Kong, Israel, Singapore, South Korea, and Taiwan (treating Hong Kong and Taiwan as separate countries for these purposes). If one treats the Yangtse Delta region of China, centred on Shanghai, as a separate economic entity, it may also qualify for developed status and one could perhaps add to the list Malaysia, Turkey and some of the Emirates. But that is about it – only perhaps five of about 160 nations have clearly graduated to developed status in the past 60 years. Given that the predominant approach to development over this period has been the Washington Consensus, this suggests its policies are a development failure.

Of these nations that have undoubtedly developed, governments have enjoyed a much larger role in Singapore, South Korea and Taiwan than Washington Consensus policies would permit. Governments in those countries have directed much economic activity. Indeed, the only nation to develop in the past 60 years following largely Washington Consensus policies has been the island state of Hong Kong.

The nations of East Asia have enjoyed decades of extraordinary and sustained growth. For over 20 years China has grown at an average rate

---

[16]   Thomas I. Palley, 'Toward a New International Economic Order: Goodbye Washington Consensus, Hello Washington Alternative', accessed 2 September 2010, <http://www.thomaspalley.com/docs/articles/economic_development/new_intl_economic_order.pdf>.

[17]   IMF, *World Economic Outlook* (2009).

[18]   Ibid.

above 9 per cent; Malaysia, Singapore and South Korea have all grown at annual average rates above 6 per cent, and Taiwan and Thailand at 5.5 and 5.9 per cent respectively.[19] When Japan was outperforming the world, from 1950 to 1965, its economy expanded on average at over 10.4 per cent per annum.[20]

The success of Asia, especially East Asia, in general has highlighted the weaknesses of the Washington Consensus policies as the region generally has not embraced consensus policies. A comparison of the economic performance of China and India provides further evidence of the failings of the consensus.

China and India are two very different nations, with different political systems, development paths, financial systems, and economic policy settings. Yet both nations have far outperformed those implementing Washington Consensus policies. It is arguable that China and India have unique advantages not available to other developing nations. China's advantages include a massive supply of relatively well-educated, cheap labour and a huge potential domestic market which China has used adroitly to lure inbound FDI (and ensure high technology comes along with it). India's advantages include a similarly large, cheap workforce coupled with a widespread facility with the English language, the English common law legal system and other institutions, and a tradition of excellence in mathematical and scientific education.

So comparisons between China or India and other developing countries may not be fair or informative. However, comparisons between China and India provide further proof that the policies of the Washington Consensus are misguided. Government has a much smaller role in the Indian economy than in China's. The market is the major allocator of financial and other resources in India, much less so in China, where the government uses its control of the financial sector to direct economic activity. So, of the two nations, India's policies are closer to those of the Washington Consensus than China's. Yet China has consistently outperformed India, and, given

[19] Jayati Ghosh, 'China and India: The Big Differences', accessed 2 September 2010, http://www.networkideas.org/news/aug2005/news25_China_India.htm. Statistics for 2006–08, CIA Factbook, accessed 2 September 2010, https://www.cia.gov/library/publications/the-world-factbook/, except for statistics for Taiwan, which are from *Key Indicators for Asia and the Pacific 2008*, Asian Development Bank. Statistics for 1995–2005 from *Key Indicators for Asia and the Pacific 2008*, Asian Development Bank. Statistics for 1989–94, *World Outlook 1995*, Economist Intelligence Unit; and for 1987–89, *World Outlook 1993*, Economist Intelligence Unit.
[20] K. Beida, *The Structure and Operation of the Japanese Economy* (1970), 12.

the increased investment in the health and education of its people which China's economic growth and national priorities have made possible, it is likely to continue to outperform India in the foreseeable future.

The final word on the Washington Consensus goes to Professor Hal Scott: 'there is little evidence that IMF conditions, usually requiring contractionary fiscal and monetary policies, have worked'.[21]

Indeed, the US and other nations should be grateful that China and other East Asian nations have largely ignored the Washington Consensus and charted their own paths, because for decades the stellar economic growth of East Asia has lifted that of the world. China's capacity to produce manufactured goods, clothing and other items ever more efficiently and cheaply has kept a lid on inflationary pressures in virtually all developed economies. For Australia, Brazil and other commodities exporters China's growth has provided a massive market for minerals and other commodities. Indeed, the rise of East Asia generally underpinned global prosperity in the two decades leading up to the global financial crisis in 2008, and has continued to play a pivotal role since that crisis.

However one assesses the performance of the Washington Consensus policies, their record is abysmal. And this is why the growth of the CMIM into a policy-generating institution is so exciting, because one can logically expect any form of Asian Monetary Fund to research, develop and recommend policies that have a proven record of success in Asia.

WHERE THE CMIM MIGHT LEAD

Most analysis of the CMI and the CMIM focuses upon the potential of the credit facilities to shore up national banking systems and deter market panic in times of crisis. This is undoubtedly important. When capital markets froze in the wake of the global financial crisis, the US Federal Reserve extended large facilities to 14 central banks, including those of Japan, Singapore and South Korea, to provide liquidity in US dollars to foreign financial institutions, and the Korean facility proved important in stabilizing South Korea's economy in the latter half of 2008.[22]

However, my particular interest is more structural and long-term than crisis amelioration and harks back to Japan's original motivation in promoting an Asian Monetary Fund in 1997. Part of Japan's motivation in

---

[21]   Hal S. Scott, 'A Bankruptcy Procedure for Sovereign Debtors?', *The International Lawyer* 37 (2003): 115.

[22]   Henning, above note 11, 7.

pushing for an AMF was to expand its influence and leadership within the region and to promote its own economic interests by protecting its bank loans to, and investments in, the region. However, another part of its motivation lay in advancing an Asian model of development in opposition to the IMF's strongly neoliberal policies that were imposed as part of its bailouts of South Korea, Thailand and Indonesia. By promoting an AMF, Japan sought to promote a policy alternative to the prescriptions of the IMF.[23] And US opposition to the proposal was in part so strong precisely because the US perceived the AMF could become a 'powerful voice for international financial policies that were not inclined towards Western interests and ideas, creating a division between the Western-backed IMF and the Asian-backed AMF'.[24]

Japan's push for an AMF in 1997 would probably have failed even with strong Chinese support. However, without such support it was doomed, and China withheld its support because it was more concerned at the time with the rise of Japanese influence in the region than the continuation of US hegemony.[25] This has since changed. The development to date of the CMI into a CMIM is largely the result of Sino-Japanese cooperation (as evidenced, in part, by China – including Hong Kong – and Japan each making the same contribution to the credit facilities of the CMIM). In 1997 China was still wary of becoming involved in regional institutions. In the intervening years, however, China has worked assiduously and adroitly to increase its regional leadership and has become much more comfortable with regional institution building and membership. This in turn has motivated Japan to increase its regional influence, and the Japanese see financial cooperation as an area in which their more sophisticated financial system allows them to compete well with the Chinese.

Two further factors have served to bring the region together in the 13 years since 1997. The first is the region-wide resentment about the way the IMF rode roughshod over the policy prerogatives of sovereign nations and imposed, as part of its bailouts, policies that proved to be utterly inappropriate and founded upon a profound misunderstanding of the region and its crisis.[26] The second is that the nation that historically has wielded the most economic influence in East Asia, the US, contributed not one

---

[23]   Yong Wook Lee, 'Japan and the Asian Monetary Fund: An Identity–Intention Approach', *International Studies Quarterly* 50 (2) (June 2006): 340.

[24]   Chey, above note 8, 458.

[25]   Ibid., 459.

[26]   R.P. Buckley and S. Fitzgerald, 'An Assessment of Malaysia's Response to the IMF during the Asian Economic Crisis', *Singapore Journal of Legal Studies* (2004): 96–116.

dollar in its hour of greatest need to the bailouts. China, Japan and other regional nations have since come to view the US as having taken advantage of the East Asian crisis to advance its own agenda in the region generally, and in particular to promote the IMF-organized bailouts as a way of ensuring Western banks were repaid as the bailout funds were required to be used to repay debt then due, all while being too mean to even contribute to the bailout funds.

This sense of shared victimhood has been reinforced by a sense of shared neglect, as US foreign policy became consumed by its focus on terrorism and the Middle East from 2001 to 2008. The Obama administration in Washington is now circumspect in opposing regional initiatives, appearing to fear, probably correctly, that strong opposition by it to what China and Japan want to do in their own backyard is only likely to backfire and increase anti-US sentiment in the region.[27]

When all these factors are coupled with the massive advances in the past decade in China's economic power and in its self-confidence in acting in the region, the stage is now far better prepared for China and Japan to work together to lead regional economic cooperation than it has ever been before. The establishment of a well-resourced Asian Monetary Fund would provide the capacity to develop an Asian Consensus on the types of economic and other policies that support development and could become a 'powerful voice' to promote those policies.

At the moment, the debate is framed in terms of the 'Beijing Consensus' versus the Washington Consensus. The phrase Beijing Consensus was coined in 2004 by Joshua Cooper Ramo,[28] a former foreign editor of *Time* magazine and a Professor at Tsinghua University at the time his essay was published.[29] It has been widely used, because of the nice contrast with the Washington Consensus, the way it taps into US fears about the rise of China, and the way it encapsulates the battle for global hegemony which many Americans believe has begun. It is generally used as short-hand for the policies that China has adopted, rather than for what Ramo meant by the term, which is fortunate, for Ramo's analysis was inchoate and problematic.[30]

---

27   Chey, above note 8.
28   J.C. Ramo, *The Beijing Consensus: Notes on the New Physics of Chinese Power* (London: The Foreign Policy Centre, 2004).
29   Yang Yao, 'The End of the Beijing Consensus: Can China's Model of Authoritarian Growth Survive?', *Foreign Affairs*, 2 February 2010.
30   For a useful critique of Ramo's formulation of the Beijing Consensus, see Scott Kennedy, 'The Myth of the Beijing Consensus', *Journal of Contemporary China* 19 (2010): 468–72.

Yet viewed from a global perspective the Chinese economic miracle is only a subset of the Asian economic miracle, and if a new approach to development has evolved in Asia that offers much to other nations, it should be derived from rigorous analysis of the policies and approaches that have worked across the region, not merely in its largest country. This approach has the benefit also of not needing to somehow pretend that there has been a consistent Chinese consensus on its economic policies. China has, in fact, approached economic development as a process of 'crossing the river by feeling for the stones with one's feet', in the words of Deng Xiaoping.[31] Pragmatism, more than any ideological consensus, has guided China's development. It is, in fact, the US focus on what matters to, and threatens, the US that has led to the ascendancy of the idea of the Beijing Consensus, a term not commonly used within China.

What Asia and developing nations throughout the world would most benefit from is the development of an Asian Consensus based on rigorous research and analysis of the economic performance data and policies of the nations of Asia. Ironically, this was recognized by Ramo in his Beijing Consensus essay, when he wrote, 'China's path to development is of course unrepeatable by any other nation'.[32]

This is not the place to attempt the analysis that will lead to an Asian Consensus. It is likely an Asian Consensus would include policies that encourage a substantial role for government, prioritize inbound equity investments over debt (particularly inbound investments that bring with them high technology and management expertise), and emphasize nation building through investment in the education and health of the local people. Very few investments generate returns for a developing nation as strong as those from investing in the health and education of their children.[33] China's current spending priorities suggest it understands this, deeply. As Susan George wrote 20 years ago, 'The IMF cannot seem to understand that investing in . . . [a] healthy, well-fed, literate population . . . is the most intelligent economic choice a country

---

[31] For a good explanation of the meaning of this aphorism, see Clinton Dines, 'Changing China Lecture', Lowy Institute for International Policy, Sydney, 25 February 2010, accessed 2 September 2010, http://www.lowyinstitute.org/Publication.asp?pid=1242; S.J. Gabriel, 'Economic Liberalization in Post-Mao China: Crossing the River by Feeling for Stones', accessed 2 September 2010, http://www.mtholyoke.edu/courses/sgabriel/economics/china-essays/7.html.

[32] Ramo, above note 28, 5.

[33] Nora Lustig, *Social Protection for Equity and Growth* (New York: Inter-American Development Bank, 2000); Nora Lustig, *Mexico: The Remaking of an Economy* (Washington: Brookings Institution Press, 1998).

can make'.[34] Recent IMF and World Bank practice suggests these institutions are still to learn this lesson.[35]

However, this is work for another day, as the articulation of an Asian Consensus demands a rigorous analysis of the economic performance data and economic and other policies of a substantial number of diverse nations. It is important that this research is done thoroughly, and not rushed, or politicized and used polemically in the way most formulations of the Beijing Consensus have been. The purpose of this chapter is simply to emphasize the enormous potential of a properly analysed Asian Consensus to serve as a guide to future policy making within Asia, and as an alternative development model for consideration by developing nations outside the region.

CONCLUSION

Washington Consensus policies have not worked in most countries to which they have been applied, and the policies that engendered dramatic and sustained growth in China, Japan, South Korea, Singapore, Malaysia, Taiwan and other countries have been quite different. An Asian Monetary Fund could develop and promulgate this Asian Consensus and thereby pioneer new approaches to the development challenge. This could serve the region, and developing nations elsewhere, far more effectively than have the IMF and its Washington Consensus policies.

The second reason an AMF represents a great opportunity is that presently the region is not benefiting as much as it could from its massive foreign exchange reserves and high savings rates. China and Japan hold nearly 20 per cent each of worldwide official foreign currency reserves[36] and Asian nations generally have the highest savings rates in the world. An Asian Monetary Fund could work to more fully develop regional bond markets and take other initiatives to keep the region's reserves and savings in the region. Greater regional financial self-sufficiency would serve to insulate the region from the volatility that comes with a dependence upon foreign capital. A virtuous cycle is potentially achievable here. Greater regional integration of financial systems through an Asian Monetary

---

[34]   Susan George, *A Fate Worse Than Debt* (New York: Grove Weidenfeld, 1990), 143, 187, 235.

[35]   Ross P. Buckley, 'IMF Policies and Health in Sub-Saharan Africa', in Adrian Kay and Owain Williams (eds), *Global Health Governance: Crisis, Institutions and Political Economy* (London: Palgrave Macmillan, 2009).

[36]   Kohlscheen and Taylor, above note 10, 323.

Fund should lead to greater regional stability; which should lead to more of these savings, both individual and sovereign, staying in Asia; which should, in turn, lead to even more regional stability. An AMF remains the logical response to the great paradox of the East Asian crisis of 1997 – a crisis brought on by foreign capital losing confidence in a region that had the world's highest savings rates. If East Asia could have kept its money at home, it never would have needed foreign capital, and there would have been no chance of a crisis provoked by its exodus.

The road to an Asian Monetary Fund is likely to be long, and difficult. But the first real steps have been taken. An AMF represents the chance to move away from a development model that is focused primarily upon ensuring poorer nations are able to service their debts and move towards a model that is genuinely focused upon the development of the nations themselves and their people. The development of the CMIM to its logical endpoint as an Asian Monetary Fund offers nothing less than the opportunity to refine and test an entirely new approach to development, one with, to date, a splendid track record.

13. The evolving role of the Asian Development Bank in the creation of an Asian Currency Unit

Nhu Vu

In 1966, the Agreement Establishing the Asian Development Bank (ADB)[1] came into force to foster economic development in Asia. Partly motivated by a desire to invest surpluses, and recognizing Asia's need for development capital, Western countries established the ADB at a time when Asia was starved of capital. Currently however, some Asian countries have much less poverty than they did 40 years ago and now generate huge capital surpluses. Because of these changes, some have argued that the ADB should lend less and focus instead on becoming an economic coordinator to ensure regional stability throughout Asia. This chapter will examine the legal authority of the ADB in pursuing such regional coordination and stabilization activities, focusing on the ADB's project to create an Asian Currency Unit (ACU).

The purpose of the ACU would be to serve as a currency index. It would be based on a 'basket' of the weighted average of currencies of Asian countries and would probably also include the euro and the dollar.[2] The primary purpose of the index would be to bolster capital markets so that regional countries could be more resistant to external shocks by facilitating exchange rate adjustments.[3] Other benefits of the ACU would include lessening dependence on extra-regional currencies to serve as regional reserves, alleviating global imbalances, reducing Asian dependency on the US dollar, contributing to the development of an Asian multi-

---

[1]   Agreement Establishing the Asian Development Bank (22 August 1966), 571 U.N.T.S. 123 (hereinafter ADB Charter), art. 65.

[2]   Masahiro Kawai, 'The Role of an Asian Currency Unit for Asian Monetary Integration', Asian Development Bank Institute, October 2008, 16, accessed 2 September 2010, http://www.obela.org/system/files/Microsoft+Word++Masahiro+Kawai.pdf.

[3]   Ibid., 17.

currency bond market, and ultimately promoting the integration of Asian economies.[4] Although comparisons are made between the ACU and the European Currency Unit, the ACU at the outset would only be used as an index and would not initially involve exchange-market interventions. Nevertheless, the President of the ADB and others have indicated that the ACU could ultimately lead to a regional currency in several years when favorable conditions exist.[5]

Yet, the creation of an ACU and the other initiatives like participation in currency swaps seem more in line with activities that the IMF would pursue, and arguably are a bit far from the ADB's purpose in poverty reduction in providing resources to countries for long-term economic development.[6] The ACU would not involve much lending, a basic activity of a multilateral development bank. The lending that the ACU would provide would be for intervention in markets and would not focus on long-term projects for infrastructure for sustainable development, as provided by most multilateral development banks.

At the May 2007 ADB summit in Kyoto, Cambodia and other poor countries angrily rejected the suggestion that the ADB abandon poverty relief.[7] If the ADB continues to pursue economic stabilization activities at the cost of providing developmental aid to poorer countries, countries adversely affected by the changes like Cambodia would be justified in asserting that the ADB is acting beyond the stated purposes of its charter.

This chapter will look at the authority of the ADB in its evolving role from development bank to regional economic coordinator focusing on the creation of an ACU because the ACU has been developed primarily under the leadership of the ADB. The first section of this chapter will examine the ADB charter and past interpretive decisions made by the ADB, and look at other regional stabilizing initiatives the ADB has undertaken to see how these fit within the purposes stated in the ADB charter. I argue that the creation of an ACU does fall within the purposes of the ADB charter. The second section of this chapter examines how to create a body that would take on such regional stabilization activities in the event such

---

[4] Bin Zhang and Fan He, 'Is Asian Currency Unit Attractive to East Asian Economies?', *China & World Economy*, 15 (1) (2007): 64.

[5] Haruhiko Kuroda, 'Transitional Steps in the Road to a Single Currency in East Asia', 14 May 2004, accessed 2 September 2010, http://www.adb.org/AnnualMeeting/2004/Seminars/presentations/hkuroda-presentation.pdf.

[6] See Paul B. Stephan, Julie A. Roin and Don Wallace, *International Business and Economics: Law & Policy*, 3rd edn (Newark NJ: Lexis Publishing/Matthew Bender, 2004), 365–6.

[7] See 'What are We For?', *The Economist*, 10 May 2007.

activities are found not to be authorized under the ADB charter. Finally, the feasibility of actually creating an ACU is explored.

As a backdrop to the motivations of the ADB's involvement in stabilization activities, one can look to the financial crisis that hit Asia in 1997. Countries in Asia looked to the causes of and responses to the crisis and formed the belief that future crisis prevention would have to start within the region. The response of the International Monetary Fund (IMF) to the crisis led to several Asian countries losing faith in the IMF's ability to handle any crisis. For example, during the crisis, Japan with the IMF convened a conference to provide financial support for Thailand. In the package to Thailand, only regional states, including Australia, China, Indonesia, Japan, Malaysia, Singapore and Korea, provided aid; the US and European countries contributed nothing. In addition to criticism for not reacting swiftly enough to the crisis, the IMF was and continues to be criticized for imposing stringent conditions on bailout packages, such as requiring raising interest rates and cutting public spending.

In the wake of the global financial crisis in 2008, Asian countries have also suffered even though the economic crisis was not of their own making. For example, Asian Pacific GDP was expected to drop 3.4 per cent for 2009 after peaking at 9.5 per cent in 2007. The global financial crisis is also expected to have kept 100 million people in developing Asia in poverty.[8]

To minimize the effects of future crises, especially like the one that occurred in Asia in 1997, the ADB has suggested that a regional self-help mechanism be created to prevent, manage and resolve currency crises through collective efforts and to head off currency speculation at an early stage.[9] Since the Asian financial crisis, the ADB's embrace of the role of a regional coordinating body to fight off crisis has been manifested by various initiatives, including the creation of the Regional Cooperation and Integration Unit (RCI) of the ADB; participation in currency swaps; issuance of local currency loans and the development of an Asian bond market in cooperation with the Association of Southeast Asian Nations (ASEAN); and, most recently, spearheading the creation of an ACU in order to allow countries to monitor how Asian currencies are moving collectively vis-à-vis key external currencies.[10]

---

[8]   Haruhiko Kuroda, 'The ADB is Helping Asia's Poorest', *Wall Street Journal*, 1 May 2009.

[9]   Masahiro Kawai, 'Regional Financial Cooperation in East Asia: Progress, Opportunities and Challenges', remarks from the Second Deposit Insurance Corporation of Japan Roundtable, 8 March 2007, 6.

[10]   Zhang and He, above note 4, 62–76.

THE LEGITIMACY OF AN ACU DEVELOPED BY THE ADB

The ADB Charter

At first glance, when looking at the statement of purpose, the text of the charter, the ordinary meaning of words, and the historical context of the creation of the ADB, the ADB charter does not appear to include within its permitted activities involvement with economic stabilization policies or the creation of an ACU. However, when looking at the implied powers of an international organization as could be interpreted from the text of the ADB charter itself, and the interpretive process as outlined in the ADB charter, the arguments that the ADB may undertake such activities are persuasive.

Textual analysis

The purposes of the ADB are laid out in the ADB charter in Article 1, which simply states that the Bank will foster economic growth and cooperation in Asia and contribute to the acceleration of the process of economic development. To achieve these purposes, the ADB is given a set of functions as delineated in Article 2 and broken down into six clauses. Yet five out of these six short clauses include the word 'development'. For example, to fulfill its stated purpose in Article 1, the Bank will 'promote investment in the region of public and private capital for *development* purposes', and 'utilize the resources at its disposal for financing *development* of the developing member countries' and 'provide technical assistance for the . . . financing and execution of *development* projects'.[11]

This purpose and function section strongly indicates that the ADB should stay focused on development, developing member countries, and infrastructural programs for the development of countries. However, in examining all of the ADB charter, there are persuasive arguments indicating that the regional involvement of the ADB in stabilization practices and the creation of the ACU are permissible. The final clause of the mission section, for example, states that the ADB will also 'undertake such other activities and provide such other services as may advance its purpose'.[12] This last clause acts like a catch-all phrase that would permit the ADB to pursue whatever activity it thinks it may need to 'advance its purpose' and perhaps is the most permissive in all of the charter because it is listed

---

[11] ADB Charter, arts 1–2 (emphasis added).
[12] Ibid.

at the very beginning of the charter among the other permitted functions. Indeed, international organizations need flexibility to respond to changing times, and scholars argue that, in reality, the expansion of the competence of organizations should be accepted, with limitations to that competence clearly recognized.[13]

Further support of the ACU comes from within the charter itself and appears next in Article 19, Special Funds. This article allows the ADB by a vote of two-thirds of the total number of governors to accept the administration of Special Funds. Such special funds could support the granting of emergency loans, or those of 'high developmental priority' as may be justified for 'any purpose of the Bank'.[14] Arguably, those funds could also be used to maintain currencies in the event of a crisis, or to create an index like the ACU to monitor currency fluctuations.

Again, in Chapter IV where the Bank's borrowing and other miscellaneous powers are listed, the charter states that the Bank will have additional powers as may be 'necessary or appropriate in furtherance of its purpose and functions'.[15] Of importance is the conjunction 'or' separating 'necessary' and 'appropriate', because this allows the ADB to pursue activities for whatever would be considered simply appropriate – a lower standard than what is necessary to give effect to its purpose.

Implied powers
The former general counsel of the IMF, Joseph Gold, commented that powers that are not directly stated in the text of a charter are the implied powers of an international organization. In examining the criteria for implied powers, one looks to what is needed for the organization. To make this determination, Gold remarked specifically on the distinction between 'necessary' and 'appropriate', writing that the two words are not to be treated as a 'unified single criterion'. Rather, they are words to be used as alternatives.[16] Gold also argued that the principle of effectiveness is a fundamental justification for an implied power. In other words, by providing a framework to oversee stabilization policies in Asia, the ADB would be giving effect to its purpose of promoting economic development.[17]

It makes sense that the ADB would want to secure the worth of several

---

[13] Nigel D. White, *The Law of International Organisations*, 2nd edn (Manchester: Manchester University Press 2005), 107.

[14] ADB Charter, art. 19, clauses 1–3.

[15] ADB Charter, art. 21, clause vii.

[16] Joseph Gold, *Interpretation: The IMF and International Law* (London: Kluwer Law International, 1996) 46.

[17] Ibid., 49.

billions of dollars in loans it provides to developing countries, rather than sitting helplessly in the event that a country's currency value is at risk. Were such a crisis to occur, member countries' economic development would be affected and they would not be able to repay their loans from the ADB.

Interpretation under the ADB

Like other Bretton Woods organizations such as the World Bank and the IMF, the legitimacy of actions at the ADB is left to the organization itself to determine as specified in the founding agreements.[18] Opponents of expansive interpretation might find that the internal interpretation procedure is inherently biased – that is, that the organization is much more likely to rule in favor of whatever course of action it has already pursued. On the other hand, an internal procedure can expedite proceedings given the complicated economic nature of the issues.[19] Another reason for an internal procedure is the contrast between potentially lengthy legal proceedings and the expediency that may be required in economic emergency situations. One last reason is that states may often prefer to resolve issues within the organization itself where they are represented and could, by their votes, influence decisions.[20] Because these internal proceedings seemed to have worked for the IMF and the World Bank, it is reasonable to assume that this is also why the ADB adopted such a procedure. Presently, if a question of interpretation or application arises between any member and the Bank, the Board of Directors determines the interpretation. Even appeals are kept within the ADB, and only the Board of Governors has the right ultimately to resolve questions of interpretation.[21]

Because the member states all agreed to an internal interpretation procedure, to determine whether the creation of an ACU would be legitimate under the ADB, analysis of other actions pursued by the ADB and their legitimacy should be reviewed. To date, the ADB has formally interpreted its charter on only six occasions. Out of these six decisions, none have been

---

[18]   International Bank for Reconstruction and Development (World Bank) Articles of Agreement (1–22 July 1944) (hereinafter World Bank Charter), art. IX, 'Interpretation'; International Monetary Fund Articles of Agreement (22 July 1944) (hereinafter IMF Charter), art. XXIX, 'Interpretation'; ADB Charter, art. 60, 'Interpretation or Application'; Tetsuo Sato, *Evolving Constitutions of International Organizations* (The Hague: Kluwer Law International, 1996) 193–5.

[19]   Sato, above note 18, 194.

[20]   Ibid., 207–9.

[21]   ADB Charter, art. 60, 'Interpretation or Application'.

appealed, and five out of the six decisions generally expanded the powers of the ADB.[22]

For example, in 1983, the Board of Directors interpreted Article 16.1 of the charter concerning commission and fees. The article begins 'The Bank shall charge, in addition to interest, a commission on direct loans made or participated in as part of its ordinary operations . . .' The Board of Directors found that the charter did not prohibit the discontinuation of a commission on ordinary operations loans when the building-up of the special reserve was considered to be no longer necessary. It is noteworthy that the text of the charter, by using the word 'shall', is written in a manner that commands the charging of a commission. Yet the Board of Directors concluded that charging a commission would no longer be necessary since the building-up of special reserves was no longer necessary, thereby justifying the change.[23]

In making the above interpretations, the Board used its implied powers, and did not comply with the higher 'necessary' standard. Such past actions indicate that the ADB will continue to interpret its charter more expansively and flexibly and would recognize the creation of an ACU.

Other Regional Initiatives

Besides looking to the formal interpretations of the ADB, other initiatives have been pursued involving stabilization of the Asian economic region. These activities and their endorsement by the ADB Board of Directors should be examined as well in determining whether the ACU would be considered legitimately sanctioned under the ADB charter. In July 2006, the Board of Directors endorsed the ADB's Regional Cooperation and Integration (RCI) Strategy.[24] Like the ACU, RCI involves the coordination of economic activities throughout Asia. The RCI Strategy has four interrelated pillars: (1) regional and sub-regional economic cooperation programs on cross-border infrastructure, (2) trade and investment cooperation and integration, (3) monetary and financial cooperation and integration, and (4) cooperation in regional public goods. The RCI report opens by asserting that the charter mandates the ADB to play an active role in regional cooperation, and for this reason the ADB in 1994 for the first time

---

[22]   See correspondence from Donald A. Kidd, Principal Counsel of the ADB (hereinafter referred to as Kidd Correspondence) (in the author's possession).

[23]   See ADB Board of Directors Meeting, *Transfer of Commission to the Special Reserve,* 29 December 1983.

[24]   ADB, Regional Cooperation and Integration Strategy Policy Paper (July 2006) (hereinafter RCI Paper), iii.

articulated how it would promote regional cooperation. Included in these initiatives that frame the RCI Strategy are efforts to prevent the spread of infectious diseases such as avian influenza, HIV/AIDs and SARS, and initiatives on energy efficiency, environmental management, and governance. Other initiatives include working with ASEAN on the Chiang Mai Initiative and the Asian Bond Markets Initiative.[25] The RCI paper states that the ADB's role in the third pillar, regional monetary and financial cooperation and integration, will be through non-lending support – a deviation from the general role of a multilateral development bank. Because of this, it is worth further examining the Chiang Mai Initiative and the Asian Bond Markets Initiative.

Chiang Mai Initiative Multilateralization
The Chiang Mai Initiative (CMI) was created on 6 May 2000 under the auspices of ASEAN. Like the ACU, the CMI was designed to bolster economic stability in Asia. The purpose of the CMI was to allow Asia to cope effectively with disruptive currency fluctuations and international capital movements, should the events of the Asian financial crisis repeat themselves.[26] The role of the ADB with the CMI, as articulated in a memorandum of understanding undertaken by the ADB and ASEAN, would be to provide support for the ASEAN Finance Ministers, commit to sharing knowledge, consult with each other on regional and sub-regional policy dialogue, explore the potential of co-financing regional and sub-regional programs and projects, exchange information, and prepare joint reports, among other things.[27] The memorandum further states that collaboration by both sides would be guided by (i) pro-poor sustainable economic growth, (ii) inclusive social development, and (iii) good governance for effective policies and institutions.[28]

The CMI began as a bilateral currency swap arrangement among 16 countries where pairs of countries would agree to exchange currencies in order to provide balance-of-payments and short-term liquidity support. Due to the ongoing criticism that in an emergency more currency would need to be rapidly disbursed, the CMI has developed into a multilateral currency swapping agreement. Since the multilateralization of the Chiang Mai Initiative (signed on 28 December 2009 by ASEAN+3 (China,

---

[25] Ibid., ix.
[26] See Henry C. K. Liu, 'The Case for an Asian Monetary Fund', *Asia Times*, 12 July 2002.
[27] Memorandum of Understanding for Administrative Arrangements, ASEAN and the ADB, 24 August 2006.
[28] Ibid., ¶ 5(i).

Japan, and Korea), which came into force on 28 March 2010), the currency swap arrangement has been renamed the Chiang Mai Initiative Multilateralization (CMIM). Under the CMIM, ASEAN+3 governments in total contributed US$120 billion to a regional reserve pool to provide emergency liquidity to countries in a financial crisis.[29] A country would be able to swap its local currency for United States dollars by an amount up to its contribution multiplied by either 5 for ASEAN countries or 2.5 for Japan, China, or Korea.[30]

Asian Bond Markets Initiative
Under ASEAN talks, Japan initiated the Asian Bond Markets Initiative (ABMI) in 2002. The ADB's involvement with the ABMI involves supporting ASEAN in bolstering Asian bond markets with the goal of increasing regional stability throughout Asia. Under the ABMI, ASEAN countries agreed to organize various aspects of creating a bond markets initiative, and one topic that China covered was the issuance of bonds denominated in local currency by multilateral development banks.[31] The reasons in favor of developing local currency bonds are several. One of the cited causes of the Asian financial crisis is that of a currency and maturity mismatch problem created by borrowing short-term capital in foreign currency to finance a long-term local currency investment. For example, instead of raising money in China by issuing local bonds, a Chinese telecommunications company would borrow money in US dollars to finance its project in China. The region would be subject to instability if all foreign creditors decided not to roll over their short-term loans, resulting in an inadequate supply of dollars. Moreover, Asian savings are sent abroad to financial centers in New York or London, for example, and then come back to Asia as short-term capital in foreign currency. Therefore, Asian bond markets would provide for (1) alternative sources for public and private investment, (2) alternative modes of wealth holdings for Asian households, (3) a more resilient financial system, and (4)

---

[29] Aladdin D. Rillo, 'Chiang Mai Initiative Multilateralization (CMIM): East Asia's Regional Liquidity Support', presentation to UNASUR Finance Ministers' Meeting, Quito, Ecuador, accessed 2 September 2010, http://www.bce.fin.ec/documentos/Eventos/Economicos/Aladdin%20Rillo%20ASEAN.pdf.

[30] Fintan Ng, 'Economist: Chiang Mai Initiative a "Compromise"', *The Star Online*, accessed 2 September 2010 http://biz.thestar.com.my/news/story.asp?file=/2009/12/30/business/5380412&sec=business.

[31] Yong Chul Park, 'Beyond the Chiang Mai Initiative: Prospects for Regional Financial and Monetary Integration', paper prepared for the Technical Group meeting of G-24, Washington DC, 27–28 September 2004, 15.

reducing the problem of currency and maturity mismatches. The ABMI would essentially facilitate Asian savings in Asian long-term investment in local currency.[32]

The ADB's role in bond market development with ASEAN would consist of technical assistance and policy advice, provision of partial credit and political risk guarantees, issuance of ADB bonds in local currencies to promote national and regional bond market development, and support of regional cooperation through examining the feasibility of a regional clearing and settlement system, harmonized credit and trading standards, and improved local credit rating systems.[33]

The ADB Board of Directors has already given its endorsement of both the CMI and the ABMI among other initiatives in endorsing the Regional Cooperative and Integration Strategy. The Dean of the Asian Development Bank Institute (part of the ADB) has defended involvement in bond issuance as an activity in which the ADB has participated dating back to the early 1970s, when the ADB opened Japan's domestic bond market to foreign issuers.[34]

The CMI and the ABMI, however, are distinct from the ADB's initiation of an ACU. To begin with, the CMI and the ABMI began as a result of efforts by ASEAN – an entirely different organization. Moreover, the role of the ADB is primarily one of support in facilitating swap arrangements and the development of the Asian bond markets. Finally, there is support for the ABMI in the ADB charter itself. The ADB charter expressly allows for the ADB to 'buy and sell securities the Bank has issued or guaranteed or in which it has invested'.[35]

Under the ACU, the ADB would be responsible for providing an index based on a currency basket containing the currencies of various countries with the goal being to stabilize fluctuation of the currencies in the region.[36] This is a goal which the ACU shares with the CMI and the ABMI.

---

[32]   Masahiro Kawai, Asian Development Bank Institute, 'Asian Bond Market Development: Progress, Prospects and Challenges', keynote address at the High Yield Debt Summit Asia 2007, Singapore, 16–17 May 2007.

[33]   Ibid.

[34]   Ibid. A samurai bond market refers to the issuance of yen-denominated bonds in Japan by non-residents. See 'Enhancing Japan's Status as an International Financial Center', accessed 2 September 2010, http://www.mof.go.jp/english/if/ks030707c.htm.

[35]   ADB Charter, art. 21, clause ii.

[36]   Bang Nom Jeon and Hongfang Zhang, 'A Currency Union or an Exchange Rate Union: Evidence from Northeast Asia', presented at the Oxford Business and Economics Conference, London, June 2007, accessed 2 September 2010, http://trintrin.com/obec/Bang%20Nam%20Jeon,%20Hongfang%20Zhang.doc.

However, because the ACU is wholly an ADB undertaking, and because it involves participation of the ADB in activities that are not clearly supported in the ADB charter, there is a strong argument that the ADB would be acting beyond its mandate by creating the ACU.

Another source of guidance may be found in comparing the ADB and the World Bank because the ADB was modeled on the World Bank. The World Bank similarly focuses on poverty relief and the promotion of development for long-term growth. Towards this goal, the World Bank dedicates 25 per cent of its annual lending to so-called fast disbursement and structural loans to address balance-of-payments problems, with conditions that are less harsh than those imposed by the IMF.[37] Because the regional economic and coordination policies that the ADB is implementing would support balance of payments, it would seem that there would be more support for the ADB's currency unit project. However, there is a noteworthy distinction between the World Bank and the ADB. The World Bank's charter specifies that one of the World Bank's purposes would be to work towards the resolution of balance-of-payments issues, as explicitly stated at the beginning of its articles of agreement.[38] In contrast, balance of payments is mentioned only once in the ADB's charter: in Article 13, titled Provision of Currencies for Direct Loans. Under Article 13, the ADB may only provide currencies other than that of the member country if the ADB determines that a project may cause a strain on the balance of payments of the member country where the project is to be carried out.[39]

Conclusion Regarding the Legitimacy of an ACU

The comparison between the ADB and the World Bank suggests that the ADB's participation in currency stabilization activities could be permissible. Although the ACU involves the ADB in pursuing a non-lending activity that is not explicitly allowed in its charter, this does not necessarily mean that the ADB's actions with the ACU are illegitimate. But there are still other reasons for questioning whether the ACU is an authorized pursuit under the charter of the ADB. For example if one compares the IMF's charter with that of the ADB, striking differences exist to the point that the creation of an ACU would seem to have originated with the IMF. And if one were to go to the intent of the parties that gathered to form

---

[37] See Stephan, Roin and Wallace, above note 6, 375.
[38] World Bank Charter, art. 1, clause 3.
[39] ADB Charter, art. 13, clause ii.

the ADB, it is very unlikely that they had intended to become involved in creating a currency index.[40]

Perhaps the most important factor to look at in determining whether the ADB may lead the development of an ACU is the principle of effectiveness, because this has been an important factor used by the ADB's Board of Directors.[41] In asserting the reasons for its involvement in the CMI and the ABMI as part of the RCI Strategy, the ADB noted how several of its activities worked toward the mission of reducing poverty. For example, the ADB pointed out how acceleration of trade and investment integration of the developing member countries with non-regional economies helps reduce poverty, and how foreign direct investment inflows have a positive impact on poverty reduction. Moreover, the ADB underscored the importance of proactively preparing for a crisis, because when the Asian financial crisis occurred, economic growth plunged in many crisis-affected countries and 'the impressive achievements in poverty reduction over the previous three decades encountered major setbacks.'[42] Even though the ACU may be an activity with which the ADB did not imagine it would become involved, it is a means to help it achieve its goal – poverty reduction. Finally, although some poorer countries might not be able to receive as much funding for infrastructural development projects, this harm could be counterbalanced by the benefits of the ACU.

CREATING THE IDEAL ECONOMIC STABILIZATION ORGANIZATION FOR THE REGION

In the event that member countries insist that the ADB focus on developmental activities and the Board of Governors finds that the ADB has acted beyond its mandate by creating the ACU, another organization would then have to take the lead with the ACU. Examining critiques of the CMIM, the ABMI and the charter of the IMF will help determine what would be the best characteristics for a regional stabilization organization, particularly since no organization except for the ADB is taking the lead in the development of an ACU.

---

[40] See White, above note 13, 89.
[41] See Sato, above note 18, 35.
[42] RCI Paper, above note 24, 8–9.

CMIM

Although it was a major multilateral achievement for bringing together several nations to prepare for economic instability, the CMIM is still in developmental stages. It will need to provide clear rules identifying when short-term lending for a crisis should be activated. Further, with the multilateralization of the currency swap agreement, even greater regional surveillance is needed to help determine when swap activation will occur. Presently, under ASEAN, the Economic Review and Policy Dialogue (ERPD) surveillance process is used, but the ERPD simply involves information sharing among countries. Talks are presently underway at the ASEAN Secretariat to determine how to conduct more rigorous regional surveillance.[43] The ADB has stated that a professional secretariat office should be created to help finance ministers and central bank governors in regional economic surveillance, and that BASEL II should be improved, while further progress is made in deepening the size and liquidity of local currency bond markets. Countries such as Malaysia are critical of the CMIM's current link with the IMF, because loans are closely tied to conditions imposed by the IMF.[44] The CMIM is dependent on and linked to the IMF because only 20 per cent of the available swap funds may be drawn by a borrowing country. If a country wanted to draw over 20 per cent of the available swap funds, that country must agree to conditions imposed by the IMF, because ASEAN and the ADB do not have strong enough regional surveillance mechanisms in Asia to ensure that countries will be able to handle the financial burdens they take on.[45]

ABMI

As for the ABMI, the president of the ADB has stated the importance of local bond markets to counter excessive reliance on banks and currency mismatches that previously contributed to the Asian financial crisis.[46] In creating a stabilization fund, therefore, member countries must have strong legal and governmental bodies for the regulation of securities issuance to ensure a robust regional issuing bond agency. Credible ratings

---

[43]   Rillo, above note 29.
[44]   Kawai, above note 2, 12.
[45]   Randall Henning, 'The Future of the Chiang Mai Initiative: An Asian Monetary Fund?', Peterson Institute for International Economics, Policy Brief No. PB09-5, accessed 2 September 2010, http://www.piie.com/publications/pb/pb09-5.pdf.
[46]   Kuroda, above note 5, 4.

agencies should also be involved, and the initiative would have to provide incentives for the private sector to become involved.[47] Other key issues that would have to be resolved include 'securitization, credit guarantees, promotion of local currency denominated bonds, and foreign exchange transactions and settlements'.[48]

IMF

Although the charters of both the IMF and the ADB involve lending and economic development, there are fundamental differences. A simple reading of the purpose sections of the two charters highlights these differences. Unlike the ADB's charter, the IMF's includes clauses that are much more in line with what an organization involved with regional stability and liquidity issues would include. For example, the IMF's first stated purpose is to 'promote international monetary cooperation through an organization that provides the machinery for consultation and collaboration'. The IMF's charter further states that it is 'to facilitate the expansion and balanced growth of international trade', and the third delineated purpose is it exists 'to promote exchange stability, to maintain orderly exchange arrangements among members, and to avoid competitive exchange depreciation'. Further, in 1987, the IMF adopted a 'stand by' arrangement that allows countries to draw up to a certain amount without examination by the IMF. Finally, Article VIII(2)(b) of the IMF charter allows members to collaborate to ensure orderly exchange.[49] This is a significant contrast to the ADB charter, which focuses on development.

Characteristics of the Ideal Organization

Taking into account these collective comments on the CMI and the ABMI and comparisons with the IMF, an organization that would take on the development of the ACU, and possibly other regional stabilization mechanisms like the CMI or the ABMI, should focus on four areas in creating its charter: (a) modeling its purpose section on the IMF's, (b) regional surveillance, (c) lending requirements, and (d) membership, including strengthening ties between and among its member states.

Because the success of initiatives would depend heavily on the

---

[47]   Jennifer A. Amyx, 'A Regional Bond Market for East Asia? The Evolving Political Dynamics of Regional Financial Cooperation', Australia–Japan Research Centre, Asia Pacific School of Economics, Pacific Economic Papers, No. 342, 2004.
[48]   Kuroda, above note 5, 4.
[49]   Stephan et al., above note 6, 373.

organization's ability to monitor economic fluctuations, member countries should agree to make themselves subject to monitoring or undertake that they will comply with BASEL II within a certain time frame, for instance. This could be a requirement for joining the organization. Such surveillance would alleviate reliance on other international organizations like the IMF, and could also allow for more flexible lending.

To further the effectiveness of initiatives, the organization might also consider creating an Exchange Rate Mechanism (ERM) as was created with the European Monetary System, using the European Currency Unit (ECU), which predated the euro. The purpose of the ERM would be to define, on the basis of the ACU, fluctuation bands in which market exchange rates could move for member countries. Ultimately, if a transition were to occur from the ACU as an accounting unit index to an actually used unit of currency, the use of an Asian ERM would probably be required to intervene to provide exchange rate stability.[50] Of course, creating the ERM and enforcing the permissible fluctuations of currencies within a band requires that the organization have strong surveillance mechanisms in place and that member countries commit their central banks to the monetary policy in line with practices acceptable to the organization. While member countries compromise their autonomy in committing to an ERM, such a mechanism would make the ACU a more meaningful tool to ensure regional stability while benefiting member countries. For example, it has been argued that Denmark and Hungary suffered greater volatility of exchange rates and higher interest rates during the global financial crisis of 2008 due to their not being members of the European Monetary Union.[51] The Asian ERM could also help stabilize exchange rates in the run-up to a possible Asian Monetary Union (AMU) and alleviate problems associated with the irrevocable fixing of exchange rates at the start of an AMU.[52]

If surveillance mechanisms were in place, the organization would be able to make it easier for countries to borrow money to counter significant currency fluctuations that deviate from whatever the permissible band would

---

[50] See Yung Chul Park, 'Regional Currency Unit (RCU) and Exchange Rate Policy Coordination in East Asia', Seoul National University, 4 November 2007, accessed 2 September 2010, http://www.petersoninstitute.org/publications/papers/park-on-ito1007.pdf (arguing that without regional exchange rate intervention, the ACU as an index will only be a political gesture towards integration).

[51] Werner Becker, 'EMU: A Role Model for an Asian Monetary Union?', Deutche Bank Research, 17, accessed 2 September 2010, http://www.dbresearch.com/PROD/DBR_INTERNET_EN-PROD/PROD0000000000234582.pdf.

[52] Ibid., 23.

be for the ACU. Currently the conditions under the CMIM may be too stringent and the conditions set forth under the IMF may be too difficult for a struggling member country to accommodate. To be eligible for a loan, the IMF may require borrowing governments to reduce their budget deficits and rate of money growth; eliminate monopolies, price controls and interest-rate ceilings; deregulate selected industries; remove export barriers; maintain adequate international reserves; and devalue their currency if faced with a fundamental balance-of-payments deficit.[53] The results of IMF policies have been criticized as questionable, especially as applied to Asia in the late 1990s. For example, the IMF called for currency devaluations and unchanged low inflation rates for its financing in Indonesia, Korea, and Thailand. Doing this necessitated massive reductions in Asian money supplies. Interest rates then increased significantly, but investors did not invest more because they were wary of defaults on dollar-denominated debts. The result was that Asian economies were stunted because consumers and businesses found it extraordinarily difficult to borrow.[54]

Instead, a regional currency stabilization organization should increase the threshold amount for automatic emergency lending while assessing the individual borrowing country's situation. This would be similar to a stand-by arrangement under the IMF, but the initial amount of funding would be higher. To reduce the risk of a moral hazard, member countries could make future lending difficult based on past performance of repayment.[55]

THE FEASIBILITY OF AN ASIAN CURRENCY UNIT

While this chapter does not focus on the viability of the ACU becoming a reality, comments are provided since this is the aim of the ADB's efforts. Many believe that the use of an ACU in achieving intra-regional exchange rate stability is desirable, but most experts agree that Asia as a whole may not necessarily be considered an optimum currency area (OCA) and therefore adoption of an ACU is still premature. Factors used to assess whether incentives exist for countries to form an OCA include openness to the area members, financial market integration, symmetry of shocks affecting area members, and willingness to coordinate on fiscal policies.

---

[53] Lawrence J. McQuillian, 'The Case Against the International Monetary Fund', in *Public Policy* 8 (Stanford University, 1999).
[54] Ibid.
[55] Park, above note 31, 40.

While East Asia as a whole is generally not considered an OCA, most experts agree that several sub-groups of the region's economies may form an OCA. For example, the following countries could form an OCA: Malaysia, Singapore, Thailand, Korea, and Japan. In fact, the level of integration in East Asian economies currently matches levels in Europe in the 1980s and 1990s.[56] Experts further contend that not all factors for an OCA need exist before a commitment to economic integration occurs. Moreover, scholars argue that once an OCA commitment forms, economies will naturally integrate such that the OCA incentives will further coalesce. Finally, with the adoption of the CMIM necessitating regional surveillance most likely through ASEAN or the ADB, arguments have been made that East Asia should at least begin informal exchange rate coordination. The initial step that Masahiro Kawai, the Dean and CEO of the Asian Development Bank Institute, argues should be taken now is to adopt a currency basket based on the US dollar, the euro, and the currencies of other East Asian countries or the ACU. Countries would then stabilize their currencies to this basket depending on each country's conditions and preferences, and national monetary authorities would maintain their autonomy similarly to what Singapore does now vis-à-vis its basket containing the US dollar, euro, yen, and other major and regional currencies. An Asian ERM would be adopted only at the second stage, when formal exchange rate policy coordination would begin.[57]

However, a few more steps must be taken before beginning even the informal coordination process. To begin with, it is still not settled which currencies to include in the basket. Which countries or organizations will determine even this fundamental issue is still unclear. The OCA rubric may help in determining which countries to target first to roll out a pilot ACU project, but OCA incentives alone are not determinative. Finally, a regional surveillance body needs to be fully established dedicated to monitoring and developing the ACU, and managing resources to handle currency fluctuations. Whether this role will be filled by the ADB, by ASEAN under the regional surveillance body of the CMIM or by another organization is still unclear. Other significant ongoing impediments include the historical absence of strong pan-Asian institutions and political commitment, the diversity of economic and political systems, and the reluctance to lose national sovereignty over economic policymaking.

---

[56] Kawai, above note 2, 8.
[57] Ibid., 17–18.

CONCLUSION

International organizations grow, change, and must adapt to survive. In the 1960s, when the ADB came into force, China was significantly poorer than it is now. Presently, China is one of the ADB's largest providers of funds, while also being its second largest borrower. China has even competed with the ADB and won in providing a loan to the Philippines – the headquarters of the ADB. The irony of these circumstances has led critics to believe that the ADB is no longer needed. In the past decade, however, the ADB has emerged as a leader in the role of regional coordinator. Its leadership role in this arena has been criticized because concentration on the development of an ACU and other regional stabilization mechanisms deviates from its general mandate to provide developmental loans to poor countries.

Nevertheless, there are several arguments which demonstrate why the undertaking of regional economic coordination falls within the ADB charter. The implied powers doctrine is the greatest argument among the various methods of interpretation because the coordination of regional stabilization mechanisms enables the ADB to give further effect to its developmental aid and is therefore legitimate. Although it is important to keep in mind the poor countries whose development projects may be reduced as a result of this new focus area, these very countries arguably will significantly benefit from an ACU.

If the participation of the ADB in the creation of an ACU is considered outside the ADB's charter, the question remains as to who will assume this much-needed role of regional coordinator that the ADB has taken on. The ADB's leadership in supporting and developing the ACU has been a key step in coordinating economic stabilization in Asia. While there are still a few more steps before the ACU may become a reality, Asia is moving toward economic integration now more than ever before.

Conclusion

Richard Weixing Hu, Douglas W. Arner and Ross P. Buckley

The purpose of this volume has been to analyze recent developments and likely future paths for regional economic integration in East Asia. Our perspective on the issue was inspired by a paradox: East Asia enjoys a high degree of trade integration but a low degree of financial and monetary integration, even though it has an abundance of capital and foreign reserves. On the trade side, the region is highly integrated in terms of intra-region trade, foreign direct investment, and GDP correlation, both formally through an ever-expanding web of free trade agreements and functionally through well-established production networks in the region. East Asia is the world's manufacturing hub. It produces over 50 per cent of global manufacturing trade. China is a global manufacturing powerhouse, and yet over 40 per cent of the value of its exports consists of inputs imported into China from the rest of East Asia.

On the finance side, however, East Asia exhibits a very low level of integration. Most East Asian economies are far more financially linked with North America and Europe than they are with other economies in the region. Yet East Asia enjoys the world's highest savings rates and China, Japan, Taiwan, South Korea, Singapore and Hong Kong have among the largest foreign exchange reserves in the world. While formal and functional regional trade integration is only likely to accelerate, financial and monetary integration is likely to continue to proceed at a much more modest pace.

East Asian financial integration hinges on how major players in the region want to pursue financial and monetary cooperation. The Asian Financial Crisis in 1997 motivated regional actors to take small steps to redress this imbalance by establishing the Chiang Mai Initiative – a series of bilateral currency swap arrangements among the ten ASEAN nations plus China, Japan and South Korea – to provide credit to central banks to support currencies in difficulty. The global financial crisis that started in 2008 triggered the ASEAN+3 grouping to take new steps to increase regional financial and monetary cooperation. In February 2009, the

Chiang Mai Initiative was greatly strengthened and multilateralized by increasing its fund size and adding some surveillance and technical advice capacity, as well as expanding membership to include Hong Kong. Yet, people see different implications from these developments. Some view them as the first steps toward an Asian Monetary Fund, which provides short-term credit and financial and technical advice to its members, as does the IMF. Others see these early steps as unlikely to lead to a regional institutionalized financial facility as ASEAN has a poor record of moving swiftly or decisively. To further complicate the picture, the two major players in East Asian integration, China and Japan, seem to have yet to come to terms on how to proceed with future financial and monetary cooperation in East Asia, although there are signs that they are learning how to cooperate on these issues.

The chapters in this volume have examined the changing dynamics in regional cooperation, as well as the recent developments and likely future paths for economic integration in East Asia. By analyzing the changing regional order and new dynamics for regional cooperation, we have sought to make sense of the implications of these developments for future regional institution building. Our analyses suggest that East Asia needs a more coherent and balanced way forward for regional economic integration, and that this must be a greatly strengthened priority of the region.

This concluding chapter attempts three more tasks. First, we discuss the implications of the present global financial crisis for East Asian regional economic integration. Second, we reconsider the issue of trade and financial integration and examine the importance of their mutual reinforcement in regional economic integration. Last but not least, we examine the prospects of East Asian economic integration and institution building in the years to come.

THE GLOBAL FINANCIAL CRISIS: IMPLICATIONS FOR EAST ASIA

The present global financial crisis is both 'bad news' and 'good news' for regional economic integration in East Asia. First, the negative side: the financial crisis has caused devastating effects on the world economy and caused serious rethinking of its financial architecture. Although this crisis was 'Born in the USA' and was less damaging to the East Asian economy than the Asian financial crisis of 1997–98, a homegrown crisis, East Asia's economic growth, and especially its foreign trade, was hit hard. The larger proportion an economy's net exports were of its GDP, the more it has been affected by the global financial crisis. Yet the region would have been more damaged had it not benefited from the reforms and substantive progress made after the Asian financial crisis in improving domestic economic regulation, particularly in the financial sector and in regional cooperative mechanisms.

It is true that economic difficulties caused by the financial crisis have slowed the pace of global trade and financial liberalization. It not only has had a dragging effect on multilateral negotiations of the WTO Doha Round but also has delayed work on regional trade liberalization, although some bilateral and multilateral FTAs are still on-going. As countries have scrambled to take urgent and exceptional measures to stabilize financial markets and stimulate economies, trade protectionism and economic nationalism is on the rise, which makes regional trade liberalization more difficult. Another effect of the financial crisis is that it has refocused economic policy debates from the regional level to the global level, including structural problems of the global financial architecture. World and regional leaders began to debate how to reform global financial institutions such as the IMF and the World Bank, and the G-20 has emerged as the central forum for future global economic and financial governance. As the G-20 leaders stated at the close of their 2008 Washington summit, the global financial crisis was largely caused by the failure of leading countries to appreciate and address risks in financial markets. Other major underlying factors, including global economic imbalances, also contributed to 'inconsistent and insufficiently coordinated macroeconomic policies, inadequate structural reforms, which led to unsustainable global macroeconomic outcomes'.[1]

Correcting 'global imbalances' has become a focal issue in the debate, with the nature and pattern of East Asian economic growth receiving more scrutiny during the crisis and the region's export-led economic strategy increasingly questioned. Many argue that the growth patterns of the East Asian economy have contributed to global imbalances and were in part responsible for the global crisis. 'Global imbalances' are a range of deficits and surpluses and their underlying differences in economic performance among major economies. Most East Asian economies, especially China, are alleged to be responsible for global imbalances by exporting too much and consuming too little. Global imbalances, reflected in high and low savings rates, trade deficits and surpluses, increase during periods of high economic growth but cannot be sustained during crises. As Jeffry Frieden

---

[1]   G-20 Declaration, Summit on Financial Markets and the World Economy, 15 November 2008, Washington, DC, accessed 2 September 2010, http://www.g20.org/Documents/g20_summit_declaration.pdf.

argues, the world economy needs constant rebalancing: 'Political difficulties arise when it comes to the distribution of the adjustment burden. As the popularity of a borrowing boom turns into the disaster of a financial bust and debt crisis, thorny questions about winners and losers come to the fore.'[2] Net national savings are high in East Asia while low in the United States, and these have to rise to reduce the magnitude of current account deficit. The unfolding of this debate has brought home a strong message to East Asian economies: the need for greater stress on domestic consumption in the region. To rebalance the global economy, East Asian economies are asked to readjust growth strategies between export-led growth strategies and those that focus more on domestic consumption. This alternative is particularly stark for China.

Turning to the positive side, the global financial crisis has boosted potential gains from regional cooperation and promoted support for it. The trend of regional economic integration has been gathering strength since the beginning of the twenty-first century. The present global crisis has provided more incentives for deep cooperation in East Asia. As in every crisis, nations learn to improve competitiveness in global markets. The region has become more aggressive in forming FTAs and other forms of deep integration. Nationalism tends to obscure regional integration. But the effect of the financial crisis prompted more political support for fostering greater macroeconomic and financial policy coordination, with regional surveillance and regulatory issues becoming more compelling. It has also generated more support for building stronger and deeper regional economic institutions. The trade and financial cooperation agreements initiated and finalized during the crisis are *prima facie* evidence of how the financial crisis has had positive effects on regional cooperation.

On the financial front, there has been more dialogue on how to maintain more liquid, stable financial markets and promote cooperation through free trade areas. The CMIM was adopted as an explicit reaction to the financial crisis. The Chiang Mai Initiative (May 2000) had led to a series of bilateral liquidity swap arrangements among Asian central banks. In 2007, ASEAN+3 entered a new stage, undertaking the multilateralization of these accords by opening the door to the creation of an 'Asian Monetary Fund'. East Asian countries overcame one major financial crisis a decade ago and undertook a raft of measures to reform and strengthen

---

2 Jeffry A. Frieden, 'Global Imbalances, National Rebalancing, and the Political Economy of Recovery', Council on Foreign Relations, working paper, October 2009, 4, accessed 2 September 2010, www.cfr.org/international-finance/global-imbalances-national-rebalancing-political-economy-recovery/p20464

their financial sector with a good deal of success. While Asia has the necessary resources – huge foreign exchange reserves – to manage this project, it also faces the same political and technical difficulties that have dogged the reform of the international financial institutions and similar efforts within the European Union: governance, share of contributions, macroeconomic supervision, conditionalities attached to the use of these resources. The region has never been able to overcome the inter-state differences and now, nine years later, the project is yet to take off. Could the current crisis mark a new stage for Asian monetary cooperation? More generally, which model should this regional agreement follow? And what should its relationship with the IMF be? As it did in 1997, the region confronts the need for greater cooperation and coordinated protection of reserves, cross-border infrastructure building, and integration of safety-net policies. The financial crisis has reinforced the need for more cooperation in regulating global financial markets and the need to support global macroeconomic stability.

As the G-20 becomes the main stage for global economic reforms, as Hadi Soesastro argues, East Asian nations can advance their interests through the G-20 platform while continuing to sharpen their focus on regional infrastructure development projects and cooperative institution building. They can stimulate the regional economy and recycle the region's huge reserves as well as promote structural adjustments to redress global imbalances. The region can also more effectively exert leadership on the trade front to keep global markets open, one of East Asia's top priorities in the G-20. Other priorities are ensuring adequate financial flows for development and purposeful coordination of the countries' economic stimulus packages. East Asia's strategic participation in the G-20 is aimed not only at securing its role in global economic governance but also at increasing its effectiveness in projecting the regional strategic efforts toward global economic recovery.[3]

MUTUAL REINFORCEMENT OF TRADE AND FINANCIAL INTEGRATION

Regional economic integration needs compatible trade integration and financial cooperation to support each other. East Asia has already

---

[3] Hadi Soesastro, 'East Asia, the G20 and Global Economic Governance', *East Asia Forum*, 8 March 2009, last accessed 28 July 2010, http://www.eastasiaforum.org/2009/03/08/east-asia-the-g20-and-global-economic-governance/.

undertaken numerous regional cooperation projects, ranging from those promoting trade and investment cooperation and collaboration in regulating financial markets to cooperation in macroeconomic, social and environmental issues. In order to have deeper and more balanced economic integration, the region needs to advance on both trade and financial cooperation fronts.

East Asian economic interdependence, largely supported by trade relations, is growing but awareness of the need to deepen regional financial links is still low. As of 2009, there were over 100 FTAs in force or under negotiation in Asia. Compared with other regions in the world, the density of FTAs is high and national trade policies have become more compatible with each other. As a result, the share of intra-regional trade in East Asia is more than 50 per cent of total regional foreign trade, a level only slightly below that in the European Union. Today East Asian economies trade with each other as much as they trade with developed countries in Europe and North America. They have managed to increase intra-regional interdependence while at the same time maintaining close linkages with European and North American markets. East Asia's total exports to Europe and North America have increased substantially when parts and components incorporated into final goods exported to these markets are included. FDI within the region has grown quickly over the last two decades, largely driven by expanding production networks and business process outsourcing in East Asia. The stronger economic linkages have led to a high correlation between national economic growth, national income levels, and even equity prices.

Since the Asian Financial Crisis of 1997–98, there have been a number of initiatives and projects to establish an intra-regional framework of regional free trade in East Asia. ASEAN+3 has emerged as the main vehicle for that ambition. However, a regional integrated FTA is rational but not practical for national trade policies. In recent years many regional economies have also actively pursued FTAs bilaterally. There have been a number of bilateral FTAs and RTAs in progress. Some bilateral FTA and RTA activities by major players are actually competitive, in a hub-and-spokes pattern of 'dirty' FTAs. These competitive FTAs will not be instrumental to deeper regional economic integration, but rather weaken the regional multilateral trade system, as they create the 'noodle bowl' effect of trade agreements. Other major non-East Asian players could also be a force for regional disintegration. In the 2006 APEC (Asia-Pacific Economic Cooperation) summit, the United States proposed an FTA of APEC members (FTAAP). It is foreseeable in the near future that East Asia will have a network of multi-layered FTAs, not an integrated single trade regime. As long as the FTAs among Japan, China and South

Korea are not signed, an integrated East Asian free trade area cannot be complete.

Regional financial cooperation could be helpful for regional trade integration. Although East Asian financial systems have improved since the crisis, regional economic integration could benefit more from deepening regional financial cooperation. Regional financial cooperation could dramatically strengthen national financial systems as well as regional economic linkages. Although the region's financial connections are deepening, East Asia's capital markets remain more closely linked to global markets than with each other. Many countries have restrictions on capital account transactions and on the entry of foreign banks and other financial firms. ASEAN has prepared long-term plans for developing capital markets and liberalizing capital flows and financial services. But, given the diversity in financial regulation, they cannot make more substantive moves unless the Northeast Asian countries are willing to provide due support. The global financial crisis has exposed the deficiencies of global monetary and financial arrangements built on the American financial system model. Most Asian currencies are pegged to the US dollar, which could lead to a deterioration in their competitiveness if the value of the US dollar becomes unstable. The policy of unilateral pegging to the dollar has become more expensive especially when the liquidity and flow of capital in international financial markets is high in volume and denominated in the US dollar or other non-Asian currencies. East Asian central banks often feel helpless when their financial markets are hit by strong international speculative forces.

Many East Asian economies have a common problem with managing their foreign reserves. As a result of their current account surpluses, most East Asian economies have accumulated massive foreign exchange reserves. Among the world's ten central banks with the largest foreign exchange reserves, six of them are in East Asia – China, Japan, Taiwan, South Korea, Hong Kong, and Singapore.[4] Most of their reserves are invested in US and European bonds. These foreign reserve investments face the potential risk of depreciation if inflation in the United States and/or Europe increases and the US dollar and/or the euro depreciate(s) dramatically. Alternatively, East Asian nations could invest more of their savings and foreign reserves within the region. If they do so, this could lead to the development of investment vehicles to finance regional SMEs and

---

[4]   Reuters, 'Corrected Factbox: Top Ten Central Banks with Biggest Reserves', 2 June 2010, accessed 2 September 2010, http://www.reuters.com/article/idUSTOE64P07B20100602.

infrastructure and generate more financial products to enable consumers and investors to use their incomes more productively. The Asian Bond Markets Initiative was set up to help strengthen the market infrastructure for local currency bond development.

To facilitate financial cooperation, it is important to have more macroeconomic policy coordination. East Asia needs to construct region-wide financial markets, and the markets must be liquid and integrated. The construction of regional financial markets requires more coordination in financial policies, and stronger regional institutions, to address regional governance and transnational issues. East Asia's macroeconomic policies have so far shown little evidence of convergence in terms of monetary and fiscal policies, albeit there is much commonality in exchange rate systems that are often pegged to the US dollar. Thus, there is a need to first make macroeconomic consultation and surveillance more effective within the ASEAN+3 framework. The CMIM is potentially a major step in that direction, in terms of strengthening the short-term financing facility and improving the rules under which resources are used for effective crisis management. In the long run, it could lead to more cooperation in exchange rate and macroeconomic policies and eventually serve as the precursor to a move towards an EU-type of monetary union.

FUTURE PROSPECTS OF REGIONAL INSTITUTION BUILDING

The challenges for future East Asian economic integration are formidable. To promote economic integration, regionalism offers an approach midway between national unilateralism and global initiatives. East Asian regionalism is distinctive, open, pragmatic and market-driven with growing government support. According to Katzenstein and Shiraishi, East Asian regionalism is inclusive in character and its style of integration is to establish networks.[5] Regional integration processes vary across world regions. In contrast to East Asia's network-style integration, Europe tends to build formal institutions and reinforce their exclusive character. East Asian integration is driven by dynamic developments in markets rather than by formal political institutions. In that sense, East Asia has been weak in developing formal institutions, just as it has been weak in developing domestic state structures and the rule of law.

---

[5]   Peter J. Katzenstein and Takashi Shiraishi (eds), *Network Power: Japan and Asia* (Ithaca, NY: Cornell University Press, 1997).

As regional trade and financial cooperation continues to increase, there is an increasing awareness of the need to develop more institutional capabilities to facilitate economic integration. For a long time after World War II, East Asia was perceived as being institutionally underdeveloped, lacking region-wide political and economic institutional structures except for an American-centered network of bilateral security treaties. Yet, after the Cold War and especially after the Asian Financial Crisis of 1997–98, a rising tide of regionalism and institution-building projects appeared. There is today, in East Asia, anything but a shortage of institution-building initiatives and projects. Instead, there is a proliferation of regional groupings and dialogues, ranging from ASEAN, the ARF (ASEAN Regional Forum), ASEAN+3 and the East Asia Summit to APEC. East Asian nations are organizing themselves into an 'alphabet soup' of multilateral groupings and organizations with overlapping memberships and different mandates.

There are now multi-layered 'institutional complexes' in East Asia and the larger Asia Pacific region. This multi-layered and multi-textured institution-building process has been actively promoted by ASEAN and its participants include all the major powers in the Asia Pacific region. The overlapping and sometimes competing region-building projects and groupings reflect an emerging redistribution of power and influence in the region after the Cold War. The 'ASEAN way' of regional institution building works by emphasizing informality, consultation, consensus building, conflict management and confidence building, and only progresses institution building at a pace comfortable to everyone involved. The pace of East Asian institution building has thus been slow. Everyone involved has seemed more interested in the 'process' and 'form' than in the final result of institution building.

The ASEAN-driven, multi-layered institution-building process seems to have serious weaknesses. Not only is the governance of each institution in question, but also the allocation of tasks and functions across these institutions is problematic. More specifically, the region faces some fundamental questions in institution building – which countries are in the region, what are their agendas, and what kind of institutions do they seek to build?

The membership issue of regional institutions concerns how to define a 'region'. A 'region' is not just a geographical area, but a political construct. Who is in the region and who is not cannot be determined *a priori*, but is rather a political question about the vision of regional institutions. There are three competing views of East Asian regional institution building. One school argues for a future regional institution embedded in the APEC framework, which embraces a larger Asia Pacific community including the United States and Canada. The second school favors an East Asian-only grouping – an East Asian Community – anchored in the ASEAN+3 process. The third school prefers an alternative in between APEC and the East Asian Community, based on the East Asia Summit (EAS). It is argued that the EAS, with a membership broader than ASEAN+3, can maintain balance in the East Asian Community. But the opposite view argues that it would be self-defeating to make another APEC-type of regional forum. If the idea of the EAS is to forge a long-term Asian economic, social, cultural and political community to 'balance' the United States, Europe and other emerging regional blocs, it does not make sense to ever expand its membership to the United States and Russia. However, now that this has occurred, it is unclear as to the future of the EAS and its relation to other groupings, especially APEC. What does appear clear for now is that ASEAN+3 should continue its institution building in parallel with other regional forums. This would allow the EAS to supplement ASEAN+3 as a regional platform for consultation and dialogue on broad strategic issues, without ever growing into a functional institution-building project on its own.

There is also disagreement on the models and forms of regional institutions. Should they follow the European Union's model of transferring national sovereignty to a supranational structure in the future? Or should they continue travelling down the present path to develop informal and loosely organized forums for dialogue while carefully guarding their national sovereignty? Originally, Dr Mahathir's idea of the East Asian Economic Group (EAEG) in the early 1990s was to build an Asian-only regional community in response to, and to rival, the EU and NAFTA. Initiated by the Asian Financial Crisis, the ASEAN+3 process promotes functional cooperation among regional countries. Yet East Asia remains weak in forming and empowering a common identity. A regional identity needs cultural as well as normative elements shared by all nations. As some scholars point out, behind East Asian regionalism is nationalism and it is this which constitutes a driving force for regionalization. Compared with European regionalism, East Asia lacks a convincing and acceptable normative framework for regional institutions.[6] Future developments in regional institution building will be constrained by the persistent concerns of regional nations about the erosion of their national sovereignty. It will be difficult for them to give up sovereignty for a regional supranational

---

[6] See, for example, Baogang He, 'East Asian Ideas of Regionalism: a Normative Critique', *Australian Journal of International Affairs* 58 (1) (March 2004):105–25.

structure like the EU. Moreover, regional institution building is not just about free trade in goods and services, or security dialogues. In the European Union case, a common ideology and shared concepts of democracy, human rights, individual freedom, and rule of law constitute the normative foundation of its regionalism and regional institutions. Measured by this yardstick, a *bona fide* East Asian community is a long, long way away.

Looking further down the road, who will play the leadership role in East Asian institution building: China, Japan, or ASEAN? Can the big powers continue to rely on the small states to push forward the institution-building process? There are two problems here. The first problem concerns ASEAN's own leadership capacity. Based on the vision provided in the ASEAN Concord II, ASEAN has embarked on a more in-depth community-building process, which includes building an ASEAN Security Community (ASC), Economic Community (AEC), and Social-Cultural Community (ASCC). The goal of Concord II is to make ASEAN more coherent and further integrated. Without internal cohesion and strength, ASEAN will not be able to act together and lead the big powers in regional institution building. Yet, recent developments in Southeast Asia do not suggest the organization has a strong will and the capacity to advance strongly regional institution-building initiatives.

The second problem concerns the Sino-Japanese rivalry in regional institutions. Given a number of outstanding bilateral problems and the changing geostrategic structure in East Asia, China and Japan will continue to compete and probably intensify their competition for the regional leadership role. Under the ASEAN+3 and EAS arrangements, leadership is provided and exercised by ASEAN. The Plus Three countries expect and respect ASEAN's role in the driver's seat. But how long will this last? The big powers are unlikely to let this continue for ever and eventually will surely ask ASEAN to pay due attention to their opinions. In time it is easy to imagine the big powers taking the driver's seat either by one becoming the leader, or, far more likely, by co-chairmanship in agenda-setting. To further complicate the issue, the United States remains a powerful player in the region. East Asia is of vital and permanent importance to the United States. As Kurt Campbell argues, the United States under the Obama Administration wants to 'act as a resident power and not just as a visitor, because what happens in the region has a direct effect on [American] security and economic well-being'.[7]

---

7   Kurt Campbell, 'Regional Overview of East Asia and the Pacific', testimony before the House Committee on Foreign Affairs Subcommittee on Asia, the

East Asian leaders need more time to sort out these problems and to rationalize and consolidate the expanding regional institution-building projects, and direct and enable ASEAN+3, the EAS and APEC to readjust their agendas and activities among themselves. ASEAN+3 could continue to be the engine for regional functional cooperation while the EAS becomes the forum for engaging other countries in strategic dialogues. It will be a defining issue whether ASEAN+3 and the EAS become complementary to each other or duplicative and begin to work against one another. As for the future, whether there should be an Asian-only grouping based on the ASEAN+3 process, or a pan-Asian community embedded in the EAS design, or a pan-Asian-Pacific community erected along the lines of the APEC framework, is still too early to call. In some ways, it seems most likely the future regional institutional structure will not be the product of one overall conscious design, but rather will be something that emerges 'naturally' or coalesces and comes together along the way.

It is most likely that in much the same way that China's economic policies have been driven overwhelmingly by pragmatism, and by 'crossing the stream feeling for the stones with one's feet', so will the future of East Asian economic integration.

Pacific, and the Global Environment, Washington, DC, 3 March 2010, accessed 2 September 2010, http://www.state.gov/p/eap/rls/rm/2010/03/137754.htm.

Index